# Dressing Modern Frenchwomen

# *Dressing* Modern Frenchwomen

## Marketing Haute Couture, 1919–1939

Mary Lynn Stewart

THE JOHNS HOPKINS UNIVERSITY PRESS

*Baltimore*

*This book has been brought to publication with the generous assistance
of the Karl and Edith Pribram Endowment.*

© 2008 The Johns Hopkins University Press
All rights reserved. Published 2008
Printed in the United States of America on acid-free paper
2 4 6 8 9 7 5 3 1

The Johns Hopkins University Press
2715 North Charles Street
Baltimore, Maryland 21218-4363
www.press.jhu.edu

Library of Congress Cataloging-in-Publication Data

Stewart, Mary Lynn, 1945–
Dressing modern Frenchwomen : marketing haute
couture, 1919–1939 / Mary Lynn Stewart.
p.   cm.
Includes bibliographical references and index.
ISBN-13: 978-0-8018-8803-8 (hardcover : alk. paper)
ISBN-10: 0-8018-8803-4 (hardcover : alk. paper)
1. Women's clothing industry—France—History—20th century.
2. Fashion merchandising—France—History—20th century.   I. Title.
HD9940.F8S84   2008
338.4′7687082—dc22                                    2007033661

A catalog record for this book is available from the British Library.

*Special discounts are available for bulk purchases of this book. For more information,
please contact Special Sales at 410-516-6936 or specialsales@press.jhu.edu.*

The Johns Hopkins University Press uses environmentally friendly book
materials, including recycled text paper that is composed of at least 30 percent
post-consumer waste, whenever possible. All of our book papers are acid-free,
and our jackets and covers are printed on paper with recycled content.

# Contents

# PART IV
## Modern Women

vi

# Illustrations

# Acknowledgments

So many archivists, curators, librarians, colleagues, and friends have helped me in my nearly ten-year quest to write a total history of fashion between the two world wars that I can thank only a few of the most important ones here. Pride of place among the archivists, curators, and librarians goes to Mme. Brigitte Lainé, archivist at the Archives de Paris, who introduced me to the study of fashion as objects and as commercial products through her own work, notably in the book *Objects,* and shaped my approach by guiding me through the Archives of the Conseil des Prud'hommes, Textiles, which had not yet been catalogued when I began exploratory research in 1998. I have valued our discussions about articles and papers that preceded this book.

Mme. Madame Marie-Andrée Corcuff expedited my many requests for photographs and permissions at the Archives de Paris. Early encouragement came from Mme. Valerie Guillaume, then at the Palais Gallière, Musée de la Mode, who met with me and responded positively and productively to my still-unformed project in the mid-1990s. A former curator and conservator, Mme. de Chaignon, allowed me access to the Banque d'Images and uncatalogued sample books at the Musée des Tissues de Lyon. Pascale Lascheux, the librarian at the MTL, was equally helpful about access to the minutes and bulletins of the silk syndicate in Lyon. Mme. Jacquié, at the Musée de l'Impression sur Etoffes de Mulhouse, not only made the archives fully available but also entertained a lonely visitor to her city. At the Bibliothèque Historique de la Ville de Paris, Mme. Billaud directed me to remarkable photographic and archival resources and shared some of her own experiences with couture. I truly valued those conversations.

Finally, I am grateful to all the archivists, curators, and librarians who assisted me in the above-mentioned sites, as well as at the departmental archives in the Nord and the Rhone, the Archives Nationales, Bibliothèque des Arts Décoratives at the Louvre, Bibliothèque Forney, Bibliothèque Marguerite Durand, Bibliothèque Municipale de Lille, Bibliothèque Municipale de Lyon, and Bibliothèque Nationale de France.

Many scholars read all or part of this book manuscript and made useful suggestions for revision. First let me thank Rachel Fuchs, who read the entire penultimate draft, and Linda Clark, who read an earlier draft, for suggestions about organization and identification of errors and omissions. Other French historians, notably Vinni Datta and Karen Offen, helped me revise sections of the manuscript. My colleagues at Simon Fraser University, Arlene McLaren and Marjorie Griffen Cohen, brought their expertise as a sociologist and an economist, respectively, to bear on relevant sections of the manuscript. Readers of two research grant applications advised me to use the material objects in fashion exhibits and the photographs and drawings of fashion as sources; this book is immeasurably better for their advice. Lastly, reviewers of three articles I submitted for publication in journals, as well as commentators on papers I have presented over the past ten years, have all contributed to the final manuscript.

The Social Sciences and Humanities Research Council of Canada gave me two standard research grants, which allowed me to spend a total of nearly a year in France conducting research in many different archives, museums, and libraries. Two small SSHRCC grants financed two exploratory research trips at key points in formulating and reformulating the project. These grants also paid for five research assistants over five years. Each of these assistants—Nancy Janovicek, Alisa Webb, Michael Lanthier, Shaun Richards, and Mary Shearman—is acknowledged in relevant portions of this book. I also enjoyed their companionship in this long endeavor. I wish to acknowledge the financial support of SSHRC, Simon Fraser University Vice President of Research B. Mario Pinto, and the SFU Publication Grant Fund, which allowed me to hire a wonderful indexer, Annette Lorak. Last but hardly least, I am grateful to Henry Tom, Barbara Lamb, Julie McCarthy, Carol Zimmerman, and others at the Johns Hopkins University Press for their thoughtful reading of the manuscript and helpful suggestions to make this a better book. Despite this assistance, I alone am responsible for any errors or omissions in this book.

# Introduction

This book challenges the notion that fashion, including haute couture, is a trivial or marginal subject for serious historians. In the century from 1860 to 1960, haute couture dominated fashion in Europe and the Americas. Fashion theorists consider this century "a bridge between the class-structured fashion of the past and the democratization of fashion today."[1] Especially in the years between World Wars I and II, French couture, which had been associated with classic styles and exclusivity, developed an ambiguous relationship with fashion, which values novelty and standardization.[2] The simplification of haute couture dress styles and the development of casual clothing lines encouraged imitation by confection, or ready-to-wear, manufacturers, which blurred one of the most visible markers of social distinction. The straight lines and other putatively masculine features of modern styles also obscured one of the clearest markers of gender identification. One objective of this volume is to identify the extent of marketing and "masculinization" in interwar couture. This entails describing how fashion arbiters and bourgeois women reinscribed class and gender messages onto modern couture. A related goal is untangling the multidirectional relationships between modern fashion and modern femininity.

Biographies of famous designers and studies of new styles have made little impression on twentieth-century economic, social, or gender history.[3] Even the fine cultural history of haute couture by fashion historian Valerie Steel has barely infiltrated the new cultural history. The exception to this historical indifference is Mary Louise Roberts' germinal work, *Civilization without Sexes,* which analyzes contemporary male criticisms of the tubular line of women's dress and modern women as masculine as well as feminists' representation of the new styles as liberating.[4] Instead of concentrating on male novelists and critics, or on declared feminists, *Dressing Modern Frenchwomen* analyzes how female fashion columnists, popular women novelists, and autobiographers represented the new silhouette and simplified features of interwar fashion to their largely feminine readers. This book seeks the opinions and practices of a wider segment of the female population in ten- to twenty-year runs of twelve illustrated magazines, including expensive society monthlies, modestly priced fashion and women's weeklies, and feminist magazines. It also compares press coverage of modern clothing and women to representations of modernity in fashion and femininity in women's autobiographical writing and popular fiction to gauge the degree of democratization.

One outcome of this wider purview is a recognition that modern womanhood did not seamlessly mesh with the limited democratization of haute couture. While elite magazines promoted a more comprehensive and transgressive version of modernity, popular magazines proffered a moderate version of modernity to a wider but still middle-class readership. Both types of women's magazines tried to transform masculine features by focusing on feminine fabrics or trim and by declaring other troubling features of new styles to be feminine. Their responses qualify the recent fascination with gender-subversive features of modern fashion by documenting how most bourgeois women adopted "masculine" styles selectively and diluted their disturbing qualities by adding feminine trim and accessories for a "tasteful look," one that reaffirmed the class and gender order. Aware that separating items of clothing into masculine and feminine lines enhanced profits, fashion producers and marketers encouraged their efforts.[5]

It is widely acknowledged that fashion is modern. If one adopts David Frisby's definition of *modernité* as "the more general experience of the aestheticization of everyday life, as exemplified in the transitory qualities of an urban culture shaped by the imperatives of fashion, consumerism, and constant innovation,"[6] fashion is prototypically modern. Fashion also fits Charles Baudelaire's concept of modernity as "the ephemeral, the fugitive, the contingent, the half of art whose other half is the eternal and the immutable." Baudelaire was interested not only in painting, the subject of his famous essay, but also in the dandy and the *flaneur* (the male fashion plate and the male observer walking about the city).[7] His depictions of the dandy and the *flaneur* capture modern investment in appearance and the modern idea that the entire world is consumable. It also genders modernity masculine, implicitly making femininity extraneous to modernity.

In *The Gender of Modernity*, Rita Felski dissects gendered interpretations of the modern, especially the implications of treating women as traditional in a modern polity.[8] In *Undoing Gender*, Judith Butler suggests that women, like people of color excluded from modernity, resist exclusion.[9] After examining attempts to combine modernity with fashion and femininity, this book proposes an intermediary concept: *hybrid modernity*. I borrow the term *hybrid* from postcolonial theorists for whom hybridity signifies an unsettling of fixed identities due to migration and diasporas, a process that allows for the emergence of new identities. Recently, feminist historians have applied the concept of hybridity to the phenomenon of the new woman after the First World War, especially the way that the illustrated press identified the new woman with the modern and the disruptive.[10] I extend their approaches by noting (chap. 8) the presence of a hybrid feminism consisting of coded allusions to the new, looser styles liberating women's bodies, facilitating mobility, and enabling paid labor—in the allegedly escapist and frivolous fashion press.

Through content analyses of cover illustrations in six fashion magazines and intertextual analysis of illustrations, fashion columns, and style features in twelve fashion magazines—undertaken with an understanding that both images and texts need to be decoded[11]—*Dressing Modern Frenchwomen* identifies the clothing styles and behaviors expected not of that elusive being, the modern woman, but of modern bourgeois women. Classifying the bourgeoisie is a challenge no longer met by indicating ownership of economic capital, occupation, or income. Increasingly, classifications refer to possession of social capital such as higher education.[12] Defining bourgeois women is particularly difficult, for they have been categorized by their husband's socioeconomic status as ladies of leisure or stay-at-home wives. A few historians incorporate the notion of bourgeois women possessing taste. Happily, women's and fashion magazines characterize not *the* bourgeois woman, but bourgeois women. Although society monthlies usually assumed their readers to be members of the grand bourgeoisie — aristocrats, socialites, and ladies of leisure — even these monthlies mention women in liberal professions, with no reference to husbands.[13] Indeed, husbands are almost absent from these monthlies, an absence that is part of these monthlies' promotion of individualism and recognition of their readers' desire to be individuals. Lower-priced fashion and women's weeklies also reached beyond the stay-at-home middle-class housewife to pink-collar workers. They were more likely to mention the occupations of readers' husbands, that is, small businessmen or members of the liberal professions. These weeklies were reticent about individualism, preferring to emphasize "personalizing" clothing with embroidery, jewelry, and other accessories. Appealing to readers who were tenuously bourgeois, they emphasized women dressing to affirm the social status of husbands, fathers, or families.

Fashion magazines also pinpoint changes in bourgeois women's situation. Before the First World War, an infallible indicator of bourgeois status was employing at least one full-time maid, but after this devastating war, maids were no longer universal markers of bourgeois status. Although society, fashion, and women's magazines assumed that their readers had servants immediately after the war, society monthlies soon dropped references to live-in maids, and weeklies slowly recognized that "the maid of all work is in the process of disappearing," that middle-class readers would now have to do (more of) their own housework.[14] Keeping up appearances, whether in their public attire or their household furnishings, now required considerable thought and effort. Fashion and women's magazines offered appropriate advice on housework and fashion.

The scope of this book clarifies that the *garçonne* (boyish-looking women) years, characterized by straight chemises, higher hemlines, and short hair, began in the mid-1920s and ended in the late 1920s, but extends the time line of modern fashion and womanhood into the reputedly more traditional 1930s. The only study of 1930s fashions interprets the return of the natural waistline and fuller skirts as feminine and romantic—which many correlate with a general conservative tendency.[15] Systematic comparison of fashions in the 1920s and 1930s reveals that the curvier silhouettes of the 1930s had many similarities to the straight lines of the 1920s. The longer time frame disrupts familiar assumptions about the 1930s as a step backward for women. Women accustomed to shorter, slimmer skirts resisted longer, fuller skirts—just as married Frenchwomen tenaciously held onto jobs during the depression.

### ORGANIZATION, THEORIES, AND METHODS

Guided by Ben Fine and Ellen Leopold's definition of fashion studies, *Dressing Modern Frenchwomen* treats fashion as a "hybrid subject" encompassing the overlapping spheres of production, explored in parts one and two, and consumption, considered in part four.[16] The two spheres are connected by marketing, the subject of part three. This book links haute couture to its sister industry, confection, or ready-to-wear production, as well as to its suppliers in the textile industry, and untangles the knotty ties between couture, confection, and textiles. It demonstrates that this sector of the economy developed advertising and marketing techniques used today.[17]

Because haute couture made many items of apparel, this book focuses on day dresses and suits, two staples of bourgeois women's wardrobes.[18] Eschewing discussion of evening gowns—luxuries only the wealthy could afford—it considers the controversies over skirts and slacks, clothing associated with women's sports and masculine styles. It attends to accessories like hats, because couture emphasized a total look, and it examines foundation garments, because slimmer silhouettes had implications for ideal body shape. The Lyonnais silk industry, known as the Fabrique, which pioneered rayon production, and northern woolens, which pioneered woolen blends, are representative of the even larger industry of textiles. Textile manufacturers worked closely with haute couture to develop and publicize new styles, but these manufacturers also served confection, "little," or neighborhood, dressmakers, and home sewers. Serving these customers, textile firms facilitated democratization.

Fashion has produced much theory, some of it nearly impenetrable to historians, who prefer to have more empirical evidence with their theory.[19] However, I have benefited from several French theorists, especially as appropriated by feminist theorists.

First, my work is rooted in sociologist Pierre Bourdieu's theses about fashion "revolutions" in the 1960s, namely, that individual creators should be regarded as manifestations of the whole field of cultural production and that couturiers create an aura about themselves in order to justify the elevated price of their products.[20] Bourdieu's logic of practice, specifically, his concept of "structuring dispositions, constituted in practice and always oriented towards practical functions," inform sections of the book on everyday attire and clothing care.[21] I am also indebted to Bourdieu's ideas about the importance of social and symbolic capital in defining the bourgeoisie and about fine distinctions between similar items signaling social *distinction*.[22] In particular, feminist interpretations about how human beings carry different kinds of capital helped me understand that bourgeois women's appearance was a kind of capital.[23] Most bourgeois women believed that they should wear clothing that suited their family's social status and struggled to sustain an appropriate sartorial statement in the difficult economic circumstances of postwar inflation and the Great Depression. Beatrix Le Wita's ethnography of the French bourgeoisie, which applied Bourdieu's ideas to bourgeois women's taste in clothing, helped me conceptualize these women's reserved relationship to fashion fads and their commitment to an identifiably bourgeois look.[24] Practical advice columns and women's autobiographies and novels provided evidence of bourgeois women's strenuous efforts to integrate new styles with existing expectations of bourgeois respectability.

I also accept much of Gilles Lipovetsky's argument in *The Empire of Fashion*, which considers haute couture "the most significant institution in modern fashion" and fashion "the earliest manifestation of mass consumption: homogeneous, standardized, indifferent to frontiers." Lipovetsky presents fashion as "a primary agent of the spiraling movement toward individualism and the consolidation of liberal societies." Fashion promoted modernity, defined as freedom from tradition and valuing individual autonomy.[25] His insistence that fashion allows "complex blends of refusal and acceptance" offers historians of women, fashion, and consumption an escape hatch from reductive models of modern women as fashion victims, irrational consumers, or cultural dupes. Lipovetsky describes early twentieth-century "modernity" in women's clothing as stripped-down chemises, and not, as many contemporary commentators did and some historians still do, as masculinization. He recognizes that greater equality and individuality in vestimentary expression did not override the gender cleavage in clothing styles.

The works of Roland Barthes honed my analysis of fashion rhetoric, though not through complex semiotic analysis. Barthes's idea that the language used by magazine writers does not comment upon but rather "creates" the meaning of clothing guided this book. I endorse his contention that "written clothing"—editorials, features, and captions—imparts essential information about the color and texture of material and gives garments functional and social meanings not evident in drawings or monochrome photographs. If I adopt Barthes's idea about the fashion magazine as a "machine" articulating the meaning of fashion, I qualify his generalization about fashion writing evacuating the "real" in favor of the mythic because he ignored the eminently practical advice columns. Comparisons to advice columns, which are grounded in everyday life, to autobiographies and popular novels, and to recent work in women's and gender history, help establish how realistic fashion columnists were.[26] However, content analysis of cover drawings, advertising, and articles virtually erase maternity, domesticity, religious observance, and aging.

There are certainly challenges to interpreting fashion discourse. Especially in columns entitled "Fashion and the World" or features like "Dress for Dinner," fashion writers confuse wearing a style with being the sophisticated woman dining out, attending a play, etc. In 1924, *Vogue* printed illustrations of a curvaceous woman in an S-shaped dress of 1904 and of a tall, slim woman in a low-waisted chemise dress. Under the first illustration, a staff writer wrote that the dress reflected "a fragile woman foreign to the practical realities of existence. Encumbered by flounces and a train on her skirt, immobilized by a rigid corset, how could this young woman conceive of an active life and the need for physical exercise?" Under the second illustration, the author wrote: "Simplicity, comfort, epitomize 1924 style. In creating new obligations for women, the war has suddenly swept away the excessive fantasy of the preceding years. The practical dress becomes necessary as feminine activity develops . . . women, being more independent, take on a more individual appearance."[27] Here the writer, like other reporters, assumed dress styles had significant implications for everyday activities and personality traits.

This slippage from appearance to experience was not unique to fashion magazines. In 1921, an article in the general interest paper *L'Illustration* was accompanied by two drawings of women, one wearing a typical dress of 1903 and the other wearing a typical dress in 1921. In the first drawing, the dress has a cinched waist, a full-length, semi-full skirt, puffy sleeves, and finishing touches on the bodice; it is worn with a wide-brimmed hat. In the second drawing, the dress has a low, loose waistline, the skirt is slightly flared, the hemline at mid-calf, the bodice plain, the sleeves narrow, and a head-hugging cloche completes the ensemble. The text asserts that differences in dress style accounted for differences in gestures and bodily freedom. The author commented on the disappearance of the "gasp for breath" from tight-laced corsets and of the sweeping gesture to gather up long, full skirts in order to walk. He observed that modern women were one hundred times less "packaged" than women in 1906.[28] These observations, like many others, exaggerated the differences between prewar and postwar women.

These kinds of passages were ubiquitous in the fashion press. Interwar fashion journalists presented modern fashion as simpler, more comfortable, and more practical than prewar ladies' wear, with little consideration of less comfortable and practical accoutrements, like higher-heeled shoes. They glided from detailed observations of fashion to undocumented statements about modern women being more active, independent, and individualistic than their predecessors. In the final chapters of this book, I test their correlation of these characteristics to feminism, new work opportunities, and sports by analyzing fashion coverage in a range of fashion magazines. Because not all bourgeois women could afford subscriptions to illustrated magazines, I also examined department store catalogues. In the "golden age" of commercial catalogues, most bourgeois women received catalogs distributed by department stores. Full of sketches and detailed descriptions of dress, these catalogs invited readers to imagine wearing the clothing represented.

Feminist theorists informed my approach to the relationship between fashion, consumption, and identity. I accept Judith Butler's argument about femininity as performance, or repeated practices that become naturalized through "a stylized set of acts," but I also agree with her caveat, in the second edition of *Gender Trouble,* that not all aspects of subjectivity are external.[29] Fashion discourse can be read as a script, or primer, for the performance of femininity, but French fashion reporters never claimed that clothing, cosmetics, and deportment could transform all aspects of a personality. Indeed, they insisted on a core self that one must respect to be truly fashionable. If this line of argument was largely a "selling point," it nevertheless appealed to readers and tells us something about their beliefs about the self.

I am indebted to Angela McRobbie's admonition to find out how women's understandings and uses of fashion commodities may have differed from their intended meanings or uses.[30] To learn if understandings and uses differed, I read women's autobiographies and fiction by Colette and Lucie Delarue-Mardrus, two writers who contributed to the fashion press, and other popular women novelists of the interwar years, using techniques derived from literary criticism to decode representations of fashion in fiction.[31] These sources suggest that bourgeois women had a variable approach to clothing, contributing to my thesis about fashion's meanings varying along the lines of age, social status, occasion, and individual circumstances. These sources also topple shibboleths of Frenchwomen as frivolous fashion mavens. The autobiographical and literary sources accord well with French psychoanalyst Serge Tisseron's postulate that people's contact with things is not only functional or symbolic but is also connected to individual identity and that the meanings they attach to things are not stable but situational.[32]

In a content analysis of almost every cover drawing on *Vogue* and *Femina,* and of four hundred cover drawings on four modest fashion magazines over ten- to twenty-year periods on the assumption that magazine covers depict "ideal readers" in order to attract what we now call their ideal demographic, I concentrated on human figures and the background in cover art.[33] Using gender analyses of advertisements developed by Irving Goffman and refined by feminist scholars, I found that covers depicted young, active, and independent female figures, usually without male companions or children.[34] These findings were compared to a rhetorical analysis of fashion and advice columns, style features, and advertorials (advertisements posing as articles) in twelve French magazines and three daily newspapers. Critical cultural studies gauging reader receptivity to messages in magazines informed this work.[35] After compiling definitions of common descriptors like *elegant, chic,* and *tasteful,* as well as key words like *modern* and its constant semantic companions, *youthful* and *active,* I realized that these key words appeared long after the transition from the tubular, gender-bending dresses of the 1920s to the curvier, gender-normative dresses of the 1930s—one of many indicators that the 1930s were not regressive.

To develop the thesis about a limited democratization, I surveyed illustrations in 100 mail order catalogues and more than two-dozen flyers distributed by six Parisian and two provincial department stores in the 1920s and 1930s. While the formulaic illustrations did not merit content analyses, they allowed comparisons to dress styles in haute couture collections. To reduce the number of items to manageable proportions, I followed the trends in simple fall/winter afternoon dresses in catalogs and in haute couture collections. The comparisons documented rapid adoption of the general features of haute couture styles, at prices less than a third those of haute couture originals. By tracking the styles and prices of patterns for ladies' afternoon dresses, as well as the prices of the materials needed to make such dresses, I show that home sewers could mimic couture styles at about a tenth the cost. This is a previously unexplored aspect of democratization.

By weaving together the production and consumption of ladies' fashion and dress fabrics and by stitching together a multidisciplinary approach to women's fashion between the two world wars, *Dressing Modern Frenchwomen* combines French fashion history with women's, gender, and cultural history. Instead of the usual focus on leading designers, famous style setters, or dramatic style innovations, it concentrates on the gender of designers, their most popular styles, the promotion of haute couture styles, and the sartorial strategies—and adaptations to modernity—of bourgeois Frenchwomen.

# PART

# I

# Gender,
# Genius & Publicity

*Chapter One*

# Couturiers/Couturières

S ince the seventeenth century, French manufacturers and exporters have traded on their reputation for tasteful luxury products and have represented the French as having a more refined taste than citizens of other nations. According to Leora Auslander, taste was contrasted to the more transitory, historically specific notion of style. Until the twentieth century, taste was largely an expression of bourgeois class formation and consolidation, guided by a burgeoning number of "taste professionals," who distinguished between tasteful and merely fashionable products. By the mid-nineteenth century, Whitney Walton demonstrates, bourgeois Frenchwomen were being held up as bastions of taste. In the furniture business, this meant large numbers of copies of royal styles. Rather than exact reproductions, manufacturers produced historical pastiches such as Louis XVI–style furniture. Claiming ownership of these products was difficult, even under the copyright law of 1902, which protected industrial models. One consequence was the wide-scale production and consumption of historical pastiche furniture.[1]

Since the emergence of a gendered fashion culture in the eighteenth century, critics had denounced women's taste as a response to worries about "the effeminacy of French art and the weakening of French culture."[2] One response to such critics was to proclaim the superiority of the taste of Frenchwomen. Interwar fashion arbiters employed rhetoric about the supremacy of the taste (variously and vaguely defined as discretion, distinction, finesse, grace, or tact) of Parisiennes or Frenchwomen, especially after the disruptions of international trade during and after the First World War and the Great Depression.[3] While fashion arbiters drew distinctions between good taste (*le bon ton*) and style (*le dernier cri*), they did not discount new styles, as long as all items of clothing were assembled into an elegant look and adapted to a personal style.[4] One consequence was that interwar fashion, which drew upon historical styles and "borrowed" from other cultures, was characterized not by historical or cross-cultural pastiche but by a mix of modern and traditional elements that I call hybrid modern, and others call art deco.[5]

Instead, the logic of fashion was "based on the tension between originality and reproduction," much like the logic of contemporary modern art. In *Couture Culture*, Nancy Troy argues that Paul Poiret (1879–1944) constructed himself as an artist to employ high culture and its discourses to sell his clothing to wealthy clients while following the seemingly opposite course of enhancing the popular appeal of his work. Troy compares the signature label on designer dresses and the signature of modern artists on their works, such as Marcel Duchamps's signature on art objects that fell between unique works of art and mass-produced commodities.[6] But signature styles were only one of an array of marketing practices, and Paul Poiret only one of a remarkable group of designers, male and female, who introduced new styles and new marketing practices.

## Couturiers, 1860s–1920

The transplanted Englishman Charles Worth (1825–95) launched modern haute couture in the 1860s, when he broke with the prevailing system, in which dressmakers filled individual customers' orders for styles in fabrics that customers chose. Instead, Worth insisted that the couturier was a "creator," who presented finished designs, known as models, to affluent customers and imposed his taste on customers. He elevated the status of dressmakers and introduced a house, or signature, style, two essential ingredients in haute couture.[7] Beginning as a silk salesman in a dry goods establishment specializing in Lyonnais silks that also offered customers clothing made from their fabrics, Worth first made dresses for his employers, then in 1857 set up his own business, known as the House of Worth and Bobergh (his Swedish partner for several years). He introduced the bustle and backswept skirts, which facilitated movement by comparison to the huge and awkward bell-shaped skirts that had preceded them. He also displayed princess dresses with low waistlines and empire-style dresses with high waistlines and low necklines. But Worth's designs are less distinctive for their lines than for their rich silk material, especially new purple and magenta printed silks made possible by recently discovered aniline dyes and printing techniques. Most of his designs had lavish embroidery, beading, or lace trim. Worth, who opined that "we live by and for luxury," inaugurated the "opulent era" of dress design. The houses of Doucet (1822–1924) and Pingat (1860s–1896) carried on this tradition, with their own design specialties: Doucet's less-structured dresses in more delicate fabrics suited the art nouveau aesthetic, while Pingat was the master of wraps and outerwear.[8]

These three men were part of a mid-nineteenth-century trend of men reentering the dressmaking business. The gender history of dressmakers is not unilinear, for men had dominated facets of dressmaking in the seventeenth and early eighteenth centuries. Clare Haru Crowston has demonstrated that the link between dressmaking and allegedly feminine skills was forged in the eighteenth century. The term *couturier* (as opposed to *couturière*) had nearly disappeared in the eighteenth century, when the usual designation for men in the clothing trades was *tailleur,* which implied the more skilled aspect of the trade, cutting, and fitting.[9] As late as the interwar decades, many men in the clothing trades preferred the designation *tailor* or *ladies' tailor.* After a decline in the number of men in the field in the second quarter of the nineteenth century, haute couture, and the coupled concept of the couturier as creator, was associated with male designers for fifty years.[10]

The familiar identification of creativity with masculinity is one reason that many fashion historians call Paul Poiret the preeminent modern couturier.[11] A related reason is that many art historians consider cut or form to be the essence of modern art.[12] Poiret himself claimed responsibility for the early-twentieth-century transformation of women's dress silhouette from S–curved to straight-lined. Art historian Richard Martin sees his use of geometric forms and flat profiles in dresses as reflections of "the culture of Cubism."[13] Poiret began his career as a designer for the couturière Mme. Cheruit and then for the House of Doucet before he opened his own couture house in 1904. Two years later, he introduced high-waisted, empire-style dresses and interpreted this innovation in the cut of women's dress as a revolution that freed their bodies. In one of his autobiographies, *En Habillent l'époque,* he contended that his tubular dresses rid women of the corset and thereby "liberated" their midriff.[14] More objective commentators, notably the doyenne of fashion historians, Valerie Steele, and the long-time editor of *Vogue,* Diana Vreeland, observe that Poiret mainly designed for his slender wife without theorizing about liberating women's bodies and vacillated in his dedication to bodily liberty when he introduced hobble skirts, which severely constrained mobility.[15]

Although no one doubts that Poiret was the most imaginative prewar designer, biographers are skeptical of some of his self-serving claims. Alice Mackrell treats

Poiret's prewar alterations in the silhouette less as a revolution than as a revival of the high-waisted designs of the Directory and the Empire (1796–1815). Her approach is not only based on an admirable skepticism about the hyperbolic quality of designers' promotional material and of fashion discourse more generally; she also takes a broader perspective on the chronology of modern European women's silhouettes, one initially developed by A. B. Young, who discerned two tubular cycles, the first from 1796 to 1829 and the second beginning in 1900 and lasting to 1937.[16] Because seventy years of fuller skirts, subdivided into a "bell-shaped cycle" (1830–67) and a "back-fullness cycle" (1868–99), separated these two tubular eras, the lapse of time explains why a revival might be received as a revolution. Mackrell notes that Poiret admitted that he had been influenced by his studies of the sculptures of Antiquity. In Poiret's other autobiography, *My First Fifty Years,* he wrote of learning "to use one point of support—the shoulder, where before me it had been the waist. All my gowns flowed from that point of support at the extremity of the shoulders and were never fastened at the waist. This new basic principle caused fashion to evolve toward classical antiquity." My examination of fashion modernism extends this line of argument by suggesting that modern style was based upon a combination of new and classical elements.

Mackrell demonstrates that Poiret fluctuated between Western and Eastern influences. He borrowed Far Eastern designs like the Japanese kimono, which he encountered during world travel; cultural visitors to Paris, such as the Ballets Russes, which triggered an Oriental "craze," prompted other "exotic" innovations.[17] His continuing commitment to rich Orientalism in line and fabric reflects his specialization in leisure wear for the wealthy. As Herbert Blau suggests, his highly ornamental attire was to be "worn uniquely, as if beyond the gaze, and certainly not on the street, or even at the opera or ostentatiously at a ball."[18] A mélange of classical and "exotic" features would define fashion modernism—although exoticism included Eastern Europe and colonial Africa as well as the Orient, and fashion modernism would more often imply exotic fabrics than radically different dress styles.[19]

Poiret's immediate postwar silhouette, with an ample bodice, pagoda sleeves, and long, flared skirt in the manner of Breton peasants, hardly enhanced women's bodily freedom, and customers simply did not buy these folkloric costumes. Poiret slowly resigned himself to shorter hemlines and straighter skirts. Despite a final hurrah at the Exposition des Arts Décoratifs in 1925, Poiret ceased to have an impact on style. His elaborate designs, extravagant lifestyle, and managerial style resulted in bankruptcies and reduced him to designing ready-to-wear clothing for Au Printemps department store and models for a couture house that legally could not carry his name (though aficionados knew he was the house designer).[20]

## Couturières, 1906–1939

Poiret's claims to have single-handedly smoothed the silhouette and liberated women's midriffs clash with evidence that couturières made similar alterations to the silhouette. When Poiret first showed empire styles in his collection, in 1906, the leading designer of the era, Jeanne Paquin (1859–1938), also showed an empire line. After the death of Charles Worth in 1894, Jeanne Paquin was the best-known designer of ball gowns and other sumptuous apparel.[21] Since her start as an apprentice to a "little," or neighborhood, dressmaker, she had worked as a seamstress and a designer in a couture house before she and her husband, Isadore Paquin, built her own house up to the point that it employed more than two thousand workers in 1900. That same year she was elected president of the fashion section at the Universal Exhibition in Paris, and she designed the clothing for the huge statue of La Parisienne, which loomed over the entrance to the exhibition. In 1913, she was awarded the Legion of Honor, and during the war she became the first female president of the Couture Syndicate.[22] In the first two decades of the century, Paquin conducted a legal campaign to control representations of her models in the fashion press and to use laws on artistic and industrial property rights to stop reproduction of her models by competitors in haute couture. As an early-twentieth-century couturier, Poiret has overshadowed Paquin because Paquin introduced fewer major changes than he did and because she took issue with some of the gender-bending changes that have been enshrined in the pantheon of precursors of modern design. In the fracas over Poiret's harem pants in 1911, Paquin criticized them as "unaesthetic," and she threw her support behind fuller skirts in the quarrel over the slim skirts introduced by Callot Soeurs in 1912.[23] Another reason for her relative neglect is that, like most couturières, hers was a circumspect lifestyle.

During the Belle Epoque, women designers moved into haute couture, and by the interwar period, there were more couturières of distinction than at any time before or since that period. Women's access to the world of haute couture differed in some particulars from that of couturiers. Some, like Worth, began their careers in commercial establishments selling fabrics and clothing; many, like Poiret, had previously designed for other couturiers. Textile firms, department stores, and other suppliers partially financed both couturiers and couturières. Family connections played a role in both groups' ascent, though men usually got financial assistance from fathers or fathers-in-law, while women were more likely to get start-up money from husbands or sisters. For instance, the Callot sisters began with a fancy goods shop in 1888. After Marie, whose married name was Gerber, acquired skills and clients designing for another couture house, she relocated the sisters' shop to the couture district and changed it into a couture house. Reopened in the heart of the haute couture district after a wartime closure, the firm operated under her and her husband's direction until her death in 1927, when first her sons and then her widower took over. Other couturières began as milliners; several others built up a devoted clientele as première, or head, seamstresses at established couture houses and took their clientele with them when they set up their own houses. At least two couturières got much of their initial funding—and encouragement—from wealthy customers.[24]

The most innovative and influential designers of the interwar decades were couturières, not couturiers. In the 1920s, Madeleine Vionnet (1876–1975) and Coco Chanel (1873–1971) launched the shift toward looser, more comfortable women's dresses. Elsa Schiaparelli (1890–1973) added touches of whimsy and color to the more sober designs of the 1930s. A fourth couturier, Sonja Delaunay (1885–1979), innovated in fabric and color mixes, but she was not as influential as the other three.

Although Madeleine Vionnet is now less well known than Chanel, she was very highly regarded in the 1920s. Vionnet began as a laundress, worked in London as première at Paquin's outlet there and at Kate Reilly's shop selling Paris models. When she returned to Paris, she designed for Doucet from 1907 to 1911 and set up her own house in 1912. In 1908, Vionnet's contribution to the Doucet collections included dresses draped from the shoulders. Inspired by Ancient Greek apparel on statues in the Louvre, she cut material on the bias to fall in soft folds, or tiny pleats, from the shoulder or breast to mold to and move with the body. Aside from flagging her modernist attention to cut and line, art and fashion historians discern other artistic and design influences. Richard Martin detects the influence of cubist art and Japanese design in her emphasis on form and construction rather than ornamentation. Betty Kirke also argues that Vionnet drew inspiration from Japanese designs, notably cutting her flowing tubular dresses in rectangular pieces, like patterns for kimonos, in order to increase their "fluidity."[25] Although the contemporary fashion press lauded her "cutting expertise,"[26] it was taciturn about avant-garde artistic and non-Western influences on her designs. Instead, fashion journalists paid tribute to her combination of antique and modern design: "All the sympathy of her logical spirit, her artist's imagination, remains resolutely turned toward these two points: responding to the needs of the modern woman while resting on the great Greek and Roman traditions."[27]

One reason Vionnet is less famous today than Poiret or Chanel is that she did less self-promotion. (Another reason is her retirement in 1940. Unlike Chanel, she did not reopen her house after World War II.) Far from contending that she invented the tubular line, Vionnet insisted that she was uninterested in fashion "insofar as it is unstable and changeable." Unlike Poiret, her style did not vary significantly over the next thirty years (although it became slightly more fitted in the 1930s). When praised for inventing the bias cut, Vionnet modestly maintained that she only extended the bias cut from skirts to full-length dresses. In several published interviews, she did claim to have freed women's bodies from corsets, tight bodices, and heavy skirts.[28] Believing in as many styles as there were types of women, she claimed that her purpose was to enhance the beauty of every kind of woman. In actuality, she designed for women whose physical beauty inspired her and although—or perhaps because—she was squat, she admired tall, slender women.[29] Contemporaries connected her style with greater respect for the contours of the female body. Fashion photographer Cecil Beaton wrote that "everything Vionnet created had a cling or a flow, and women dressed by her were like moving sculptures. Through her use of materials she exposed the anatomy of women for the first time,"[30] and Diana Vreeland of *Vogue* described how a Vionnet dress could be slipped over the head to reveal the body's contours without any side or back opening. Her dresses were showcases for well-shaped bodies.[31]

Although Coco Chanel championed the simplification of women's attire, she and her hagiographers have exaggerated her singularity in this regard.[32] In addition to making ladies' wear less complicated and less decorative, like other couturières, she made it more androgynous, which was less common. Financed by one of a series of well-heeled lovers, Gabrielle Chanel rented a suite at a hotel in the posh Atlantic seaside resort of Deauville in 1913. Initially Chanel sold hats, but soon she introduced striped turtleneck sweaters borrowed from sailors' uniforms into ladies' wardrobes. Because she began in sportswear, a type of clothing that should enable bodily movement, she developed loose apparel that required no corsets. By the time she arrived in Paris shortly before the outbreak of war, she specialized in sports or, more appropriately, leisure clothing. Slender, with a boyish figure, she created straight-lined dresses and suits suitable only for slim, androgynous bodies like her own. Later she added pleated inserts to allow longer strides.

If these innovations were not unique, her experimentation with fabrics was unusual. Chanel's use of wool jersey changed assumptions that knits were too limp for dresses.[33] By 1927, jerseys were ubiquitous in couture collections and within two years, in ready-to-wear apparel.[34] Chanel was never very interested in trimmings other than braid on jackets or white or ecru collars and cuffs on black dresses. This kind of trim became very popular. She eschewed padding, preferring to have clothing fall naturally.[35] In her own words, even a "suit only looks good when the woman who wears it seems to have nothing on underneath." When wearing skirts, she felt, "you should be able to see the thigh and everything that goes on, and it should be comfortable to wear." One of her objectives was to design sleeves that allowed full arm movement without distorting the bodice. On the subject of the sleeve, she said: "It just has to follow the body of the wearer, not be all over the place. It is meant to fall straight over the shoulder-blades, not bulge out."[36]

Contemporaries in the fashion world rated Chanel's innovations essential to the triumph of modern women's clothing and to the emergence of the modern woman. In the October 1923 review of the fall collections, *Vogue* magazine set the tone: "No collection reflects as much as Chanel's the thought of her creator and is as completely identified with the tastes of the present day. She knows how to give modern women the same expression of her spirit and realize a harmony in the diverse parts of her outfits. Chanel expresses the entire soul of the modern woman."[37] Decades later, the contemporary fashion photographer Cecil Beaton contended that "Chanel had literally pole-vaulted women's fashions from the nineteenth into the twentieth century" by stripping it of its frills before accessorizing with long strands of beads and "cascades of huge pearls." He described the look as "chic poverty." Like many others, he noted her focus on overall appearance and her interest in fashion (some said uniforms) for the many, rather than style for elegant individuals. "As a dress designer, she was virtually nihilistic, for behind her clothes was an implied but unexpressed philosophy: the clothes do not really matter at all, it is the way you look."[38]

Following the lead of Gilles Lipovetsky, recent fashion theorists have identified Chanel with the nineteenth-century dandy. Carolyn Evans and Minna Thornton argue that Chanel drew upon the tradition of the dandy, an "essentially masculine cult of distinction mediated through style and dress" that signified personal independence. Unlike most couturières, Chanel reveled in publicity and infused her personality into her designs so thoroughly that "wearing a Chanel" became "wearing Chanel." Like Beau Brummel and other dandies, she simplified the profile, dismantled social distinctions, and promoted a more androgynous look. It is less clear that her look signified independence.[39]

The third influential couturière between the two world wars differed dramatically from Chanel and Vionnet. Italian-born Elsa Schiaparelli was widely traveled when she arrived on the Paris fashion scene in the late 1920s. Like Chanel but unlike Vionnet, she was "hampered by none of the dressmaking traditions. Most of her designing was done in her head, often while walking to work, alone in the countryside, driving."[40] Like the other two couturières, she claimed to respect the female body, but she did not mean the undulating curves of many women's bodies as much as the skeletal structure beneath the curves. More of an architect of clothing than Chanel or Vionnet, she considered the skeleton the frame for her clothing.[41] Although she designed leisure wear that left women's bodies free to move, her leisure wear was distinctive. Starting with sports clothes in 1927, she designed hand-knit cardigans with "amusing" patterns (fig. 1). Her skeleton sweater hit newspapers that took little notice of fashion. White lines on the sweater outlined a rib cage so that the woman wearing it "gave the appearance of being seen through an x-ray."[42]

Schiaparelli's cosmopolitanism made her more open to colonial influences than Chanel or Vionnet. Schiaparelli literally appended West African masks on sweaters and capes and appropriated other West African symbols for her designs. This appropriation occurred at the same time that dress designers "borrowed" liberally from other cultures, but primarily from the Balkans, Italy, Greece, and Turkey.[43] Schiaparelli guilelessly described the exploitative process as adding "Negro-like designs . . . and strange scrawls from the Congo." In this, she was not unlike the School of Paris artists who, "indifferent to the myriad ethnographic discoveries concerning the meaning and use of the artifacts within their source culture, attended strictly to the physical characteristics of the objects. While this attitude may have granted the objects a respect . . . it also insured that appreciation could manifest itself only according to the precepts of a fashionable . . . primitivizing aesthetic of purely Occidental origins."[44] An example of this process can be found in the fashion press, where masks from "primitive" cultures were compared to the old European tradition of masks for carnival or Mardi Gras.[45]

Schiaparelli transgressed in other ways as well. Evans and Thornton interpret her outrageous clothes as "a discourse of perversity and play," offering the women who wore them an opportunity to thumb their noses at the decorum of most ladies' wear. They also construe her more outré garments as spectacle, a

FIGURE 1. Schiaparelli sweater. Classeur Redfern, Ricci, Schiaparelli. Courtesy, Archives de Paris.

way to disguise the women inside the garments.[46] Her hats, in particular, were playful (fig. 2). Gaining fame in the late 1920s and early 1930s, when many women and designers were tiring of reductive straight-lined styles, and when many couture houses were curtailing their production of sportswear, she participated in the allegedly conservative trend toward natural waistlines and longer skirts.[47] Yet she also applied eye-catching decorative details like large, hand-carved wooden buttons and incorporated military features like shoulder pads and epaulets in her suit jackets. One of the best fashion journalists, Martine Rénier, called her square shoulders and narrow skirts a "geometric mode" and "an amusing adaptation of contemporary statuary."[48] Schiaparelli's dominance in the 1930s undermines trite arguments that this decade's fashion was significantly more conservative than 1920s styles.

When Chanel and Schiaparelli showed black gowns with white trim, Schiaparelli added "unexpectedly" bright colored scarves and gloves. She is, of course, known for introducing "shocking pink" and other vibrant colors into the spectrum for women's wear. Despite art historians' and fashion arbiters' predilection for cut as a marker of modernity, prominent interwar couturiers, including Pierre Gerber, co-director of Callot Soeurs and director of the Couture Syndicate in 1931, praised color. A painter himself, Gerber contended that color gave dresses more individuality, especially in the long period of the "standardized" chemise dresses of the 1920s.[49] Authors of articles on fabrics and sewing agreed that color was important, although they also held that the texture of textile was another marker of personality and distinction.[50]

A fourth couturière, Sonia Delaunay, was a painter before, during, and after her foray into clothing design from 1923 to 1931 and her longer venture in fabric design. Her couture experiments with startling color and texture contrasts grew out of her prewar experience with the "gay colors" of her homeland, her status as a founding member of the group of early abstract painters known as Orphists, and her and her husband Robert Delaunay's simultaneous color theory about bright and unexpected color combinations giving an impression of life and movement. Her bold geometric patterns expressed her interest in and knowledge about geometry (fig. 3). One of her technical inventions was an embroidery stitch that enhanced the motility of dresses. Her commitment to fluid fabrics meant that she treated dresses as a form of moving painting and expressed the modern agenda of greater mobility for women—an agenda that Delaunay, like other designers, attributed to changes in the lifestyle of modern women.[51]

FIGURE 2. Schiaparelli suit and hat, circa 1935.
Copyright Lipnitzki / Roger-Viollet.

FIGURE 3. Sonja Delaunay coat. DEM 178 no. 8466. Courtesy, Archives de Paris.

However imaginative and exciting her art and fashion, Delaunay, like many women artists, has been dismissed by art historians for operating between the realms of high art and mass culture.[52] Because she made no significant alteration to the line, or cut, she has been accorded less scholarly attention than Chanel or Vionnet. Of course, fixating on cut ignores the fact that Delaunay had no need to alter the basic structure of dresses, because straight lines and flat surfaces, without complicated seaming or construction, served her artistic agenda. Indeed, her agenda was too avant-garde for haute couture and major fashion magazines in the allegedly groundbreaking 1920s. Her experiments with color and texture contributed to the bankruptcy of her couture house in 1931. The return to highly constructed garments in 1929–30 and the Great Depression also hastened her bankruptcy.[53]

Despite the innovations of Chanel, Vionnet, Schiaparelli, and Delaunay, Valerie Steele concluded her study of interwar couturières with an admission that attempts to correlate the less complicated and more comfortable cut of women's clothing with the special genius of women designers fail.[54] Certainly other couturières, for example, Jenny, whose house operated from 1908 until 1938, and Jane Regny, who opened her house in 1922 and operated through the 1930s, made simple and supple clothing for sportswear and leisure wear. Both popularized pleated skirts and sweaters for sports and outdoor leisure activities (fig. 4). But Jean Patou (1880–1936) was the first couturier to open a sportswear department—in the early 1920s—and he advanced the trend toward more practical styles.[55] Like Poiret's, his claim to modernize and mobilize women is complicated by contradictory designs, because he was also the first advocate of the natural waistline in 1924 and he kept showing natural waistlines until they were accepted in 1929–30. The revival of the natural waistline, accompanied by fitted bodices and longer, fuller skirts, was welcomed as a return to femininity. Fashion arbiters criticized the revival for hindering women's mobility—critiques that led to slightly shorter hemlines and less bulky skirts.[56]

A more serious objection to an argument about the special genius of women designers being responsible for the new sports line is the variety of couturières' approaches to design. Compare Chanel and Vionnet, who shared some personal traits but had quite different signature styles. Both had humble beginnings, a strong desire for independence, and interest in freeing women's bodies from "false shackles." However, Chanel barely knew how to sew, whereas Vionnet was a trained seamstress. Chanel, who did not know how to draw, only designed on living mannequins.[57] Vionnet cut and fitted on wooden dolls before approaching the living body.[58] Chanel displayed her designs on her own boyish body; Vionnet preferred to wear androgynous outfits with a Trilby hat rather than her flowing, sculptural designs. Today, Chanel is best known for the little black dress and boxy tweed suits that she introduced in the 1920s. If these fashion statements are now clichés, they were initially controversial.[59] For instance, her tweed suits trespassed on masculine territory, because tweeds had been used for Englishmen's casual wear.[60] A major element of her success was her pared-down, essentially cross-dressing style.[61] Conversely, Vionnet preferred indubitably feminine silks, notably crepes de chine, satins, and tulles, which were supple enough for the draping effect she sought,[62] and she loved beaded fabrics.[63] Chanel defended the homogeneity of her ensembles, insisting that however homogeneous, they enhanced individual beauty.[64] Vionnet's credo was clothing to express the body's singularity, though

FIGURE 4. Jenny sports skirt and sweater. Séeberger Frères collection, Etampes, box 12, M158159. Courtesy, Bibliothèque Nationale de France.

few woman without a svelte body dared to express their bodies' singularity in her subtly revealing styles.

While almost all couturières produced leisure clothes, all but Amy Linder, Jenny, and Jane Regny built their reputations upon other styles. Nicole Groult (Poiret's sister) developed two complimentary styles: simple black dresses with a discreet touch of color and afternoon—tea or bridge—dresses embroidered with colorful flowers.[65] Louise Boulanger, whose house operated from 1922 to 1938, was known for dresses with sashes, bows, and even trains; her penchant for sashes and bows on the hips was emblazoned in her advertising: "Louiseboulanger authorizes woman to have hips" (fig. 5)."[66] She introduced a studio dress made of "sumptuous" fabrics intended "uniquely for the interior—specifically for the studio, a new "semi-intimate room where we like to receive friends at tea time or to have a cigarette"—which fashion commentators considered a feminine alternative to evening pajamas.[67] Both of these couturières emphasized the skilled needlework involved in intricate finishing, a feature that contemporary customers appreciated. Articles in the fashion press more often used descriptors like "*habillée,*" or "dressy," than "simple" or "modern," to describe their models. These women have attracted less historical attention than Chanel, Vionnet, and Schiaparelli because they stressed decorative details, which Cubists and other modern artists dismissed as feminine and passé.[68] Their dedication to decorative detail and fine sewing also clashed with the fashion journalists' tenet that cut was "the essence of chic Parisianism."[69] No doubt their subdued personalities also played a role in their historical neglect.

Something similar happened to Jeanne Lanvin (1867–1946), who was best known for her "romantic" mother-daughter outfits (fig. 6), bridge dresses for card parties, and "*robes de style,*" full-skirted long gowns reminiscent of eighteenth- and nineteenth-century evening gowns.[70] She was prescient in opening children's clothing and sportswear departments and was the first couturier to introduce menswear lines.[71] Like many other couturières, she began as a seamstress and, in her case, opened a house specializing in girls' dresses that was so successful she soon added ladies' wear. She designed herself, drawing inspiration from the styles of Antiquity, which she strove "to adapt . . . to our modern taste and give a constantly new face to the things that are eternally beautiful."[72] In a 1929 interview, and later as head of the fashion section of the international exhibition of 1937, she defined a kind of hybrid modernism in fashion. Couturier Karl Lagerfeld considers her "a great, great, designer" who has been almost forgotten because she was mature by the 1920s and was never a "fashion personality like Chanel."

Valerie Steele adds that Lanvin has been neglected because motherhood is "the one aspect of female sexuality that has not played a significant role in twentieth-century fashion."[73] I will add that haute couture did not even offer much in the way

FIGURE 5. Louise Boulanger dress, 1928. D3U 10B, no. 58, modèle 90.
Photograph by Françoise Rivière. Courtesy, Archives de Paris.

of clothing for baby nurses, babies, or children.[74] One of the paradoxes of inter-war design history is that haute couture avoided the maternal body and babies precisely when government, lobbies, and media other than fashion magazines were promoting maternity and natality. One reason for this curious neglect is that agents promoting natality showed little regard for, and made few improvements

FIGURE 6. Lanvin mother and daughter outfits. Séeberger Frères collection,
Etampes, box 12, M158259. Courtesy, Bibliothèque Nationale de France.

in, the actual conditions of pregnancy, birth, and nursing.[75] Fashion magazines
shared their disregard for the conditions of maternity and their distaste for the pregnant body. Only women's weeklies ran articles about "clothes for future mothers,"
and they never showed an obviously pregnant body. But fashion media reflected
Frenchwomen's resistance to the constant campaigns to increase the birth rate. Cer-

tainly, the French birth rate—notably among the bourgeoisie—rose only briefly immediately after the war, then stabilized in the mid-1920s, and fell in the 1930s.[76]

One explanation of fashion magazines' avoidance of maternity—and a partial explanation of Frenchwomen's decisions to limit pregnancies—was the obsession with youth and slenderness, an obsession that transcended couture.

## Branding and Spectacle

To entice customers to buy their expensive and innovative designs, couturiers and couturières engaged in a kind of branding based on name recognition and personality. The nearly universal expression of this practice was naming businesses after themselves (Louiseboulanger and Augustabernard ran their first and last names together, perhaps because their last names were very common). As their personal name brands became known, they marked products with their initials, notably on accessories like purses and belt buckles (when belts reappeared on women's dresses in the early 1930s).[77] By comparison to today, external labels remained the exception, because people who mattered could distinguish haute couture apparel by subtler means, such as the quality of the fabrics used. Fashion magazines endeavored to teach their readers precisely how to discern telltale details.

Another technique was developing and publicizing a persona as an artist. Nancy Troy demonstrates that Poiret "self-consciously staged his performance as a couturier, designer, art collector, etc." His theatrical approach included establishing a small theater in his couture house before the war and another one on the grounds of his couture house after the war. His extravagant and exotic costume parties are more evidence of his penchant for spectacle. Indeed, Poiret believed that designing was not his greatest "service to my époque . . . because what I did in this order, another might have been able to do. It was in inspiring artists, in costuming plays . . . that I served the public of my time."[78] Poiret imported theatrical elements into the couture business. He presented his models in a "first-night" party, with live mannequins mingling with the guests, showed his collections in his theaters, and directed mannequins on the runway, much like directors treat actors on the stage.[79] Subsequently, many couturiers presented models on mannequins at evening parties and had mannequins mingle with the guests; they also "directed" their mannequin parades.

However, a Canadian, Lady Duff-Gordon in her guise as the couturière Lucile, first adopted theatrical elements in fashion shows held at her London and Paris shops. Having dressed the "Gaity Girls" on and off stage in 1890s London, she had live mannequins saunter down a runway to music in the early 1900s, making her fashion shows forerunners of today's fashion shows. Lucile also held themed fashion shows and replaced the numbers on models with seductive names like "Passion's Thrall." Lucile's techniques and shops being resounding successes, Poiret imitated and surpassed her.[80]

So did other designers. Consider the names two of the understated couture houses gave their dress models in 1926 and 1930. Augustabernard and Boué Soeurs bestowed mildly erotic, exotic, and sinister nomenclature like "Seduction," "Ali Baba," and "Fleurs de Mal" on evening gowns. For day dresses, they favored floral or arboreal designations like "Cornflower" and "Under the Foliage," based on the colors of the fabrics or the motifs in the prints used in these garments.[81] More imaginatively, they called daytime suits "Stadium" and "Clear Morning," to evoke such activities as attending sports events or taking morning constitutionals, and they named afternoon dresses after the elegant places they might be worn, such as "Café de Paris" or "Chateau d'Amboise." Most of these designations appeal to a desire for pleasure and status.[82] A fourth category of sobriquets, attached to more dignified styles, evoked mythical or biblical characters, such as Pénélope or Esther. A fifth category was familiar or facetious feminine names—"Jeanette" or "Frivolene" (a pseudonym adopted by more than one fashion journalist). While most of these names were French, very few evoked national symbols, for example, "Joan of Arc." Finally, dress names evoked attractive types of modern women—"Gamine," "Sportive," or "Parisienne."[83] This kind of nomenclature is part and parcel of a marketing technique known as "fashion typing," whereby styles are associated with glamorous types of women, such as modern young women or sportswomen, and the names subtly suggest that women who wear such styles are equally glamorous.[84]

Textile firms often named fabrics after flora and fauna in their designs, the color of the material, or a distinguishing quality of the fabric (e.g., "Undulating"). They also applied historical names like "Directory" or "Empress," women's names like "Arlette," and fashion-type names like "Sportive."[85] In the 1930s, when much attention was accorded to dress fabrics, textile manufacturers often used motifs and names from distant lands, which textile reporter Françoise Arnoux thought inspired those who wore clothes made of the fabric, and those who viewed them, to dream of foreign travel (though not, significantly, to travel abroad).[86] I return to the issue of imaginary versus practical uses of fashion magazines in subsequent chapters; here suffice it to say that the magazines offered visions of faraway places and fantastic lifestyles and practical advice on how to experience some of the pleasures of both.

Predecessors and competitors of Poiret also allied themselves with the theater. Charles Frederick Worth, who initially relied upon prominent court women to wear and thereby publicize his designs, soon added famous actresses to his bevy of mannequins. Many of his successors counted more on dressing leading actresses on and off stage than on grand dames to publicize their designs. Ads on theater programs, usually showing actresses in designer attire, routinely announced that a particular designer dressed the female star on and off stage. Similar ads appeared in fashion magazines.[87] *Femina* had a regular column called "Fashion in the Theatre." The great director Sasha Guitry often chose Paquin designs for the actresses in his plays, notably for Jacqueline Delubac, dubbed by *Paris Match* "the best-dressed women in Paris." Costumed in Paquin models, Delubac played "La Parisienne" in a theater tour of South America that stimulated demand for French fashion there.[88] In April 1922 alone, Poiret and three other couturiers designed costumes for several plays running in Paris.[89] Cultural critics considered stage actresses wearing couture outfits to be the couturier's best agents. Some, like Arletty, had been models for fashion illustrators before stage and film careers. Once famous as a performer, Arletty employed leading couturiers—Poiret, Patou, Schiaparelli—and she continued to pose for fashion shots of designer models.[90]

Famous stage actress Cecile Sorel and musical performer Mistinguette gave interviews that pointedly mentioned their favorite couturier or couturière.[91] Although society magazine writers were skeptical about the example set by stage actresses, arguing that only maids and *nouveaux riches* followed their "bad example," their very warning implies that some of their readers tried to imitate these stars.[92] Dramatists who intended to offend bourgeois sensibilities were also disturbing to conservative fashion arbiters. Sonja Delaunay, who comes closest to Poiret in her commitment to the performing arts, designed costumes for a notoriously avant-garde Surrealist performance with music by Stravinsky and Satie, a film by Man Ray, and poems by Cocteau. Along with Picasso, Matisse, Braque, Brancus, and Leger, she participated in the famous 1924 costume ball held by the Union of Russian Artists. She designed a gown for this ball that inspired the Dada poet Blaise Cendrars to write his famous poem "On Her Dress, She Had a Body."[93] Most interwar designers contented themselves with displaying their designs on style setters at opening nights at major theaters and the Opera.

Designers grew disenchanted with stage actresses, who had lost some allure since being "at the heart of bourgeois society between 1890 and 1910." Designers noticed that film actresses were likelier to have the slim and boyish figures that best displayed their straight silhouettes.[94] Milliners also began to employ film stars in their publicity, presumably owing to their popularity rather than their figures, which were not on display in millenary advertisements.[95] The fashion press began to print photographs of movie stars alongside the older staples: photos of baronesses, countesses, and other socially prominent style setters. They ran photo essays of French and American movie stars wearing outfits designed by French couturiers.[96] These essays rarely described how to replicate star styles, a genre of article common in American fan magazines but rare in French movie magazines. Yet French fashion magazines celebrated the cinema as "the school for women" and Hollywood star Jeanette MacDonald as "the ambassador of "French chic," and they chided French film stars for being less glamorous than Hollywood stars.[97] Literary evidence suggests that many young women did try to emulate movie stars.[98] Both Hollywood and French films included fashion shows, which may have assisted viewers' efforts to look like style setters.[99]

As cinema became popular, Chanel realized that cinema "was how fashion can be imposed today." Another master of fashion promotion, Lucien Lelong, believed that "we . . . can no longer live without the cinema."[100] Poiret designed costumes for seven French films between 1912 and 1927, and Schiaparelli was almost as active costuming French films between 1933 and 1937. At least four other couturières collaborated on four French films apiece between 1927 and 1938. Chanel's distinguished collaborators included Cocteau ("*Le Sang d'un poete*," 1930) and Renoir ("*La Marseillaise*," 1939, and "*La Regle du jeu*," 1940). Couturiers and couturières also lent their talents to Hollywood films. Chanel's first two Hollywood films were "vestimentary checks," insofar as she was ignorant about what was photogenic in the cinema, and her "little dresses" and "poor style" did not show well on the screen. However, her two years as a Hollywood designer improved her finances and enhanced her prestige at home.[101] As the costume designer for six Hollywood films between 1934 and 1939, Schiaparelli had a greater impact in Hollywood. One of her collaborations, "Artists and Models," was essentially a parade of haute couture. Her broad-shouldered designs, introduced in the 1930–31 collections, corrected a cinematographic problem with the fuller-skirted clothes of the 1930s. Without broad shoulders, these outfits made almost all actresses appear pear-shaped. Her stylistic playfulness and use of exaggerated details also showed well on the screen.[102] In general, fashion illustrators like

Georges Barbier (1882–1932) and Erté (Romain de Tirtoff, 1882–1990) had more impact on Hollywood, especially after they moved there.[103]

The gender history of the productive end of haute couture has been circular. Whereas male designers dominated in its first half-century, 1860s–1910s, women played key roles in the 1920s and 1930s. Even the familiar identification of modern art and design with cut or line does not privilege couturier Paul Poiret over couturière Madeleine Vionnet. If Poiret has attracted the most attention and acclaim for "liberating women's midriff" before the First World War, Jeanne Paquin and Madeleine Vionnet were equally responsible for the high waists of 1908. Like most couturières, these two simply did not engage in as much self-promotion as Poiret did. Coco Chanel, who had no inhibitions about publicity, made as many claims about modernizing—meaning simplifying and streamlining—women's clothing as Poiret. While her innovations in stripped-down dresses and suits were important and lasting, they were hardly unique; Vionnet's draped bias dresses contributed as much to the shift toward looser, more comfortable clothing. So, too, did couturières Jane Regny, Amy Linker, and Jenny, who specialized in sports, otherwise known as smart casual clothing. Finally, Elsa Schiaparelli enlivened the sober designs of the 1930s with bright color, humor, and exoticism. All participated, to a greater or lesser extent, in the marketing methods of branding, spectacle, and other forms of publicity that marked couture's emergence as a model of modern business practices.

*Chapter Two*

# Hybrid Modern

Since the eighteenth century, French fashion producers had to contend with an aesthetic theory that assigned them to the lesser category of a craft, not the more prestigious category of an art. One of their tactics in combating this assignation was claiming status as artists.[1] Twentieth-century couturiers and couturières positioned themselves as artists, patronized the fine arts, publicized their artistic influences, and called themselves "creators" to raise their status and prop up claims to property in their own designs. Despite some designers' penchant for collecting avant-garde art and collaborating with avant-garde artists, most designers, and their publicity, focused less on their associations with cubism or surrealism than on their alignment with other decorative artists to revive the reputation of French luxury and decorative goods industries after the war, notably at the 1925 International Exhibition of the Decorative Arts held in Paris. In the 1960s, art historians relabeled much of what was called modern art in the 1920s "art deco," after the name of the 1925 exhibition. Art deco emerged as an eclectic style, combining the traditional and the modern, the functional and the decorative, the familiar and the exotic, the fine and applied arts, even hand-crafted and machine-produced goods.[2] The exhibition itself promoted a kind of "hybrid," or feminized, modernity. Art deco fabrics incorporated "exotic," especially colonial, elements, while art deco fashion illustrations depicted modern women as youthful, nonmaternal, and active.

*analyse their Presentation*

The founding father of modern couture, Charles Frederick Worth, dressed as an artist to raise the status of couturiers and to attest to his respectability as a man in what had, in the immediate past, been a female occupation.[3] Although the best-known example of artistic dress in France is the Romantic and Bohemian refusal of fashion, the association between artists and bohemianism was in decline by the time Worth donned artistic attire in the 1860s.[4] When Gwen John, an artist in her own right as well as being the sister of Augustus John, adopted an artistic appearance in the Belle Epoque, she assembled a mix of fashionable garments purchased at shops with apparel she designed and made herself, thereby signaling that she was aware, yet not a slave, of fashion.[5] In the interwar decades, few couturiers or couturières followed Worth's sartorial example. Although several couturières wore their own models at public events to publicize their designs, few of their models qualify as artistic in the bohemian sense. Even when Chanel's spare chemise dresses and tweed suits were new and mildly controversial, they did not communicate either bohemianism or Worth's extravagance.

Nevertheless, designers continued to patronize the fine arts. Worth and Paquin employed the Russian artist Bakst, better known for his fantastic stage designs for the Ballets Russes.[6] Before the First World War, Jacques Doucet collected eighteenth-century art and acquired seminal works of modern art, including *Les Demoiselles d'Avignon*. Couturières were equally supportive of the fine arts. Jeanne Lanvin was among the small number of French collectors of Impressionist art.[7] Poiret's sister, Nicole Groult, who left her brother's employ to show her own designs in 1912, was closely tied to art deco artist Van Dongen and Futurist artist Fuzito. Unlike her brother, she designed by subtraction, using decorative detail only to emphasize dress structure, which helps explain her success just as her brother was losing popular appeal in the early 1920s. Although her fashion house also ended in bankruptcy, this did not happen until well into the depression.[8]

Many interwar designers stressed that they were influenced by the fine arts, and the fashion press repeated their assertions. Press commentary on Vionnet invariably mentioned her inspiration from classical art and her individual genius.[9] Schiaparelli, who had encountered Italian futurists and French fauves and cubists in her adolescence, worked with surrealists Cocteau and Dali after settling in Paris. Fashion writers called her a "proponent of modern art."[10] She borrowed surrealistic elements for models, such as the scarlet fish wriggling on a bright blue bathing suit, handbags in the form of birdcages, and the famous hat shaped like a telephone.[11] Similarly, she absorbed the futurists' interest in bright colors and startling color combinations. But she attributed her introduction of "shocking pink," which she described as "bright, impossible, impudent," to exotic locations in "China and Peru," not the West."[12] The fashion press, which was not enamored of avant-garde art, was more interested in her "exotic" than in her surrealistic influences. Likely their readers were similarly inclined.

Only two interwar couturières were practicing artists. Alix, later known as Mme Grès, had been a sculptor before she opened her couture house. Like Vionnet, she was influenced by ancient sculptures at the Louvre, though her austere designs drew more on the restrained lines of Roman statuary than did Vionnet's flowing lines, which were inspired by Greek statues.[13] Alix was more successful than Sonia Delaunay, an abstract artist, which suggests that the fashion market was more open to representational art and classical style than to abstract art or clothes. Society magazines rarely wrote about cubism, and when *Vogue* did, it was condescending: "After the total check of cubism in art, it is amusing to study its decorative possibilities for feminine costume." Generally, the fashion press was more open to cubism in textiles, shawls, and scarves than in the construction of ladies dresses.[14] Conversely, society magazines regularly covered such representational artists as Van Dongen, known as "the most expressive painter of modern women."[15] Society magazines promoted the identification of fashion with some, not all, modern art. The men's style magazine *Adam* expressed the policy of qualified modernism succinctly: "A modern spirit, very up to date. . . . *But no cubism or dadaism.*"[16]

A more common way of linking couture to artistry was for designers to call their models *créations* and label themselves *créateurs*. When *L'Officiel de la Couture et de la Mode* was founded in 1920, the subtitle was *Organe de propagande et défense de toutes les industries de la nouveauté.* From 1924, the subtitle was *Organe de propagande et d'expansion de l'art français.* For several years, it made frequent use of the terms *création* and *créateur*, even applying *création* to models of the major *confectionneurs* among their sponsors.[17] In the society and fashion press, photographs and drawings of designs by couturiers and couturières were captioned "Créations Jean Patou" or "Créations Jeanne Lanvin," etc.[18] Use of the word *création* spread in response to couturiers' uncertain property rights to their designs and models. Soon designers employed by textile manufacturers and under contract to department stores adopted the nomenclature. This wholesale usage debased the term, causing couturiers to be more selective in their terminology.[19] Schiaparelli refused to use the word, saying it "strikes me as the height of pretentiousness." Yet she considered dress designing "an art, not an occupation."[20]

Finally, fashion arbiters taught that fashion was an art and dressing well was also "artistic." Princesse Marthe Bibesco, a fashion writer, called it "an art that is movement, movement that supports countless industries; it is a methodical, minute and creative effort." According to Bibesco, "native Parisiennes performed the service of being pleasing to observe." (In her book, *Noblesse de Robe,* Bibesco acknowledged that couturiers could make a Parisienne of an Italian, an Argentine, a Greek or an Irish woman.)[21] *Vogue* distinguished between women who treated fashion as an expression of their personality, or the "*créatrices,*" and those who limited themselves to existing types, or the "*imitatrices.*"[22] Less socially prominent journalists, writing for more modest readers, simply declared that composing an ensemble was an art.[23]

Efforts to educate everyone in the clothing business about the artistic nature of couture extended to new professional schools for women working in couture, where Daniel Gorin, director of a couture firm, instructed teachers that "couture proper . . . that is to say, creation," is not just chic, "which by itself does not suffice." Couture was "the beautiful" in a classical sense, having to do with harmony. It was "rare and different."[24]

## Art Deco Fabrics

Poiret made three important contributions to art deco, two of which involved fabrics. First, Poiret's travels introduced him to new methods of textile design. In the Belle Epoque, textile design had become fashionable among artists like Fortuny in Italy and the Wiener Werkstätte in Vienna. When Poiret traveled in Central and Eastern Europe, he discovered the Wiener Werkstätte, with its naturalistic style of woodblock fabric design. Impressed by the work he saw in children's schools, he set up a school, L'Ecole Martines, for working-class teenage girls in Paris. Instructors took the pupils on excursions to parks and zoos and encouraged them to paint freely in watercolors. Large, naïve flowers were their favorite motif. Although Poiret closed the school after the Great War, he continued to commission designs from a few talented graduates. Textile producers imitated the naïve flower motif.

Second, Poiret employed artists of the stature of Raoul Dufy (1877–1943) to design fabrics. By 1910, when Poiret first hired him, Dufy had exhibited at major salons and galleries, been a member of the fauves movement, and experimented with cubism. He had encountered "*l'art munichois,*" the decorative style consecrated in Munich in 1908 and celebrated in Paris in 1910, when the entire ground floor of the Grand Palais at the Salon d'Automne was given over to the Exposition des Arts Décoratifs de Munich. At the Salon, Munich designers furnished and decorated a whole room, including wallpaper and window treatments. When Dufy decorated a pavilion for Poiret's Thousand and Second Night extravaganza in the spring of 1911, it was in "Munich" style, with panels painted with bold flowers similar to Bavarian folk art. Around this time, Dufy was making woodcarvings to illustrate Guillaume Apollinaire's "*La Bestiaire ou Cortège de l'Orphée.*" Flora and fauna would be recurring motifs in the fabrics Dufy designed for Poiret and later for Bianchini-Férier, a prominent Lyonnais silk firm.[25] Working for Poiret until 1925 and for Bianchini-Férier until 1928, Dufy formulated the principles of modern fabric design: the use of vivid colors, clean lines, and an eclectic mix of traditional and exotic elements.[26]

Textile producers contributed more to popularizing modern fabric design than Poiret did. Bianchini-Férier, a company founded in 1888 by three former employees of a large Lyonnais silk store, had a history of innovation in the mechanical weaving of luxury silks, the integration of production, and the elimination of commercial intermediaries by establishing outlets in Paris (1897), London (1902), and New York (1909) to deal directly with couture houses and other customers.[27] One of the partners, Charles Bianchini, registered new fabric designs called "Poiret type" in 1911 and designs called "Dufy genre" after 1912. Although Lyonnais manufacturers traditionally employed local designers, Bianchini-Férier hired Dufy in 1912, provided him with a design workshop, and renewed his yearly contract until 1928. Dufy determined the style and quantity of designs he submitted; Bianchini examined and approved every design to be produced.[28] From 1919 onward, Dufy commanded the annual sum of 2,000 francs for the "absolutely exclusive" right to his designs in dress and furniture fabrics.[29] Although Dufy cut back on designing dress material in 1922, he designed furniture material until 1928. Meanwhile, Bianchini employed prominent art deco artists and illustrators, for example, Georges Barbier and Paul Iribe.[30]

The silk industry, in conjunction with Lyonnais municipal authorities, mounted an impressive exhibit, "The Renaissance of French Art," as part of the effort to revive French decorative arts after the Great War. In 1927, they subsidized the impressive Exhibition of the Art of Silk in Paris, which excluded traditional or copied fabrics in order to introduce couturiers to new fabrics their designers produced. The organizers felt that the exhibition promoted closer collaboration with couture.[31] The municipality of Lyon financed schools to develop skills needed in the silk industry, schools with courses—including ones for women—on "industrial design applied to textiles." The Lyonnais Fine Arts School offered instruction on silk design that emphasized artistic training. Michel Dubost taught a master class, "The Flower as Applied to Decoration," from 1918 until 1923, when he was hired by a prominent silk firm.[32] François Ducharne installed Dubost and thirty-three associates in the capital to collaborate directly with couturiers.[33] Breaking with the Lyonnais tradition of profuse, detailed flower motifs, largely due to his exposure to Japanese prints, Dubost set stylized flowers against an expanse of blank space. He published luxurious albums of prints of his designs on vellum paper with text by no less an author than Colette.[34] His successor in the course on flowers in decoration, M. Durieux, was not as inventive, but he encouraged a modern approach, defined as more minimal and serene than art nouveau style. Durieux arranged class visits to Paris couture houses so that students could learn directly about couturiers' needs and requirements.[35] Dubost, Durieux, and their students and associates contributed to the vogue for silk prints with large, vividly colored flowers against a black background, prints that became "a part of the patrimony of Parisian haute couture."[36] Floral and plant motifs dominated silk print collections through 1931.[37]

Although floral designs defined art deco textiles in the 1920s, geometric designs made headway from the mid-1920s.[38] Here the Rodier firm, founded in 1853, made an impression on textile design similar to Poiret's influence on fashion, insofar as Rodier introduced "exotic" elements into fabric design. Whereas Poiret was influenced by the impact of sub-Saharan art on cubism and by his travels in the East and Middle East, Rodier and a new generation of textile designers were shaped more by the texture, straight lines, and sober colors of North African textiles and the motifs of South Asian textiles they had seen at colonial exhibitions.[39] As Elizabeth Ezra writes in *The Colonial Unconscious,* the French public between the world wars was "inundated with images of sub-Saharan Africa, the Mahgreb, southeast Asia, and the West Indies in books, film, advertising, and exhibitions." By the 1920s, the French colonial policy of assimilation—which implied making French citizens of colonial subjects—was being challenged by the policy of association—which emphasized the cultural distinctiveness of each colony. Both of the operative policies were rhetorical devices that obscured a fundamental contradiction: French domination over the colonies. Central to the discourse of difference between the metropolis and the colonies was the concept of the primitive as opposed to the civilized, mediated by notions of the exotic as something that could be consumed and thereby domesticated.[40] Textile manufacturers and haute couture alike contributed to this consumption and domestication.

France already exported textiles to former colonies and contiguous areas in North Africa, the Middle East, and South Asia. One of the twelve branches of the Lyonnais silk fabrique, or industry, known as Articles for the East, the Middle East, and the Indies, supplied heavy cloths interwoven with silver and gold, scarves, shawls, and handkerchiefs for Muslims "from Morocco to the Indies and as far as China." Annual business in this branch amounted to 40 million francs in 1919.[41] In the 1920s, as the silk industry faced challenges due to a fluctuating currency and protectionist barriers in European and American markets, they put more emphasis on the colonial market. When crushing tariffs were imposed on silks during the Great Depression, the fabrique relied even more on the colonial market. By 1935, French colonies were taking 23 percent of its exports.[42] Accordingly, textile manufacturers were well represented among the exhibitors and were inspired by colonial displays at exhibitions.

As one of nearly three thousand metropolitan exhibitors at the national colonial exhibition of 1922 in Marseilles, Paul Rodier wandered among the African and Indo-Chinese colonial exhibits, taking notes on the composition and motifs of colonial textiles. Unlike earlier colonial exhibitions, the colonial products on display were not behind windows, with tiny labels, but spread out where the public could examine and touch them. Like colonial exhibits at world fairs and earlier colonial exhibitions, there were disturbing elements of the "exhibitionary complex," or spectacles with live colonial subjects acting French scenarios about primitive life, as opposed to their actual, hybrid kind of colonial experience, and illustrating a racialized myth of progress whereby colonial administrators claimed to be moralizing "brothers of different colors."[43]

Inspired by Indo-Chinese and North African textiles, Rodier blended wool with silk or cotton, introduced color combinations borrowed from sub-Saharan Africa, and included Indo-Chinese motifs in his next collection of fabrics. He publicized the colonial theme in the names he gave to blends ("Phnom-Penh," "Tchin-Sou") and prints (stylized South Asian flowers on "Djersador de Mampikong"). In subsequent years, Rodier traveled to many colonies and established workshops in Indo-China that, although directed by French artists, wove in the native manner to ensure the primitive and exotic quality of the fabric. Textile reporters called him "the inspiration of fashion" and "a renowned creator of new fabrics.[44] In turn, Rodier and other textile producers called themselves "créateurs" and their products "créations."[45]

The 1931 colonial exhibition was held in Vincennes on the outskirts of Paris, a site "redolent of romantic associations as the home of marginal people exiled from Paris proper." On site, the exhibition segregated the metropolitan section, which consisted of 42,000 square meters of commercial exhibits of goods produced for the French colonies, from the colonial section, visibly replicating the appropriately hierarchical economic relations between metropolis and colonies. Despite the intentions of the chief organizer, Marshall Hubert Lyautey, who wanted to avoid the carnivalesque aspects of previous exhibits, the exhibition required that "natives" (racialized colonials) wear indigenous clothing instead of the mix of European and local attire that they usually wore. Directors also demanded that natives demonstrate archaic techniques, rather than the combination of traditional and modern techniques they normally employed.[46]

After the colonial exhibition in Paris in 1931, many fabric designers blended different textures, mixed black, brown, and beige colors in geometric designs, and named new blends and designs after colonial sites and events. The new fabrics soon made their way into couture collections.[47] Marshall Lyautey had asked Georges Lepape (1887–1971) and other French artists to make sketches of colonial artifacts; Bianchini-Férier and other major silk producers wove or printed fabrics from these sketches. The silk firm Chatillon Mouly Roussel produced a silk print covered with animals and zigzags based on a Vera Schoukhaieff sketch. Coudurier, Fructus, et Descher launched prints inspired by Crozet's Cambodian courtside sketches. Colonial motifs—as appropriated by French artists and designers—continued to be part of fabric collections through the 1930s.[48]

## Exposition des Arts Décoratifs, 1925

At the exposition, Adornment (*Parure*) was one of the sections. Almost all leading couturiers showed models in boutiques on the esplanade along the Seine, on the Alexander III Bridge, or on Poiret's specially designed barges anchored along the river.[49] "Being rather weary of the habitual shop windows of preceding expositions," the designer Drecoll wrote, "we resolved to group all the chef-d'oeuvres of couture into an interesting ensemble, which is why we built, beside the grand central stairway in the Grand Palace, a two-story display space

composed of various salons, reception rooms, etc."[50] The grand stairway slop-
ing down to a runway would become a staple of fashion shows. Jeanne Lanvin's
prize-winning exhibit of an inanimate mannequin dressed in a Lanvin gown seated
at a dressing table full of Lanvin cosmetics represented femininity and consumption in a theatrical manner. According to Tag Gronberg, this shop epitomized the fair's motif of Paris as a fashionably dressed Parisienne.[51] The motif
recalled an earlier association of the Parisienne with Paris world fairs, notably,
the enormous statue of La Parisienne above the entrance gate to the 1900 fair.
However, the statue had been imposing and remote, unlike the human-scale and
more accessible mannequin.[52]

Before and after the exhibition, couturiers employed interior decorators and
furniture makers, other groups seeking recognition as artists that also marketed
to women.[53] Vionnet, a successful couturière, used the opportunity of moving
to new premises in 1923 to renovate a Beaux Arts building in a strikingly modern
way. In her sales salon, furnishings were in complementary shades of pale gray,
set on a white carpet flecked with black, and against walls covered with frescos by
a symbolist painter whose depiction of women as strong and (some thought) cruel,
aroused controversy.[54] Newcomer Jean Latour redecorated his "sumptuous hotel in Louis XIV style . . . according to modern conceptions of a couture house,"
conceptions that included a wide staircase of pink marble up to the second floor,
where collections were presented in large rooms decorated in Louis XIV wood-
work, with carpets, curtains, and walls in a "soft dull green enhanced with gold."
On the third floor, fitting-room walls were covered and furniture was upholstered
in Rodier fabrics "in pretty shades of gray and golden brown."[55] Doucet, Jane
Regny, Mme. Paquin, and other couture houses commissioned furniture from the
leading art deco furniture designer, Jacques-Emile Ruhlmann (1879–1933), who
tried to reconcile tradition and modernity and saw affinities between the art of
the decorator and that of the couturier.[56]

The art deco exhibition showcased modern design for shop premises. As one
art critic wrote: "For the aesthetic of curves, modern art has substituted that of
straight lines and angles; for ornamentation, the bare mass. . . . These principles should apply in architecture and interior decoration, including those of retail shops, all of which are affected by the mobility and fast pace of modern life.
All should be 'calm and sober.'"[57] This alignment with modern décor raised some
difficulties about the gender of modernity, which was usually cast as masculine.
Fashion journalists drew analogies between modern decorative arts and modern

women (as represented in fashion illustrations), highlighting "the same simplicity of long lines."[58] Others found "the rigorously simple, geometrical, and unadorned style [of the displays] . . . too austere for elegant women of today. Whitewashed walls, bare floors, uncovered windows, and angular furniture are no setting for the life of a woman of the world."[59] General-interest magazines retorted that the Elegance Pavilion was less angular than other pavilions and included fewer modern and more feminine touches of pale blue and rose colors. One reporter called it "a harmonious home," using the English word *home* in the text. The official reporter for the Adornment Group noted that presentation salons "most often borrowed their décor from styles of the past."[60] In short, the pavilion represented feminized, or hybrid, modernity. Something similar characterized much of modern fashion.

Tag Gronberg credits the International Exhibition of the Decorative Arts (and changes in regulations for building façades in 1923) with new investments in shop façades and show windows—and linking fashionable feminine allure to sales displays.[61] Ghislain Wood considers the fusion of art deco with shopping and, in particular, women shoppers "the greatest legacy of Paris 1925."[62] Before and after the war, architects had been trying to "modernize shops" through better lighting and ventilation, wider aisles for customers to stroll through the merchandise, and spotlighted product displays inside the shop and in the show windows—in short, to make products visible and attractive to actual and potential customers.[63] The 1925 exhibition, followed by three years of prosperity, encouraged these initiatives, until monetary problems stalled them in 1928.[64] Luxury goods shops used "the clean lines" of polished steel and aluminum and mounted minimalist window and counter displays.[65]

As a mélange of traditional and new elements, couture shop design, like the Elegance Pavilion, should be classified as hybrid modernity. Many couturiers renovated seventeenth- or eighteenth-century buildings using the harmonized colors and clean lines of modern décor.[66] Couturiers and their publicists understood that "an ambiance of good taste and great luxury" mattered to their clientele and considered décor "an indirect kind of publicity . . . that operates by the association of ideas, spatial continuities." Drawing on a nineteenth-century notion of bourgeois taste, they argued that bourgeois women responded best to older buildings and antiques.[67] Jean Patou furnished his main sales room with forty-seven Louis XVI–style chairs but installed a "modern bar with mural mirrors" in his central fitting room.[68]

# Art Deco Illustration

Poiret's support of artists extended to hiring academy-trained artists to illustrate his designs. Here his intervention was decisive. In 1908, Poiret commissioned Paul Iribe to create an album of Poiret dresses, and three years later, he commissioned Georges Lepape for a second album of fashion plates.[69] Poiret's art gallery, next to his couture house, displayed Lepape's original plates, along with works by artist friends Pierre Brissaud (1885–194) and Bernard Boutet de Monvel (1884 or 1891–1949).[70] Although these albums copied fashion journal practices of including fashion plates, the term *album* referred to an art publication.[71] Once again art was called upon to obscure an essentially commercial purpose. Influenced by Japanese prints, Iribe and Lepape foregrounded mannequins and used few props to set the scene. Both artists employed the *pochoire* technique of using several stencils, one atop the other, to build up a design layer by layer. The albums were printed on heavy vellum, and a thin opaque sheet protected each plate. The layering process and paper quality made these very expensive publications: forty and fifty francs apiece. Only 250 copies of Iribe's and 1,000 copies of Lepape's were printed.[72] Albums by individual illustrators continued to promote haute couture for more than a decade, with a hiatus during the Great War.[73] Even in the golden age of catalogs between the wars,[74] couture houses preferred artistic albums—which were less original versions of Poiret's prewar albums.[75]

Despite their limited distribution, these lavish albums represent a fundamental break between the nineteenth-century tradition of fashion plates and the twentieth-century apogee of illustrated fashion magazines. French illustrators had submitted fashion plates to women's magazines since the eighteenth century and to the new genre of fashion magazines since the nineteenth. At least as early as 1815, when a fashion periodical first employed the word *artistic* in its title, fashion illustrators aspired to be considered artists. In 1829, the first exhibition of fashion drawing was held. A group of painters who drew for the fashion press, several of them women, formed an association in 1880 to publish a large journal of "artistic fashions."[76] Fashion plate settings evolved from timeless landscapes featuring gardens and balconies to scenes from contemporary urban life, similar to impressionist paintings.[77] However, many nineteenth-century illustrators were constrained by magazine style preferences and a teamwork approach that required individual artists to work only on layouts, or draw figures, or apply washes. Another constraint on individual artistic expression was the need to convey the details of the garment's construction and the number and types of buttons and trim to serve the neighborhood dressmaker who copied the designs.[78]

Long allied with the genre of fashion magazines, fashion illustration was swept along by the surge of new publications after removal of the stamp duty in 1870 and of government authorization and financial bonds in 1881. In the following decade, developments in offset- and helio-gravure initiated the era of the modern magazine, with its increased visual content. These changes meant illustrated newsprint magazines could be produced and sold for as little as ten centimes and better quality paper versions for fifty centimes. In the 1890s alone, eighty-eight new women's, fashion, and society magazines began publication (though there was much duplication and many of these publications were ephemeral). The modest fashion weekly appeared then. *La Mode Pratique* (1891–1939) was published by Hachette, which had a monopoly of the 1,081 railway bookstands in 1900. Circulation rose after the addition of a pattern per issue, notably in *La Petite Echo de la Mode,* which boasted 210,000 readers in 1893. A handful of publishers who maintained closer contact with the fashion industry than with the journalistic world controlled one-quarter of the new magazines. Publishers put out illustrated bimonthlies on paper thicker and shinier than the newsprint used by more modest fashion magazines. Pierre Lafitte, who published *La Vie au Grand Air* (1897), added a bimonthly titled *Femina* (1901–54). The prospectus read: "Elegance. Worldly Affairs. Fashion. The Home. Theaters. Sports, Music, Literature, and Art." Because *Femina* ran more ads than other society magazines, it cost only fifty centimes per issue. Pierre Lafitte borrowed his advertising policy from Anglo-American magazines, with which he had many agreements.[79] *Femina* also innovated in running photographs of socialites at the races, and soon at other sites where high society gathered, reflecting readers' interest in what society ladies actually wore, not just clothes shown in the collections (fig. 7). This practice spread to other magazines and newspapers.[80]

In this propitious context, Lucien Vogel, a former art student and son-in-law of the publisher of the major illustrated paper, *L'Illustration,* launched a monthly printed on thick matte paper that included several *pochoire* prints per issue. Vogel called upon academy-trained friends like Georges Lepape to collaborate on *La Gazette du Bon Ton.* His goal was ambitious: "Now that fashion has become an art, a fashion gazette must also be an art revue." He employed promising young artists who also drew for Cheruit, Doeuillet, Doucet, Paquin, Poiret, Redfern, and Worth—"those creators of masterpieces who have made the entire world envy and

FIGURE 7. Socialites in Schiaparelli, Paquin, and Worth models worn
at Longchamps, 28 May 1933. Séeberger Frères collection, Etampes,
Oa381, box 19, M 166112. Courtesy, Bibliothèque Nationale de France.

admire French fashion."[81] Not coincidentally, these same designers (and prominent silk firms) subsidized the new publication. After the Great War, *La Gazette
du Bon Ton,* which cost twenty-five francs per issue, reached a circulation of
20,000. However, it filed for bankruptcy in 1925.[82]

Happily for Vogel, his father-in-law had purchased a biweekly magazine entitled *L'Illustration des Modes,* to which he appointed Vogel director and his

daughter fashion editor. When the American publisher Condé Nast purchased *L'Illustration des Modes* in 1922, he changed it to a monthly and nearly halved the price of an annual subscription to twenty-five francs. The retitled *Jardin des Modes* lasted until the fall of France in 1940 and was revived after the war.[83] As director for a few years, Vogel continued to promote art deco illustrators, though he and his replacement employed less-talented illustrators over the course of time.[84] One reason for the decline was the departure of Erté and other imaginative illustrators to the United States.

Condé Nast called upon Vogel when he started a Paris edition of *Vogue* in 1920.[85] For a few years, the Paris edition was run from London and bore a striking resemblance to the London edition.[86] The Paris edition cost six francs per issue until 1924, when it became a monthly and lowered its price to four francs. As artistic director of *Vogue* Paris, Vogel commissioned many of the illustrators he employed at *La Gazette du Bon Ton* and *L'Illustration des Modes*.[87] Georges Lepape drew more covers than any other *Vogue* illustrator in the early and mid-1920s, but Georges Barbier, Pierre Brissaud, and Erté also signed covers. Most of these illustrators simultaneously served designers who distributed drawings of their models to magazines and used them for other publicity purposes.[88] Many of these illustrators also worked for *Femina* and other fashion magazines, including the two men's fashion magazines.[89]

Drawings predominated on French magazine covers long after photographs had taken over the covers of glossy magazines in the United States and Great Britain.[90] French designers preferred drawings, which maintained couture's connection with art and which were more amenable to manipulation to display the best features of an outfit. Advertising experts maintained that line drawings drew attention to the silhouette and appealed more to consumer desires than photographs did.[91]

## Gender, Race, Maternity

Very few cover artists were women, and, like most fashion illustrators, they are not profiled in reference books on illustrators.[92] Best known are Gerda Wegener (b. 1889), who drew for *Femina* and two other magazines before and after the war; Helen Dryden and Harriet Meserole, who signed covers at *Vogue* until the Paris edition became more independent; Elisabeth Branly, who drew for *La Gazette du Bon Ton;* and Catherine Marioton, who worked for the in-house magazine *Art-Goût-Beauté,* the luxury publication *L'Art et la Mode,* and the humbler fashion biweekly *Chiffons*. Like many well-known illustrators, Helen Dryden tried her hand at fashion designing.[93]

If there are differences based on the gender of the illustrator, they are minute. Based on a comparison of the 22 *Vogue* covers by Helen Dryden and Harriet Meserole and 226 covers drawn by their male counterparts between 1920 and 1940, women were slightly more likely to portray women outside in gardens or parks, shopping, or on vacation. The setting of one Meserole cover was tropical, making it one of only four "exotic" backdrops for *Vogue* Paris covers. Although these backdrops included a few non-Caucasians, figures in the foreground are clearly Caucasian; indeed, almost all the figures on art deco covers are pale-skinned. Inside, some advertisements depicted dark-skinned and exotically dressed women to sell cocoa and rum, but these images were not as pervasive as they had been in fin-de-siècle posters.[94] They were not deployed to market haute couture.

Photographs were slightly more diverse and inclusive, largely because fashion photographers participated in the cultural phenomenon called "Negrophilia," or the Parisian "craze" for what was (often incorrectly) considered to be African in the 1920s. One manifestation was fascination with the African-American dancer Josephine Baker, although society and fashion magazines were less interested in photographs of her revealing dance costumes than in promotional photographs in which she posed, like a modern woman or a French socialite, in couture models identified by designers.[95] Another form of diversity was manifest in the photographs showing visiting Indian "Princesses," a reassuringly elitist, foreign, and temporary inclusion. Among the many "missing persons" on fashion covers and inside illustrations were Frenchwomen of color.[96]

Whatever the gender of the artists, illustrations conformed to the emerging art deco style, which was spare and streamlined. In the 1920s, the style was angular and geometrical and, in the 1930s, more sinuous and botanical. Covers and advertisements focus on the female silhouette, a flat, stylized, and fully clothed outline of the female form. As Roland Barthes observed in his study of the art deco illustrator Erté: "All sexuality and its symbolic substitutes are absent."[97] Specifically, all signs of the maternal or the mature female body—obvious breasts or distended abdomens—are erased. Content analysis of 600 female figures on covers and in fashion spreads in *Vogue* and *Femina* found none with prominent breasts or protruding bellies. The only exceptions to the slim, boyish profiles were internal photographs of plump society women at charity events, photographs belonging to the genre photojournalism. In short, fashion illustrations did not represent or acknowledge the very real phenomenon of the aging of the female population. This virtual erasure is closely connected to the culture of youth in the press.

Maternity and maturity were slightly more evident in the less-expensive fashion and women's press than in the society press. Yet none of the 400 covers of fashion and women's weeklies surveyed for this book shows perceptibly pregnant figures, and even internal illustrations accompanying features on "future mothers" do not include visibly pregnant women. A few drawings illustrating articles about clothes for "women past forty" or "*femmes fortes*" include stocky figures.[98] Readers of weeklies got less indoctrination in the youthful, slim, and childcare-free aspects of modern womanhood than did the readers of society monthlies.

## Ideal Readers, Real Women

Covers were supposed to appeal to a magazine's "ideal reader" through depictions of attractive figures in interesting settings, visual narratives of what their target readers fantasized about doing.[99] But cover drawings were also supposed to display fashions, which is why they favor full-length drawings over headshots, except on the covers of special hat issues. This commercial purpose explains why the heads on fashion figures on the covers were small compared to the length of the torsos and why their facial expressions are ambiguous or aloof. In magazine illustrations, as on show window mannequins, facial features were effaced to encourage the viewer to focus on the product.[100] Very few of the faces are smiling on society monthly covers, though women's weekly covers show more smiling faces. The disparity in facial expressions is less significant than the chasm between the scowls on models in elite fashion magazines and the smiles on models in women's magazines in contemporary America. These disparities reflect not only class differences in self-presentation and marketing but also national variations in self-presentation and marketing.[101] One French exception was *Marie Claire,* which began publication in 1937 and copied many practices of American women's magazines, including more headshots of smiling faces on their covers than appeared in older fashion magazines.

Who were these magazines' ideal readers and what did they do? *Vogue* and *Femina* covers portray a largely feminine world of leisurely but not indolent pursuits, a significant proportion of them outside the domestic sphere.[102] The term *leisure* here means "the state of having time at one's own disposal; time which one can spend as one pleases; free or unoccupied time."[103] Most scholarship on leisure has studied its articulation with class privilege (which certainly applies here), but very little of this scholarship is about women's access to leisure time, no doubt due to cultural assumptions about women's relegation to the domestic sphere and to the cultural reality that most women fulfilled time-consuming duties as housewives, mothers, and paid workers.[104]

What has been written about women's leisure focuses on remarkable sports pioneers.[105] Several of the photographs employed on magazine covers are full-length shots of famous sportswomen dressed in couture sports clothes, sometimes accompanied by their sports equipment.[106] Most, though not all, of these sportswomen were amateurs, and their sports activities could be considered leisure activities. Inside the covers, articles lauded explorers and travelers, representatives of "feminine activity in modern life."[107] One cover and several articles in *Femina* featured an aviatrix wearing quite masculine coveralls, and all the fashion magazines surveyed for this book ran at least one photograph of these icons of modern womanhood (fig. 8). As Siân Reynolds has demonstrated, stringent military restrictions on flying licenses ensured that there were very few women pilots in France. The pioneering few fascinated the readers of all kinds of periodicals.[108] Their daring exploits, disregard for gender boundaries, and representation as androgynous accounts for this fascination.

Interwar society magazine covers share the elision of work and the proposition that "all pleasure is dynamic" that Barthes found in the fashion magazines of the 1960s.[109] Covers of monthlies regularly represented nondomestic, dynamic leisure. Most covers show a single female figure or a pair of them standing (243 of the principal figures), with fewer (89) sitting. Most seated figures are in dressing rooms, but over the two decades, more are located in commercial settings, such as tearooms or theaters. Most of the upright figures are outside, in private gardens, though several are at the threshold of the larger world, framed by a doorway or the pillars of a terrace. These covers are emblematic of the limited mobility and qualified modernism promoted by these periodicals.

However, dozens of monthly cover figures are located in public parks or on city streets, in the countryside or mountains, or at the beach. Several are boarding trains or ocean liners. The captions on these drawings, and the articles about travel inside the covers, refer to travel, not tourism—that is, a privileged phenomenon, not a mass experience.[110] Most figures taking long strides or swinging their arms are skating, skiing, hiking, or playing tennis or golf. In *Femina*, a few

FIGURE 8. Cover of *Femina*, 1927. Courtesy, Bibliothèque Nationale de France.

are canoeing and one group is kayaking.[111] Inside the covers, ads and advertorials promote sportswear and sports gear. If these are ladies of leisure, in the sense that they appear not to work, they are not the idle creatures of nineteenth-century fashion magazines. Only eleven of the female figures are reclining on divans like the languid ladies of leisure represented in women's magazines of the mid- to late-nineteenth century.[112]

In stark contrast to the models that assume subordinate postures in the ads in American magazines analyzed by Erving Goffman and feminist scholars, these active, upright female figures are not subordinate. One indication of their autonomy is the absence of dominating masculine figures.[113] All sixty-three male figures depicted on fifty-one covers are companions of female figures and most are in the near background, almost like props. Sometimes all that is visible is the male upper body, helping a female figure into an automobile, or one arm and hand, giving the female figure a bouquet. Very few female figures lean toward or gaze at the male figures as if for approval. Society magazine covers, like the photographs in *Vogue* New York in the 1940s, portrayed an independent feminine world of pleasure and active leisure.[114]

The most distinctive feature of French society magazine covers is how rarely they showcase the family and children. Only twenty children appear on *Vogue* Paris or *Femina* covers, mostly in summer vacation and Christmas issues. Only thirteen covers depict women with babies, a striking underrepresentation of babies in an era of pervasive propaganda for more births. Only five covers show women in a realistically or sentimentally maternal manner, supervising children's piano practice or gazing fondly at children. For comparison, ten covers showed women walking dogs. Few articles discuss children, and most of them focus on maternal selection of girls' clothing or shopping for children's Christmas gifts. The principal message is one of "consuming motherhood" and raising appropriately feminine daughters. Of course, consuming femininity was a touchstone of fashion magazines. However, there are intimations that instructing girls about clothing and shopping with them were pleasures as well as responsibilities and that these activities fostered mother-daughter bonds.[115]

The abundance of nonmaternal images and the scarcity of articles on maternity in these magazines mirror bourgeois Frenchwomen's resistance to being defined primarily as mothers and their stubborn opposition to having many children. Between the wars, expectations about maternal childcare, especially childhood hygiene, and the hours per day French mothers actually devoted to childcare rose steadily. State subsidies for having more than two children were too meager to encourage most women, and especially bourgeois women, to have three or more children. The results are clearly documented in the decline in the national birth rate from 21.4 to 16.2 per thousand people between 1920 and 1933.[116] Perhaps overworked women read fashion magazines for fantasy escapes from the realities of childcare?

Modest fashion and women's weeklies appealed less often to the "modern woman." Like society magazine covers, most of the fashion and women's magazine covers show a single woman or a small group of women, occasionally with a male companion. Comparatively more female figures interact with children and are situated in the home, where a few do domestic chores, usually with an appliance or product advertised in the issue visible on the cover. Articles offer advice about mothering beyond clothing children, such as assuring proper hygiene and physical fitness.[117] Clearly the ideal readers — and presumably the actual readers — of fashion and women's weeklies were more domestic and maternal than the ideal or actual readers of society monthlies. *C'est la Mode* was quite realistic: "For Your Moments of Leisure" implied that leisure had to be squeezed in between maternal and housewifely duties.[118] *La Mode Illustrée* ran one of the few articles on housedresses in these magazines; the author encouraged readers to make "simple, clean, and attractive" housedresses, "appropriate for domestic and maternal duties in the morning [and] for [indoor] leisure activities in the afternoon." The most modest weekly spilled more ink on peignoirs than on housedresses. The rationale was that "one must be elegant at home."[119] The reason was that haute couture and confection made and marketed lingerie.

*La Mode Pratique* and *La Mode du Jour* ran articles on clothing for "future mothers,"[120] breaches in the wall of silence about pregnancy that offer clues about the reasons for the silence. The writers recommended "dresses that do not draw attention," specifically, dark-colored dresses with vertical stripes and pleats to dissimulate the rounded belly, and without "any ornamentation encircling the bust or the hips, which tends to enlarge the silhouette." Swelling bellies and hips were supposed to be concealed. Although medical columnists warned about corsets and tight clothing compressing the fetus, no fashion columnist expressed concern about the fetus.

Not all readers recognized that covers were idealized representations of women. Responding to a letter from a reader criticizing a cover, the editor of *La Mode,* Mme. Georges Regnal, explained: "A cover has never been a true fashion engraving. It involves fantasy, amusement of the eyes. . . . Consider the background of these color illustrations, and you will see skies, waters, nuances that do not exist in nature. Modern decorative art wants it that way."[121] Her explanation accords with Catherine Marioton's description of the process of illustration: she received sketches and swatches of material from couturiers and then she would "work up whole scenes with different dresses and accessories against an imaginary background."[122] No editor acknowledged that the tall, slim, straight or slightly curved silhouettes on these covers might be equally misleading.

In the 1920s and 1930s, couturiers and couturières sought to raise the status of their work from a craft to an art by associating with artists, collaborating in theatrical and film productions, collecting art, publicizing their artistic influences, and calling themselves creators and their products creations. For the most part, however, designers were more closely aligned with other decorative artists, for example, interior decorators and furniture designers, who were also trying to improve their standing in relation to the fine arts and at the same time to restore the reputations of the French luxury goods industries after the Great War. The pinnacle of their joint efforts was the 1925 International Exhibition of the Decorative Arts. The type of art and design promoted at the exhibition was later dubbed *art deco,* though the mélange of the fine and applied arts, the functional and the decorative, and the familiar and the exotic might better be termed *hybrid modern.* What has been known as art deco influenced fashion through fabric design, notably by introducing prints with large, vividly colored flowers against a black background and by adopting (and adapting) the textile blends, straight lines, and sober colors of North African fabrics and the motifs of Indochinese prints as seen as colonial exhibitions. Designers favored fashion illustrators who emphasized more angular and geometric silhouettes, with little attention to the curves of art nouveau or the signs of a maternal or mature female body. But as extensive as designers' efforts to position themselves as creators were, they were only one aspect of the promotional strategies of haute couture.

*Chapter Three*

# Publicity

A ccording to Fred Davis in *Fashion, Culture, and Identity,* fashion feeds on the unstable aspects of consumers' social identities, and "designer-artists" who initiate new styles somehow "intuit the currents of identity instability" and try "to lend expression to them, or alternatively to contain, deflect, or sublimate them." Davis recognizes that fashion cycles respond to a "complex of influences, interactions, exchanges, adjustments and accommodations among persons, organizations and institutions." Usually, the process "is sustained through some complex amalgamation of inspiration, imitation, and institutionalization," but major fashion revolutions (like that of the 1920s) draw more on inspiration than on imitation or institutions. By contrast, the average fashion cycle is "institutionally constrained by numerous aesthetic conventions, publicity practices, and merchandising requirements."[1] In 1925, a year of little change, Jeanne Lanvin elucidated: "We proceed by successive adjustments and imperceptible modifications. We must avoid bewildering customers and they scarcely ought to perceive the transition."[2]

This chapter adapts Davis's insights about the fashion process as a shifting amalgamation of inspiration, imitation, and institutionalization. Despite widespread assumptions that designers imposed their will on fashionable women, designer accounts of their relations with fashionable women, these women's accounts of their role in selecting and rejecting styles, and the number of unsuccessful models presented in every collection reveal that the connections between designers and consumers were much more complicated. The multitude of magazines devoted to publicizing haute couture is equally compelling evidence for an interactive relationship between designers and consumers.

Influenced by postmodern feminist critiques of liberal ideas about a single, stable, and independent self and notions about more flexible identities, I want now to investigate both how fashion magazines affirmed the possibilities of exploring new personas along with new styles while reaffirming women's belief in a core self. Though recent feminist scholarship revolves around gender or sexual identity, fashion magazines, and presumably their readers, were as obsessed with redefining or modernizing class-specific conduct and apparel. They were not prepared to abandon grounding notions of an essential self.

## Dictating or Divining?

Public opinion held that designers dictated to passive consumers.[3] Their position echoed Enlightenment criticisms of women's susceptibility to the seduction of consumer goods and also reflected uneasiness about the new visibility and status of couturiers and couturières.[4] Neither designers nor their customers were enamored of these views.

Coco Chanel claimed that she created her simple chemises and suits in response to consumers' new economic, social, and leisure opportunities. Fashion reporters in the 1920s and many fashion writers since then barely rephrased her promotional copy. Especially after Chanel aligned her styles with adolescence and mobility, characteristics of the modern women, journalists and biographers paraphrased her promotional copy.[5] Her publicist, Lilou Marquand, had a different perspective. She believed that Chanel dreamed of transforming "the woman in the street" with slim skirts, pullovers, and suits. "Beyond appearance, she sought to form the person, her way of life, her way of thinking."[6] The novelist Colette agreed that Chanel tried to "sculpt" women, not just get rid of "doo-das" on clothing.[7] Edna Chase, editor-in-chief of *Vogue*, called Chanel "a super saleswoman," who insisted that fashion magazines use full-page photographs of her mannequins, posed standing, because this pose best displayed their simple, straight lines. Michel de Brunhoff, editor of Paris *Vogue*, found her very demanding. She refused to let editors select among the fashion shots she sent them or to release photographs of models "unless they [were] shown alone on the page, the facing page not containing models from different houses."[8] These insider views suggest not so much dictation as complex negotiations between designer intentions and consumer interests.

Interwar designers contended that they understood the desires of women. Jean

Charles Worth (son and heir of Charles Frederick Worth) summed up their position: "Couture is intimately, profoundly associated with the feminine mentality of an epoch, one of its most precious reflections."[9] How did designers acquire their knowledge of women's desires? Once again, Jeanne Lanvin lifts the curtain on backstage practices: couturiers observed their customers and decided the direction of fashion "by the way the customers react before such and such a dress in the collection." *Vogue* reported that couturiers studied "the daily needs of woman and helped her to meet them without sacrificing her femininity and personal style," adding that "more than one couturier" hovered around fitting rooms and tearooms eavesdropping on their clients' conversations.[10] Couturiers' new social status allowed them to socialize with elite women at the theater, the horse races, and galas. When they donated models to charitable auctions or organized charitable fashion shows, they used these opportunities to see what styles were popular at these events.[11]

Fashionable women differed about their servitude to fashion. In 1926, when the weekly supplement *Eve* asked a handful of Parisiennes about "The Tyranny of Fashion," the answers ranged from an unqualified yes from Mme. Jeanne Prost, who called women "slaves of fashion," to an adamant no from Mme. Germaine Sallandri, who held that "an intelligent, tasteful woman only takes from fashion what emphasizes her charms and erases her disadvantages."[12] Ten years later, the Countess de Pange took a cultural approach. She argued that fashion, which was the contrary of fantasy, "implied uniformity." It depended upon the history and psychology of people.[13] The Couture Syndicate and the fashion media took Sallandri's position. The syndicate considered "the Frenchwoman . . . a precious collaborator for couturiers," for "she tempers fashion and adapts it to her person." *Eve* held that women select styles that suit their "personal tastes" and particular circumstances.[14]

Weeklies serving modest middle-class women believed that women should dress in a manner appropriate to their station in life. As Catherine Horwood found in interwar England, differing strata of the bourgeoisie adopted different sartorial strategies, with the modest middle class more concerned about "keeping up appearances" than the *haute bourgeoisie*.[15] However, French women's weeklies insisted on *personalization*, a term these magazines and presumably their readers preferred to *individualization*. Although personalizing usually meant colorful embroidery or other decorative details, it was a way of applying "the façade of individuality to an essentially conformist environment."[16] Decorative details, especially those crafted by the wearer, reconciled middle-class devotion to feminine respectability with a more elitist desire for individuality.

Only one respondent to the 1926 survey, stage actress Cecile Sorel, attributed transformational powers to fashion: "Fashion is a way of renewing oneself, physically and morally. It is the occasion for the woman to be multiple." Self-fashioning arguments were common in articles about Hollywood stars in American and French movie magazines, but rare in French fashion magazines, even after the latter began to publish interviews with film stars. The exceptions were a few articles on fashion as rebirth in American-owned *Vogue* (and an ad campaign promising cosmetic "Metamorphoses" by the American company Elizabeth Arden).[17] Star culture, with its standardization of beauty and fashion norms, was less prevalent in France than in the United States, no doubt due to the competition of other, socially prominent celebrities, like *"les élégantes."*

French fashion magazines did run articles about transforming dresses by wearing long, loose blouses known as tunics over sheath dresses in the 1920s or adding cuffs, collars, or sleeves to fitted dresses in the 1930s.[18] In addition to the obvious appeal of keeping up with fashion economically, these articles tapped into their readers' wish to try out new personas in a period of rapidly changing expectations of women. But these kinds of article never suggested a fundamental change in the wearers. Couturiers and journalists who suggested that fashion helped a woman to be "always new, always unexpected," added: "without ceasing to be you, before all else, after everything."[19] This sort of comment suggests that fashion arbiters believed that readers liked the idea of presenting different personas but did not want to abandon the notion of a core self. These journalists rarely detailed what exactly this core self was, allowing readers to answer from their own self-understanding. Extrapolating from the overall contents of these magazines, this core self included religious and family values.

The popular novelist, feminist, and fashion chronicler Magdeleine Chaumont gave *Eve* a rare psychological answer: "Clothing offers the woman certitude of success and love; well dressed, the ugliest is passable." Although her argument was purely speculative and highly generalized, fashion columns repeated it.[20] An article by cultural commentator Georges Masson made a subtler psycho-vestimentary argument: clothing was a form of "supplementary confidence."[21] Implicitly, many fashion reporters agreed; explicitly, they rarely referred to psychology. Research into the psychological bases for fashion choices was less developed in France than it was in the United States.[22] French advertising experts sought general psychological expertise on how to persuade people in theories about perception and suggestion. They were interested in how visual images and repetition captured attention and converted potential into actual customers.[23] Although fashion magazines drew on this academic material, they did not cite it.

Fashion magazines also ignored psychoanalysts who linked the sexual instinct to a desire to be beautiful (which included well-dressed) to attract mates.[24] In general, these magazines avoided direct references to sexuality. More than concerns about propriety motivated their erasure of sexuality. Fashion magazines profited from couture's design-centered approach to marketing, one that emphasized promotion, as opposed to today's market-centered approach, with focus groups and other research into consumer needs and desires.[25] Fashion journalists occasionally discussed "seductive" styles, which they associated with mystery. However, they were more inclined to use the adjective to describe clingy fabrics, not dress styles. A *Vogue* staffer who mentioned "sex appeal" attributed it to American (meaning Hollywood) fashion, which the staffer contrasted to the "charm" of French fashion.[26] Charm implied a subtler, indirect kind of seduction.

The only contemporary research into why Frenchwomen bought the clothes they did were fashion magazine interviews with style setters, which give a snapshot of the opinions of fashionable Paris. In 1920, *Femina* asked ten style setters, "For whom do women dress?" Most of the respondents thought that women dressed for themselves, citing women on desert islands who cared about their appearance.[27] Their answers conformed to fashion magazine claims that women dressed for themselves, their comfort, and the occasion. Eighteen years later, the Countess Elie de Ganay defined elegance as "knowing how to adapt yourself to fashion or, if you prefer, adapt fashion to yourself. It means knowing how to dress strictly according to the minute or the occasion." Daisy Fellowes claimed to dress "simply to be comfortable, at my ease and without the least disguise."[28] Her answer was fashionably correct but disingenuous. According to fashion photographer Cecil Beaton, she "invented the sequin coat cut like a man's dinner jacket" and "wore it with audacity and a green carnation." Schiaparelli, who often dressed Fellowes, lauded her "courage" in wearing outré models.[29] Fellowes liked to attract attention by standing out; most bourgeois women decidedly did not want to follow her example.

Several of the women interviewed in 1920 gave nuanced answers. Two contended that women subconsciously dressed to please men, but two others held that women who dressed for male attention did so "to eclipse" other women. Male commentators in the general-interest press espoused similar views, which were simultaneously flattering to men and insulting to women. Typically, these male commentators wrote as if all women were the same.[30] Fashion magazines did not publicize their opinions, which were neither complimentary to their readers nor consistent with their message about individuality or personalization. Other respondents to the 1920 survey recognized that different women adopted different sartorial strategies. One drew distinctions between coquettes, who sought male attention; the elite, who pleased themselves; and "the mass," which wanted "to put a distance between themselves and others." Another respondent argued that age affected women's sartorial strategies: at eighteen women sought male attention; at thirty, they wanted to be noticed by other women; and at fifty, they acted for "their own satisfaction." Fashion magazines advised wearing clothing that suited one's age and size – their gesture toward the not-yet-developed concept of market segmentation.[31]

Further insight into why women dressed as they did can be found by reading autobiographies. Care is required because most women's autobiographies tell more about special occasion gowns than everyday clothing. Many autobiographies hint at different motives for wearing different items of clothing; these motives include the wearer's disposition and social expectations. When Catherine Pozzi was recuperating from a bad bout of tuberculosis, she recorded in her diary that a Callot evening gown made her "beautiful again . . . and younger." When she was in better physical and emotional condition, her diary entry noted that a designer afternoon dress was simply "as it should be."[32] Female characters in popular women's novels also selected fancy dinner frocks to feel attractive but chose dresses and suits for family gatherings to conform to familial and social expectations. On the basis of wide reading in women's autobiographies and popular novels, I posit that bourgeois Frenchwomen, like the elite Canadian women interviewed by Alexandra Palmer, saw special-occasion outfits as long-term investments and peer-group uniforms and, accordingly, took considerable care purchasing and maintaining these dresses.[33] The French material suggests that dressing for church and extended family events was more important in interwar France than in postwar Canada.

Advice on apparel for weddings, christenings, and family gatherings in women's and fashion magazines confirm the custom of dressing for these rituals according to familial conventions. These conventions included composing a look that communicated the social standing of their (implicitly bourgeois) husbands and extended family.[34] Society magazines never mentioned spousal or family approval of clothing. The difference mirrored the disparity in the social standing of *haute bourgeois* and middle-class families and greater disposable income among *haute bourgeois* women.

The saying, "The couturiers propose; the Parisienne disposes," captures the symbiotic relationship between designer and buyer. M.H. of *Vogue* elaborated: "The great collections launch various themes. Only when the Parisienne has taken them up do 'the fashions' become 'the fashion.'" M.H. claimed that *les élégantes* "now play the role actresses and mannequins played in the past. . . . The time when couturiers imposed their fantasies upon us is over."[35] Rejecting the notion that couturiers dictated to customers, Martine Rénier asked: "You think that you follow him? What an error! He precedes you, but in the direction that you want to go."[36] In short, "he" divined what "you" wanted.

Perhaps the most persuasive evidence for the interdependence of couturiers and customers are the percentage of models shown annually that sold well enough to recoup costs. Even in the boom years 1927–29, only about one-tenth of the models shown in collections sold well, and most of them sold to commissionaires and foreign buyers.[37] Vionnet's sales records for the mid-1920s suggest that her house made more than ten "repetitions" apiece of only fifteen to twenty models per collection. Most of her successful models did not sell more than 60 units, and none sold more than 165.[38] One effect of this sales pattern was that about fifteen very successful models from each collection were "seen everywhere" in Paris, prompting fashion reporters to complain about a lack of individuality.[39]

Another indication of couturier's dependence upon customer preferences involved designers taking cues from a rejection of styles in their last collection, as happened when they abandoned efforts to restore fuller skirts and pagoda sleeves in the early 1920s. Other times, designers persisted but made concessions to customer resistance. When Jean Patou showed dresses with a natural waistline in 1924, few fashion writers predicted a change in silhouette. When several designers included dresses that "discretely outlined the female form" in 1925, many fashion journalists reported that women, discontented with the uniform-like chemise dress, would not accept the new style unless dresses remained comfortable and practical.[40] For three more years, fashion columnists warned designers that Parisiennes would only accept the new style if it avoided the tight waists and billowing skirts of previous eras. During these years, most Parisiennes did not adopt the new line, and many designers continued to show the straight silhouette alongside a curvier one, leaving fashionable women with a dilemma: "obvious or hidden waist?"[41]

As late as the spring of 1929, when the summer collections were shown, a handful of couturiers did not include garments with natural waistlines. One fashion columnist claimed that "among those who battle for the resurrection of the truly feminine woman, men are prominent. . . . From the woman's point of view, they resist, no doubt because they fear losing the advantages conferred . . . by the masculine look and in order not to abdicate the independence and prerogatives we have obtained in modeling ourselves on the masculine sex."[42] Writing for the general-interest publication *Le Journal* and the feminist publication *Minerva,* a fashion journalist, Juliette Lancret, reported on women's resistance to the supposedly more feminine curvy silhouette, saying that Parisiennes refused to buy longer hemlines and fuller skirts. Her articles goaded the president of the Haute Couture Syndicate into a public protest, which spurred other fashion columnists to support Lancret.[43] When resistance to long, full skirts continued for two years, designers raised the hems slightly and reduced the volume of daytime skirts.[44]

## Print Publicity

Another testimonial to the commingling of designer initiative and customer interest is the amount of publicity designers deployed. The advertising field was expanding. A syndicate in existence since 1906 had more than 1,600 members in 1931. Most members resided in Paris, and most of the remainder lived in Lyon and Lille. While most members were print media directors, a growing number came from publicity agencies. Women entered this expanding field.[45] Courses on publicity had existed since 1906, and schools were founded in the 1920s; three journals specializing in publicity and marketing existed in the interwar decades. While most agencies, schools, and concentrated on the larger and more lucrative areas of department store and small shop marketing, some agents served haute couture and a few scholars studied their publicity.[46]

In addition to signature styles and cultural events to display models, couture houses used print publicity to develop brand-name recognition.[47] However, haute couture was selective. Although advertising agents declared that posters, with their visual content and repetition, were good vehicles to reach women, couture houses never used outdoor posters, presumably because these posters were too public to persuade wealthy women. This must have been a gendered decision, since automobile manufacturers employed posters to persuade wealthy men.[48] In any event, advertising took a new direction in the interwar years. After a slump in the early 1920s, poster advertising revived, and new print technology fostered brightly colored commercial posters. But by the 1930s, over 90 percent of advertising budgets went to other kinds of advertising.[49] Economists and publicists believed that urban pedestrians and transit passengers paid little attention to posters precisely because they were so ubiquitous.[50]

Couturiers also shunned regular advertisements in the daily press, which reached between 200,000 and 3 million readers per newspaper.[51] They did allow fashion drawings and photographs to be distributed by press agencies to major dailies and weekly supplements, though the captions did not always identify the couturier, as opposed to their provenance (Paris).[52] Moreover, couturiers admitted to their shows fashion columnists from prestigious national dailies like *Figaro*, as well as from major regional and provincial dailies, like *L'Echo du Nord*, in Lille, or *Le Progrès*, in Lyon. They sent drawings and photographs to illustrated weekly supplements and to Parisian dailies and to major provincial dailies. *Nos Loisirs*, the women's supplement to *Le Petit Parisien*, reached a circulation of more than 3 million, while *Eve* (1920–40), an illustrated supplement to ten to eighteen provincial newspapers, reached provincial readers who wanted to follow Parisian fashion.[53] Although *Nos Loisir*'s coverage of haute couture was sporadic, *Eve* regularly published two complementary columns: "All the Fashion," on the latest trends, and "Fashion for the Economical Woman," on sewing one's own stylish clothes.

Dry goods shops and department stores placed sales ads in the daily press near the new women's pages, which emerged as publishers realized that the wife and mother decided which newspapers came into the home.[54] Retail outlets may have avoided the women's page because ads on special topic pages cost more than ads on other pages.[55] Even without a designated women's page, newspapers grouped items of interest to women. In *Le Progrès de Lyon*, "The Workbasket" (knitting and mending basket) appeared near the weekly column "Women's Life. Paris Fashion." So did small ads for such products as food supplements and household cleaning products. Textile producers advertised in the daily press but were less satisfied with these black-and-white ads than they were with multicolored ads in fashion journals.[56] Major producers like Rodier deftly built up brand-name recognition through fashion journal ads and advertorials.

Haute couture and textiles preferred niche advertising in media devoted to their products. Before the war, the silk manufacturer Maison Albert Godde et Bedin (AGB) published a free eight-page bulletin filled with illustrations of couture creations identified by couturier—a kind of indirect publicity only worth the expense if the firm already had brand-name recognition. After the war, the bulletin became the society magazine *Art-Goût-Beauté*, with a circulation of 15,000 to 20,000. Publicity for one of AGB's successor companies, Wilmart, continued in the fashion column and ads.[57] From 1919 through 1935, the Lyonnais Silk Manufacturers Syndicate subsidized a lavish bimonthly, *La Soierie de Lyon,* which in 1927 became a monthly with cultural coverage in vain hopes of doubling circulation to 3,000. Soon after the syndicate stopped its annual subsidy of 23,000 francs in 1934, *La Soierie de Lyon* folded.[58] Although *La Soierie* was a trade publication with reports on exports, taxes, and tariffs, it always included fashion coverage.[59]

In a patriotic and profit-motivated response to the need to revive demand for French fabrics after the war, a publicist for Hachette, which had purchased *Femina,* informed the Lyonnais Silk Manufacturers' Syndicate that *Femina* and one of its daily newspapers, *Excelsior,* would run regular features on fabrics.[60] This initiative had the intended effect of increasing textile advertising. As supply and demand improved, wool and silk manufacturers bought full pages on the inside front or outside back covers of fashion magazines and in close proximity to features on their products—which were really advertorials for their products.[61] Textile ads and advertorials pioneered the routine use of photographs in French fashion magazines. After the demise of *La Soierie de Lyon,* the Silk Manufacturers Syndicate contributed 150,000 francs to the Central Silk Committee for publicity in fashion and general-interest illustrated magazines but soon redirected its advertising away from the drawing-dominated *L'Illustration* toward the new photo-journal, *Vu* (a Lucien Vogel magazine, similar to *Life*). To fund these initiatives, the Central Silk Committee raised and spent 250,000 francs.[62]

Couturiers did not have the financial resources to establish house organs and did not engage in collective advertising on the scale of textile manufacturers associations.[63] Instead, groups of couturiers sponsored magazines. After the war, Cheruit, Doucet, Jenny, Lanvin, Paquin, Patou, Poiret, Worth, and nineteen other designers sponsored an "official" publication, *Les Elégances Parisiennes,* which gave advance information about forthcoming collections.[64] When *Elégances* succumbed in 1922, *L'Officiel de la Couture* replaced it. When the depression hit, the couture syndicate added an official bulletin in a smaller format. The four-man executive board, all business directors of major couture houses, informed members about new import duties on their goods and legal protection of their models.[65]

A plethora of theoretically "independent" fashion magazines sprang up. Their independence was tenuous, since much of their revenue came from advertising for couture and textiles and since their columnists had to have good relations with couture houses and textile firms to access their collections. Usually, fashion columnists made only mild criticisms of collections. When they went further, the couture syndicate retaliated. By the early 1930s, more than two hundred of these magazines were being published in France. Although several were distributed in other European countries, most targeted different strata of bourgeois French-women.[66] Individual issues were displayed in refined magazine shops—not in the more plebian tobacco shops.[67] Circulation soared in the 1920s, sank in the early 1930s, and slowly revived in the late 1930s.[68] During the depression, several changed title and format, merged with other periodicals, or stopped publishing.[69]

In the 1920s, these magazines introduced innovations in layout. They increased visual content, sold advertising space in larger blocks, and placed full-page ads on the first few pages of each issue, instead of burying ads in the final four pages, as most had done before the Great War. Marketing experts promoted advertising through "evocation," meaning greater use of graphic images than of textual description.[70] Assuming women to be emotive and impulsive shoppers, they considered evocative advertising particularly appealing to female consumers. Marketing experts advised producers who wanted to "reach a feminine clientele" to purchase large blocks of space in fashion magazines and women's supplements of daily newspapers,[71] as couture and textiles were already doing.

The twelve magazines analyzed below were published by eight publishers in Paris; many of these publishers also put out apparently rival magazines. Magazines hired publicity agencies, located in the couture district, to handle their advertising.[72] Soon couturiers filled the inside pages of magazines with full- and half-page ads, although they rarely paid the premium for cover ads. For a full-page ad, *Vogue* and *Femina* charged 5,000 francs in 1927 and 7,000 francs in 1934 (with a dip in price in between, when the depression hit).[73] Fashion weeklies asked 1,900 francs per page in 1927 and 4,000 francs per page in 1934. They sold more advertising by the line, which was cheaper, and charged even less for "a mention" in a shopping column. When a prominent couture house went into bankruptcy in the Great Depression, it owed 8,500 francs to *Femina*'s publicity company and 6,000 francs to *L'Officiel de la Couture*.[74]

Other than citing couture houses and textile firms in quarterly reports on seasonal collections, the fashion media did not acknowledge close ties with advertisers.[75] Ads for these women's magazines claimed that their readers leafed through issues at their leisure; scholarly studies of how present-day women read contemporary women's magazines confirm that women browse through them.[76] Casual readers might have been unaware of the tangled web of relations between magazines and marketers. Unlike the advertising-saturated and media-savvy readers of today, readers of interwar magazines might not have suspected the incestuous relationship between magazines and marketers. But they became more discerning. Not long after a new kind of women's magazine, *Marie Claire,* came on the market in 1937, it placed the following disclaimer beside its table of contents: "We remind readers that our pages of text contain no publicity of any sort. All the products cited, all the firms and brands mentioned in our articles, are there for the sole purpose of rendering service to our readers."[77] *Marie Claire*'s circulation hurtled to 900,000 in 1939, far beyond the circulation of the magazines discussed below.[78] In addition to using more photographs, *Marie Claire* had more beauty and fitness columns than fashion magazines did. However, *Marie Claire* adopted many fashion magazine formulas, such as referring to readers as "*chères lectrices*" and setting up a Friends of Marie Claire House with courses on cooking, cutting fabrics, and physical culture, as well as advice on "elegance, beauty, household and legal matters." Like department stores, the Marie Claire House included a tearoom, lounge, travel bureau, and ticket office.[79]

Magazine directors tried to develop a rapport with readers by employing long-term editors or columnists who personified the magazine. What distinguished fashion magazines from other illustrated magazines publishing then, apart from their focus on fashion, was their women editors and columnists. All the long-term fashion editors and named columnists were women.[80] Among them were Jeanne Ramon Fernandez (J.R.F.), fashion editor of *Vogue* Paris from the early 1920s through the 1930s, and Martine Rénier (M.R.), fashion editor of *Femina* from 1925 through the 1930s. Many columnists, like Camille Duguet, who penned the "Elegant Visions" column in *Chiffons* from 1918 to 1932, wrote for more than one fashion magazine.[81] Columnists who used pseudonyms chose familial ones like *aunt, cousin,* or *godmother.* They addressed readers as "*lectrices amies.*"[82] We can safely infer some subscriber identification with long-term columnists. Because many contributors only initialed their articles, it is difficult to know how many were women, though their knowledge of social niceties marks them as bourgeois. Reporters who signed first names invariably chose sobriquets like "Francine" or "Sylvène," presumably on the long-standing assumption that *lectrices* paid more attention to women's opinions on fashion and women's issues. Pseudonyms also allowed the journalists to write for several periodicals at the same time.[83]

Management developed reader loyalty by giving out coupon books, opening shopping and needlework academies, and selling dress material and notions by mail.[84] *Eve* published an annual *Almanac* advertised as "an agreeable companion," with advice about sewing and embroidery.[85] Another strategy was "Letter to a friend" or provincial relative advising readers how to dress and where to buy the latest products. Because correspondence between friends and relatives seemed personal, these features were deemed to be effective ways of persuading women to purchase products.[86] Like other service columns, these articles used the first- and second-person pronouns, *I* and *you,* to construct subject positions through synthetic personalization, a process by which personal pronouns create the impression that the writer knows the reader.[87] *La Mode* and *La Mode du Jour* published "*Entre Lectrices,*" letters between isolated readers that must have contributed to a feeling of belonging to a like-minded community. Occasionally readers chided editors and columnists, and the journalists responded by explaining or changing their position.[88]

Given that these magazines were marketing vehicles, their advice was relatively restrained. Even *Vogue* suggested that the chic woman did not pursue every trend, kept models from previous seasons in her wardrobe, and did not have a wide variety of outfits in her wardrobe. Why? "The costume that gives her a young look, that responds to her taste and comfort and activities, should not be set aside for some arbitrary novelty that will not give her as complete satisfaction." Other reasonable guidelines were mixing and matching pieces to vary outfits and building a wardrobe around a basic piece, such as a coat.[89] The 1999 wardrobe exhibit at the Musée de la mode (Louvre) confirms that style setters did not own very many designer outfits and wore good couture pieces for many years.[90]

## Magazine Marketing

At the apex of the bourgeois women's press were two society bimonthlies that became monthlies in the mid-1920s. *Vogue* called itself a lifestyle magazine: a counselor on "the choice of a dress, a perfume, a residence, a restaurant."[91] *Femina* claimed to be a guide to "the art of pleasing others, distracting oneself."[92] Both reported on the couture collections in illustrated columns with such titles as "When Looking at the Collections" (*Femina,* 1917–1923), or seasonal pieces, such as "First Echoes of Spring Fashion" (*Vogue,* Feb. 1926). Another regular feature, "Fashion in the World," detailed new styles and where they might be worn. Articles on wardrobes—good indicators of the social status of readers—included specialized ones for travel and entertainment.[93] Individual issues cost between 3 and 4 francs in the early 1920s and 8 to 10 francs in the late 1930s. Subscription rates between 75 and 100 francs in the late 1930s suggest that only wealthy women could afford subscriptions. Each magazine had about 20,000 subscribers in the 1920s; *Femina* reached a peak readership of 40,000 in 1934–35.[94] Their influence extended beyond subscribers because neighborhood dressmakers took these magazines to show customers couture models, and many women could afford the four seasonal collections or annual wedding issues, which were advertised separately in fashion and women's weeklies.

In articles, advertorials, and advertisements, *Vogue* and *Femina* showcased "exclusive" fabrics, haute couture designs, expensive cosmetics, art deco furnishings, and automobiles. These society magazines bear some resemblance to late-nineteenth-century women's magazines, which reconfigured the chic *parisienne* as an artistic consumer who expressed her individual taste in fashionable attire and interior decorating. By linking personal chic with home decorating, these fin-de-siècle magazines redefined shopping as a domestic duty and alleviated anxieties about female consumers walking through the city, window shopping, and behaving like *flaneuses*.[95] By the 1920s, society magazines presumed that their readers were consumers and promoted hybrid modern/art deco rather than pastiche antique furnishings.[96] In place of fin-de-siècle covers depicting women reclining on divans, interwar covers showed active women attending tea dances, balls, and the theater.[97] These magazines advertised cruise lines, hotels, and Vuitton luggage. Most ads for household products touted appliances, such as refrigerators, which were too large for most French apartments.

*Vogue* focused on aesthetic pleasures, stating that "elegance is one thing, the practical sense is quite another thing."[98] Yet *Vogue* Paris was less committed to promoting avant-garde art (or queer life styles) than *Vogue* London under Dorothy Todd's editorship, from 1922 to 1926, though it was more open to avant-garde art and alternative lifestyles than the New York flagship.[99] Moreover, *Vogue* and *Femina* were useful to their elite readership. Following the fashion-plate tradition, they printed black-and-white drawings of designer clothing with captions explaining the dresses' construction and text referring to "your dressmaker" making them up.[100] Evidently readers of society magazines did not dress only in couture clothing. Until the mid-1920s, *Femina* ran periodic features about easily sewn dresses intended for home sewers. It warned readers about saleswomen's tactics of persuading indecisive customers with flattering and trendy language. In the 1930s, saleswomen replaced sales pitches like "that makes you look young" or "that flatters your figure" with "that hilarious phrase: 'This is a Parisian look.'"[101]

*Vogue* and *Femina* differed primarily in geographic focus and gender consciousness. Like its sister periodicals in London and New York, *Vogue* Paris was fascinated by the international set. Directed by Michel de Brunhoff, who promoted automobiles, *Vogue* often led with articles about automobiles, some of which did not mention women drivers or passengers. However, automobile advertisers in *Vogue* and other magazines shared modernist adjectives like *svelte* and *slim* with fashion magazine descriptions of modern women.[102] In this way, *Vogue* and Brunhoff's other magazine, *L'Officiel de la Couture,* pioneered cross-promotions of couture and automobiles in France.[103] Otherwise, French automakers, or more precisely, French subsidiaries of American companies, adopted this kind of advertising later than American automakers did, perhaps because automobile ownership was lower in France (more than 1.5 million registered automobiles in 1930). One factor must have been calculation about the smaller size of the potential market among Frenchwomen.[104] *Vogue* also published more articles by men than *Femina* or any magazine discussed below.[105] Edited and staffed by women, *Femina* covered automobiles in relation to fashion and cosponsored an annual contest on "feminine elegance in automobiles."[106] In general, *Femina* offered more coverage of women's charities, including maternal feminist charities. In the "society" pages, reporters focused on fashionable attire and events; in articles about social issues, they concentrated on issues.

In line with society magazine covers' elision of marital and maternal representations of society women, their tables of contents excluded wifely or maternal advice.

The fashion weekly *La Mode Pratique* (1891–1939) and bimonthly *Chiffons* (1907–32) cost one-quarter as much as society periodicals—one to two francs per issue—and attracted 42,000 and 200,000 readers, respectively. These prices suggest a middle-class readership. Although they routinely described haute couture collections, they reported on a wider array of clothing and materials than society magazines did. Ads for clothing and textiles used adjectives like *elegant*, which was favored in society magazines, but made greater use of the more pleasing adjective *charming*.[107] Other ads plugged less-expensive household products like cleansers rather than household appliances, which one weekly acknowledged were too expensive for their readers.[108] The notable exception was sewing machines, which all society, fashion, and women's magazines promoted.

These two magazines also took a more cautious approach to the fashion and social changes of the 1920s than that of society magazines. They ran more articles on dressing suitably for family occasions than dressing in the latest style for plays or restaurants, which surely reflected their readers' family values, status anxieties, and limited disposable income. Yet these magazines, and presumably their readers, were not puritanical or retrograde. The occasionally chiding tone of Camille Duguet, editor of *Chiffons,* contributed to the demise of the magazine in 1932. When *Chiffons* revived as the glossy monthly *Françoise,* costing five francs per issue, the prospectus referred to "the fresh, young, attractive, and elegant magazine" that was also "ingenious, convenient, practical and useful."[109] In short, it exploited almost every fashion buzzword associated with modernity. Although the new director, Françoise de Perval, was upbeat about fashion trends, *Françoise* did not survive financial problems as the depression deepened.[110] In a lateral move typical of fashion journalists, Perval joined *La Mode Pratique,* where she wrote a shopping column, "The Pretty Things I've Seen."[111]

Despite their titles, these two publications resemble Cynthia White's category of middle-class women's magazines whose purpose was to serve more than to entertain their readers. Like *Nos Loisirs,* they wrote about general wardrobes. In *Nos Loisirs,* "Clothing Suitable for All Occasions" listed three categories of apparel: city wear, for shopping and visiting; travel wear, for weekend excursions and vacation trips' and ceremonial wear, for weddings and baptisms. Recognizing that many readers could not afford a special travel wardrobe, the author, Marcey Ducray, recommended sturdy and versatile everyday clothing for travel. By ignoring ocean travel and automobile trips, as well as theater and sports apparel, she recognized that her readers were in the lower echelons of the bourgeoisie. One of her articles asserted that weekend travel was a new experience for readers.[112]

All three magazines included advice columns about sewing one's own clothing and updating last year's garments. *Chiffons* and *La Mode Pratique* also offered sewing, knitting, and crochet courses and sold patterns, material, and notions by mail order.[113] These services suggest that more women were following fashion, if only by changing the length of a hem or adding cuffs to sleeves. Like their English counterparts, these magazines offered "both a dream of unattainable glamour . . . and an opportunity to realize some of that glamour through economy, home-production, and adaptation."[114]

Fashion supplements to Paris newspapers paralleled society monthlies and fashion weeklies. *Excelsior-Modes,* a quarterly published by the daily newspaper *Excelsior,* cost five francs when it appeared in 1929 and ten francs a decade later, when it was thicker and glossier. *Excelsior-Modes* claimed the same number of subscribers (20,000) as the daily *Excelsior.* Appearing after the seasonal collections, it spotlighted models that "our best qualified elegant ladies" will wear.[115] In addition to printing photographs of *les élégantes,* it published articles by style setters and aristocrats. Like society magazines, it ran articles about travel and advertised hotels in the posh Atlantic seashore resorts of Biarritz and Deauville.[116] *Les Modes de la Femme de France,* a Sunday supplement, was more conservative about clothing trends. Coline, the fashion columnist, was one of the few fashion journalists who warned that low waistlines and high hemlines were not flattering to heavy-set women.[117] At a cost of one franc per issue in 1919, *Les Modes de la Femme de France* claimed "more that 200,000 *lectrices* among the elite of society." At a cost of one franc fifty centimes one decade later, it no longer claimed as large or distinguished a readership. Although it survived the depression, it never attracted as many readers as it had in the 1920s.[118] The decline may have been due to its increasingly sclerotic attitude toward new styles.

Other weeklies were more reasonably priced and widely distributed. Older weeklies *La Mode Illustrée* (1860–1937) and *La Mode* (1896) and two newer ones, *La Mode du Jour* (1921–56) and *C'est la Mode* (1932–38), cost less than a franc per issue in the 1920s and most of the 1930s. These four weeklies identified their readers as modest in income but respectable in conduct, which translates as lower middle class.[119] Like other weeklies, they were slow to welcome modern home decoration, largely because of cost concerns.[120] Each magazine had the familiar combination of a column following haute couture and another column on economical variations on fashionable attire. They characterized "real elegance" as "a perfect adaptation of the toilette to the person, the circle, the circumstance. Graceful gestures, a seductive voice, posture, and face, an ease, an absolute, innate distinction, all this is elegance."[121]

All four were really women's magazines. *La Mode Illustrée* promised to help readers "make the house as attractive and comfortable as possible." Cousine Jeanne, editor of *La Mode,* penned a column called "Talking Cooking"; *C'est la Mode* had "The Perfect Housewife." All these magazines gave advice on such marital responsibilities as purchasing a husband's clothes or correcting a husband's bad habits.

Some comparisons to the Catholic women's weekly *Le Petit Echo de la Mode* help establish the degree to which fashion reached petit bourgeois women. At a cost of twenty-five to sixty centimes per issue between the wars, *Le Petit Echo*'s circulation reached 1,125,000. The domestic activities of the female figures on the covers and regular columns on mothering, childcare, and cooking identify its ideal readers as lower-middle-class housewives.[122] This weekly even devoted the occasional column to "attractive housedresses." Despite, or perhaps because of, identifying with the ladies who staffed Catholic charities for families and children, *Le Petit Echo* expressed concern for the economic problems of working-class women. Going beyond the usual complaints about the "domestic crisis," or middle-class women's problems hiring domestic staff, they suggested that employers improve maid's working conditions. *Le Petit Echo* even published letters from women who were factory workers.[123]

Although *Le Petit Echo* distanced itself from other fashion publications, it claimed expertise in fashion:

> The outfits in the *Petit Echo* capture the essence of Parisian elegance. Without delay, we publish the creations of the most celebrated couturiers; no other journal can offer you such certain and rapid information. Perhaps you find the luxury publications more seductive? All they have over the *Petit Echo* is the superiority of their beautiful paper. Our paper is beautiful also, and if we do not put gloss on it, it is simply so we can sell our publication for 40 centimes. And we do not limit ourselves to presenting delicious new models of inaccessible elegance; our pattern service is at your disposal to furnish you with an excellent pattern of impeccable cut with which you can easily execute the pretty model in our collections.[124]

In actuality, the Baronne de Clessy, who wrote the "Revue de la Mode" column, was mildly critical of low necklines, high hemlines, short sleeves, and sheer fabrics, and Liselotte, who wrote the morality column "Jardin des âmes," could be scathing about revealing clothing "loosening morals."[125] Although all the magazines considered here presumed a Catholic readership (most obviously in features on christenings), *Le Petit Echo* alone devoted cover drawings to women attending church and covered Vatican pronouncements on women and the family. Franceline, who wrote the "Pages féministes" column, advocated subsidies for "families with many children" and railed against depopulation. She supported services for mothers and children.[126]

One can interpret the elaborate infrastructure of haute couture institutions and marketing instruments as evidence of top-down dictation to fashionable women or as testimony about designers' dependence upon stylish women. Designers and style setters themselves stressed negotiation and interdependence. Sales figures confirm that designers might propose, but Parisiennes and foreign buyers disposed. The sheer number, variety, and circulation of fashion magazines substantiate a complicated two-way relationship between couturiers and customers, as well as a democratization of fashion consciousness.

# PART

# II

# Business
# & the Workplace

# Chapter Four

# Business

Haute couture, confection (ready-to-wear), and textile manufacturing were closely connected export businesses in a sector susceptible to the dramatic business cycles of the interwar economy. Since their interests were not completely complementary, they both cooperated and engaged in internecine conflict, which they tried to reconcile through corporate structures. Each of these businesses adapted to the new economic instability with efforts to expand their markets without abandoning their long-standing policy of positioning French textiles and clothing as tasteful commodities in limited supply. Clothing was more successful than textiles at this balancing act.

## Connections

Despite differences of scale and clientele, haute couture and confection had historic connections. The initial Worth and Bobergh firm was a self-designated "Special House of Confections." The professional syndicate founded in 1868 represented couture and confection. In the 1890s, both branches presented two seasonal collections annually. Both prepared models for reproduction, not unique designs, albeit with considerable differences in the quantities made. Couture houses produced many models but authorized only a small number of any one model to be reproduced by foreign clothing manufacturers or select ladies' wear shops and supplied precise directions for the production of models. Confection sold fully and partially ready-made clothing cut in series and machine sewn. Couturiers and couturières distinguished their models from ready-made dresses by publicizing their artistry, "exclusive" fabrics, rich trim, careful fitting, and fine hand sewing—and by charging up to ten times more than good ready-made clothes cost.

By 1911, a separate syndicate for haute couture formalized the differences between the two branches of the garment industry.[1] More than a dozen couturiers and almost as many couturières provided made-to-measure apparel for wealthy and stylish women who purchased clothing at the couture houses. Individual customers were allowed only slight alterations to conform to their bodily proportions and personal requirements. Before an outfit left a couture house, it was inspected to assure that it met all the specifications on the production certificate.[2] This system of quality control, with some scope for personal expression, fostered publicity about the good taste or *distinction* of the fashion-conscious aristocratic and haute bourgeois women, as well as leading stage and film actresses, whom the fashion press dubbed *les élégantes.* According to the fashion press—and students of the fashion business—these privileged women were fashion arbiters. In the 1920s and 1930s, they inspired provincials and foreigners more than mannequins on the runway did.[3]

Confection put more emphasis on standardization to appeal to a wide customer base, but major firms offered made-to-measure or partially made-to-measure clothing and retailers emphasized their similarities to couture houses.[4] Although listed in trade publications under the rubric *"Nouveautés et Confections,"* not under *"Couture,"* up-market department stores appeared under a new heading, *"Sports Costumes–Haute Couture."*[5] It was not a coincidence that the type of clothing that emphasized simple, clean lines and symbolized the modern women blurred the boundary between haute couture and confection. The Samaritaine department stores opened a "luxury branch" replete with a fur salon and a tearoom.[6] In the 1920s, the luxury branch advertised in society magazines, and in the 1930s, *Femina* devoted a regular column to it. *Femina* columnist Françoise Arnaux detected "an atmosphere of elegance and refinement" in the luxury branch. In its couture department, premières who had previously been employed in couture shops prepared collections that served as a basis for a limited number of ready-to-wear dresses.[7] The Bon Marché imitated couturiers by showing their "latest creations" and employing some of the same illustrators used by the fashion magazines. In these catalogs, the Bon Marché used sales pitches similar to haute couture publicity: "All Bon Marché models are made in our workshops following *original designs* and reflect a constant *creative* effort to keep pace with Fashion" [italics mine].[8]

Au Printemps and Galeries Lafayette copied couturiers' practice of giving their late afternoon and evening gowns evocative names like "Enigma." While expensive by comparison to other dresses in their catalogs, their tea, cocktail, and evening gowns cost about one-fifth as much as comparable couture apparel.[9] Until 1932, Au Printemps' mail order catalogs sold partially ready-made day dresses that permitted personalized fitting by local dressmakers or astute home sewers but cost approximately two-thirds as much as ready-made day dresses in the same issues of these catalogs.[10] Even worse, from the perspective of haute couture, department stores displayed new styles "in the manner of" this or that couturier weeks after these styles had been introduced in the couture house collections.[11] All these practices made haute couture style, if not haute couture itself, more accessible to more bourgeois consumers.

Although textiles had never been mere suppliers for the fashion industry, the textile and fashion industries had always been interdependent.[12] In addition to serving milliners, haberdashers, and furniture, drapery, wallpaper, and automobile makers,[13] textile producers cooperated with couture in shaping fashion trends. Two designers explained this phenomenon. Jean-Charles Worth wrote that "designing a collection began, not with drawing, but with viewing and choosing from fabric collections." According to Madeleine Vionnet, "You must know the material, by look and feel" to imagine how it would "fall" or hang, especially draped or loose chemise dresses.[14] Beginning in 1923, Sonia Delaunay provided more than fifty designs annually to a silk manufacturer in Lyons. The following year, with the help of the fur merchant Heim, she opened her famous Simultaneous Shop, which sold both fabrics and clothing. Soon she began a long collaboration with the Dutch department store Metz and Company. Over the years Metz bought some two hundred of her designs for clothing and home decoration. Her work was sold at Liberty's in London and at department stores in New York. In 1928, Jane Regny and her husband designed prints with her signature on "every yard of the salvage" for an American manufacturer, Alcot Fabrics. In the early 1930s, Chanel collaborated with English and Scottish manufacturers of cottons and woolens.[15]

Couture houses purchased classic materials outright and reserved new materials "in exclusivity" so that they could claim exclusive rights to use these materials, but they often bought novelties "on condition," so they could return unused material for reimbursement. Usually, couture houses took more fabric than they needed in order to avoid supply problems if individual customers, and especially foreign buyers, purchased many garments made of certain fabrics. Returned remainders, including "exclusive" fabrics, were sold to "little" dressmakers and department stores that used the fabrics to make "imitations" of haute couture styles. Remaindered fabrics caused much friction between couturiers and textile manufacturers. At any time, a good house might have nearly half a million francs' worth of material on hand. By postponing payments on materials, textile magnates effectively bankrolled many couture houses.[16]

The silk industry had been enmeshed with couture since the eighteenth century.[17] Lyonnais silk manufacturers pioneered national and international advertising of fashion as well as fabrics. They sent dolls dressed in the latest Parisian styles to major cities in France and to European court cities to generate orders to be made up in Paris or by local dressmakers. In either case, dressmakers would be expected to order Lyonnais silks. By the 1920s, the fabrique exported two-thirds of its fabrics, as well as accessories like shawls, well beyond Europe and North America, to the Middle East, India, and Indo-China.[18] Silk magnates recognized that cooperation with haute couture helped their sales because French couture dominated the international and domestic markets. Already, prominent silk firms had opened outlets in Paris to provision Parisian couture and confection. These firms subsidized couture houses not only by generous return policies for unused materials but also by delaying payment for materials until collections sold.[19] But when suppliers helped talented designers set up businesses in competition with former employers, there were complaints. And when suppliers cut off credit during the depression, many couturiers were forced into liquidation or bankruptcy.[20]

## Wartime Adaptability

During the German occupation of the northeastern departments, centers of French woolen and cotton production, many mills were destroyed, dismantled, or deprived of their labor force.[21] A year after the onset of hostilities, over half the spindles in wool spinning were out of commission because they were in the invaded territories or had been immobilized. Nearly all the looms weaving woolens for clothing were in the invaded or immobilized territories. About one-tenth of the cotton looms were in the invaded regions or unable to operate because they were too near the front lines. Nearly 20 percent of the remaining cotton looms lay idle because of labor shortages.[22] Over the course of the war, the occupation amputated two-fifths of the textile industry's productive capacity. Cotton and woolen mills in Normandy and other parts of France scrambled to supply material to clothe the armed forces and the civilian population.[23]

The Lyonnais silk fabrique, dispersed throughout southeastern France, was not devastated. Historically, the fabrique comprised the production of silk fiber and fabric, but there had been a secular decline in the domestic production of fiber since the Méline tariffs of 1892. The much larger contingent of silk weavers organized a silk fabricants syndicate, which was in turn subdivided into fifteen groups according to the type of cloth woven, the destination of the cloth, or the purpose for which the cloth would be used. For instance, weavers of light fabrics dyed in pieces formed one group; weavers using dyed threads constituted another group.[24] Seventy-five percent of silk fabric was exported in 1913.[25] Between 1914 and 1915, silk exports to the United States doubled in value, thanks to the prosperity of the luxury goods market in the still-neutral country. When the United States entered the war in 1917, the value of French silks exported there fell by two-thirds.[26] Internally, silks remained more available than woolens or cottons.[27]

Like other branches of the textile industry, the fabrique adapted to wartime privations. As the silk industry revamped to supply the war effort, it transformed dress material for use by the air force. After the war, techniques developed to make silk parachutes were applied to production of light yet durable silks for lingerie and afternoon dresses.[28] The industry also accommodated couturiers' demands for lighter but durable fabrics for loose chemise dresses by investing in artificial silk (later named *rayon*) and blending it with natural silk, which made light silks more practical.[29] Haute couture mainly used artificial silks and blends in lingerie and loungewear.[30] One particularly successful blend was Bianchini-Férier's Rosalba (49% natural, 51% artificial silk), which was registered in 1918 and renewed through the 1950s. Used primarily in corsets and girdles, Rosalba also found favor with Madeleine Vionnet for her bias-cut dresses.[31] Even silk firms specializing in brocades, damasks, and lamés expanded production of lighter silk blends and introduced artificial silk versions of some of their richest materials.[32]

After not presenting winter collections in 1914, haute couture rallied for the 1915 collections, which were very sober and martial. Jackets and coats had the cut and pockets of military uniforms. Although some couture houses closed during the war—Jean Patou designed uniforms for the armed services—others continued to operate. The couture syndicate proposed a four-meter per dress restriction, which encouraged straighter, simpler silhouettes and shorter hemlines. In response to requests for practical outfits from bourgeois women acting as volunteer Red Cross nurses, who toiled in military hospitals as well as in civilian dispensaries,[33] wartime couturiers designed the simple chemise, a move that also eased problems

of limited supplies of materials for civilian clothing due to declining textile production and the redirection of much of the existing production to military use.
In the case of shorter hemlines and looser skirts, couturiers followed the example of bourgeois Frenchwomen involved in wartime work. These women had removed their trains, raised their hemlines, and adopted more practical shoes to fa-
cilitate travel around the city in buses, given the lack of civilian automobiles and
carriages. These changes also helped solve supply problems. When couturiers
lowered hemlines and amplified skirts after the war, many of these same women
resisted, since they still took public transit, liked moving around more freely, and
thought that shorter skirts were more "becoming." After three years, couturiers
raised the hemlines and introduced slimmer skirts.[34]

Chanel's resort to plebian fabrics to replace luxury materials is an example of
wartime improvisation. The leading wartime woolen manufacturer, Jean Rodier,
whose plants were in Normandy, offered her a huge stock of natural-colored jersey (a knit woolen) at a discount. Unable to imagine women buying couture garments made of jersey, which was normally reserved for underwear, Rodier insisted
that she try the fabric before he would make any more.[35] She persevered and prevailed. In 1917, fashion columnist Camille Duguet described jersey as light, supple, and "fitting for feminine bodies freed from the constraints of corsets." Two
years later, another columnist welcomed silk jerseys and pronounced jersey a
better fabric than linen for chemise dresses. By the 1930s, jersey was deemed
"the classic element . . . for all times, all circumstances, and all seasons."[36]

## Postwar Volatility, 1918–1922

During the First World War, 1,310,00 French soldiers died or disappeared. This
figure represented more than a quarter of Frenchmen aged twenty to twenty-seven.
Another 1,100,000 men suffered permanent disabilities. Among the mourners
were at least 600,000 war widows, approximately 450,000 of them mothers of
minor children. The actual number of war widows varied, as some 400,000 re-
married and as veterans wounded in the war died years after hostilities had ceased,
leaving new war widows.[37] In response, the state revised its system of war pen-
sions. While widows still received graduated sums based on the rank and cause
of death of the fallen husband, widowed mothers of minors could now access subsidies for the care and education of war orphans up to the age of thirteen. Even
supplemented by subsidies from the Wards of the Nation program, widow's pen-
sions did not suffice for widows of low-ranking war dead. Although many small

charities sprang up to serve them, many war widows had to work for pay.[38] Lacking reliable figures for the number of war widows who entered couture, confection, and textile work, we can only note that these industries employed large numbers of widows. Most widows who applied for apprenticeships for their children
to the Paris Conseil des Prud'hommes-Textiles (the industrial relations board for
textiles and clothing) were war widows. Both couture and confection had special
programs to hire wards of the nation as apprentices.[39]

Estimated material losses to France totaled 55 billion francs, one-quarter more
that the national income in 1913. Industrial production was 57 percent of its 1913
level and would take five years to return to the prewar level. Because the government mainly financed the war by borrowing, the national debt rose tenfold, and
because most of the debt was short term, the financial burden was unstable and
difficult to manage after the war. Hoping that German reparations would pay off
the debt, the government responded slowly to the looming financial crisis, and
government securities dropped to less than a fifth of their former value. Bourgeois
families who had invested in government securities before 1914 saw their income
from government bonds plummet.[40] Benjamin F. Martin subtitled his book on the
politics and diplomacy of Après-Guerre France "Illusions and Disillusionment."[41]
The subtitle also applied to private life.

During the postwar inflation, financially ruined families were in straightened
circumstances. Most of these families tried to "keep up appearances," which required heroic efforts, especially from housewives. Fashion magazines charted
women's efforts. From 1917 to 1920, *Femina* oscillated between encouraging
readers to buy clothes, dress up, and work as their contribution to the war effort,
on the one hand, and providing ideas and instructions for "little" dressmakers,
"easy to sew" patterns for home sewing, and advice on coping in difficult times,
on the other.[42] Women's magazines geared to middle-class housewives gave
equally contradictory advice. In preparation for the visit of allied heads of state
in 1919, *La Mode* told readers that "to be pretty and well dressed is a homage
publicly rendered to the courage and heroism of our soldiers, their sons, their
brothers." Conversely, *La Mode Illustrée* counseled careful household budget-
ing and employing war widows and orphans to do sewing and other household
work. As this magazine began to report on a serious housing crisis, it advised
readers to "reestablish your budgetary equilibrium" by working at home.[43]

Attitudes toward servants are another sign of consumer illusions about a return to a Belle Epoque–style household economy clashing with harsh new eco-

nomic realities. In the immediate postwar years, magazines as diverse as *Femina*, *Vogue*, *La Mode Illustrée*, and *Nos Loisirs* assumed that their readers had servants. In 1921, *Nos Loisirs* published an article on how to dress a maid; by 1923, it recognized that "the maid of all work is in the process of disappearing" and that readers would now have to do their own housework.[44] Aside from having less money in their household accounts, many middle-class women could not find women willing to work as domestics.[45] In the early 1920s, *La Mode Pratique* reported a "domestic crisis" increasing the housewife's workload; in the late 1920s, it recorded that housewives were forced to make "concessions" to domestic servants; in the midst of the depression, it finally acknowledged that housewives had halved the number of their servants from four to two, or two to one.[46] Society magazines dropped references to live-in maids but rarely referred to readers doing housework—unless you count interior decorating as housework.

While the fashion columnist for *La Mode* ran an article on attractive aprons for the housewife as early as 1921, society magazines eschewed comment on aprons. Even in the late 1930s, when *Vogue* acknowledged that some readers had to do housework, it advised wearing washable housedresses, not aprons. After asking why aprons were "out of favor," the author ducked the question by alluding to "psychological reasons that go beyond the scope of this article." These psychological reasons must have included the association of aprons with maids.[47] The only *Femina* cover that included a maid was published in 1934. Depicting a maid in the prototypical black dress with white apron catering to a semirecumbent lady in a negligee, it was a throwback to fin-de-siècle cover drawings.[48]

Reconstruction began in the formerly occupied departments as early as 1919, led by the city of Lille, which organized an international exhibition to revive commerce, industry, and agriculture in the "devastated Nord."[49] Efforts to rebuild and refit industrial plants were remarkable: 78 percent of the industrial establishments damaged during the invasion and occupation were fully or partially operational in 1923.[50] A decade later, British Board of Trade analysts considered French wool textile equipment "very modern," thanks to the replacement of war-damaged equipment during the postwar years. However, the analysts also noted that few mills were large and that integration of the stages of production was "uncommon." The Board of Trade study gave a similarly mixed review to the cotton industry: it had advanced technology due to postwar reconstruction but had not integrated production or built large, rationalized plants. These industries remained "divided and specialized" and dependent upon imports of cotton and wool fibers.[51]

External events harmed the export sectors of textiles, in general, and of woolens, in particular. The abrupt withdrawal of British and American support of the franc and the British decision to abandon the gold standard resulted in a dramatic drop in the value of the franc.[52] When the French government depreciated the franc in 1919, wartime inflation ended. Shortly thereafter, a worldwide recession spread to France, causing the franc to move up on foreign exchanges. Textiles were seriously squeezed. On the supply side, manufacturers paid higher prices for imported fiber; on the demand side, many foreign orders were canceled. The crunch damaged the textile sector, which employed nearly a third of the industrial labor force and over a quarter of the female labor force in manufacturing. Massive unemployment ensued.[53]

In the immediate aftermath of the war, more Lyonnais silk firms set up outlets in Paris, some of which included design workshops that collaborated with couturiers to create the textures, colors, and prints that couturiers desired. Simpler and straighter silhouettes required a softer and suppler fabric, which could be draped or finely pleated to allow mobility without altering the line or amplifying the contours of the body.[54] Accordingly, Lyon specialized in crepes de chine, which remained in vogue throughout the 1920s. The fabrique also made older fabrics less bulky (velour) and less stiff (taffeta) so that they could be used in the new chemise dresses and straight-lined suits. Chiffon velour and delicate taffetas enjoyed renewed popularity in late 1920s.[55] Printed silks came into fashion in the 1920s. Older motifs—flowers, Persian gardens, Japanese scenes—were "modernized," meaning that they became bigger, bolder, and more clearly delineated. A few cubist and geometrical patterns entered the repertoire.[56]

A few couturiers prompted innovations in textile products. Vionnet, who preferred crepe de chine and satin, which were pliant enough for the draping effect she sought, was the first to employ blends of natural and artificial silk. To accommodate bias-cut dresses, she prodded silk manufacturers to produce fifty-four-inch-wide dress material for the first time.[57]

After the war, woolen manufacturers briefly reclaimed their overseas markets.[58] The leading innovators were the Rodier brothers. Between 1853 and 1924, the House of Rodier registered 1,600 new blends, textures, and designs.[59] After the war, the brothers experimented with old and new yarns, revived artisanal production, made new blends, adopted new motifs, and wooed the fashion press.[60] Typically for French producers, the Rodiers specialized in fine, luxury fabrics and built small plants. Jean Rodier ordered artisanal production of Kasha, a blend including expensive Tibetan cashmere yarn. He escorted fashion journalists around his artisanal weaving centers, and journalists responded enthusiastically to his seasonal collections of fabrics, scarves, and shawls. One gushed that his kashas were "so supple, so personal, so feminine, and so seductive, too." Kasha, with its "exquisite softness and surprising lightness," replaced rougher, heavier woolens. Whole winter collections were "nearly entirely conceived with Rodier woolens."[61] Kasha and djersa (a fine jersey) introduced in these years remained in Rodier collections for more than a decade.[62] Initially intended for sportswear, kashas and djersas were adapted for afternoon and dinner dresses.[63] Chanel may have initiated fabrics' crossover from sports to formal wear, but she was hardly alone in this venture.

During the war, when rich fabrics were scarce, embroidery was the principal form of decoration on ladies garments. During the antebellum years, all fashion magazines advised readers to embroider to update and personalize their garments.[64] Embroidery being a feminine accomplishment,[65] they assumed that bourgeois women embroidered. Embroidery patterns were staples of the *Journal des Ouvrages de Dames* and *La Broderie Lyonnaise,* both women's bimonthlies that predated the Great War. Annual subscriptions to these magazines cost eleven and twenty francs, respectively, or up to seventy-eight francs with monthly patterns, yarns, and other supplies necessary to execute some of the patterns. Only bourgeois women could afford to subscribe, though working women might buy a single issue for one to two francs and use patterns in it for years. These magazines printed patterns for embroidery not only on linens, cushions, handkerchiefs, children's clothing, and women's underwear but also on women's blouses, dresses, and jackets. For women's under- and outerwear, the most common design was a traditional garland of flowers, though some floral motifs took on more abstract shapes over time. While editors of this genre of magazine could be critical of short hemlines as decadent and straight lines as masculinizing, their fashion columnists welcomed the trend toward looser, more practical clothing.[66] In short, these journalists were conservative but not retrograde. After the war, specialized magazines combined embroidery designs and up-to-date fashion coverage. Fashion and women's magazines found space for embroidery designs.[67]

Couture houses were starved of fine fabrics just when their clientele longed to put aside wartime drabness and the predominance of military colors as well as to offset the visual monotony—and reminders—of large number of women in dull black widow's weeds.[68] Because most of the available textiles were plain, they were

FIGURE 9. Davidoff embroidery. DEM 178 no. 7608. Courtesy, Archives de Paris.

embellished with rich embroidery. After the Russian Revolution, nearly 150,000 white Russian exiles arrived in Paris, and many Russian women, including aristocrats, did handicrafts to support their families. They embroidered handbags and blouses for the fashion industry and sold them at charity events. When these products were well received, many enterprising Russian women opened embroidery workshops to supply couture houses with embroidered blouses and dresses (fig. 9). The Grand Duchess Maria Pavlovna Romanova (1890–1958) opened her own house, called Kitmir, on the basis of an exclusive contract with Chanel. Chanel sent fabrics cut in her workshops to Kitmir's to be embroidered with patterns based on Maria Pavlovna's studies of old Slavic motifs and stitches that Parisians found "quite original."[69] In the early 1920s, Chanel made tunics in dark colors adorned with vividly colored, "exotic"—meaning Slavic—embroidery. Everyone from the young couturier Jean Patou to the long-established couturier Beer used heavy Slavic-style embroidery in 1921.[70]

## Prosperity, 1923–1928

As a consequence of the disruptions of the Après-Guerre, France did not duplicate prewar production levels for several years. The government's commitment to restore the franc to prewar parity on the gold standard, Germany's default on reparations, and the French occupation of the Ruhr, followed by hostile foreign and internal speculation on the franc, drove the value of the franc down to less than four cents American. Foreign trade improved, but higher taxes and internal inflation of almost 100 percent between 1922 and 1926 hurt French people on fixed incomes—some of whom might have bought an item or two of haute couture.[71] The government stabilization of the franc in 1926 provoked a recession in 1927. Poincaré's 8 percent devaluation of the franc in June of 1928 ended a decade of inflation and currency instability. Although growth picked up late in 1928, it had little effect on textiles.[72]

Unfortunately, existing economic statistics do not separate the figures for the overall production of clothing into ready-to-wear and haute couture. Together, exports soared through 1926, when the value of foreign exports of French clothing reached 1,970,638,000 francs. The declining value of the franc on foreign exchanges fueled the upswing, and the International Exhibition of the Decorative Arts boosted exports in 1926. By 1928, the monetary crisis and the devalued franc had caused a slump, with the value of exports falling to 1,434,608 francs in 1929, when the Great Depression hit. While Britain continued to be the largest foreign market for French clothing, the United States took second place by the mid-1920s. Western European countries came third through seventh place in these years, but New World countries Canada and Argentina moved up to eighth and ninth place among importers of French clothing.[73] Nevertheless, couture remained dependent upon two major overseas markets, Britain and the United States.

Couture houses increased in number and size in the 1920s. At the beginning of the decade, twenty-five leading houses catered to two distinct groups. The smaller group was composed of individual customers, some of them wealthy

Parisiennes and others rich foreigners residing in Paris. Commissionaires placed orders for, billed, and mailed purchases to stores outside Paris in return for a commission, and a rising number of foreign buyers for department stores, ladies' wear shops, and clothing manufacturers visited Paris for the four seasonal collections or set up offices in Paris.[74] In the mid-1920s, at least seventy-five couture houses each produced between 100 and 300 hundred models a year.[75] By the late 1920s, major houses employed between 1,000 and 3,000 workers apiece to produce 150 to 300 models annually, displayed in two seasonal collections and two midseason shows. At that time, haute couture directly employed between 200,000 and 300,000 women in the Paris region (the variation reflecting the seasonality of the couture market). Individual houses reported annual earnings of up to 80 million francs. Haute couture also indirectly stimulated the employment of 150,000 other workers, largely women, in associated industries, for example, embroidery and glove-making.[76]

Haute couture was highly competitive and very speculative. When Jean Patou reopened his house after the war, he "lifted" a première and all the seamstresses from Jeanne Lanvin's lingerie workshop by offering wages higher than the current labor contract, which Lanvin honored. In the boom years of the mid- to late-1920s, less famous couturiers made similar "raids" on rivals.[77] These raids are distinct from counterfeiting cases, in which premières took patterns from their previous employer to be duplicated by their new employer, part of an epidemic of copying (see chap. 5). Because only one-tenth of the models sold well enough to recoup the costs of designing, producing, and displaying them, designers assumed a high degree of risk. To prevent bankruptcy, most houses became limited liability companies and separated their artistic and business managements. This was especially true of married couturières, some of whom could not conduct financial affairs without their husband's consent; the 1907 law on married women's property rights did not abolish "marital authorization" of expenditures, which many bankers and notaries continued to require.[78] Couture houses also worked more closely with textile manufacturers, cooperating to produce fabrics suitable for the new, looser silhouette.[79] Finally, designers reduced risks by diversifying their product lines. The emblematic examples are Chanel's numbered perfumes, all bearing her name but each one numbered differently, to indicate particular scents.

The couture house of Jean Patou, located at 7, 9, and 11 rue Saint-Florentin, near the Place de la Concorde, began in June 1914 as a partnership between Jean and his father, Charles. In 1923, the house reincorporated as a limited liability company and issued 2,000 shares at 500 francs apiece, with most of the 1-million-franc capital held by Jean and Charles (610,000 francs and 360,000 francs, respectively). Jean was the "sole administrator." In concert with several other houses, the House of Patou added a sports department and a fur salon in the mid-1920s and sold accessories—scarves, boas, gloves, purses, jewelry, umbrellas—throughout its sales salons. The business owned a limousine and another luxury automobile, which were used to convey important customers to fittings and buyers to the collections, as well as seven Renault vans to deliver finished products.[80] Like Poiret, Patou employed unusual marketing techniques, such as presenting his models at an evening party, worn by mannequins who mingled with the guests, and inviting reporters and photographers to his redecorated home to write and illustrate magazine features about his home.[81] This aspect of personality advertising mirrors the practice of stage actresses and movie stars displaying their residences—and explicitly their good taste and implicitly their personalities—to the media.[82] Patou was a life-long bachelor, a man about town, and a gambler. Because he was the major stockholder and sole director, his personal behavior had serious implications for his business. When his house went into liquidation in 1935, he owed large sums of money to gambling casinos.[83]

Another couture house, Premet, located in the heart of the couture district, at 8 Place Vendôme, was headed by Mme. Charlotte, who was known in the 1920s for her "straight," "simple," and "youthful" day dresses and pleated sports skirts. Her model called "La Garçonne" took the United States by storm.[84] Mme. Charlotte followed the trend of hiring a business director and a publicity agent and diversifying by selling negligees, costume jewelry, and perfume.[85] Like Patou, she was an early proponent of a fitted bodice, telling Martine Rénier of *Femina* that "we are tired of the little sports outfit and the straight dress." When Rénier expressed surprise, Mme. Charlotte explained that the new models "would not hug the waist, as in the past, but merely draw attention to it.[86] Her predictions were premature, but accurate in the medium term, as a survey of fashion photographs and illustrations from 1929 to 1932 attests.[87]

When haute couture prospered, suppliers prospered. Between 1920 and 1923, most of the major Paris couture houses offered models "*à la russe,*" based on the traditional lines of Russian national costumes. The House of Caris, established in the early 1920s, showed only Russian-style dresses, Caucasian scarves, and handbags. At least five other houses with similar specialties opened in the same period.

Russian embroidery firms flourished. In 1923, Maria Pavlovna rented a building at 7 rue Montaigne and established an office and a showroom on the first floor and workshops on the other two floors. She employed more than fifty embroiderers. When the news of the discovery of Tutankhamen's grave hit Paris in 1923, it kindled "Egyptomania" among Parisians and a new fashion trend for geometric designs, precise lines, and color contrasts drawn from Egyptian art. To survive, the House of Kitmer added Coptic motifs and beaded fringe, which they displayed in a prize-winning exhibit at the 1925 Exhibition of the Decorative Arts.[88]

In the 1920s, Lesage established his famous embroidery and beading firm and produced some fifteen hundred pieces of embroidered and beaded fabrics for Vionnet alone.[89] In 1926, there were thirty-six other suppliers of embroidery and laces for ladies' wear and eighty-six wholesale/retail shops selling buttons. Some wholesalers specialized in one type of button, such as bone buttons. Related commerce also benefited. At least forty-seven shops sold cotton, woolen, silk, and artificial silk stockings.[90] With hemlines rising to mid-calf in the mid-1920s, sheer stockings were in great demand.

As early as 1927, the Silk Fabricants' Syndicate identified a decline in demand for silks in the expanding market for sportswear, and its members worried about increasing competition from the British, German, and Austrian sportswear industries.[91] The syndicate lobbied to ensure that artificial silks were labeled as such and that blends had labels indicating the proportion of artificial silk. Because prominent members, including the president of the syndicate, Férier, had invested in artificial silk, the syndicate merely joined the national and international silk federations in discussions about the proper name for artificial silk. After long discussion, the name chosen was *rayon*.[92] In the meantime, both pure and artificial silk producers and their associations engaged in a bitter promotional battle.[93] Ads for artificial silk touted its practicality and economy, and a new kind of ad, for "real" silk, proliferated.[94] One full-page ad had the following message in large type: "Real Silk is the true luxury and real economy. Madame, ask for natural silk and you will never have a bad surprise."[95] The "bad surprise" was likely shrinkage, which bedeviled some artificial silks.

Woolens expanded production until 1927, thanks primarily to exports favored by the depreciation of the franc. Blin and Blin Company, which specialized in rich and expensive fabrics, diversified, but mainly—and typically—into the production of other luxury fabrics. Along with other woolen producers, Ernest Blin exported directly to as many countries as possible, set up an export service with an office in Paris, sent agents on "study tours" to South America, and developed relations with Scandinavian countries. Despite these efforts, Great Britain remained the main client of Blin and Blin and of French woolen producers in general.[96] Although producers of dress-weight woolens complained about the competition of artificial fabrics and blends, few invested in artificial fabrics or integrated all stages of production, as major silk producers had presciently done.[97] In 1927, woolen producers complained to the government about heavy import duties on raw materials and drew the authorities' attention to high unemployment and even higher under-employment rates in northern textiles.[98] A fall of more than 850 million francs in wool exports in one year prompted demands for preferential duties on wool imports. The government launched a series of inquiries into the industry that revealed a secular downturn beginning before the Great Depression.[99]

## Crisis, 1929–1939

The Great Depression began internationally, with a dramatic decline in French exports in 1930–31 due to the stock market crash of 1929 and steeper duties on French imports. But the depression was aggravated by internal deflationary policies, so the depression that arrived later than elsewhere lasted longer than elsewhere.[100] After Britain and twenty-two other countries left the gold standard in 1931–32, France remained in what was known as the gold block, with deflationary effects. Not until 1936, when the Popular Front government devalued the franc and signed agreements with the United States and Great Britain to minimize exchange-rate instability, did international trade improve noticeably.[101] Although some economic historians query elements of the foregoing interpretation,[102] it explains the impact of the depression on textiles and clothing. Protective tariffs favored national markets for these commodities. Great Britain, France's largest foreign market, imposed 15 percent "emergency tariffs" on French couture and textiles. After threatening retaliation against English woolens, the French government opened trade talks Great Britain.[103] Like other economic diplomacy in the 1930s, these talks dragged on for years.

After the stock market crash of 1929, many American buyers stopped coming to Paris to buy couture clothes; some formed cartels to buy a few models in common and others relied upon style bureaus—new businesses to inform foreign buyers about trends—which meant that the buyers did not have to buy any original models.[104] American purchases fell 64 percent between the 1930 and 1931 mid-season collections, a plunge only partially accounted for by smaller collections and reductions of 20 percent on the average price of couture models. At individual houses cuts went deeper. Lanvin nearly halved the average price of her models: from 6,650 francs in 1930 to 3,940 francs in 1931. Vionnet cut the average price per model by a quarter, from 4,866 francs to 3,466 francs. A dramatically higher American duty on couture came to public attention when American customs seized a temporary collection of models because the American Embassy in Paris had not added the new duty onto the prices. This "crisis" accelerated public/private initiatives to get bilateral agreements to end unfair practices and unfavorable tariffs. These efforts stalled for several years.[105]

In the United States, some ready-to-wear firms appealed to Americans who had patronized haute couture to "Buy American," and Hollywood films that had elaborate cross-promotional relations with the American fashion industry began to compete with couture in defining fashion.[106] As well, domestic clients demanded less costly clothing, which meant cheaper fabrics and more artificial fabrics.[107] Fashion and women's magazines explained bourgeois women's new interest in lower prices, home sewing, and more reliance on neighborhood dressmakers. In *Figaro,* the fashion columnist reported that dressing luxuriously was no longer in good taste (*bon ton*).[108] *bon ton!*

Between 1929 and 1933, the maximum price of afternoon dresses dropped by more than 50 percent, from 4,200 to 2,000 francs, and overall earnings also fell more than half. A leading house in Paris, with a turnover of 70 million francs in 1929, only earned 30 million francs in 1932.[109] The houses of Premet, Cheruit, Doueillet, Doucet, Nicole Groult, and Philippe and Gaston went out of business.[110] Premet was a limited liability company with a capital of 3,100,000 francs divided into 100–franc shares. It had paid annual dividends of 8 francs per share in 1920, 1921, and 1922; 9 francs in 1923; 15 francs in 1924 and 1925; and 20 francs in 1926. As Premet felt the effects of the business slowdown over the next four years, it paid no dividends. In 1930, shareholders authorized a capital offering of up to 2,600,000 francs and appealed to Lloyd's Bank for credit. Suppliers, owed 3 million francs, pressed for payment, and when that did not transpire, for liquidation. Among the suppliers was Bianchini-Férier, which was owed 96,589 francs, and Coudurier, Fructus, et Descher, which was owed 80,959 francs. Two hundred and five individual customers had outstanding bills ranging from 710 francs (Dame Somerset Maugham) to 9,718 francs (Dame Babette Laurence Lyon).[111]

Patou went into liquidation in 1936, shortly before he died. Profits, which had risen steadily to 1930, fell by 8 million francs between 1930–31 and 1931–32. The company had to ask its lenders for an extension. With a capital of 300,000 francs, Patou created a perfume boutique in Paris and another one in New York. As the financial situation deteriorated and his debt rose to nearly five and a half million francs, he turned to suppliers and creditors for help, but they refused, without liquidation. The major creditors were M. Bader, of the Galeries Lafayette (1,000,000 francs), and four big textile producers: J. Remond and Company of Paris (561,696 francs), Alliance Textile of Lyon (304,380 francs), Bianchini-Férier (153,248 francs), and Rodier (175,777 francs). To avoid bankruptcy, Patou had to close some outlets and promise to repay 60 percent of his loans over a ten-year period.[112]

Couturiers survived by focusing more on the domestic market, by offering better prices, and by promoting "investment" dressing. As early as 1925, one of the most successful interwar designers, Lucien Lelong, declared that "dressmaking nowadays is an art, but an industrialized and organized art. . . . There is no question of creating fantasies but of establishing a collection of models on a solid basis. . . . Dresses are expensive at the present time, and women—as chic as they may be—can no longer permit themselves to renew their wardrobe each season; it is however indispensable for them always to possess a few new creations." First he reduced the embroidery and trim on his clothing.[113] Next he borrowed pleated skirts from ladies sportswear for city wear and called his new line "The Cinematic Mode." Advertising for this line, with its swingy skirts, targeted "the mobile profile of the woman of today."[114] Then he diversified by producing makeup with names like "banana flesh" cream and perfumes with his name and alphabetic indicators for different scents: Lelong A, B, and C.[115] In the 1930s, Lelong used more artificial silk and introduced "limited-edition dresses" at 1,500 francs apiece.[116]

Another couturier made hundreds of limited-edition dresses at 300 francs per item; if the client paid 350 francs, she got a made-to-measure version based on one fitting and one alteration.[117] Launched in 1930, Toutmain (all by hand) was a more extreme effort to extend the boundaries of haute couture. This house, located on the Champs Elysées, sold dresses at 150 francs that were comparable to dresses costing 450 francs at major department stores. The Toutmain shop sold a hundred items a day and also sold by mail order.[118]

In 1932, 1933, and 1935, Nina Ricci, Robert Piguet, and Mme. Grès opened new houses.[119] Although knowledgeable observers considered new ventures "foolhardy," fashion commentators felt that Piguet had made a sensible decision to specialize in "simple and sober" dresses in material of the finest quality, at reasonable prices.[120] Ricci, born in 1883 in Turin, worked at a couture house until

1929, when the owner of that house died. Encouraged by her sons, she set up her own house. Designing directly on a mannequin, like Chanel, she was a technician "without an equal." Renowned for her "impeccable" fittings, she was also known for prices about a third lower than prices for comparable items at Lanvin or Schiaparelli. She also offered a relatively inexpensive "young women's line," keeping costs down by offering only two fittings. Another practical innovation was a suit with two skirts. By 1939, the business covered eleven floors in three buildings and employed 450 workers in twelve workshops.[121]

Although less is known about ready-to-wear manufacturers, they may have suffered less. While the production of textiles for furniture, drapes, and other household and business purposes fell precipitously, the number of workers making fabrics for clothing only fell by about 11 percent. Economic historian Alfred Sauvy shows that the average prices of selected ladies wear—not couture clothing—dropped by almost half between 1929 and 1935 and then nearly recovered by 1938. He speculates that purchases of ready-made clothing probably did not decrease markedly and that better upkeep of clothes compensated for whatever cutbacks occurred.[122] My survey of fashion and women's magazines supports the suggestion that consumers took greater care in the selection and maintenance of clothes. Even couturiers began to talk about "investment" dressing.

Suppliers also suffered. Without a professional manager or much business sense, Maria Pavlovna was forced, on the eve of the Wall Street crash, to sell the House of Kitmer to a French embroidery firm. Most of the Russian houses went out of business shortly thereafter.[123] Prevost, Constantin, and Company, which sold wholesale lace and embroidery in the couture district, went into liquidation in 1930. Beginning as a partnership in 1909, the business did well until 1927, then reported losses of 19,502 francs, 84,617 francs, and 29,859 francs in the last three years of operation.[124] The Artistic Workshop, a smaller putting-out embroidery shop owned and operated by a Lithuanian emigrant, Natalie Davydoff, did not survive liquidation the same year.[125] Lesage's beading and embroidery firm outlasted the depression, thanks in large part to the patronage of Schiaparelli, who had whimsical motifs embroidered on her signature capes. Other embroidery firms shrank but continued to operate.[126]

In the silk fabrique, the depression was deep and long. Exports of crepe de chine—the market the fabrique had developed in the 1920s—collapsed. Between 1930 and 1932, the number of silk companies going out of business doubled and the number of judicial liquidations and bankruptcies quadrupled. In 1935 the fabrique exported just over half the total exports for 1928. Although the Silk Fabricants Syndicate tried to cope by decreeing a twenty-nine-hour workweek, factories had to shut down, either for several months or forever. In 1932, the textile workers' union estimated that nearly half of the plants in the Department of the Isère had been closed, either temporarily or permanently. In 1937 exports improved due to the devaluation of the franc, a commercial accord with the United States, reviving sales with Germany, and the coronation of George VI in Britain (which boosted sales of silk and couture).[127] Profits for firms that survived rose the following year.[128]

Consider the trajectory of a major silk firm. Bianchini-Férier's exports to their New York branch fell by 75 percent from 1928–29 to their low point in 1934–35. Sales to Great Britain dropped by an astonishing 86 percent between 1928–29 and the low point in 1935–36. Redirecting their attention to the internal market, the firm encountered a buyers' market. Instead of placing big, speculative orders, Parisian buyers tended to order according to demand, limit their stocks, and insist on rapid delivery. Bianchini-Férier and other textile manufacturers introduced new lines for department stores to compensate for lower demand in haute couture. During these years, the firm could no longer self-finance, and debts that had never before surpassed 1 percent rose to 4.56 percent of turnover in 1931. Dividends were not paid between 1931 and 1938. To cut costs, Bianchini-Férier reduced hours and employees in their factories. The number of workers in its weaving factories outside Lyon fell by half between 1920 and 1935 (from 50,000 to 25,000). But personnel at the headquarters in Lyon, where most of the staff did research for the collections, increased from seventy-two in 1928 to seventy-five in 1935.[129]

The impact on woolens was more serious and enduring, due to external conditions—dependency on foreign imports and higher duties on its products in major foreign markets—and to internal inadequacies, notably, entrepreneurial inflexibility, partially linked to the predominance of small-scale producers. As the chairman of the French Central Woolen Committee reported in 1928, "By the very nature of our industries, which are subject to the variation in quality of the raw material, to the changes of fashion, and to special processes, a large part of the so-called methods of rationalization present to them only a very limited interest. . . . Neither women nor even men wish to wear standardized fabrics. . . . Under these conditions how can standardized production be practiced?" English analysts did not believe in the French industry's sensitivity to fashion dictates, noting that the secular trends had been toward wool blends and durable fabrics of the knitted, tweed, and homespun type—suitable for the popular new mode of sports clothes—had been substituted for the older serges, worsteds, and dress goods. The French industry, best known for fancy and novelty goods, had not adapted to these secular trends.[130]

⚜

In 1932, a marketing expert investigated the condition of haute couture. Fitz Bénard reproached couturiers for extending credit to customers for long periods of time, during which they could not pay suppliers, and he blamed some couturiers for offering discounts of 10 to 15 percent to women of the world who wore their clothes to special events, because news about the discounts spread and other women demanded the same consideration. Bankers told Bénard that they had no interest in investing in or offering more credit to couture and associated industries. He faulted suppliers for forcing many couture houses into liquidation or bankruptcy and for encouraging four premières who left houses they had worked for to establish competing houses in the same neighborhood. Like many others, he found the "remainders" system deleterious because it "immobilized" stock for long periods of time and then sold extra stock below cost. He censured some textile manufacturers for launching "shadow brands" similar to those of higher quality materials—yet another manifestation of the democratization of fashion. His proposed solutions were cooperation and concentration—"an organized economy," or corporatism. Although he recognized "the ferocious and ruinous individualism of couturiers," he recommended that they cooperate in a common purchasing scheme to eliminate "an impressive army of parasitical intermediaries" and in a collective advertising policy.[131]

Couturiers and textile producers tried some of Bénard's recommendations. In response to the crisis unfolding in the textile sector, they engaged in collective advertising. As early as 1928, the silk syndicate joined with the Couture and Millinery Syndicate and "some women of the world" in a Luxury Goods Committee to "make sports costumes more elegant and to employ silk in lieu of woolens." The Lyonnais syndicate financed a contribution of 150,000 francs to the campaign by raising fees by 50 percent; Parisian syndicates put up 100,000 francs, and the silk manufacturers of Saint-Etienne added 75,000 francs. In less than a year, the Luxury Goods Committee raised 836,000 francs and spent 344,000 francs on fêtes in Paris, Deauville, and Biarritz, 71,000 for a press campaign, and 47,000 franc for films and other propaganda vehicles. A similar campaign was mounted in the United States. The silk syndicate exhorted manufacturers to create new fabrics for sports dresses and to consider making silk blends, as Rodier had already done. When the press campaign had some effect, another promotional effort was launched in 1932. Working with a group called "Paris Seasons," composed of "personalities from couture" such as Patou and the directors of the Houses of Lanvin and Vionnet—M. Labusquière and M. Trouyet—they tried to revive the Paris season.[132]

The economic crisis and the political and social disruptions it entailed evoked efforts to impose a corporate structure on silk weaving. Although silk fabricants had historically been advocates of liberal economic policies, a minority began to debate collaborative schemes for the purchase of raw materials, management of sales, and defense of their common interests. When the crisis of 1929–30 lingered into the mid-1930s, talk turned to a compulsory entente to impose minimum prices, limit the number of new factories, buy up redundant looms, etc. By 1934, a government inquiry proposed a law giving employers' associations the power to purchase and destroy looms. The following year a legislative bill would have extended the compulsory entente to any industry in which a majority of producers agreed to it. The bill died in the Senate, owing, in part, to opposition within the fabrique. Kevin Passmore, who studied this corporatist venture, insists that it had "authoritarian potential" but was not fascist."[133]

When les élégantes wore new dress styles, their selections had implications beyond what stylish bourgeoises would wear in France and elsewhere. The few hundred haute couture models that sold well annually were end products of a complex of closely connected and highly competitive businesses in two sectors of the French economy. Successful models produced by twenty-five to a hundred Paris couture houses (in the early and late 1920s, respectively) influenced not only confection, the larger branch of the garment industry, but also the textile industry, both industries dispersed throughout France. In addition, haute couture and confection had implications for thousands of businesses making jewelry, gloves, scarves, and other accessories, as well as ladies' hats, purses, shoes, and other accoutrements, mostly in and around Paris. Couture and confection were also supplied by businesses that produced notions, such as bindings, piping, and thread, and finishing touches, such as beads, buttons, and lace, located throughout France.

These interconnected businesses all struggled through difficult economic circumstances between the two world wars, beginning with the destruction of plants at home and the loss of markets abroad during the First World War, a postwar recovery in a period of rampant inflation, and, after a brief period of prosperity, the drastic reduction in demand and numerous bankruptcies during the depression. Although haute couture and textiles adapted to each of these economic challenges with technological and organizational innovation and efforts to expand their markets without abandoning their specialization in tasteful goods, their endeavors were hindered by the system of financing and their fierce competitiveness. In the end, haute couture succeeded better than the textile sector, which was devastated in the Great Depression.

*Chapter Five*

# The Workplace

o fulfill international and national commitments, haute couture and textiles had many work sites and huge workforces. In the mid-1920s, more than 1,200,000 French people, mostly women and girls, were employed in the production and retailing of textiles, apparel, and accessories. In the Paris region, nearly 300,000 people, mostly women and girls, made ladies' wear, lingerie, and millinery. Counting all Parisians engaged in the production of textiles, embroidery, lace, buttons, braids, beads, fringes, feathers, flowers, and notions, nearly a quarter of the population of more than 4 million worked directly or indirectly in the women's garment industries.[1] To underline the economic importance and class dynamics of the allegedly "frivolous" luxury industry known as haute couture, this chapter goes behind the beautifully appointed showrooms of couture houses to reveal the humble workrooms and crowded working conditions on the upper floors of these houses and further afield, to the textile factories located throughout France that supplied them. These workplaces were not trivial to the million or so men, women, and children who worked in them. Nor were these workers' efforts to protect and improve their livelihood peripheral to the fractious industrial relations that characterized the interwar decades and culminated in the massive labor unrest of 1936.

## Couture Houses

Couture houses combined production and sales in one location, which often encompassed several contiguous buildings. The House of Premet had one building with a reception room and an apartment on the ground floor, a large commercial space with a grand salon, eight smaller salons, and a boutique on the first floor (second story, in North America), ten workshops on the second, third, and fourth floors, and garret rooms for fourteen maids on the fifth floor. The grand salon was richly furnished with eight Regency chairs worth 800 francs apiece and two Louise XV marble-topped gilded wood consoles worth 2,000 francs; the foyer contained another Louis XV–style chest worth 1,000 francs.[2]

More has been written about the glamorous public space of couture houses than about the shabby work space in upper stories and annexed buildings.[3] During the business and social whirl of the "great fortnight" in February, when couturiers displayed their wares morning, afternoon, and evening, fashion magazines described sales salons in seasonal features called "Visits to Couturiers."[4] Fashion writers and general-interest publications were intrigued by the spectacle of the fashion show. The Countess Riguidi referred to it as "a religious ceremony. They prepare the chapel; decorate it with plants, organs are replaced by a jazz ensemble."[5] In the mid-1920s, men attended fashion shows as a form of theatrical entertainment, though women customers were quite serious about shopping at the spectacle.[6] One visitor, Louis Gillet of the Académie française, explained that salons "have one rule, which is to observe in very grand luxury, a décor of extreme sobriety . . . it is only a frame, nothing should distract attention from, or compete with, the living scene." His visit began with saleswomen seating clients on satin-upholstered chairs, then "the rustling of rich curtains through which a dozen mannequins slipped." Starting with simple morning suits for walking or shopping, the show proceeded to the more elaborate five o'clock, cocktail, tea, and supper frocks, and culminated with sumptuous ball and wedding gowns. Each mannequin wore a garment with a number or a name, and each spectator received a notebook listing those numbers or names, making it easy for customers to order items that interested them.[7]

At some houses, only one mannequin walked the catwalk at a time, pausing to turn around two or three times to show all perspectives on and features of her attire; other houses had up to four mannequins pacing and pivoting at any one time. Some couturiers and couturières hired only one "type" of mannequin (e.g., all blondes), so mannequins seemed interchangeable. Most couturiers prescribed the accessories worn; Chanel even dictated the shade of the stockings. She trained her mannequins to assume the "Chanel pose" (one foot in front of the other, one hand in a pocket), which she believed best exhibited her "minimalist chic."[8] According to Louis Gillet, mannequins had a haughty walk, which "somehow resembled an aristocratic walk."[9] Although they were not as tall, young, or emaciated as today's models, they had to be at least one meter seventy centimeters tall, under twenty-five years of age, and slender (significantly, no measurements survive, if they ever existed). For a major collection, each mannequin might be fitted for dozens of models. In larger houses, mannequins specialized in certain kinds of attire. Underneath their outerwear, they were naked except for a girdle to compress their hips and cover their private parts. In a dressing room adjoining the runaway, dressers helped them into and out of models.[10]

A very few couture houses prepared two sets of outfits, one for mannequins and the other for fuller-figured customers, so that customers larger than mannequins might have a better idea of how outfits would look on them.[11] *Vogue* warned readers that they would be disappointed if they were swayed by the way clothes looked on mannequins or by sales ladies' patter that did not take the customer's physique into consideration.[12] Between shows, customers could consult a sketchbook of models and have a mannequin display models that they thought they might purchase.[13] Some houses had a miniature fashion show several times a week, to which they invited good customers in advance.[14] Savvy Parisians waited for post-season sales.

Wendy Gambier argues that relations among dressmakers and customers in the United States could be quite intimate.[15] Insofar as French customers collaborated with "little" dressmakers on outfits and were loyal to good dressmakers, French customers may have had close relations with neighborhood dressmakers.[16] Evidence about the nature of their relationships is rare, because going to a local dressmaker was part of everyday life, of the "taken for granted."[17] Haute couture was another world. A reporter called the transition from a neighborhood dressmaker to a couture house a revolution.[18] Consulting, measuring, and fitting a client required several appointments with a première seamstress, the head of a workshop within the house. Fittings alone involved ten measurements and several checks after basting the model to ensure that it fit the client.[19] One of the most famous style setters, Daisy Fellowes, wrote about leaving a couture house "very tired, but radiant," which hints at the time and rewards involved in a fitting.[20] Because only premières did fittings, only they had much physical contact or conversation with customers. These contacts could be lucrative; customers financed a handful of premières who set up their own houses. Most employees in haute couture had little communication with customers.[21]

Observers who described the workspace called it a labyrinth. When Georges Le Fèvre visited Vionnet's back rooms in 1929, he contrasted the neat, well-lit, and "surgically clean" sewing rooms to the cluttered, dark, and dusty rooms he had seen elsewhere. Every morning teams of cleaning ladies came in, at an annual cost of 250,000 francs. He noted that even the six hundred seamstresses dispersed in Vionnet's thirteen workshops were scrupulously clean. Vionnet explained that she kept her workrooms clean and "transparent" because they produced goods that were a "pure expression of Parisian taste." She prided herself on providing a kitchen, a dining room, an infirmary, clothes closets, and bathrooms for her personnel, precisely because these were unusual amenities. Although her background as a seamstress may account for her investment in healthy working conditions and such services as a savings plan for pregnant and parturient workers, improving working conditions probably helped retain personnel during the boom years.[22] Most designers displayed little interest in employees' health or welfare. Aside from sponsoring two morale-boosting events, an annual seamstresses ball and a contest to identify the best young seamstress, the employers' syndicate, in conjunction with the clothing union, subsidized country vacations for some personnel.[23]

## Couture Workers

Employees of couture houses were divided between front rooms and backrooms and were arranged hierarchically within each category. Initially, waged workers were officially divided by sex, with women earning about half to two-thirds the wages of their male colleagues, even in the same job categories. After a decade and a half of formal commitment to equal wages, the leading union in the clothing sector removed some of the sex-specific language in labor contracts but made no significant headway in cutting the wage gap between the sexes.

Little is known about the receptionists and sales personnel in the public spaces beyond their monthly salaries under the 1936 labor contracts (not always respected in subsequent years): receptionists could expect 800 francs, a new saleswoman 700 francs, and an experienced one 1,000 francs.[24] The contracts do not mention commissions for saleswomen, which would have made them inexpensive substitutes for premières.

More is known about mannequins. Initially, couturiers chose mannequins among saleswomen. By the early twentieth century, major couture houses hired "slim and well-mannered" young women to display outfits in their salons. After the Great War, socialites dressed in the latest couture outfits posed for photographers like the Séeberger brothers at fashion showcase events, for example, the Longchamps races. They posed in the studio for magazines but did not walk the runway.[25] Couture houses recruited mannequins outside France in order to present "ideal types" attractive to foreign buyers. In New York, Jean Patou advertised for "three ideal types of beautiful young American women who seriously desire careers as mannequins in our Paris atelier. Must be smart, slender, with well-shaped feet and ankles and refined of manner." (The emphasis on feet and ankles reflected the trend toward rising hemlines and the sightline of seated spectators.) Patou brought six of the nearly four hundred Americans who replied to this ad to Paris and thought that they drew more American buyers to his next show.[26]

To remain slender, mannequins resorted to diets, slimming "salts," massages, and exercise regimens. Those who did not remain slim and youthful-looking lost their jobs or took other positions in a couture house. Mannequins received monthly salaries similar to those of the sales personnel. While a few mannequins had contracts with couture houses that ensured them work during the off-season showing dresses to important customers, most mannequins were unemployed between the busy seasons leading up to and during the four seasonal collections.[27] These two patterns of employment account for conflicting depictions of mannequins, one as gold diggers taking advantage of their position to rise on the social scale by attracting the attention of wealthy men, another as demoralized women vulnerable to sexual exploitation by wealthy men and depressed from observing the contrast between their working and nonworking environments.[28]

Backroom workers were officially divided by sex. A 1920 contract covering couture and clothing workers set minimum monthly wages by sex, from 300 francs for female packers to 650 francs for female designers, and from 600 to 850 francs for men. There were gender differences within the same occupations, whereby a male fitter earned 700 francs and a female fitter 500 or 600 francs, depending on the number of workers the female fitter oversaw.[29] But most of the wage gap was due to wage differences between occupational categories: the largely male cutters won a weekly wage of 127.10 francs in 1920, while female seamstresses in the same firms settled for 67.20 francs.[30] Cutters were skilled, but both cutters and seamstresses underwent apprenticeships. Some of the wage difference reflected the devaluation of any work associated with women, such that the skills involved were regarded as naturally or essentially feminine (a stereotype reflected in and reinforced by training girls to sew at home and in school).[31]

By 1936, labor contracts were less openly gendered. Ten categories of secretarial and financial staff earned between 950 and 1,300 francs a month, nine categories of packers, porters, and drivers earned between 800 and 1,250 francs, and three grades of stock worker earned 800 to 1,300 francs. The contracts only specified gendered wage differences for a few job categories, and when they did, stipulated that women earned about two-thirds what men did. However, tailors still earned more than premières, and male assistants earned between 33 percent and 45 percent more than female assistants.[32] These figures resemble the average wage disparities between male and female factory workers and retail employees in the late 1920s.[33] Being a feminized industry and serving a feminine clientele did not override societal attitudes about the appropriate wages for men versus women.

Initially the Clothing Workers Federation accepted wage differentials by sex.[34] However, with a significant female membership encouraged by lower union dues for women and with ties to the Confederation Générale du Travail Unitaire (CGTU), the radical labor federation, the Clothing Federation paid lip service to pay equity.[35] The provisional wartime executive board consisted of five women and four men, and immediately after the war, four of the eleven regional delegates to the National Federation were women. Thereafter the number of women on the executive board fell to one.[36] At the 1924 congress, a feminist delegate, Alice Brissat, proposed a male and a female secretary. When most delegates opposed, President Millerat persuaded them to accept the principle but apply it at the next congress. Despite this compromise, no women were elected to the next board (although more women were elected to regional councils).[37] At its first congress, the CGTU constituted a commission for feminine propaganda. Intrepid women like Jeanne Chevenard, who led a 1919 clothing strike in Lyon,[38] undertook grueling propaganda tours throughout France urging greater effort to organize women and to gain equal pay.[39] Male allies were more equivocal. They qualified their support for pay equity, saying it "does not mean that women should do all men's work. We must take into account their physical inferiority."[40] The result was little change.

At the top of the elaborate backroom hierarchy were the premières, who headed the workshops that prepared models. They cut *toiles* (patterns made of muslin) on the basis of sketches of designer's models drawn by artists trained at the Ecole des Beaux-Arts or at the new professional school for the couture industry.[41] Premières received allotments of material and notions, cut the material, directed the sewing of models, fitted mannequins and important customers, and sold models in return for a salary plus a commission on sales.[42] As the number of employees in major houses rose to one to two thousand, divided into fifteen or twenty workshops, the existing hierarchy became more complicated. Premières specialized, with one preparing *toiles* and another assembling models. Other than those making coats, jackets, and capes, few workshops specialized in a type of clothing. Many premières became more like supervisors or managers. Salesclerks and fitters did much of what had been their work, with the exception of consulting with clients about their special needs.[43] As the point of contact with customers, premières were essential to the business. A première who made mistakes preparing *toiles,* measured inaccurately, or was insensitive about a delicate subject like body size could damage a house's reputation.[44] The departure of a talented première might mean a loss of customers who were more loyal to a person who knew their personal needs so well than they were to a house. Because premières were often closely allied with their assistants, their departure might entail the loss of their closest associates, the second hands, and the seamstresses under their direction. Competition for capable premières and seconds became so furious that couturiers insisted on contracts for the duration of the busy season and later for several years, as well as six months' notice of intention to quit. Dozens of cases of broken contracts were brought before the Conseil des Prud'hommes (the industrial relations board).[45]

Below the premières came the seamstresses, known internally as "little hands" and externally as *midinettes* or *cousettes.*[46] Second hands finished a model by placing and attaching pockets to the garment (a tricky job, which required alignment of patterns and textures), hand working buttonholes and button loops, stitching on facing, piping, bindings, and other edgings, as well as appliqués and other decorative elements. "Little hands" added the lining, hemmed, and attached buttons, hooks, and other closures.[47] These processes were important, because handwork inside garments was then, as it is now, a hallmark of couture clothing.[48] Seamstresses took pride in hand stitching entire garments. During the depression, they complained that limited-edition dresses encouraged several houses to resort to piecework.[49]

Weekly wage rates varied according to the job category. After labor unrest under the Popular Front government in 1936, many couturiers signed contracts specifying a weekly pay scale of 208 francs for a première, 149 to 173 francs for second hands, depending on their qualifications and experience, and 195 for little hands.[50] For comparative purposes, recall that haute couture dresses cost between 1,500 to 4,500 francs after price reductions during the depression.

Three caveats are in order. First, the figures cited above exaggerate the rise in real wages between 1920 and 1936 because they do not take into account massive inflation between 1921 and 1926 and devaluation of the franc in 1928. In general, these financial and monetary variations meant a 10 percent decline in real wages from 1921 to 1926, followed by a commensurate rise in real wages from 1926 to 1930. Between 1930 and 1935, the cost of living fell, albeit less dramatically than wage rates did, leaving most workers worse off than they had been in 1930 but better off than they had been in 1920.[51] Second, weekly, biweekly, and monthly wage rates cannot be multiplied to get annual income because textiles and clothing were seasonal industries, where workers experienced seasonal unemployment and/or underemployment. Third, wages in Paris, like the cost of living in the capital, were higher than in the provinces; wage rates for Lyonnais premières and their assistants in the 1936 contract (with the Lyonnais Haute Couture Employers Syndicate) were one-quarter lower than the rates for their Parisian counterparts.[52]

Compared to the nineteenth century, seamstresses encountered less criticism in the twentieth about inappropriate clothing and sexual behavior. One reason was the advent of less ornate and elaborate couture clothing—or the democratization of couture—which meant that seamstresses could reproduce clothes similar to those of their customers without seeming to overstep their social standing. Another reason was increased labor organization and militancy, which were at odds with moralistic appeals about sexual misbehavior or pathetic appeals about poor women's vulnerability. Organized seamstresses could be prim and proud. They had cool relations with mannequins because, as a mannequin explained, "They consider us luxury dolls, kept women, fast-living women who were insults to the work of proletarians."[53] When Toutmain introduced low-cost dresses in the 1930s, the couture union denied that Toutmain had hired unemployed couture workers. In haute couture, union activists explained, seamstresses served a five-year apprenticeship—including two or three years as little hands—in fine handwork. Hand stitching could not be done rapidly enough for establishments like Toutmain.[54]

## Confection Work

In ready-to-wear, or confection, work sites and working conditions were very different. Sweated labor, meaning domestic or small workshop labor combined with low wages and seasonal employment, was a serious problem. Seamstresses doing piecework in their homes or small workshops were most subject to insecure seasonal employment and long periods of underemployment during dead seasons.[55] Criticism from organized workers, public health doctors, consumer groups, and feminists forced the Ministry of Labor to conduct an inquiry into sweated labor in the lingerie industry between 1905 and 1909. The final report found workdays exceeding the legal standard of ten hours for women and piece rates that converted into ten to twenty centimes per hour. The report also criticized overcrowding, poor lighting, and inadequate ventilation. The major recommendation was a minimum wage to curb excessive domestic labor.[56] Years of negotiations on how to set minimum wages in different industries and dispersed work sites meant that sweated labor continued in clothing as in other sectors of the economy.[57] In 1915, an act set regional minimum wages based on "the ordinary hourly or daily wage of a nonspecialized worker in the region." Regional committees had to calculate minimum wages from piece rates and soon after had to factor in the regional cost of living. Because such calculations were time-consuming, the rates were revised only every three years, even though the cost of living doubled in the immediate postwar years.[58]

After the First World War, the feminist Office of Domestic Labor, under the leadership of Jeanne Bouvier, tried to use the Conseil des Prud'hommes to enforce the minimum wage.[59] When employers appealed an early decision favorable to the Office of Domestic Labor, the Appeal Court rejected the competence of any association or union to initiate complaints under minimum-wage legislation.[60] Thereafter, Jeanne Bouvier ran for the Conseil des Prud'hommes, and the Office of Domestic Labor successfully sued two subcontractors for paying piece rates that did not ensure a minimum daily wage.[61] After 1924, the Office put most of its effort into extending the 1915 law to men and all the intermediaries involved in putting-out work (and a social insurance law).[62] Other suits, mounted by individual workers, failed because of intractable problems trying to translate piece rates into daily wages. The Clothing Federation lobbied for a union label to be placed near the trademark on garments to signal consumers that the workshop was "hygienic," meaning it did not employ sweated or domestic labor.[63] A decade of lobbying resulted in the extension of the domestic labor law to men and the calculation of minimum wages on the basis of an eight-hour day.[64]

These changes did not satisfy the Clothing Federation or the CGTU. In 1932, Jeanne Chevenard, the union activist from Lyon, documented the expansion of domestic work in the Lyonnais countryside and attributed it to the electrification of the countryside and the use of automotive transport.[65] Unions lobbied unsuccessfully for wage parity with workshop workers and for coverage of domestic workers under the social insurance law of 1928. After the social insurance law and the favorable labor accords of the mid-1930s, manufacturers turned to domestic work to avoid paying insurance premiums or implementing the forty-four-hour workweek. Approximately 23,000 women toiled long hours in their homes in dispersed villages south of Lille.[66]

In the 1920s and 1930s, employers enlarged ready-made clothing workshops and reorganized them according to "the industrial method." In confection, the industrial method meant many workshops, each making only one part of a garment, and large numbers of women arranged along long tables in front of sewing machines for easier supervision. When the Belle Jardinière department store reopened its Lille workshops after the war, it purchased a building that could accommodate 300 to 400 workers in 101 divisions, each of which specialized in a type of apparel, such as jackets, or one feature of an outfit, such as collars. By 1930, the Belle Jardinière employed 4,552 people, 2,230 of them in the mother store by Pont Neuf, 1,417 in nearby workshops, and 907 in branch stores and workshops around France.[67] In 1936, a seamstress employed at such a workshop did almost everything on sewing machines. Other machines cut seventy-five layers of fabric at a time.[68]

Confection workshops were as stratified as couture workshops. Confection workers who did fine handwork might earn the same wages as couture workers, but machine operators had separate contracts. According to the 1936 labor contracts, machine operators at the Charles Levy confection firm continued to be paid by the piece with assurances of minimum weekly wages. While premières in confection workshops earned the same 208 francs weekly that premières in couture earned, sewing machine operators were paid 190 to 200 francs weekly and finishers 140 to 150 francs, depending on the articles they finished. In knitting, embroidery, and fur workshops, even more complicated pay scales prevailed. In the embroidery shops, weekly wages ranged from 170 to 315 francs, with the highest sum going to designers.[69]

## Apprenticeships

Haute couture and confection had long relied upon a partially trained workforce, thanks to girls receiving sewing instruction in the home, primary schools, complementary courses after primary school, and private workshop-schools.[70] One designer, Jacques Worth, suggested that simpler styles in the 1920s permitted the employment "of women barely trained in couture work."[71] But foreign observers paid homage to the large pool of Frenchwomen skilled at fine hand sewing as an explanation for the preeminence of French couture.[72] Most seamstresses began as apprentices at the age of thirteen or fourteen, though a few were as young as eleven. Many parents complained that employers did not teach their daughters the finer points of the craft, but used them as maids and errand girls. In the early 1920s, the Conseil des Prud'hommes resolved many conflicts over the treatment of apprentices by conciliation boards, but a handful of egregious cases (involving physical correction or verbal abuse) went to the tribunal.[73]

In response to mounting dissatisfaction, a new law mandated occupational training in commerce and industry that would culminate in a certificate of occupational aptitude. Municipal public schools introduced occupational training and the Paris Chamber of Commerce established preapprenticeship workshop-schools, with both programs including sewing courses. In the capital and regional centers, private schools taught advanced sewing techniques.[74] Like other employer syndicates, the Parisian Clothing Syndicate did not finance these efforts until the crisis of 1929–30, when they and the Chamber of Commerce opened a school with fees of 200 francs a year. Auditors could attend some classes for free.[75]

New regulations in 1928 imposed formal apprenticeship contracts, which obliged employers to provide occupational courses to prepare apprentices for a professional certificate. In 1928, Callot Soeurs took on forty-five apprentices, ten of whom were war orphans (wards of the nation). Callot Sisters paid slightly above the base rates of 45.60 francs per forty-eight-hour week the first year and 55.20 francs the second year. In the early years of the depression, no couture house took on more than twelve apprentices at a time. The Société Parisienne de Confection, a major confection company, always took more apprentices than couture houses, but they too cut back in the early 1930s. Numbers rebounded in the mid-1930s.[76]

Fathers of apprentices signed most contracts, with mothers signing the remainder. These signatures offer a glimpse into yet another hierarchy within the clothing industry. Most apprentices in haute couture came from a blue-collar background and lived in the Parisian suburbs and exurbs. Most fathers were tradesmen, followed by skilled workers at railroad or gas companies, or other major utilities; almost all of them resided in the Paris suburbs. Most mothers who signed contracts were widows registered as housewives or seamstresses, often located in exurban communities around the capital. More widows signed the contracts of apprentices in confection, suggesting that confection workers came from a lower social stratum than those who entered couture.

## Industrial Relations

Given earlier prejudices about seamstresses being more interested in their appearance than their working conditions and widespread assumptions about the quiescence of largely feminine, low-wage, dispersed labor, industrial relations in the garment and textile sector were surprisingly contentious. Both clothing and textile workers organized before the war and were active during the war. Textile and garment workers participated in the three major labor federations and almost all strike movements between the wars. Industrial relations were primarily shaped— and limited—by the stratification of the labor force and by divisions between the labor federations. Clothing union activists blamed wage hierarchies and other differences between premières and *midinettes* for hindering their efforts to organize couture houses.[77]

Encouraged by feminists like Marie Bonneviale, president of the League for the Rights of Woman, Mme. Avril de Sainte-Croix, and Maria Verone, Parisian clothing workers had organized in the first decade of the century. Most clothing workers who struck during the war were in confection, especially menswear or wartime production. However, forty seamstresses demonstrated before a leading couture house in 1910, and seamstresses struck at Galeries Lafayette workshops in 1913.[78] During the war, *midinettes* participated in the 1917 strike wave. A committee of the Clothing Workers Union, composed of four union executives—two men, two women—and three striking seamstresses negotiated an agreement with Paquin and five other couture houses that introduced forty-eight-hours of work per week, overtime pay, and promises of a "cost of living indemnity." Similar agreements were concluded between the presidents of the Clothing Workers Union and of the Syndicate of Ready-to-Wear Manufacturers, men's and women's wear branches.[79]

In 1919, the issues were how the newly enacted eight-hours law would be implemented and the pay rates adjusted to ensure that workers would not be paid less. Under the aegis of the minister of labor, representatives of the clothing unions and of clothing employer syndicates renegotiated the workweek they had accepted in 1917 with guarantees of a minimum wage and promises that no foreign workers would be recruited. (As part of their doubly chauvinistic protection of jobs, union activists denounced foreigners and women, especially women working at home, as unfair low-wage competitors.)[80] A year later, the Couture Syndicate and the Clothing Workers Union signed an interunion convention covering most occupational categories. The convention reaffirmed the forty-eight-hour week and introduced the right to paid vacations. It set the minimum monthly wages detailed above.[81]

The settlements were not easily applied. After a strike at the Samaritaine department store, the employer, M. Cognac, closed a workshop and fired fifty-seven women, some of them with more than twenty years' seniority, without severance pay. Taking the case to the Conseil des Prud'hommes, the clothing federation won severance pay of 100 to 200 francs per fired worker, depending on the length of his or her employment.[82] Within a year the clothing federation demanded raises of 50 percent on the 1920 contract, which had not anticipated the rapid rise in the cost of living. Many employers granted raises of about 40 percent, but 100 of 150 confection workshops locked their workers out. When they reopened, they cut wages and refused benefits.[83] During the following two years, the Conseil des Prud'hommes heard cases against eleven couture houses and two department stores that refused vacation pay to workers they had fired or who had left work without notice. The issue was still contentious enough to warrant an amendment to the 1930 strike settlement specifying that workers fired after at least nine months in employment had the right to vacation pay proportional to the time they had worked that year.[84] Eventually, most Paris houses and department stores accorded vacation pay, but their provincial counterparts did not.[85]

Clothing strikes recurred throughout the 1920s. After a 1923 inquiry into the rising cost of living, the Seamstresses and Ladies' Tailors' Union of the Seine approached the employers' syndicate demanding 150 francs per week for premières. When some houses accorded a raise of 12 to 14 francs per week, but only to male cutters, seamstresses walked out of Callot Soeurs, Alice Bernard, and three other couture houses. Police had to break up demonstrations outside these houses. According to Nancy Green, this strike implanted the image of the militant *midinette* in Parisian memory and the demonstration impressed upon contemporary observers the feminization of workers' protest.[86] The union formed a strike committee and withdrew workers from fifty-four leading couture houses. Employers locked out 15,000 *midinettes* who went on strike. During the agitation, free (Catholic) unions settled for 108 francs for the premières, 75 francs for second hands, and 55 francs for "little hands." The last two sums represented pay cuts. After four weeks, the remaining strikers returned to work for 120 to 130 francs a week plus paid vacations.[87]

When the clothing union reiterated its demands the following year, they were by and large successful, due to prosperity.[88] Two years later, as the rate of inflation declined, clothing union demands for 15–30 percent raises for workers in small workshops met more resistance. (Because many of the owners and workers were Jewish—and no doubt because of anti-Semitism—both *L'Humanité* and the police refer to them as Jewish workshops.) In 1928 and 1929, the CGTU simply reacted to wage cuts and free unions approved tiny raises.[89]

Even after the "crisis" of 1929–30, strike action did not halt. In 1930, there were eighteen strikes in clothing, including one at Chanel and one at a major confection firm, the Société Parisienne de Confection. In the Chanel action, the all-male ladies tailors asked for a 20 percent raise and the all-female seamstresses did not join them. At the Société Parisienne, the strikers asked a more equitable increase of 15 percent for those paid less than 200 francs a week and 10 percent for those earning more. Women workers, who formed the bulk of the lower-paid workers, were active and several were arrested.[90]

## Textiles

Textiles workforces had organized by branch, region, and occupation, and most of them belonged to a national federation adhering to the Confédération Général du Travail (CGT), the less radical communist confederation, or to the Confédération Français du Travail Chrétien, the conservative, Catholic federation.[91]

In 1919, several unions approached the Chamber of Lyonnais Silk Fabricants with a proposal to link the eight-hour day to raises proportional to the reduction in the workday from ten or eleven hours. After talks with the National Silk Federation, the chamber, composed of 298 silk manufacturers, accepted the proposal. Specific syndicates with up to 160 members, who employed up to 18,000 workers, implemented their version of the forty-eight-hour week—eight hours Monday, nine hours Tuesday through Friday, and four hours on Saturday—with raises proportional to the reduction in weekly hours.[92] Strikes ensued when some employers did not respect the agreement. Individual strikes lasted from three weeks to three months; the strike wave went on for more than six months and extracted many concessions from employers.

A few examples will indicate the sweep of the strike wave. In the city of Lyon, all 1,300 tulle makers employed by the 247 tulle manufacturers struck for five weeks before settling for eight hours and piecework pay with an assured minimum wage of 90 francs per week. Settlements did not alter wage differences by sex, so women still earned about half of what men did in these workplaces (9 to 12 francs vs. 19 to 22 francs per day).[93] A month later 700 skilled spinners, all women, struck for a week and won an augmentation of 2 francs a day, or one-third more than their previous wages. When 3,000 women struck 160 silk-weaving and -spinning firms in the autumn, they encountered more opposition. The Mayor of Lyons arranged a compromise based on a calculation of average production in "normal working conditions." Other Lyonnais women, some represented by all-women strike committees, got concessions through arbitration.[94] In towns around Lyon, local authorities intervened to get raises commensurate with reductions in the workday. Pay rates remained lower than in Lyon and local wage gaps remained. In the nearby town of Tarare, 160 men won a raise of 2 francs a day and women 1.75 francs a day, leaving men's daily wage at 12 francs and women's at 8.75.[95]

From 1922 to 1929, more isolated strikes occurred in textile towns, initially to gain cost-of-living supplements but later against employer attempts to cut wage rates. In half of these strikes, women strikers predominated; women delegates from the CGTU traveled to these towns to help sustain the strikes.[96]

In the north, Christian unions in the woolen and linen industries put more emphasis on social services. The Christian, also known as free, unions ran placement bureaus and a mutual aid society that provided sickness insurance. They offered girls and women self-improvement courses in cutting, sewing, and drawing, as well as in French, English, accounting, and cooking. The courses were free for union members; most of the students were thirteen- to eighteen-year-old girls. These unions stressed collective efforts to improve hygiene in factories and offices, with special reference to tuberculosis, which was then the "scare disease" for young women. Other services included eighty low-cost rural retreats, women-only restaurants in Arras and Valenciennes, and a mixed-sex restaurant in Roubaix-Tourcoing. Some locals added classes in gymnastics, hygiene, home economics, and childcare, as well as Red Cross training.[97]

When the CGT and the free unions tried to negotiate with northern employers, they encountered one of the first real employers' consortiums.[98] In 1920, the Consortium of Roubaix-Tourcoing Textile Industries represented the owners of 312 factories employing 700,000 workers. The mostly Catholic Consortium mounted a protest campaign against neo-Malthusians propaganda, just as agitation mounted for the infamous antiabortion and anti-female-controlled contraception law of 23 July 1920. More positively, the consortium offered family pay and a birth bonus of 200 francs per infant. To get the subsidies, the beneficiaries had to sign a contract stipulating that they would lose the subsidies if they participated in collective interruptions of work. When some beneficiaries joined a strike in 1922, their subsidies were withdrawn. In 1924, the consortium disbursed 39,000 family allocations and 3,344 birth bonuses, not quite half in the form of 100–franc payments to a parent who worked in one of their plants, and just over half in the form of 200–franc payments when both parents worked in one of their plants.[99]

Although silk and woolen workers in and around Lyon and Lille had to acquiesce to the imposition of a shorter workweek and smaller pay packets in the early 1930s, they remained vigilant about other employer responses to the crisis. In 1930, more than 30,000 northern textile workers in CGT unions participated in a general strike occasioned by the consortium's attempt to substitute a "fidelity benefit" for a cost-of-living raise.[100] Three years later, over 5,000 workers in northern textile towns, including towns that had been organized by free unions, struck against a new regulation requiring weavers to operate four semiautomatic looms apiece and a new system of calculating wages. They wanted to return to the wage rates they had won between 1914 and 1922. Martha Desrumaux, a member of the regional executive of the CGTU, intervened at a critical moment to radicalize the strike. Finally, the government-appointed work inspector mediated a settlement that addressed some wage issues but kept the four-looms-per-weaver provision.[101]

In February 1934, the CGT took a leadership role in the general strike to defend the Republic against radical right-wing leagues, a strike that mobilized 4 million workers. While other sectors, like metal, provided most of the leaders, CGT-affiliated textile unions fully participated. Over the next few months, as the CGT and CGTU struggled toward reunification, members of the CGTU pursued such economic issues as an enforceable forty-hour week and wage guarantees.[102] Although women made up more than 80 percent of the labor force in artificial silk production, the never-high number of women involved in union federations and congresses had declined.[103] Because of women's prolonged experience with falling wages and reduced hours, their participation in strikes came in reaction to employer methods to combat the depression by imposing further cuts in hours and wages or imposition of more looms per worker. Often, all women won after a long strike was a slight reduction in hourly wage rates. This did not distinguish them from their male co-workers in the same regions.[104] After another intervention by Martha Desrumeaux, the mixed-sex strikers in northern villages held out for several weeks.[105]

Of the 12,000 plus strikes during labor agitation to force the Popular Front government to enact the labor reforms promised by the Front, 9,000 involved factory occupations. In concord with most organized sectors of the labor force, members of textiles unions occupied dozens of factories in the Nord and almost as many in the Rhone.[106] The Matignon Accords of June 1936, between the CGT and employers' syndicates, put an end to the extreme agitation. In conjunction with other labor legislation passed then, the accords stipulated the forty-hour workweek, paid vacations, collective contracts, wage guarantees, and amnesty for strikers.[107] Implementation was spotty, especially after the fall of the Popular Front government.

Working conditions in the backrooms of couture houses, in clothing workshops, and in textile factories were far different from what the posh salons of couture houses or of department stores implied. Few improvements came at the initiative of couturiers, confectionneurs, or textile magnates. Industrial relations during the interwar years were discordant and disruptive. Despite recurring agitation and temporary concessions, couture, clothing, and textile workers could not count on eight-hour workdays or avoid seasonal unemployment. But instead of investing in improved industrial relations, some couturières put their greater energy into campaigning against illegal copying.

# PART III

# Democratizing Fashion

*Chapter Six*

# Copying and Copyrighting

From its inception in the 1860s, haute couture displayed contradictory attitudes toward imitation of its models. Couturiers followed a long French tradition of publicity for their models throughout Europe and the New World. Publicity invited imitation. In the first two decades of the twentieth century, many designers became suspicious of the major form of publicity, the rapidly expanding fashion press, because models in the press "could be filched," in the blunt words of Elsa Chase, long-time chief editor of *Vogue.* Chase explained, "If they wanted publicity and fame, which they did, they had to risk the copying by individuals."[1] In actuality, most couturiers tolerated copying by "little" dressmakers for individual customers and were only hostile toward larger-scale commercial counterfeiting. After 1905, many struggled to have their ephemeral models covered under national and international laws protecting artistic property and industrial designs from plagiarism or piracy. In the 1920s and 1930s, designers waged a legal assault on commercial counterfeiting. Fashion theorist Gilles Lipovetsky captures the paradox: "No other fashion institution has had to keep on mobilizing a legal arsenal to protect itself against plagiarists and imitators; no other has benefited from the steady, intense publicity of a specialized press."[2] The basic problem was legal vulnerability to piracy, but internal differences between upholders of the tradition of style for the few and advocates of the modern system of fashion for the many exacerbated the problem. Directly and indirectly, the interplay of these factors fostered a modest democratization of fashion.

# Publicity

One reason for mounting tensions over copying was increased publicity. Paris first set fashion trends in the seventeenth century, certainly because of the political predominance of the French state and the cultural ascendancy of the court of Versailles but also because Lyonnais silk manufacturers pioneered national and international advertising. A few sent dolls dressed in the latest Paris style to other major cities in France and to European court cities to generate orders to be made up in Paris or by local dressmakers. In either case, dressmakers would be expected to order Lyonnais silks.[3] In the twentieth century, the textile industry retained considerable influence on haute couture because it provided the essential materials and because manufacturers often financed couturiers by the returns system of delaying payment until the collections had sold and then settling for a percentage of the previously negotiated price for unpopular fabrics. Of course, textile manufacturers were not only interested in promoting haute couture; they sold some fabrics returned by haute couture to "little" dressmakers and cheaper versions of "exclusive" fabrics to ready-made manufacturers and department stores.[4] These sales facilitated emulation and democratization.

Between 1890 and 1914, French publishers quadrupled the number of long-running women's and fashion magazines. Fashion plates, fashion albums, and society magazines like *La Gazette du Bon Ton* became more exquisite.[5] Only two of these extravagant magazines survived the First World War, and they only survived for six years. But less expensive society periodicals, such as *Fémina* and *Vogue*, commissioned artists to draw their covers after the war. Less famous illustrators made art deco drawings of designer models in the full-page advertisements that appeared inside the covers.[6] These fashion illustrations evoked elegance and revealed obvious features—for example, the silhouette—but obscured subtle design features. Only very accomplished dressmakers could reproduce the gowns in these illustrations.

Although few women's magazines were founded during the war, eighteen new magazines appeared in the 1920s and endured for at least a decade between the world wars.[7] At any one time dozens of illustrated magazines depicted and described the "highlights" of the seasonal collections. To do so, editors and reporters had to have access to the collections. As couturiers became more vigilant about who could attend their seasonal shows, in response to pirating, editors and reporters had to maintain good relations with them or resort to subterfuge to report on the collections. The already indistinct line between reporting and publicity was further blurred. Magazines also published sketches and photos with captions about what *les élégantes* wore to the theater and to balls during the winter, to major horseracing events in the spring, and on the beaches of the Riviera or Atlantic coast in the summer. Like art deco drawings, these sketches and black-and-white photos provided too few details for neighborhood dressmakers to duplicate them exactly.

The same magazines printed black-and-white drawings of apparel "inspired by" couture styles with accompanying captions explaining their construction and materials, usually alluding to having "your dressmaker" make them up. Some patterns were not just inspired by but were the work of famous designers. Charles Worth permitted *Harper's Bazaar* and the illustrated magazine *Le Printemps,* with a circulation of 10,000, to publish patterns of some of his models.[8] Jenny advertised signed patterns in *L'Illustration des Modes* at the not-exorbitant price of twelve francs. She had an arrangement with the Soieries Real firm to sell the "original material" for these patterns. Less-famous designers allowed *La Mode Pratique* to market patterns for some of their designs.[9]

Although these kinds of articles and marketing disappeared from society magazines after 1928, weekly magazines and supplements for middle-class women continued to run columns on how to sew apparel similar to couture models.[10] Many weeklies included patterns "influenced by" recent designer models or "inspired" by recent collections. Less than a month might elapse between the presentation of the original model in the seasonal collections and the publication of these patterns in weeklies, which had twenty times the circulation of any society monthly. Together with pattern catalogs promising Parisian styles, these weeklies suggest that more bourgeois women were following Parisian trends, if not buying or exactly copying haute couture.[11]

Haute couture was uneasy about the new technique of fashion photography. Beginning in the 1880s, designers hired photographers to record their models for deposit at the Conseil des Prud'hommes in order to document their claims to have created the models. The live or inanimate mannequins displaying models were brightly lit to highlight design features rather than to create an overall impression. When it was technically feasible to reproduce photographs in the press in the 1890s, magazines did not print many photographs, because the technology was new and expensive. But designers released photos of *les élégantes* dressed in their models at the Longchamps races and other fashion showcase events to the press.[12] These photographs mix two genres: news photographs, intended to document, and celebrity photographs, intended to flatter the subject. In the early twentieth century, a few shots were reproduced in color. Most of these shots are more literal than evocative; they denoted rather than connoted meaning.[13] During the interwar years the Séeberger brothers (Louis, 1874–1946, and Henri, 1876–1956) shot up to 150 black-and-white photographs of *les élégantes* wearing designer dresses at the six major Longchamps races, four Auteuil prize races, as well as at Cannes and other beach resorts during the summer season. Some of these photographs were released to the press.[14] A skilled dressmaker might be able to sew a reasonable facsimile of the outfits in these photographs.

In the first decade of the twentieth century, fashion magazines began to include a few studio photographs taken by photographers. Early fashion photographers favored soft-focus shots and the vague pictorial conventions of fashion plates. Then Poiret began to employ art photographers.[15] With the 1911 publication of Edward Steichen's photographs of Poiret dresses in *Art et Décoration,* the modernist preference for sharp focus and clean geometric lines entered fashion photography.[16] As director of *La Gazette du Bon Ton* and the Paris edition of *Vogue,* Lucien Vogel used fashion shots to promote photography as art. For instance, the chief photographer for *Vogue* in 1926, George Hoyningen-Huene, imported surrealist elements, such as shooting plastic mannequins to simulate real mannequins.[17] These photographs vacillated between the fashion magazine's need "to report the dress" and the artist's desire to take risks,[18] but they never had the documentary quality of the photographs deposited at the Conseil des Prud'hommes. Couturiers preferred the documentary photograph for property claims and evocative photography for public consumption.

During the First World War, the Chamber of Couture, Milliners, Lace Makers, and Embroiders complained to the Ministry of Commerce and to the Paris City Council about photographs taken of "the most outstanding models" worn at the Longchamps races and other showcase events. Convinced that color photography constituted "an immense danger" to their models, they asked that "appropriate police measures be taken to remedy this prejudice to their interests." In 1913, the City Council supported their request for a police ordinance forbidding anyone taking pictures of models in shop windows "or in any public place" and for a law with the same restrictions. The council added the qualification that the law should only repress the criminal use of photographs for counterfeiting. Because the National Office of Industrial Property did not support such draconian censorship, nothing came of this improbable proposal.[19]

As the number of photographs rose, designers hired specialized fashion photographers to represent their ensembles. In the late 1920s, the House of Worth employed Séeberger Frères and three other photography studios, eighteen professional models, and a dozen style setters, including a princess and a baroness. Through the interwar years, the firm employed forty-five photographers, including three women: Helen MacGregor, Mme. d'Ora, and Mme. Perstel.[20] Most of their publicity photos were studio shots of a single mannequin with few props, although some were shot outdoors and included a natural background, usually tall, slender trees, mirroring the tall, slender appearance of the mannequins. Only the natural backgrounds in any way beckoned "into a world of unbridled fantasies by placing fashion and the body in any number of discursive contexts."[21] Up to a hundred photographs were distributed to twenty-eight magazines and three newspapers in France, Great Britain, Germany, Sweden, the United States, and Canada. Among the French magazines were the monthlies *Femina, Vogue, L'Officiel de la Couture,* and *L'Illustration des Modes,* and the newspaper supplements *Figaro Hebdomadaire* and *Excelsior Modes.* English outlets were *Eve* (English version), *Queens, Harper's Bazaar, World Traveler,* and *Westminster Gazette;* American outlets were the *Ladies Home Journal,* the *New York Times,* and the *Cleveland Plain Dealer;* and Canadian outlets were *Chatelaine* and *Mayfair* Canada.[22]

Abroad, French designs were prominently displayed in fashion magazines. Especially in the 1920s, when the number of glossy fashion magazines increased in the United States and Great Britain, many of the illustrations in the American and British editions of *Vogue, Harper's Bazaar,* and other magazines were of Parisian couture. Their Paris correspondents covered the seasonal collections and wrote articles about specific designers; both types of article had more illustrations than text.[23] *Vogue* London put out special issues on the Paris collections.[24] *Women's Wear Daily,* the trade organ of American "Retailers, Jobbers, and Manufacturers," maintained a Paris bureau and routinely published illustrations of the latest Paris creations, as well as reviews of the seasonal collections, usually on the front page. *Women's Wear Daily* also ran photographs with captions like "Worn in Paris" or "Seen at St. Moritz."[25]

A pivotal figure in the distribution of fashion photographs to the United States was Thérèse Bonney, an American expatriate, fashion model, photographer, Paris Fashion Editor of the *New York Times* between 1925 and 1935, and owner-operator of the first American illustrated press service in Europe (opened in 1923).

Her fashion photographs appeared in the *New York Times* and other major newspapers in the United States, as well as in advertisements in *Vogue* New York and *Harper's Bazaar.* Bonney also introduced Americans to art deco art and design, notably in the Lord and Taylor department store's Exposition of Modern French Decorative Art held in 1928. With her sister, Louise Bonney, she wrote for visiting Americans the user-friendly *Shopping Guide to Paris,* which spotlighted major couture houses, among other luxury good businesses.[26]

Most couturiers and couturières encouraged publicity in high-end publications and used the opportunity to establish how couture differed from ready-made clothing. An ad for the House of Chantal in *Vogue* New York explicitly appealed to snobbish readers: "Chantal makes no pretence of giving the public what it wants. She does not cater to the crowd. There is no mass production in the House of Chantal."[27] French designers were less sanguine about *Women's Wear Daily,* because of the number of American clothing manufacturers that engaged in piracy. They were openly antagonistic toward a dozen illustrated fashion magazines published in Paris but distributed in Germany and Austria, because, in their words, these magazines helped Austrian and German manufacturers "pillage" French couture.[28]

Textile and clothing makers' associations had long presented their creations at international, national, and specialized trade fairs. Many couturiers were represented at the 1900 fair in Paris, and Paquin mounted a show at the 1914 Lyonnais fair (the second largest sample fair in Europe). Other couturiers did not attend the fair because silk producers had outlets in the capital.[29] After the war, couturiers participated in specialized fairs, like the Silk Fête, which was organized by the Silk Manufacturers' Syndicate in March 1923. With the help of the Association of Daily News Journalists of Lyon, the syndicate publicized the forthcoming event in appropriate media in France and selected foreign countries. Twenty couture houses, including Callot Soeurs, Drecoll, Doueillet, Jenny, Lanvin, Poiret, and Worth, brought thirty-three live mannequins with them to present their models. Eight local dressmakers, members of the Dressmakers Syndicate of Lyon, had only wax mannequins.[30]

After the war, textile manufacturers resumed international publicity at the Lyonnais fair. For the 1925 fair, held before the art deco exposition in Paris, the organizers sent invitations in French to potential exhibitors and buyers in fifty-seven countries, in English to thirty-one countries, in German to twenty-one countries, and in Spanish to eight countries. One hundred thirty nine of the 1,580 stands at the fair displayed textiles, 157 displayed ladies ready-to-wear, and 147 displayed men's ready-to-wear. Foreign buyers came from forty-four countries, mostly European, but also North and South American and Asian. Some "faithful buyers," such as the major Paris department stores Au Printemps, Bon Marché, Galeries Lafayette, and Aux Trois Quartiers, rented stands for their representatives. Four hundred and twenty-two buyers for thirty-two department stores acquired entry cards; individual Paris department stores sent eighteen to thirty buyers apiece. Ten percent of the foreign buyers came to buy silks alone, while 8.5 percent came for other textiles, and 9 percent came for ladies' ready-to-wear.[31]

Couturiers resumed international outreach before the armistice. In October 1918, Maurice de Waleffe (later the impressario of Miss France beauty pageants) gave a talk on couture in Zurich illustrated by a parade of "the most delicious models of our great couture houses, accompanied by an orchestra." As the fashion columnist for *La Soieirie de Lyon* exclaimed, "What propaganda!"[32] Especially during crises, couturiers revived the tradition. In January 1929, the director of the Martial and Armand House, Mme. Valle, organized a "French Fashion Show in London." She also arranged a fashion show in Cairo, Egypt, where Parisian mannequins and "one of the famous Parisian actresses, Regina Camier, paraded in 120 of Mme. Valle's new models."[33] During the Great Depression, Lucien Lelong flogged the superiority of French couture originals over copies in foreign markets through interviews, speeches, and fashion shows in major markets.[34]

The 1925 Exhibition of the Decorative Arts helped increase exports from 57,169 million to 77,966 million francs.[35] Encouraged by the results, experts had high expectations for the 1931 colonial exhibition. In 1927, planners made contact with the national and foreign press; in 1930 and 1931, they distributed monthly information bulletins to 1,100 French and foreign-language newspapers and spent 4 million francs on ads in the French and colonial press. They also employed cinema and conferences. Despite the colonial themes, most foreign publicity was directed to major markets—Great Britain, the United States, and Germany.[36] The class of exhibitors known as the "luxury clothing industry destined for use in the colonies," presided over by Jeanne Lanvin, consisted of a central stage and nine stands, with nine couture houses, including Lanvin, Worth, Cheruit, and Drecoll, presenting models on four live mannequins. Nineteen furriers, thirty-five embroidery firms, and even more lace and trim makers participated.[37] Textile manufacturers were better represented than couture at this and other colonial exhibitions, so the main impact on couture styles was the introduction of new fabrics and colors.[38] The exposition was credited with staving off the full impact of the world depression.

Especially after France devalued the franc in 1936, an unusual alliance of the Popular Front government, export industries, and luxury good industries put their hopes on the 1937 world fair boosting the economy.[39] Planners spent more than ever before on publicity. The government paid 765,778 francs to Paris daily newspapers, 647,392 francs to provincial dailies, 628,475 francs to the periodical press, and 198,445 francs to business publications.[40] For the first time, a world fair included a "Publicity Palace" and hosted an international congress on publicity.[41] Representatives of haute couture and the ready-to-wear industries worked closely with government to ensure that fashion would have a prominent site and role.[42] The president of the Republic invented the post of "Lady of the 1937 Exposition." Instead of mounting "some stylized statue of the Parisienne"—a reference to the huge statue at the 1900 Paris fair—he selected Daisy Fellowes, who was welcomed by the artist Jean Cocteau as "a Parisienne in flesh and bone."[43]

In planning the 1937 exposition, Jeanne Lanvin and the adornment group decided to abandon the formula of commercial sampling adopted by the preceding expositions and "to imagine a new presentation theme permitting all four classes to be grouped together in a decorative ensemble." The Elegance Pavilion cost 2,110,874 francs, 1,458,174 of which exhibitors raised, while the government contributed 652,700 francs. Alix, Chanel, Heim, Jane Duverne, Jeanne Lanvin, Lucien Lelong, Lucien Paray, Maggy-Rouff, Martial et Armand, Molyneux, Nina Ricci, Patou, Schiaparelli, Vionnet, and Worth invested 24,400 francs apiece; twelve others, including Callot Soeurs, Jane Regny, Jenny, and Louise Boulanger, each paid 7,400 francs.[44]

Although the economic impact of the 1937 exhibition was not as great as those of 1925 or 1931 had been, couture welcomed the return of the "Parisiennes in passing" and "elegant foreigners." They also began preparing for the next major international fair. At least twenty couture houses exhibited in 1939 in New York.[45]

## Copying

As an informed insider remarked, "counterfeiting started at the same time as haute couture, at the very moment when Worth began confecting a series of models destined for export."[46] Counterfeiting of couture models expanded along with the international market for haute couture in the Belle Epoque. The custom of presenting models to foreign buyers before domestic customers allowed unscrupulous buyers to sell advance information to unscrupulous domestic copiers, who produced cheaper copies before the originals had been formally presented domestically. The custom of selling models and instructions for reproducing the models to foreign manufacturers also facilitated foreign copying on a far greater scale than couturiers had intended. In 1896, a defense committee of members of the Couture, Lace, and Embroidery Syndicate tried to prevent domestic piracy by refusing to sell to foreigners before set dates, on the premise that this would reduce the opportunities for preemptive domestic copies.[47] Designers began to present two seasonal collections a year, and counterfeiters scrambled to anticipate trends in the collections. Industrial espionage abounded.

In the 1920s and 1930s, changes in the nature of haute couture intensified the problem of counterfeiting. With the simplification of women's dress, fashion was easier to copy and hence more accessible. Looser dresses could more easily be copied from sketches than form-fitting styles; simple, loose styles also reduced sizing problems in manufacturing. Most of Chanel's garments required little material, and her nearly straight cuts could be made from less expensive materials.[48] Some designers advocated introducing fancier styles requiring intricate cutting and sewing, as well as more fittings, as a solution to the problems of counterfeiting and undercutting prices.[49] But even when Paris successfully launched fitted bodices and fuller skirts in the late 1920s, the new line did not require the sewing skills or meters of material involved in prewar designer clothing. Copying merely became a less pressing problem.[50]

A dramatic increase in and redistribution of export models had a similar effect. Great Britain, the largest foreign market for French clothing, and the United States, the second largest market from the mid-1920s, engaged in widespread piracy. Some British and American department stores and lady's wear shops advertised that half their ladies' wear stock was French. In the United States, high duties on French fashions and a regime of temporary exemptions for models displayed in America and then returned to France meant that 80 percent of the models made in France were displayed in exclusive events in New York, dismantled to create patterns, then reassembled and returned to France. The patterns were used to produce copies, with French labels, that cost considerably less than the French originals. In the 1920s, a group of New York businessmen specialized in buying models temporarily admitted into the United States, transporting them or patterns based on them to Canadian and South American dressmaking networks, then "importing" copies made in these countries at much lower duties than those imposed on French apparel.[51]

Serving the rapidly increasing foreign clientele contributed to the dilemmas of copying. Interwar designers resumed the practice of two showings per season, the first for foreign buyers and the second for individual customers.[52] The two to three week delay between these two shows allowed counterfeiters enough time to copy popular models before the originals were introduced in the domestic market.

Large foreign department stores like Bloomingdale's, Bonwit Teller, Macy's, and Gimbel's in the United States, Harrods in England, and T. Eaton in Canada established their own buyers' offices in Paris.[53] Most foreign buyers only came to the twice-yearly seasonal collections, hiring agents to attend the midseason collections. As their numbers overwhelmed experienced agents, less reputable agents filled the gap.[54] Buyers and agents usually bought five to twenty-five models apiece and received for each model a certificate with information about the fabric and notions needed to produce them. Implicit if not always explicit in the production certificate was the right to reproduce the model, albeit in limited quantities. Although couture houses made up some models in the two or three weeks visiting foreign buyers were willing to wait for their purchases before returning home, couturiers knew that far more models would be duplicated in the buyers' home countries.[55]

Some foreign buyers and their agents hired women to attend collections, memorize models, and sketch them to be reproduced. As a young woman, Elizabeth Hawes (an American designer who apprenticed in Paris) was paid $1.50 per sketch for up to fifteen sketches per collection. To ensure that they could replicate the materials and trimmings, buyers and agents ripped swatches of material, trim, and accessories from models in the salons after runway shows. Hawes described one buyer who "tore fringe off all the fringed dresses so she could have it copied in New York." Even some resident buyers, with permanent offices in Paris, were complicit in this activity. The French head of Macy's office authorized Hawes "to obtain some modern sweater designs in Paris and send them to Vienna to be copied at $3.25."[56] In 1930, several couturiers accused a resident American buyer, Mrs. Ida H. Oliver, and another American, Mrs. Carolina Davis, of selling sketches of registered models to manufacturers. Police raids led to seizures of 800 sketches in Mrs. Davis's apartment and 115 more in the apartment of one of her employees. Mrs. Oliver admitted that she possessed sketches of coats and suits designed by Callot, Lanvin, Patou, Vionnet, Worth, and four other couturiers but insisted that she did not realize that this was illegal, "since sketches of couture models were bought and sold openly during the seasonal openings."[57]

Although couture houses refused to sell the rights to reproduce their designs to French firms,[58] between two hundred and five hundred copy houses operated in Paris in the 1920s. Many of their copies went to foreign buyers; others were sold as haute couture models in France, notably in provincial cities.[59] Twenty of these copy houses grossed over 5 million francs a year. Several of these large houses joined together to purchase sketches or actual designer models of the most popular styles through intermediaries (who changed frequently, as designers identified the complicit individuals). Since copy houses did not pay designers, made only popular styles, and sold them at lower prices than the originals, they moved most of their merchandise and were very profitable.[60] A few *maisons de belle copies* located in the heart of the couture district in Paris offered knockoffs with imperceptible differences from original Chanel, Patou, and other designers' models. One kept stolen *toiles* and original models in a room that could be locked electronically from a distance, in case of a police raid. Yet most copy houses were humble places, located upstairs on side streets, in order to avoid prosecution and taxes.[61] Savvy Parisiennes bought counterfeit couture models at a fraction of the price of the originals there.[62]

Copy houses acquired designer models by various devious means. They hired women to pose as customers to buy models or they rented models from foreign buyers, mannequins, and individual customers. Individual customers left designer clothes overnight at the copy house on the pretext of having alterations done, despite couturiers' policy that alterations must be done in house. Couture houses justified this policy in terms of maintaining standards, but they also hoped that it would limit counterfeiting. Overnight, the copy house dismantled the model to make patterns from the pieces and then made knockoffs from the patterns. In addition, copy houses enticed top seamstresses and saleswomen from couture houses into their employ and expected them to bring with them patterns, customers, and expertise gained in their previous job.[63]

At least two interwar couturières—Madeleine Vionnet and Augusta Bernard—began their careers copying couture designs.[64] Ironically, Vionnet would lead the second phase of the legal battle against pirating.

## Designs and Models

Haute couture and textiles were vulnerable to copying because of an uncertain legal position regarding protection of their products.

Textiles patented their products; haute couture rarely did. Despite patenting the mix of raw materials and designs in new products, the Lyonnais silk fabrique experienced counterfeiting both of composition and motifs on their fabrics when customers sold their sample books to unscrupulous textile firms. Several American manufacturers hired key employees of major silk firms who brought their knowledge or samples of their previous employers' fabrics with them to copy.[65] Few couturiers bothered with patents, except for technical innovations, such as a method of weaving beads into fabrics patented by Madeleine Vionnet in 1923. Vionnet thought this method could be applied to partially ready-made as well as made-to-measure dresses. Because the method worked better on draped than tailored dresses, and because beaded fabric was very expensive, it was not widely adopted.[66] National and international patent laws, which mandated exploitation of inventions within three years of registration,[67] were not compatible with haute couture because couture models were rarely completely original, instead being new combinations of existing design elements, and because only a small fraction of all models found favor with buyers, and then only for a season or two. The challenge was to protect models before and after their introduction in seasonal collections, when copiers could rush out cheaper imitations, undercutting designer prices and consumer demand for expensive designer models.[68]

Many textile manufacturers and couture houses registered brand names and trademarks under an 1857 French law and under international conventions of 1891, 1900, and 1911.[69] Registration was part of a larger French trend, as the number of brand names registered annually quintupled between 1886 and 1920. Many recorded the company name or initials—often in antique letters—but more and more included a graphic symbol on the assumption that symbols were more easily remembered than words or initials. Couture, like liquors, employed hieratic silhouettes, signifying elegance.[70] Designers commissioned stylized art deco labels and logos.[71] Silk manufacturer Bianchini-Férier had bees on its labels.[72] Fashion magazines advised readers concerned about the quality of their dry goods and clothing to recognize trademarks and buy brand names.[73]

However, brand names and trademarks could more easily be simulated than models. During Poiret's trip to the United States in 1913, he discovered knock-offs of his models selling for as little as fifteen dollars apiece and copies of his dress label being "freely hawked." After he returned to Paris, he met with prominent fashion magazine publishers to propose that leading couturiers form an association to protect their interests. To avoid arousing suspicions about his motives in this hypercompetitive business, he asked publishers to approach other designers. The publishers persuaded Jacques Worth (another son and successor of Charles Worth), Jeanne Lanvin, Jeanne Paquin, the Callot sisters, and the Rodier brothers to constitute the Protective Association of French Couturiers, "to bring to an end counterfeiting of labels and illicit use of their names."[74] The war interrupted this promising development.

After the war, Madeleine Vionnet tried to foil label forgers by including her signature, fingerprint, and a specific number for each model on her labels. As Molly Nesbit has explained, this was a perfect expression of a new legal definition distinguishing between cultural and industrial labor on the basis of the imprint of an individual personality.[75] However, dishonest label producers quickly duplicated signature, fingerprint, and numbers. Despite inventions like secret seals, phony labels proliferated.[76] In 1931, one police raid alone turned up more than 52,000 fake couture and millinery labels, as well as evidence of ten years of dubious transactions by manufacturers, buyers, and agents. In response to this exposé, the French Wholesale Dress Association tried to negotiate a deal with the couturiers' associations to authorize reproductions of models bearing the creator's label and to sell these reproductions domestically and internationally.[77] Couturiers' commitment to limited production and their distrust of wholesalers stymied this initiative.

In the nineteenth century, branches of the garment industry had tried to protect models under two separate French laws, neither of which explicitly applied to their industry. Hat, corset, and lingerie makers either appealed to the 1793 law on literary and artistic property rights, which applied to "designers," or to the 1806 law protecting industrial design, which applied to manufacturers. The 1793 law was enacted to protect authors and artists from plagiarism, primarily by depositing copies of printed or graphic works at the Ministry of the Interior and eventually at the Bibliothèque Nationale, in order to prove that the depositor had created the literary or artistic work and could collect royalties. The 1806 law on industrial property rights required manufacturers to deposit a sample of a product, or a depiction and description of a product, to the appropriate Conseil des Prud'hommes in order to prove their invention of the product. After an 1887 judicial interpretation of this law, manufacturers had to reserve products "as exclusive property" for three to five years or in perpetuity. Until 1902, commercial courts had to determine whether dress models were works of art or manufactured products, whether dress models were unique, and what constituted a counterfeit.[78]

Despite many court cases, no clear jurisprudence emerged. As early as 1857, the Commercial Court applied the 1806 law to millinery on the grounds that the sample hat deposited by the plaintiff at the Conseil des Prud'hommes had "a special cachet of novelty that constituted a kind of individuality" and fined the defendants for making "servile imitations." Although milliners hailed this decision, it had a fatal flaw: "servile imitation" precluded reproductions with such a slight alteration in detail as the exact position of trim on a hat. In 1860, the court denied that the same law applied to hats on the grounds that the sample hats in this case merely "reconfigured" familiar forms. The same year, the Civil Court ruled that neither law covered clothing, because an item of clothing was "neither a work of art, nor a new invention, but a compilation . . . of objects of a known form." Other rationales for refusing coverage were the ephemeral nature of fashion and the practical nature of clothing.[79] With these kinds of rulings, it is hardly surprising that couturiers did not pursue counterfeiters in the courts.

In 1902, the law on artistic and literary property was amended to encompass designers of ornaments, whatever the artistic merit or destination of the ornament.[80] Although the amendment did not mention couture, it seemed to apply to clothing designers, since they too designed and produced goods that were both aesthetic and commercial in nature. In practice, depositing examples at the Bibliothèque Nationale, predicated on the eternal value of literature and art, did not suit the changeable and competitive clothing industry.[81] After intensive lobbying by the French Association for the Protection of Industrial Property and by the Paris Chamber of Commerce and Industry,[82] the legislature passed an act that met some of the needs of industrial designers. The 1909 law applied to "all industrial objects that differ from similar objects, whether by a distinct and recognizable configuration . . . or by one or several external effects giving it a new and distinct physiognomy." Drawings or photographs of up to one hundred models at a time could be deposited at the Conseil des Prud'hommes; these models were then the legal property of the depositor for five years without any requirement for exploitation of the designs. Deposition in perpetuity was reduced to fifty years. Publicity, such as a fashion show, did not cancel ownership. Before any publicity, the depositor could have officers of the court seize alleged copies. Anyone found guilty of copying models was subject to fines of 25 to 2,000 francs.[83]

The 1909 law had several disadvantages. Photographing and paying deposit fees for 250 to 300 models annually was costly, given that perhaps only one-tenth of the models would find favor with customers. Depositing photographs also meant twenty to thirty trips per year to the office of the Conseil des Prud'hommes.[84] Clothing associations worried about the potential for piracy of models implicit in the system of keeping depictions and descriptions of models at the industry-specific offices of the conseil. These associations came up with a scheme for deposition at the National Industrial Property Office, which protected designers and producers by publishing details about deposits in the *Bulletin Officiel de la Propriété Industrielle.*[85] The further expense of publication ensured that fewer deposits were made to the National Industrial Property Office than to the industrial relations board.[86] A third defect of the law was the absence of provisions prohibiting unfair competition *(concurrence déloyale),* which meant that stealing *toiles* and selling them to competitors were not legally linked to counterfeiting. Instead, articles 425 and 426 of the penal code covered industrial espionage and theft by competitors. Penalties were limited to fines and expenses.[87]

Internationally, protecting models was even more difficult. Several importing countries had no laws on artistic and industrial property rights, and other countries only extended the protection of these laws to foreigners if they had bilateral treaties with that foreigner's country. Application for coverage under these laws involved complicated and costly formalities. A provision of American copyright laws required registration of the product before publicity for the product, a requirement incompatible with the seasonal fashion shows in France, which identified the models worth importing and reproducing. American officials often refused to register any item of practical utility, like clothing, under their design patent law. Finally, there were quarrels about which country had registered a model first. Although the International Bureau of Industrial Property, in Bern, Switzerland, kept a registry, not all companies or countries sent documentation on their designs to the bureau.[88]

Despite recent European Union laws, international piracy of luxury goods has not abated. France, with 70 percent of the brands counterfeited worldwide, is the principal victim, due to the importance of luxury goods production in France.[89] Outside France, court rulings still recognize "acceptable knockoffs" if they can be construed as a "remix" of elements or an obvious fake.[90]

## Internal Differences

Economists who observed the volatility of the luxury goods and textile industries recommended better coordination of industrial and commercial interests, not in trusts or cartels but in a corporative form. Syndical efforts had some success in textiles, but not in couture, where designers were hopelessly divided on how to cope with copying.

The Central Woolen Committee, the French Silk Federation, and the French Cotton Cartel scrutinized legislative bills and treaty negotiations that might affect their industries and engaged in collective bargaining.[91] Couturiers were neither as financially secure nor as easily organized as silk manufacturers. Although they belonged to the Union of Textiles, Clothing, and Furnishings Producers, its sixty-five employer associations were too diverse to take concerted action on behalf of couture.[92] The Chambre Syndicale de la Couture Parisienne, with 241 members in 1928 and a central committee composed of representatives from twenty-six houses, could not agree on the appropriate response to copying. Not until 1936, in response to massive labor and social unrest, was the Syndical Chamber reorganized by Lucien Lelong and Daniel Gorin and reoriented toward unity.[93]

Despite the deficiencies of the French legislation, textile manufacturers tried a combination of corporate vigilance and court actions to protect their models. The Silk Manufacturers' Syndicate monitored the distribution of sample books that domestic and foreign silk manufacturers could plagiarize and kept a list of domestic and foreign companies plagiarizing their members' fabrics.[94] In 1924, the House of Ducharne accused an American firm already identified as a copier of "poaching" two of its key employees and copying Ducharne fabrics. The Silk Syndicate modified its constitution to sanction William A. Weiner, first by warning him, then by informing the Silk Association of America of his deeds, and finally by expelling him from the Lyonnais Syndicate. In the course of investigations, the syndicate's newly formed Designs and Models Committee discovered that Mrs. Weiner, a former première at the House of Doucet, had taken advantage of her connections to procure samples to be copied. In another important case four years later, Ducharne successfully sued a Lyonnais company for plagiarizing two designs.[95] Rejecting several proposals for binding arbitration, the syndicate relied on voluntary arbitration and publication of arbitration decisions. The system, which did not reveal the companies implicated, was ineffective.[96] In the Great Depression, the Lyonnais Silk Syndicate looked to the National and European Textile Congresses for international arbitration about designs and models, and to the International Chamber of Commerce to deal with a serious new international threat: Japanese copying.[97]

Meanwhile, a division appeared between manufacturers of simple silks and of "*haute nouveautés*" (more elaborate prints and textures). Bianchini-Férier, which produced both, stopped defending the texture and composition of one of its most famous light silks, georgette, though they did pursue competitors that used the

name *georgette*. The two principals banded together with other producers of *haute nouveautés* to guarantee their "creations" against counterfeiting. Although the *haute nouveautés* group avoided the commercial or criminal courts to pursue plagiarists, they resorted so often to syndical arbitration that critics worried about the growing number of expulsions from the syndicate, which was already losing members due to the depression.[98]

By contrast, couturiers acted alone or in small groups. Some focused on preventing illegal actions. During the Great War, Poiret returned to the United States with a line of ready-made clothing described as "genuine reproductions . . . exclusively for the women of America."[99] He hoped to institute a system whereby Americans could copy these models and pay a royalty for every copy, but American manufacturers were not prepared to pay royalties. (Thirty years later, when the American industry was more developed and secure, they adopted such a scheme.)[100] Chanel issued invitations to her shows, reserved the right to refuse entry to guests suspected of copying, and confronted suspects. However, most designers were wary about confrontations, because they risked insulting a buyer who might purchase a dozen or more models.[101] Most designers worried about commercial counterfeiting simply multiplied the labor-intensive and luxurious details that distinguished couture models from ready-made clothing, while the fashion press promoted the doctrine that real distinction meant combining all the details into a "look." Nevertheless, designers like Coco Chanel realized that copies did not reduce sales of the original models, because copies did not offer the fit, fabric, and finishing touches of the originals; these designers recognized that overseas copies would popularize their designs in the lucrative overseas fashion market.[102] Two consequences were the spread of commercial knockoffs and a democratization of haute couture styles.

## Legal Campaigns

In the first two decades of the century, the leading couturière, supported by a dozen designers, launched a legal campaign to control representations of her models in the fashion press and to use existing laws on artistic and industrial property rights to stop reproduction of her models by competitors in haute couture. When designers made peace with the fashion press in the early 1920s, a younger couturière who believed in a distinctive style for a select clientele, backed by another association dedicated to protecting models, pursued the new counterfeiters, known as copy houses, in a series of widely reported court cases.

In 1906, Jeanne Paquin brought two important complaints about piracy to the courts, one about the publication of photographs of new models before they were presented in her collection under the 1902 law on artistic and literary property, and one about the reproduction of her models by another couture house under the 1806 law on industrial property. Five years later she instigated a suit against another competitor, citing the 1909 law on designs and models. A defense group composed of twelve leading couturiers supported her during twelve years of trials and appeals.[103]

In 1905 and 1906, *Le Chic* and *Le Chic parisien* (magazines about French fashion published in Paris but sold in Germany and Austria) included drawings of models by Paquin not yet presented in her collection. Paquin sued the Parisian publishers of these magazines, Bachwitz, Brentano, Gruenwald, for plagiarism, citing their publication of engravings of four models she had deposited, in the form of photographs, with the Conseil des Prud'hommes. Her representatives cited the 1902 law on artistic property and the 1806 law on industrial models. Because the models had not legitimately left her workshop, Paquin's lawyers argued that they had been removed fraudulently and alleged infraction of articles 425 and 426 of the penal code against counterfeiting. The first court refused to consider deposits in the form of drawings or photographs as works of art subject to plagiarism and therefore refused to grant any protection under the law on artistic property. That court also declared that drawings in the press could not be illegal copies, which could only be made in workshops in the same way as the original. However, this court ruled that there had been a "quasi-infraction" of the code that constituted a "prejudice" to the "novelty" of the models, and it fined one of the newspapers. After examination by a panel of experts, including a fashion illustrator, the appeal court overturned the decision and declared that a drawing in a periodical could result in reproduction of a model. The court ruled that drawings depreciated the value of designs and promoted "unfair competition" by other designers, who could copy them.[104]

In 1906, Paquin successfully sued the Beer couture house for copying several models that, her lawyers argued, were her exclusive property, because she had deposited photographs of the models at the Conseil des Prud'hommes in accordance with the century-old law on industrial property. The court convicted Beer and ordered him to pay Paquin 8,000 francs in damages. When Beer appealed, the court confirmed the original decision. The appellate court consulted another panel of experts, which contended that slight differences in design details between the originals and the knockoffs did not preclude charges of piracy. The decision appeared to override earlier judicial decisions limiting coverage to "servile copies." Contending that the complainant had to prove "bad faith" or intentional reproduction on the part of the copiers, Beer launched several more appeals. Ultimately, the original ruling was upheld.[105] Despite this setback, Beer continued to show collections into the 1930s.

In 1911, Paquin decided to test the 1909 law on designs and models. She had learned from one Mme. Moissenet (who was likely a "plant," sent to a ladies' tailor shop to get evidence) that a ladies' tailor had promised to deliver to Mme. Moissenet a red striped dress and a belted jacket that resembled Paquin models. Paquin contended that the offending outfits were "servile copies" of models she had deposited at the Conseil des Prud'hommes but not yet revealed to the public in her seasonal collection. Assuming that someone in her employ had been bribed to sketch the models or to sneak their *toiles* out of her workshops to be reproduced, she filed a complaint that led to a police seizure of these two costumes at the ladies' tailors shop, and she sued the owners for 20,000 francs in damages. Her business manager also asked authorization to publicize the judgment in twenty newspapers and magazines. The first court rejected Paquin's attempt to prove "bad faith" by mean of similarities between the knockoffs and the originals without stolen toiles or other tangible evidence. After two appeals, the appellate court appointed a panel of experts composed largely of couturiers, and it accepted their decisions that the seized outfits differed from the Paquin models only "in the dimension of the collar [on the dress] and the cut of the jacket" and that these differences did not modify "the general character of the costume." The panel concluded that the similarities between the seized outfits and the designer originals could not happen fortuitously and "sufficed, by themselves, to constitute undeniable proof of bad faith."[106] The appeal court ruled in Paquin's favor on 31 December 1918. Designers hoped this decision would provide guidelines in a murky area of jurisprudence. Women's magazines, which had been selling patterns "in the style" of various couturiers, started to clarify that they "interpreted" rather than imitated designer models.[107]

After the war, discouraged by governmental "inertia," syndical groups made peace with the fashion press. They supported a glossy new trade organ, *L'Officiel de la Couture et de la Mode.* Couturiers gave *Officiel* reporters "free access into their houses, closed at all times against the attempted inquisitiveness of some foreign buyers." The purpose was to defend couture and confection against "the practices of certain foreign clients and . . . to provide information for buyers of models."[108] The trade organ closely followed a series of legal cases against counterfeiting that dragged through the commercial courts, and it lobbied for changes in the laws against copying. The editor, Lucien Chassaigne, tried to rally the entire French press against the audacious pillage of fashion plates from fashion magazines. Although his principal targets were foreign buyers, he also castigated "our own counterfeiters . . . who present collections from Paris in large foreign cities and offer to reproduce these copies."[109] Soon society magazines began reporting couturiers' campaign against counterfeiting, and women's legal guides instructed consumers not to buy copies.[110] In the early 1930s, the *Bulletin Officiel de la Chambre Syndicale de la Couture Parisienne* also followed court cases. The editors were incensed when the court of appeal refused to confirm a lower court conviction of a première who had copied one of her previous employers' models exactly and had produced thirteen models that were "not of original inspiration," on the grounds that these did not constitute "repeated plagiarism."[111]

Madeleine Vionnet knew about copying from her early years in couture, when she had cut, fit, and supervised seamstresses sewing copies for Kate Reilly's London shop, which advertised that it sold "Paris models and dresses of the season in the very latest styles at about half price."[112] When Vionnet set up her own house, she made models in many colors, and *les élégantes* who found styles that suited them bought many differently colored versions of the same styles. *Vogue* and American manufacturers and importers referred to a "Vionnet type" dress, though the manufacturers and importers likely meant illegal copies of her dresses. Even while reporters repeated Vionnet's claims that she designed simple, loose outfits for the modern woman, they recognized that her models, many of them in exquisite silks with elaborate beading, represented an older tradition of style for a limited number, not the emerging system of fashion for the many.[113] In 1923, Vionnet's new business manager, Louis Dangel, entered into an agreement with a made-to-order firm. When other American manufacturers continued to put out "Vionnet-type" or "Vionnet-cut" garments, Dangel took out full-page advertisements to identify authentic Vionnet models in the European editions of American newspapers. In the mid-1920s, Vionnet signed deals for exclusive American rights to reproduce her models wholesale; one deal involved production of one-size-fits-all ready-made dresses, which were produced and marketed as "Repeat Originals" at $150 apiece. These dresses were not marketed for long.[114]

Domestically, Vionnet used publicity, legal suits, and in-house surveillance to combat piracy. Beginning in 1920, her advertisements included the declaration

that "Mme. Madeleine Vionnet does not sell to agents or to dressmakers. The 1909 law protects models. All Madeleine Vionnet's creations are her property. Copies and reproductions will always result in legal suits against their authors." (Other couturiers confined themselves to notices that all their models were registered at the Conseil des Prud'hommes.)[115] Other couturiers and the fashion press nevertheless closely watched Vionnet's first legal suit over copying. On 31 December 1921, she won a ruling that recognized that designing clothing was an artistic endeavor and therefore covered by the 1902 law on artistic property.[116] Recognizing artistic endeavor in clothing design bolstered legal arguments about copying based on design elements alone, without corroborating evidence about the theft of *toiles* or other intentional acts. Of course, courts would still have to sort out which law applied in particular cases. However, payment of a 1,000-franc fine and 12,000 francs "damages and costs" did not deter one of the convicted couturiers from operating for several more years.[117]

Throughout the 1920s, Vionnet lodged complaints against copy houses, prompting police seizures and trials. Her manager, Dangel, formed an association, the Artistic Protection of Seasonal Industries, dedicated to defending creators from "theft of their ideas and counterfeit of their models." The association sustained court actions against counterfeiters and kept a blacklist of buyers suspected of using unethical methods.[118] Dangel also used the pages of the *Bulletin Officiel de la Chambre Syndicale de la Couture Parisienne* to exhort couturiers to mount only two collections per year, winter and summer, and "to have the courage to refuse the undesirables that they know very well enter into their salons."[119] The association often orchestrated visits to copy houses by women posing as customers in order to acquire copies for prosecution, which led in some cases to initial judgments against the couturiers for "provocation."[120]

Dangel exercised so much surveillance over Vionnet's workshops that it occasionally poisoned the working environment. Suspecting that sketches of Vionnet models were being surreptitiously removed from the workshops to be copied, he ordered some henchmen to search the workshops overnight, without warning, and did not return the sketches they seized immediately. When a sketcher by the name of Mlle. Constantine Martiale and one of her assistants threatened to sue over the unauthorized search of Martiale's desk and the removal of her drawings and personal effects, the director fired her on the spot. Subsequently, he disingenuously wrote to her explaining that her work had been unsatisfactory for some time due to her tardiness and "spirit of revolt and anarchy"—not because of her legal threat. Martiale sued, claiming "abusive rupture of contract" and failure to pay wages owed as well as an indemnity for breaking her contract. The Conseil des Prud'hommes ruled that Vionnet must pay the wages owed and a small indemnity for not giving Martiale notice but awarded no damages for "abusive rupture of contract."[121]

Jeanne Lanvin, who had fought copying since 1910, founded another society that laid charges against counterfeiters and offered "insurance against copying" by photographing models and depositing them at the Conseil des Prud'hommes.[122] Its office was located in the Society for Author's Rights, which had 35 agents in Paris and 740 in the provinces.[123] The economic crisis of 1930–31 spurred Jeanne Lanvin, Jeanne Paquin, Jean Patou, and Charles Worth to join Vionnet's association to protect French couture models from piracy. In the following years, one of the association's cases involved a notorious *"maison de belles copies,"* whose proprietor admitted making knockoffs of several prominent designers' models priced from 3,000 to 5,000 francs, and selling them at 1,500 to 1,800 francs. Chanel, usually aloof from these cases, joined Vionnet as complainant. Another suit resulted in an award of 260,000 francs in damages, for twenty-six separate copies.[124] Fashion commentators compared the dramatic police seizures to the struggle to enforce American prohibition, noting the presence, in both, of bootleggers and police raids.[125] Other employers in the luxury trades disapproved of the police raids and repeated court cases.[126]

Although constant vigilance reduced copying, to be effective, legal intervention had to be swifter and fines had to be higher. Both protective associations lobbied for amendments to the 1909 law but split over the only serious legislative proposal. A 1930 bill would have increased fines, which was acceptable to all, but would also have permitted seizure of alleged copies before photographs of the models were deposited, which was controversial because it could be abused by unscrupulous couturiers and couturières. A more effective law was not enacted until the 1950s.[127]

By the 1930s, many couturiers were trying another approach toward copying: producing and selling their own ready-to-wear clothing. In the mid-twenties, Jean Patou and Sonia Delauney opened ready-to-wear sports boutiques; in the midthirties, Elsa Schiaparelli added another ready-to-wear boutique (like others before her, she claimed to have invented this kind of boutique).[128] Lucien Lelong introduced limited-edition dresses to be sold in authorized dress shops.[129] Schiaparelli, who understood the new dynamic of fashion, considered laws protecting models "vain and useless. The moment that people stop copying you, it means that you are no longer any good."[130] Of course, Schiaparelli's humorous and outrageous outfits with colonial artifacts, military details, and bright colors were unlikely to be copied, because few bourgeois women considered them tasteful. A new generation of couturières was beginning to accept that fashion was about emulation and was learning new ways to distinguish haute couture from copies.

*Chapter Seven*

# Shopping and Sewing

A t the beginning of the eighteenth century, a rigid system of clothing prevailed in a stable social order; midcentury saw a major rupture: as a more confident bourgeois society emerged, bourgeois men renounced elegance for a sober appearance, while women's clothing continued to display decorative elements.[1] Daniel Roche's study of the birth of consumption in France, 1600–1800, documents that urban bourgeois and petit bourgeois women spent twice as much on attire and owned far more garments than their husbands did. New consumption patterns brought lighter fabrics, more types of apparel, and regular variation in styles to urban areas, while peasants still valued sturdier fabrics and fewer items of apparel, and they mended their clothing repeatedly.[2] By the 1920s, the system of fixed clothing was over, except in remote villages. Although the age of opulent ladies' wear had passed, ladies still spent more on clothing than men.

In *Fashioning the Bourgeoisie*, Philippe Perrot studied the development of modern clothing consumption based not primarily on purchasing power but on social and cultural discrimination or purchasing know-how. In particular, he demonstrates how bourgeois women's clothing became showpieces of family status. Two mid-nineteenth-century developments—confection and department stores—were implicated. Most bourgeois women could not afford many, and many could not afford any, items of haute couture, but they could afford quality ready-to-wear. However, bourgeois women had to be lured into department stores and their clothing consumption legitimized by "an unprecedented spectacle of permanent temptation in a respectable setting."[3] In this chapter I follow the extension of haute couture style by department stores, their publicity, and their mail-order catalogs into the 1920s and 1930s and introduce a little-studied explanation of democratization: the widespread practice of home sewing of patterns "inspired" by haute couture.

Contemporary fashion commentators noticed and accepted a limited degree of democratization of haute couture, as long as Frenchwomen personalized their clothing. They correlated "the diffusion of elegance" with several factors: greater social "fluidity," the spread of department store catalogs to the provinces, "the rapidity of modern transport, the triumph of democracy, and the school of cinema."[4] Few mentioned the prevalence of home sewing. The practicality of shopping at department stores, browsing through catalogs, and home sewing resembles Frenchwomen's experiences of making do during the First World War. These practices also prefigure the adaptability of Frenchwomen to the privations of the German Occupation and the Vichy Regime.

## Department Stores

The *grand magasin* was a nineteenth-century innovation. The volume, variety, display, pricing, and departmentalization of their merchandise made these stores models of modern marketing.[5] Between 1850 and 1914, Paris department stores exploited a "consumer revolution" stimulated by rising disposable income, the introduction of consumer banking services, including deposit and checking accounts, and a series of international exhibitions that emphasized marketing. Department stores contributed to the consumer revolution by selling on the installment plan and establishing their own credit companies.[6]

The retailing revolution began in dry goods stores known as *magasins de nouveautés* in the 1830s and 1840s. Most department stores began this way and many department store pioneers began as clerks in *magasins de nouveautés*.[7] These stores sold fabrics and linens and also shawls, hosiery, and gloves. They assembled similar product lines in specialized departments and permitted free entry (shopping unaccompanied by a salesclerk). As early as the 1830s, a few had fixed and clearly marked prices, which eliminated haggling. These innovations began the transformation of stores from places people went to in order to buy specific items to "theaters for exploring your desires." This transformation entailed enlarging stores to permit more display and introducing glass display cases.[8] By the 1850s, *magasins de nouveautés* offered easy exchanges and regular sales.

Stores specializing in ribbons, lace, and other trimmings introduced a form of mass production, making large quantities in many small or large workshops, without mechanization beyond the introduction of sewing machines. Some put work out to a network of small workshops; others set up large workshops with industrial sewing machines. Many of these workshops made ready-to-wear clothing. Around 1845, these stores had begun selling cloaks and coats, garments that did not require meticulous measuring and fitting. Although most of these fancy goods stores did not survive the 1848 Revolution, one flourished.[9] La Belle Jardinière, founded by Pierre Parissot, sold fabrics and work clothes—smocks, overalls, and aprons. Dedicating to making "new clothes in conditions that permitted prices much lower than tailors charged and barely higher than second-hand clothiers charged," the store exploited the recently invented sewing machine. After several expansions, it moved to a large building near the Pont Neuf on the Right Bank.[10] Although considered a popular store because it sold work clothing, La Belle Jardinière appealed to bourgeois customers. In the interwar period, it advertised in *Femina* alongside more prestigious department stores.[11]

The prototypical Parisian department store was Le Bon Marché, begun in 1852 by Aristide Boucicaut and a partner. By 1863, Boucicaut bought out a second partner, and in 1869, opened the first multistory building purposely built as a department store. It had the large horizontal display windows and colored skylights that became hallmarks of Paris department stores. Located on a square on the Left Bank of the Seine, it annexed other buildings in the vicinity over the decades. Boucicaut diversified, adding ladies' ready-to-wear, children's wear, rugs, and other household goods, and later still, travel goods, perfume, stationery, and toys. Throughout, textiles and clothing remained the mainstays. Other Bon Marché innovations included electric lighting, escalators, and cash registers, each of which made shopping more convenient. Before the First World War, Le Bon Marché was the world's largest department store. Its turnover of 227,000,000 francs in 1910 far exceeded that of its nearest competitor, the Louvre department store in Paris (founded in 1855). Revenues at Au Printemps (1865) or La Samaritaine (1870) fell far behind those of the two leading department stores.[12]

The Bon Marché used entertainment and in-store services to attract and retain customers. In the 1870s, it organized concerts that drew thousands to the environs and forged a lasting bond between shopping and entertainment. Together with other stores, the Bon Marché encouraged leisurely counter shopping by offering services to make customers' "stay in the store more agreeable, comfortable, and less fatiguing." After introducing cafes and tearooms in response to suggestions from exhausted and hungry provincial customers, major department stores multiplied their services. They installed lounges, banking wickets, travel agencies, and ticket dispensers (and in the 1930s, cinemas). Although stores hoped that customers would use the time spent in the lounges to decide on purchases, the lounges must also have functioned as places of respite in these emporiums of goods arranged to entice.[13] Couturiers borrowed one of these services. They opened tearooms, where "the latest sandwiches, washed down with tea . . . serve as pretexts to talk about fashion."[14]

Aux Trois Quartiers was founded in 1827 by a couple, Charles-Armand and Marguerite-Augustine Gallois, near the Madeleine Cathedral on the Right Bank of the Seine. Marguerite and her sister had operated a shop nearby, to which the couple added an annex selling mourning clothes and a dry goods outlet with the name Aux Trois Quartiers on the Boulevard Madeleine. In the first decade of the twentieth century, architect P. I. Friesé rebuilt the two buildings. In 1910, the store had counters for silks, linings, and other fabrics, lingerie, shoes, purses, and gloves, as well as household linens and rugs. The Articles de Paris department offered small furniture, decorative items, watches, clocks, and wallets; other departments sold perfume, porcelain, china, and glassware. By 1913, Aux Trois Quartiers had a tearoom and a hair salon. Their catalog service switched to better-quality paper, included more drawings, and added articles on fashion, cosmetics, and recipes. Some catalogues even had a correspondence corner.[15] Like fashion magazines, their catalogs tried to build up customer loyalty.

The second city of France followed a similar course. During massive urban renewal under the Second Empire, Lyon acquired two department stores. A former employee of a dry goods store, Henry Perrot, opened a dry goods store that also sold ready-made clothing. Inspired by the Bon Marché, Jean Dabonneau opened a more popular department store on a major artery. When that popular store went into liquidation in 1892, Perrot took over the property, expanded the merchandise to more than one hundred types of product, and called the new enterprise Le Grand Bazar de Lyon. Bazaars had earlier specialized in household goods, but by 1892 the term connoted immense stores with a many products for sale. Perrot installed electricity and took out full-page advertisements in local daily papers. The largely male employees, many of whom lived in a dormitory attached to the store, were subject to strict discipline, including wearing a uniform of black trousers and white shirts. Nearly half the personnel ordered, tagged, arranged, and delivered merchandise. Before the First World War, the Grand Bazar delivered purchases to the Lyon suburbs in a large truck with the company logo painted on the sides. A new manager, Fernand Pariset, launched weekly sales to move products that lingered in the inventory and updated catalogs to resemble fashion magazines.[16]

During the war, department stores had to cope with inadequate supplies of products and personnel and with destruction of property. In 1914, La Belle Jardinière workshops for the confection of work and woolen clothing, located in Lille, were destroyed. Initially, this forced the department store to put out sewing to home workers around Paris, but as home workers moved into wartime employment, the store expanded its own large workshop on the Rue Didot in Paris.[17] Whereas department stores had previously employed men with prior experience as shop clerks, they now hired more women, many of them younger and less experienced in retail work than their predecessors. This hiring pattern continued after the war. Women mixed with men in shoe departments, for example, but only rose to the level of department heads in departments with an all-female staff, such as ladies' wear.[18] After the war, schools trained girls to be retail clerks. The school in Paris offered a four-month course of academic and practical studies, including hygiene, product display, rapid addition, and psychology. Young women who took the academic courses and paid their own tuition passed on their knowledge of sales techniques to other employees. Employees who took the practical courses received bursaries of 500 francs from their employers.[19]

Although Le Bon Marché lost its leadership position after the war, it renovated and expanded in 1930. A brochure entitled "Modern Palaces," published in celebration of the opening of the new buildings, reported that the improvements were based on "a commercial science of modern necessities" and provided "maximum well-being and comfort."[20] Other Paris stores were more dynamic. Galeries Lafayette, which began as a shop in 1895, diversified rapidly. Even before the Great War, it pursued a policy of integration by buying silk and other textile factories. In 1919, it took control of the previously mentioned Société Parisienne de Confection, a company specializing in ready-to-wear clothing. By 1920, Galeries Lafayette had 142 departments, a tearoom, hair salon, and reading room. Bolts of material filled the counters on one whole floor. In the 1920s, personnel reached a high point of four thousand.[21]

As pioneers of horizontal merchandise display windows, electrical lighting, and elevators, department stores were already considered modern.[22] Most of their buildings had been erected between 1877 and 1920 in art nouveau style. Between

1921 and 1924, Au Printemps rebuilt after a fire razed the previous premises. The hugely successful Anglo-American department store developer H. Gordon Selfridge contributed an essay to a brochure announcing their reopening. Selfridge applauded "the ingenious systems that Au Printemps has imagined to speed payments for purchases and inter-departmental communications to accelerate the delivery of packages." An architecture critic praised the monumental entrance doors for facilitating access "without effort, without a fight"—implicitly contrasting them to pedestrian jams at the doorways of the old buildings and of other department stores. To allay fears about fires, a technician lauded the ease and speed of escalator egress from upper stories and basements.[23] The 1925 Exhibition of the Decorative Arts primarily affected department store window decoration and outdoor displays by reducing the number of items on display and by spotlighting them. These improvements further distanced department stores from most small shops, with their densely packed, dimly lit window and counter displays.[24]

Another legacy of the art deco exhibition was more extensive use of modern wax and metal mannequins to showcase ladies' clothing in window displays. Some of the art deco mannequins evoked controversy about their lack of facial features and "haughty stances" (like the female figures on the covers of fashion magazines). In response, experts insisted that these mannequins encouraged women to pay attention to the outfits they wore, not their facial beauty or bodily perfection.[25] Over the next five years, Parisians accepted that "elegance requires more grandeur and less coquetry" in mannequins (and, by extension, modern women). Here coquetry means makeup and pleasing expressions; in fashion magazines, it implied well dressed. By 1927, provincial department stores realized that these controversial mannequins were "real draws" for potential customers.[26]

Department stores adapted in other ways. Aux Trois Quartiers continued to advertise major Paris sales in the provincial press and to display sales items in local mail-order outlets.[27] Other stores set up local branches. Calculating that local branches better served local customers, they opened many outlets in the provinces and in the colonies.[28] Often they took over local department stores in difficulty, renovated them to look more like a Paris store, and renewed the stock to attract "a more distinguished and elegant clientele."[29] In Lille, Au Printemps refurbished the Galeries Lillois and renamed it Au Printemps (Galeries Lillois) to attract new and old customers. To reduce competition in the mid-1920s, Printemps and Galeries Lafayette agreed that neither would install an outlet in a city that already had a branch of the other store; this agreement lasted until 1941.[30]

Although Bouchara, a *magasin de nouveautés* in Marseilles, expanded to the capital and other French cities, expansion from the provinces to Paris was rare.[31]

In the 1920s and early 1930s, provincial department stores modernized their premises and retail techniques. Between 1922 and 1933, the Grande Bazar de Lyon annexed contiguous properties and held concerts, puppet shows, and other theatrical performances on the fourth floor of the store. After the art deco exhibition, the façade and windows were "embellished" in a prize-winning manner.[32]

In Nantes, the Decré family had taken over a grand bazaar, built a "modern" building in 1901–2, extended delivery service to the surrounding region, and renamed their store a grand magasin before the First World War. In the 1920s, the store added textiles and a catalog. During the early 1930s, the business opened an office in the capital to purchase "the latest creations" and opened a new store built with "transparency," meaning with the large windows, mirrors, and metallic trappings favored by modern architects. Before long, the store had a food department with refrigerated counters, a restaurant, cinema, hair salon, travel agency, post office, and (it claimed) the first self-serve cafeteria in Europe.[33]

Even confection firms independent of department stores did well in the 1920s. Weill and Sons operated a small ready-to-wear business outside the couture district at the end of the Great War. The business sold women's clothes without labels to department stores and ladies' wear shops that affixed their own labels. In 1922, father and son created "Albert Weill Jeune," specializing in girls' and modern (i.e., youthful) women's attire, and moved into the clothing district at the foot of Montmartre. The new company flourished. When the sons took over in 1929, they consolidated all stages of production into one building and formed a close association with a textile wholesaler. Four sales agents, one for each region of France, traveled four months a year, covering 40,000 kilometers by train.[34]

Rocked by the depression, department stores had to make major adjustments. Between 1929–30 and 1937–38, turnovers in individual stores fell between 17 and 44 percent. In 1939, the Louvre asked for judicial liquidation.[35] Although sales at Galeries Lafayette dropped by 35 to 40 percent between 1931 and 1936, management took advantage of low costs to renovate the main store, reorganize stock management, and withdraw investments in confection.[36] As sales dropped 53 percent in the first five years of the 1930s, La Belle Jardinière added shareholders and directors, including the former director of Le Bon Marché. The Board of Directors lowered prices, fired workers, closed workshops, and reorganized the remaining ones into assembly lines. The work-related changes provoked "lively resistance."[37]

Following American and British models, Paris stores established discount stores. Printemps set up "Prisunic" in 1931, Galeries Lafayette "Monoprix" in 1932, and the Bon Marché "Prixinime" in 1933. Unlike the founding stores, these "popular" stores had centralized buying, fewer articles for sale, smaller premises, no extra services, cash-only sales transactions, and prices posted on countertops, not on individual items. These features facilitated faster customer service and rotation of stock. Their profits helped most Paris department stores survive the depression. Some provincial department stores suffered more. With an aging management and surplus inventory, the Grand Bazar de Lyon fired staff and closed annexes. The store did not really revive until 1951, when it affiliated with Printemps. It is now in receivership and is permanently closed.[38]

## Department Store Publicity

In the interwar decades, major department stores appointed publicity directors to generate and coordinate publicity. Their purview encompassed arranging merchandise displays to appeal to buyers and entertainments to attract buyers, as well as developing customer loyalty by contests, prizes, and rebates. But their principal responsibility was print advertising.[39]

In the daily press, department stores advertised a wide array of products, "considerable choice" within product lines, "good quality," and reasonable prices. All department store ads listed several products ranging in prices, such as a 1927 Au Printemps (Galeries Lilloises) ad for dresses from 30 to 125 francs.[40] As store ads became more pictorial in the 1920s, sales ads took on the appearance of a crowded catalog page. Ads for ladies' wear did not contain as many sketches and captions, making them more visually appealing. Compared to advertising copy today, the accompanying text put more emphasis on the quality of the fabric and trimmings used on garments, no doubt because many customers sewed for themselves or consulted with dressmakers about fabrics and trimmings. Paris department stores placed ads in shopping newspapers, society monthlies, fashion weeklies, and supplements to daily newspapers. Inside the front cover and on the back covers of fashion magazines, they alerted potential customers to upcoming sales or seasonal presentations of the latest styles.[41] They put sales inserts into magazines, to be removed and taken to stores as guides to the sales.[42]

Provincial department stores advertised in local and regional dailies. Many proclaimed that their ladies' wear was au courant with Parisian ladies' wear, using slogans like "the latest fashion from Paris" or "a large choice of Paris models."[43]

While some dress shops had names like "Au Paradis des Dames," more shops included "Paris" in their name and publicized the Parisian provenance of their products. In Lyon, "A la Parisienne" advertised that they had Parisian styles. In Lille, "Aux Modes Parisiennes" made similar claims.[44] Local clothing stores and local branches of clothing chains such as Henri Esders marketed women's clothing at lower prices than ladies' wear shops. Their ads trumpeted "the lowest prices in town."[45]

Special flyers used more personal appeals, more vivid language, and more varied typeface than newspaper ads or magazine inserts. A flyer for Le Bon Marché promised "Madame" that she would enter "THE TEMPLE OF FASHION." Other flyers posed as invitations to special exhibitions of new fabrics or dress styles. Some left blank spaces for notes about individual items, like the notebooks handed out at couture shows.[46] Flyers for ladies' wear borrowed terminology like *elegant* from society magazines, but were more partial to the adjective *charming,* which was more common in women's magazines. Probably flyers, like women's magazines, were distributed to a socially mixed clientele that included women who did not necessarily self-identify as elegant.

In addition to advertising in bound shopping guides, department stores published diaries with a calendar of sales dates and theater and cafe addresses. Some diaries constructed the reader as a modern woman and clever shopper. In a Galeries Lafayette *Agenda for 1934,* Paul Reboux, a prolific popularizer of history, literature, and fashion, described "a svelte young women" going to sales at Galeries Lafayette, which attracted "the modern girl who thinks about her exams as much as her appearance," the good client, "who knows what she wants, pays, and goes," and "the practical spouse who sends her husband to other departments . . . knowing full well that his purchases will deprive him of the right to criticize Madame's purchases." Reboux included *les élégantes,* because, he reported, it was now acceptable for them to go to the Galeries Lafayette. Indeed, they called the store "the galleries, with affectionate familiarity."[47] His flattery of *les élégantes* was one of very few examples of the kind of ingratiating language about customers regularly used by North American department stores advertising French couture.[48]

## Mail-Order Catalogs

Major department stores had large catalog departments. The Galeries Lafayette department employed twenty-five illustrators, printed 2,000 copies of each catalog, and sent just over half of them to the Paris region, the rest to the provinces. The editor believed that their audience first leafed through a catalog "recreationally," for the "pleasure of discovery." Subsequently, readers studied particular items and made calculations about quality and price. Each page was "a sort of window display"; it should not be crowded or disorganized, because a messy layout discouraged further perusal. In short, the catalog constructed the reader as a spectator first and a consumer second. It also brought consumption into the home.[49] Some Bon Marché and Au Printemps special catalogs respected these principles, but general catalogs were filled with small drawings of many items, without any background and with short, dry captions. By the mid-1930s, an analyst complained that French catalogs, with their tiny drawings and "cold language," lagged behind catalog developments in the United States. The analyst recommended displaying fewer items, using livelier language, and mixing photographs with line drawings. After all, a catalog was supposed to "create the desire to possess" and "hypnotize the reader/viewer into an irresistible impulse to satisfy . . . desire."[50]

Provincial department stores also published catalogs. In Bordeaux, Aux Dames de France (founded in 1908) produced two catalogs per season, one for household products and one for fabrics and fashions. They delivered fifty-page catalogs in thirty delivery vans within a radius of 100 kilometers around the city. On the bottom of most pages were slogans "judiciously edited to produce the best impression," such as "Buying hats at the Dames de France confers a true sign of elegance."[51]

Publicists considered the catalog "the most precious form of publicity." Ideally, catalogs were supposed to be clearly illustrated, "with good, plain type, on thick, semiglossy paper," so that they would last and could be scrutinized frequently. To encourage customers to keep catalogs for the whole season, some had a notice emblazoned on the front cover: "Don't lose this catalog! You will find it useful all season." Actually, there were two kinds of catalog, a bland kind on newsprint with precise descriptions of products for the "methodical" buyer, and a "stimulating" kind on semiglossy paper intended to catch the eye and spark the imagination.[52] Department stores published both kinds of catalog. Their biannual general catalogs were bland; their smaller, glossier, and more specialized catalogs—particularly those for clothing and textiles—fell in the stimulating category. Stores advertised their clothing and fabric catalogs in fashion magazines.[53]

After the war, more stores tried to imitate fashion magazines by hiring talented illustrators like Georges Barbier to draw covers, and writers like André de Fouquières (a regular contributor to *Vogue*) to write "chronicles" advising readers how to dress. One well-received Galeries Lafayette cover depicted an idealized female figure interpreted as "the image of the woman combatants dreamed about."[54] Soon, though, the cover figures were represented slightly more realistically, notably shopping (fig. 10). A few Au Printemps special catalogs used thick matte or glossy paper throughout the issues.[55] Even La Belle Jardinière occasionally employed an illustrator such as Pierre Brissaud and used gold foil on its covers.[56] In the 1930s, when French fashion magazines began using photographs on covers, major department stores did the same.[57] Copywriters lifted adjectives like *elegant* and *distinguished* for afternoon and evening wear, *simple* and *practical* for morning and sportswear, from fashion magazines.[58] Headings like "Details That Count" in these catalogs read like the headings on fashion spreads in magazines.[59]

With the exception of covers on La Belle Jardinière general catalogs (which showed more men, including workmen), most catalog covers depicted tall, svelte, fashionably dressed female figures. Except for illustrations of clothing for *"femmes fortes"* (plus-size clothing), the female figures inside the covers were slender.[60] Otherwise, the quality of the paper, crowded layout, and appeals about lower prices distinguished catalogs from magazines. Most department store catalogs were still made of newsprint, "modernized" by using color and depicting human figures in livelier poses on the covers.[61] Interior drawings were tiny, black and white, and lacking in background details. Many captions promised reasonable prices, implying that the ideal reader/customer was a bourgeois or petit bourgeois woman of average income.[62] Only the Belle Jardinière catalogs included work aprons or blouses on their "Work Clothing" pages.[63]

Other indications of catalogs' social purview are the inclusion of clothing for mothers, children, and housewives, and for everyday comfort. Unlike society monthlies and many fashion magazines, catalogs displayed breastfeeding bras and slips, aprons and housedresses, and cotton and woolen stockings.[64] Lingerie that might reveal the female figure's torso or upper legs was depicted alone or on a wooden stand, not on a body, presumably to avoid offending readers. Their diffidence about bodily exposure stands in contrast to the drawings and photos of women wearing corsets and girdles in society and fashion magazines. Catalog editors who knew that husbands and children might browse through their publications were more attuned to middle-class propriety than magazine editors were.

Special catalogs and flyers for ladies' wear targeted a more established bourgeoisie. "Invitation" flyers for presentations of seasonal clothing showcased more expensive clothing than general catalogs and described the clothing displayed as more fashionable and made of better-quality materials. A dress in the "latest style made of good quality crepe georgette in fashionable colors or black" cost

FIGURE 10. Cover of Au Bon Marché summer catalogue, 1927.
Collection Au Bon Marché. Courtesy, Bibliothèque Fornay.

395 francs in the Bon Marché summer 1929 clothing catalog, while a dress made of "good quality crepe georgette" was 250 francs in that summer's general catalog.[65] Prices also varied according to the material used. In a 1926 flyer, Aux Galeries Lafayette offered women's suits from 195 francs, for one made of "good gabardine," to 595 francs, for one made of "extra supple wool and cashmere."[66]

At these prices, most bourgeois women could not afford a new suit every year.

In a series on household budgets in the depression years, *La Mode Pratique* posited an average family income of 80,000 francs annually, which, the journalist calculated, allowed an expenditure of 1,500 to 2,000 francs a year on ladies' wear. She made lists of annual purchases totaling these sums. A reader who "made do" with 1,000 francs annually for her personal wardrobe protested that many women, "even from good families," could not afford 1,500 francs for their wardrobe. Chastened, the journalist compiled a 1,000-franc shopping list that focused more on basics and long-term planning—purchasing a sturdy winter coat every three years and a new suit in only one of the intervening years.[67] There were no recorded reader complaints about this list.

## Expanding Markets

Improvements in the layout, goods, and services offered by department stores, combined with massive publicity, attracted clientele, even wealthy women. In 1921, a Parisienne told the journalist Roger Allard that "the idea of penetrating one [a department store] sickens me," but she did enter because "it is so practical. It is shopping." Allard concluded that the department store "meets all needs. To be more precise, say that it creates new needs, that it is itself a new desire."[68]

Provincial campaigns and advertising had considerable effect. Initially, Paris-based fashion journalists associated provincials with unfashionable styles, but after noticing that provincial readers bought many of their patterns and solicited their advice, they became more respectful.[69] In the early 1920s, journalists targeting provincial readers expressed reservations about slavishly following Paris fashion. While they reported on the collections and *les élégantes*, they suggested that readers mainly needed to know about Parisian style for trips to the capital.[70] By the mid-1920s, most fashion magazines promoted Parisian style for urban women in the provinces. Camille Duguet explained that better transportation and communication, notably fashion journals "addressed to provincial women," accounted for the emergence of "provincial Parisiennes."[71] A less interested observer, the Countess Riguidi, attributed a new provincial consciousness of fashion to catalogs and films. By the mid-1930s, couturiers and couturières themselves reported that provincials were now wealthier, more familiar with couture, and wanted to dress "*en Parisiennes.*"[72]

Other evidence implies a more uneven, age-based pattern of adopting modern styles in provincial towns and villages. As late as 1931, advice books instructed women from the provinces and the colonies on how to dress in the capital.[73] A recurring plot line in popular women's novels of the interwar period is a young provincial woman visiting or moving to Paris and realizing that her wardrobe is outdated. In the 1931 novel *Anne Fauvet,* the heroine notices even as she steps out of the railway car bringing her to the capital that "fashion in Paris is not the same as fashion in Andilly"(her natal village). Generally, exposure to haute couture and high society—or becoming a dressmaker—partially or fully transforms the heroine into a Parisienne, with the degree of transformation directly linked to the heroine's income. Anne Fauvet learns from her mistakes about sartorial nuances, by observing sophisticated Parisiennes at social events and by training as a dressmaker. Seeing the lighter, simpler styles in vogue in 1920s Paris, she decides that the provincial "morning costumes are complicated, the coats restrictive, the hats enormous. . . . A woman dressed in this way looks ten years older than women in Paris." She learns "a Parisian pleasure, *flanerie,*" wandering around and window-shopping, which, she recognizes, can only happen "in a big city, where you are not noticed." Once "initiated into Parisian women's tricks," she "rushes to the grand couturiers' sales and flatters and pesters the sales clerks to get advance information about sales."[74] Returning to their natal city or village, these heroines are often treated as Parisiennes, with young women showing intense interest in their attire and elderly women harshly condemning it.

Even this essentially conservative literature suggests that fashion made inroads in the provinces. Some women welcomed the returned heroine and took pleasure in her sophistication. In her study of professional and businesswomen, Colette Yvers reports that farmwomen who brought their produce to town and city markets had begun to dress in the latest styles. She adds that their neighbors did not know what to make of this.[75]

Perhaps the most persuasive evidence of democratization of haute couture styles can be found in less prestigious mail-order catalogs. Not far from the pages on work clothes in La Belle Jardinière catalogs are pages of "Entirely Ready-Made Dresses." These dresses consistently followed trends in haute couture day dresses, although they were made of lower quality fabrics and had fewer intricate details than the originals. The prices of these dresses ranged from 175 to 575 francs in 1926 and from 195 to 375 francs in 1931 (when the categories "partly ready-made" and "entirely ready-made" as applied to dresses were retired). Prices for their replacement, "Our Dresses for Ladies," remained at the lower range throughout the 1930s.[76] More evidence comes from Helen Harden Chenut's comparison of two sales catalogs, one from La Samaritaine department store and the other from a provincial workers cooperative in the 1930s. While Chenut found a wider array of women's clothing, in better quality fabrics, in the Samaritaine catalog, both catalogs presented a slender, modern dress silhouette, with little overt display of class differences or appeal to opulence in either.[77] Of course, in life, the cognoscenti recognized the quality of the fabric, the fit, and other marks of distinction between haute couture and confection.

## Home Sewing

Although most fashion and women's magazine had columns about home sewing (often disguised as instructions for "your little dressmaker"), fashion histories have paid little attention to these columns or to the widespread practice of home sewing, which contributed to the democratization of couture. Perhaps sewing is too much of an everyday activity to warrant attention? Or is home sewing too domestic an occupation to warrant a historian's attention?

We have noted that most French girls had to take sewing classes in primary school and many took "complementary courses" afterward. Primary school taught them about the properties of different fabrics, how to find the bias in a piece of cloth, how to lay and cut out patterns, and how to hem and hand stitch bindings on a garment. They also learned simple embroidery and crochet stitches. Practical exercises included making a sleeve, an item of lingerie, and a young girl's dress. Other lessons covered washing different fabrics and mending clothing. The official purpose was to "give the young girl a taste for feminine manual work" and "to teach her everything needed to prepare for her future role as a mother of a family and mistress of a house." Complementary courses upgraded needlework and cutting skills and culminated in students sewing a more complicated dress with darts or pleats.[78] Embroidery, knitting, and crochet yarn companies published booklets that school girls could keep for reference after their school years; Dollfuss-Mieg et Cie. (DMC), for example, brought out *The ABC of Sewing*, with drawings and details about various stitches and yarns.[79]

As adults, bourgeois women could access many sources of information on home sewing. Women's and fashion magazines advertised reasonably priced, plainly illustrated sewing booklets with practical information on choosing fabrics for different styles, adjusting patterns to fit individual bodies, and cutting patterns without wasting any material.[80] Housekeeping books had sections on sewing your own and your children's clothing, with entire chapters devoted to sewing difficult new features like pleats. Sections on fabrics described the draping qualities and durability of fifteen different kinds of silk and woolen material and listed the items of clothing for which each one might be suitable. Other sections dealt with washing, ironing, and mending clothing, paying due attention to the right water temperature and washing powders, iron temperature, and thread for each task.[81] Clearly, the custom of maintaining clothing had not died out.

These sections resemble articles in fashion and women's weeklies, with instructions on how to dye, remove stains, and mend clothes.[82] Many ads touted laundry soaps, stain removers, and dyes.[83] Studying these instructions and ads reveals the situation of women without easy-care fabrics or automatic washing and drying machines, as well as a respectable bourgeois world where clothing was expected to last. These instructions and ads offer a glimpse of the end of fashion cycles, advising when a garment was no longer amenable to alterations, mending, or other cleaning to keep up with trends or simply keep up appearances. The end of fashion cycles is a subject rarely discussed in fashion writing.[84]

Regular features on fabrics in fashion and women's weeklies were vague about whether their target audience was home sewers or women who went to neighborhood dressmakers. Maintaining that the latter was ideal, they nevertheless defended readers who made some of their own clothes, especially simple items like capes, leaving the impression that not all readers relied solely on dressmakers for their everyday clothing.[85] (Home sewing children's clothing was widely accepted.) *La Mode Pratique* even acknowledged that some readers sewed special occasion clothing. For instance, a "fiancée with initiative and imagination" could make her wedding dress.[86] The number of sewing courses, including correspondence courses, publicized in fashion and women's weeklies reinforce the impression that many of their readers sewed.[87] In addition to regular columns on "economical" styles to be home sewed, many magazines published diagrams of patterns arranged on a piece of fabric so that readers could multiply the measurements of the pattern pieces to create their own patterns.[88] When readers wrote asking how to make new styles inexpensively, columnists responded with addresses of reasonably priced dry goods shops and reliable name brands.[89]

Women's weeklies like *La Mode, La Mode du Jour,* and *C'est la Mode* enticed readers with bonus patterns, either free or at a reduced price.[90] *La Mode Illustrée* offered subscribers twelve patterns on large sheets of thin paper, with the pieces marked and laid out on the sheets, at 1.25 to 4 francs apiece. Soon the magazine supplemented this rigid system with a variety of patterns for everything from slips to suits costing from 2.40 to 12.50 francs apiece (in 1930).[91] *La Mode Pratique*

contended that "an amateur dressmaker, a cultivated woman," could make complicated dresses like the full- and long-skirted *robe de style*. Beside drawings of gorgeous *robes de style* by Lanvin and Poiret, the magazine appended the question: "Your budget does not permit you to order one of these marvelous outfits? If you cannot afford to order one, you could use similar designs by less-renowned couturiers." Their service measured customers and created "made-to-measure" patterns for 7 to 30 francs per pattern. In the mid-1930s, this service also arranged for expert seamstresses and tailors to make dresses and suits "in the latest fabrics" for 150 francs and up. The service sent orders for haute couture dresses and suits at 175 to 875 francs to "a workshop of one of the best houses on the Rue de la Paix" (presumably Toutmain).[92]

The fashion bimonthly *Chiffons* distributed complete packages—patterns, fabrics and notions—for outfits. *Chiffons* claimed to reproduce "the most interesting haute couture models." "Thanks to our relations with producers," their ads proclaimed, "we are always aware of what is new and elegant and can offer our subscribers very advantageous prices."[93]

Society magazines did not include patterns and only exceptionally promoted patterns in their monthly issues. They addressed sewing advice columns to "little dressmakers," though an adept home sewer might follow their instructions.[94] In the first issue of *L'Illustration des modes,* the lead article declared that the monthly would not cover fashion in the sense of "the dress to be worn this year, a pattern to cut out, and the latest crochet or knitting stitch."[95] However, after it became *Le Jardin des Modes,* it put out four seasonal albums of drawings and patterns for 100 francs annually. In 1933, the quarterly became a monthly album called *Soyons Pratiques: Patrons et ouvrages du Jardin des Modes,* at 40 francs annually. Patterns had to be purchased at further expense, ranging from 4 francs for precut paper patterns to 25 francs for precut muslin patterns.[96] In short, their subscribers and customers were hardly petit bourgeois.

Pattern catalogs provided information to home sewers and "little" dressmakers. The Paris office of Butterick Company—located in the heart of the couture district—published *La Miroir des Modes,* a translation of *The Mirror of Fashion,* which was distributed in English-speaking countries. *Le Miroir* consisted of drawings of clothes made from their patterns and a column called "For Amateur Dressmakers" by an American, Eleanor Chalmers. It sold by subscription, at 20 francs annually, or by individual issue, at 2 francs per issue, which meant that customers who could not afford subscriptions could buy single issues. Butterick printed extra copies of special wedding issues.[97] *Patron-journal* and *Pariser Illustiere Mode Zeitung,* published in Strasbourg, displayed photographs and drawings of haute couture models beside pattern information for styles similar to these models, long after the clampdown on copying.[98] Both of these publications were sold outside France.

During the depression, the publisher of *Le Petit Echo de la Mode* issued a 200-page quarterly called *Guide Pratique de la Mode de Paris,* which followed seasonal fashions. Information about patterns was on blue newsprint, articles on white newsprint. At 2.50 for a premeasured dress to 12 francs for a "made-to-measure" dress, these patterns cost less than patterns sold in fashion magazines. In one issue, the blue pages displayed twenty-eight day dresses, including sports dresses, country dresses, and city dresses. The descriptors in the captions— *elegant, chic,* and *charming*—read like descriptors in fashion magazines and flyers. Another magazine-like feature was regular reports on fabric collections, though the *Guide* spotlighted less exclusive and expensive fabrics than society magazines did. The *Guide* also sold wooden dressmaking mannequins for 95 to 110 francs.[99] Although these sales items suggest that many neighborhood dressmakers bought the *Guide,* articles on how to sew particular features hint that readers included bourgeois women who were not as skilled as professional seamstresses.

Patterns were available in major department and dry goods stores and through their mail-order catalogs. Ads for *Soyons Pratique* patterns directed interested buyers to seven Paris stores, two department stores each in Lyon and in Lille, and at least one store apiece in 116 other cities in France (not to mention London and Lvov, Poland).[100] Other department stores set up pattern departments in their stores and sections in their general catalogs. Au Printemps promised that "all the models presented here were created in our workshops and are our EXCLUSIVE PROPERTY." To help home sewers choose fabrics, some general catalogs inserted swatches. In summer catalogs, most of the fabrics were silks, though the number of cottons increased as beach and country vacations became more common.[101] In 1923, light silks for lingerie and blouses cost 10.90 per meter, more substantial crepe de chine for dresses 19f90 per meter, and artificial silk jersey 15f90 per meter. Better quality silks, like taffeta, sold for 20–25 francs, and the most expensive silk, called la Reveuse, for 39 francs per meter. Ten years later, in the depths of the depression, Au Printemps was selling crepe de chine at 12–19f90 a meter and "supple" taffeta for 14.90–18.90.[102] Fabric prices dropped, then stabilized in the depression. Astute consumers sought lower prices at dry goods sales.

Based on a sample of twenty-five patterns for simple afternoon dresses, the average length of one-meter-wide fabric recommended was (a generous) four meters per dress. Calculating the prices of dress-quality crepe de chine at 19.90 a meter and an average pattern at 4 francs for a simple day dress, the basic cost of a home-sewn silk dress was 83.90. Lining cost from 3.25–26.90 per meter in 1925. In 1938, a good rayon lining cost 8.90 per meter.[103] Since lining was mainly used under skirts, requiring about two meters of material, the average cost of lining material at 8.90 per meter was 17.80. Although most women could embroider using patterns from the *Journal des Ouvrages des Dames* or *Modes et Travaux Féminins,* they bought small pieces of lace for collars, cuffs, and other garnishes at 2–15 francs apiece. In the 1930s, they likely purchased leather belts at 15 francs or stiff cloth belts (to be covered with the dress fabric) for 6 francs.[104] A reasonable estimate for a good quality home-sewn silk dress would therefore be about 120 francs, 40 to 100 francs less than similar ready-made dresses in catalogs. Evidently there was an economic incentive to make one's own dresses.

Dresses followed trends in, but were not close copies of, haute couture models. Dresses made with patterns "inspired" by haute couture cost more, and dresses based on designer's pattern cost a good deal more, both for the patterns, which cost at least 12 francs, and for the recommended fabric, which was essential to imitate haute couture.

Perhaps the best evidence of the prevalence of home sewing is the ubiquitous advertising for home sewing machines. Sewing machine manufacturers placed recurring ads in all the fashion and women's magazines and near the women's page or fashion column in daily newspapers. In her study of the Paris garment workers, 1750–1915, Judith Coffin traced sewing machine manufacturers' development of family-size sewing machines and the aggressive advertising campaign to gender the machine feminine and appeal to working-class women by representing smaller sewing machines as furniture in a middle-class home.[105] By the interwar period, fashion magazines were suggesting that sewing machines were found in middle-class homes but were disguised as another piece of furniture.[106] Sewing machines remained a major purchase: 660 francs on sale at the department store, Dufayel, in 1923.[107] Singer ads made pitches about convenience and gratification: "Fairy work, without fatigue, with pleasure," or about economy: "A thrifty young woman's best friend is her sewing machine." Singer, with its head office on the Avenue de l'Opéra in the couture district, had 400 branches throughout France.[108]

Popular women's novels document the phenomenon of bourgeois women

sewing some of their clothing. While most female characters in popular women's novels preferred to have a dressmaker make special-occasion dresses, they made their own everyday dresses and, in a pinch, dinner and evening gowns. These characters also knew how to mend worn or torn apparel.[109]

As knit tops and sportswear became more popular in the mid-1920s, fashion and women's magazines added knitting patterns. Although most of the patterns were for children's clothing, patterns for women's pullovers were the second-largest category.[110] The same magazines ran small ads for yarn and gave courses on knitting and crocheting. The rise of La Redoute is testimony to the popularity of knitting. A manufacturer of wool yarn employing 500 workers in Roubaix, La Redoute began retailing yarns in 1922. It advertised widely in women's magazines and gave yarns evocative, often floral names—"*Gladiola*," "*Azalea*"—to appeal to the largely urban, leisured group of women who read these magazines. In addition, La Redoute subsidized a magazine, *Pénélope, Travaux de Laine et Modes*. In 1928, the company welcomed its 600,000th client. That year it put out its first free catalog, offering forty-three different articles, as well as a series of luxurious albums displaying completed versions of sweaters, dresses, scarves, caps, and other items of clothing made with their wools and patterns. Soon Aux Trois Suisses followed suit. When the depression slowed development, La Redoute's marketing slogan changed to "Value, Quality, Economy."[111] This sales pitch no doubt appealed to the practical and realistic side of Frenchwomen during the depression.

Much evidence points to a democratization of haute couture styles, if not haute couture models. Department stores were avatars of modern merchandising, including couture house marketing. Long after the introduction of price tags, counter and window displays, and in-store services in the nineteenth century, department stores continued to improve product displays by minimalist and artistic arrangements and spotlighting and to add conveniences and attractions, such as escalators and films, to entice shoppers. Moreover, department stores advertised continually in newspapers, magazines, and mail-order catalogs. Some catalogs looked like fashion magazines and were distributed throughout France, reaching a wide range of bourgeois and petit bourgeois, as well as some working-class, households. Many of the clothes advertised in these catalogs were "influenced" or "inspired" by haute couture.

Department stores and mail-order catalogs sold sewing machines, dress material, notions, and patterns, and fashion magazines advertised sewing machines, offered sewing courses, marketed patterns, and ran features on how to sew, alter, and maintain clothing. Pattern books proliferated. All these outlets advertised clothes or patterns "influenced" or "inspired " by haute couture models. A good-quality department store dress that resembled a haute couture model could be purchased for a third the price of the couture dress; a qualified home sewer could approximate a haute couture style for hundreds of francs less than the original and up to a hundred francs less than a comparable department store dress. Clearly department stores, mail-order catalogs, and home sewing contributed to the democratization of haute couture style.

# PART IV

# Modern Women

# Chapter Eight

# The Politics of Modern Fashion

Students of modernity often associate it with notions of individualism and equality that in France were wed to the concept of fraternity, a wedding that meant that modernity and citizenship were conceived as masculine and women were excluded from both. In the 1920s, fashion arbiters linked modernity to greater autonomy, more than individualism, and a limited equality, but they offered a counter discourse about modernity in the feminine, wherein modernity implied active women with more opportunities and independence than their predecessors. The modern woman became "a resonant symbol of emancipation,"[1] as long as emancipation was understood in terms of economic and physical activities, not political rights. The politics of modern fashion were primarily economic, physical, and cultural.

A new body of scholarly literature connects the straighter silhouette, higher hemlines, and shorter hairdos of post–World War I fashion with the emergence of the "flapper" in the Anglo-American world and the "modern girl," or "moga," in Japan.[2] Scholars found that voluble members of the cultural elites, most of them men, denigrated the modern girl in erudite periodicals and books. American, British, and Japanese critics engaged in a discourse about gender instability associated with rapid social and cultural changes, not least of which was a "surplus" of unmarried women and new occupational opportunities for single women following the war.[3] This scholarship demonstrates that best-selling novels, Hollywood films, and the mass circulation press publicized the modern woman, which is to say, the socially and physically, not politically liberated woman. Scholars treat the flapper or moga as "highly commodified cultural construct(s)" associated with Western urban culture after the First World War. They suggest that the modern girl, like the new woman before her, was a commercial "appropriation of the cultural space of feminism . . . minus most of the politics."[4]

In France as elsewhere, the modern woman is invariably represented in clothing that enabled easier movement and facilitated economic endeavor. Accordingly, the fashion press can be a source for the study of modern womanhood. Always discounting the inflated language of the fashion press, one can decode its discourse about modern styles and women. In addition to interrogating key words in the fashion media, in this chapter I assess advertisers' contributions to the image of the modern Frenchwoman. These magazines and marketers promoted a "highly commodified cultural construct," a kind of "commercialized femininity," and claimed to be "cultural intermediaries" for a new femininity.[5] Mme. Saisset, a Paris school inspector and a critic of modern women, blamed fashion magazines for spreading the ideal of modern womanhood.[6] In fact, fashion magazines reacted to criticisms of modern fashion and cross-dressing as masculine by claiming some items of masculine clothing for a new feminine, but soon respectably bourgeois, look. The result was a hybrid modernity that shaped the way devoted readers understood and adopted modern femininity and fashion.

Fashion arbiters' mix of the modern and the feminine had some specifically French features. The fashion press was engaged in a campaign to restore and sustain haute couture and textiles internationally. Their patriotic appeals to restore the fashion business as detailed in previous chapters differed in three ways from Nazi and fascist efforts to distinguish their German and Italian national styles from hegemonic French (a.k.a., international) style by reviving regional costumes and introducing elements of paramilitary uniforms.[7] First, haute couture was not trying to develop a national style but rather to revive Parisian style as international style. Second, French fashion discourse defended new styles as modern and protofeminist and eschewed nostalgia for earlier feminine styles and roles. Third, although haute couture flirted with elements of military uniforms, it did not promote paramilitary uniforms.

To be sure, in all three countries, women resisted postwar campaigns for a return to regional costumes. In France, as Poiret learned to his misfortune in the early 1920s, style setters did not buy Breton folkloric styles. They preferred Russian peasant style, which was coded "exotic," and the vivid colors of the Ballets Russes, which fashion arbiters called "naïve, primitive, and barbaric."[8] Confidence

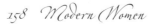

about the ability of haute couture to appropriate foreign design elements led to such condescending comments about other ethnic costumes, even if, as in this case, the comments were intended as compliments or at least inducements to buy. As Mariana Torgovnick has shown in *Gone Primitive*, the primitive is a Western concept closely aligned with modernity and could have positive outcomes for Western societies.[9] In this case, the positive outcomes were more and brighter colors in Western women's wardrobes. Other than the Russian émigrés who served haute couture, it is unclear who, among the sources of inspiration, benefited.

## Parisienne Chic

Most couturiers and couturières depended upon the international market for prosperity. Society magazines like *Vogue* followed the international set, and trade magazines published feature articles in English and Spanish for international readers. Fashion and women's magazines sold subscriptions in Francophone countries, Spain, Italy, and England. In the tenuous years of the antebellum recovery, internationally oriented society magazines made some arrogant remarks about the superiority of Parisian fashion and the "provincialism" of the rest of the Western world. Domestically oriented fashion magazines made fewer derogatory comments about other nation's clothing, mainly because magazines targeting Frenchwomen were indifferent to clothing from other countries, with the exception of British menswear, and later American sports clothes and Nordic ski togs, which French consumers admired. As haute couture adapted to the depression and prepared for the colonial exhibition of 1937, which everyone hoped would stimulate international demand, fashion arbiters resumed making statements about the supremacy of French—meaning Parisian—couture. Even then, they made relatively few dismissive remarks about other countries' clothing.[10]

At first reading, fashion magazines seem to address Parisiennes alone. They covered Paris more thoroughly than any other place and devoted more ink to Paris than to all other locations in the world. In society magazines, regular columns reviewed Parisian theater and occasional pieces described Parisian galas. Aside from a few specials on major provincial cities, the society press ignored provincial cities. In addition to setting Paris up as a privileged site for fashion consumption, magazines presented Parisiennes as style setters to be emulated. Magazines serving regional markets assigned far more column inches to style setters in the capital than to their counterparts in provincial cities. Regional supplements acted as if their readers were intensely interested in the Parisian scene in order to replicate it. When *les élégantes* came into conflict with designers' campaign to revive longer, fuller skirts in the mid-1920s, provincial columnists supported the style setters.[11] One reason for their focus on the capital was that most journalists who followed haute couture resided there. If they had originally come from the provinces, they moved to Paris and became Parisian correspondents to provincial papers. Another reason was that regional weeklies that promoted local couture did not last very long.[12]

The fashion media asserted that Parisiennes, the first private customers to see the seasonal collections, eliminated "the oddities that could lead us to errors of taste if we contented ourselves with adopting them without discernment." A correspondent for *La Soierie de Lyon* elaborated, "Once a style gains her acceptance, it starts off on its conquest of the world. Ask the Parisienne why we no longer have the long trailing skirts and unspeakably pointed shoes so dear to American women. It is because she knows that the short skirt and slightly rounded shoe are wonderfully becoming to her slender silhouette, small feet, and eternal youth."[13] This dig at American clothing reflected concern about the competition of American clothing manufacturers.

A closer reading of fashion journalists reveals that they knew Parisiennes did not dictate to the world. They reported that designers prepared two separate collections every season—one for foreigners, one for Frenchwomen. They cited an unidentified couturier who contrasted the flamboyant models presented to foreign buyers, especially the North and South Americans buyers who "saved" haute couture in the 1920s, to the subdued models reserved for Frenchwomen.[14] Fashion columnists for provincial dailies emphasized that Parisiennes rejected bizarre styles and selected styles worthy of provincial attention: "Quite apart from some eccentricities worn by the mannequins . . . we admired the grace, the distinction of our most famous worldly women."[15] Of course, fashion magazines themselves promised to weed out unrealistic and ridiculous designs. *Femina* ran series with titles like "Very Femina," spotlighting the models in every collection "dedicated to you . . . dresses new and discreet at the same time, in which taste compensates for audacity, dresses in equilibrium in a word." Another magazine pledged: "After conducting you into the mysterious world of haute couture, *Marie Claire* presents a practical set of little dresses, costumes, coats, evening wear."[16]

When the media referred to the Parisienne, they ran the risk of evoking a dubious type of women developed in a body of literature and sketch albums since

the 1880s. Although biographies, novels, and plays occasionally referred to the Parisienne as "small footed, slender waisted, and beautiful enough to tempt a saint,"[17] they were more likely to describe her physical attributes as plain than pretty. Instead, the Parisienne excelled at assembling stylish clothing and had a flair for interior decorating. Although these books resembled women's advice literature of the Belle Epoque, biographies of courtesans and actresses, who were still assumed to be promiscuous, did not function as taste arbiters for bourgeois women. Many of the albums of Parisiennes were intended for male viewers and included sketches of men peeking into women's dressing rooms.[18] Advice books about being Parisienne ostensibly written for young women, literally addressed "gentlemen" and were equally voyeuristic.[19] These nonfiction works overlap with fiction about the femme fatale, the woman who was irresistibly and usually tragically attractive to men. The Parisiennes fatales did not have to be Parisian, or even French, by birth. Many were foreigners appreciated for their "exotic beauty"—which, before the advent of Clairol, included Scandinavian blonds—but all femmes fatales wore the seductive staples of Parisian lingerie: black silk or lace stockings.[20] Even fiction promoted Parisian products.

A more respectable kind of nonfiction addressed to women accepted the basic premise of Parisian women being plain but able, through artifice, to personify beauty. Octave Uzanne's *The Woman in Paris*, printed and reprinted from 1904 through 1910, contended, "Woman is a hundred times more feminine in Paris than in any other city in the universe." Why? Because Parisiennes had more "bewitching seductiveness, sickly, unhealthy delicacy, attractive coquetry." According to Uzanne, fashion and style are "her offensive armor, her artists' brush."[21] Although influenced by the Goncourt brothers, who had revived the eighteenth-century style moderne, a way of representing aristocratic women as works of art,[22] Uzanne wrote for bourgeois women. He assured readers that a "clever woman" could have an acceptable wardrobe on 1,500 francs a year—five times the average woman's annual wage—if they bought department store clothing. Here he tapped into publicity in favor of feminine finery mounted by department stores.[23]

Although male contributors occasionally evoked the literary image of the femme fatale,[24] society magazines did not want to be associated with this tarnished image of the Parisienne. When many bourgeois families were in straightened circumstances due to loss of income from deflated government bonds in the early 1920s, *Vogue* alluded to Uzanne's "clever woman" in a column entitled "To Be Elegant with Economy." The columnist insisted that "real elegance is not a matter of fortune; one can supplant that with ingenuity and reflection."[25] Generally, society magazines distanced themselves from the struggling bourgeoisie.

An early article in *Vogue* defined "society" as composed of the nobility, who had distinction, and the *nouveaux riches* who followed fashion. According to the article, the latter might have the latest style, but not chic, which implied knowing how to assemble outfits and accessorize them to create "an atmosphere." While some fashion weeklies contended that Frenchwomen understood chic better than other women, *Vogue* insisted that in Paris even an "ugly French Canadian woman" could identify "what was seductive in her appearance and emphasize it." *Femina* took the more positive approach of identifying "a North American Parisienne . . . a Slavic Parisienne . . . and a Parisienne from Paris." Even if all three were dressed by the same couturier, each one had particular characteristics.[26] With the assistance of the fashion press, all would find the apparel and accoutrements of seduction in Paris.

Like other *Vogue* articles treating distinction in the early 1920s, this one wavers between affirming and denying that distinction could be cultivated.[27] This sort of article reads like an unstable blend of Pierre Bourdieu and Yvette Delsaut's differentiation between the "sober elegance" of the established upper bourgeoisie and the audacious style of the nouveau riche bourgeoisie. Such articles recall Bourdieu's theories about distinction as a culturally acquired sense of how to distinguish good taste from bad, the chic from the tacky.[28] Later issues of *Vogue* stressed the more promising and profitable line of argument about acquiring distinction, or "chic." *Vogue*'s definition of *chic*—knowing how to put together clothing and accessories to create an aura—was one of the more cogent definitions in a medium that rarely used the term reflectively. *Eve* offered more details: for a woman, chic was "the science of knowing herself well and knowing how to choose what flatters her, hides her faults, and enhances her natural gifts."[29] Chic, like distinction, was somehow innate and acquired. One reason for confusion about the source of chic was the rapid changes in fashion in the early 1920s. In that period of instability, journalists had to reassure readers that they were women of good taste, while enhancing journalists' roles as guides to good taste in a changing market.

If chic was a mysterious trait emanating from women wearing fashionable clothes, it was closely correlated with an overall look.[30] Although fashion magazines did not define elegance precisely, they described the components of an ensemble in detail. In the 1920s and 1930s, descriptions of an elegant look drew upon classical definitions of beauty as harmonious.[31] Well-dressed ladies were expected

to wear hats, scarves, and jewelry, shoes, purses, and gloves, that would complement their garments, be suitable for the occasion, and flatter the wearer.

Let us take hats as an example. Fashion magazines devoted an annual issue,
seasonal issues, or supplements to hats. At the Exhibition of the Decorative Arts,
M. Manonviller, president of the Millinery section, intoned: "Can one possibly
consider a hat a simple accessory? Style is the man himself but the hat is the woman.
A hat, a little hat sums up all the subtle and delicate grace of Paris and the Parisienne. The hat specifies and completes the figure of a woman."[32]

Hats had to coordinate with dress styles. When dresses were simple, small hats
with shallow crowns, little if any brim, pulled low on the head, were de rigueur—
except for summertime or outdoor activities, when wide-brimmed hats were acceptable.[33] In 1926, one milliner, Mauricelle Robert, made many cloches that varied only in their materials (felt, velour, etc.) and arrangement of decorative
elements. In line with marketing trends, Robert called her catalog an album, her
designs "creations," and individual hats portentous names like "My Success."[34]
In the 1930s, milliners produced hats with wider, often asymmetrical brims, with
many decorative touches, to draw the viewer's eye up to the head and to balance
the longer, fuller skirts popular then. Whereas fashion arbiters were restrained in
their use of the term *revolution* about the return of definite waistlines and longer,
fuller skirts in the early 1930s, they used the term more freely in descriptions of
the return of larger hats.[35] Over the next few years, the shape and tilt of the brims
and decorative touches varied from season to season and year to year. "Nearly masculine" shapes like straw boaters (think of Maurice Chevalier's signature straw
hat) and jaunty peaked caps accompanied suits.[36] Schiaparelli's surrealist hats—
like the telephone-shaped one—were the exception.

In turn, hat styles had implications for hairstyles and the wearer's physiognomy.
Cloches looked best with the short haircut known as the bob and with a permanent wave. Eve Lavallière and other prewar stage actresses had popularized the
bob after it appeared on Poiret models in his 1908 collection. In the antebellum
years, the chemise gave the bob and the permanent wave new leases on life.[37] Conversely, wide-brimmed hats looked better with longer hairstyles. Finally, women
with prominent noses were advised to wear hats with large, floppy, richly decorated front brims, so that the shadow of the brim would obscure, and the ornamentation distract from, the size of the nose.[38] How one simultaneously fulfilled
various mandates—prescribed in different articles—was never explained to this
reader's satisfaction.

Society monthlies ran columns on other accessories and accoutrements (necessary items like shoes). As the list of accessories and accoutrements—often lumped together as accessories—lengthened to include watches and cigarette cases, *Vogue* advised reducing them to a minimum. Still, *Vogue* thought that the woman with "few dresses, but numerous hats, purses, and shoes" exhibited "an interesting type of elegance."[39] Fashion and women's magazines endorsed accessories, because changing them transformed a simple dress into several different-looking outfits.[40] As Alice de Linières remarked, "Shoes, stockings, and gloves give notice of good taste." Writing for bourgeois women of modest means, she recommended accessories that went with "all sorts of outfits."[41]

"Details," such as mixing fabrics or contrasting-colored collars and cuffs on a dress, signified chic. During the long reign of the straight silhouette, *Vogue* admired using three materials in one dress, "that indefinable nothing by which we confidently identify a new dress." When the gently curved silhouette held sway in the 1930s, designers altered bodices, collars, and sleeves to differentiate current from last year's styles. Upper body details diverted attention from the lower torso, which helped solve the problem of the pear-shaped silhouette projected by fuller skirts. Martine Rénier saw these alterations as "the kind of novelty . . . an elegant woman consents to wear."[42]

Mixing fabrics and adding details solved maintenance problems and facilitated keeping up with fashion economically. Women's weeklies advised using different materials to refresh clothing with worn or stained areas. Ads suggested embroidering and knitting adornments themselves. Annie Blatt marketed pattern and yarn packets for "cache-misères"—ties, collars, and vests—"to rejuvenate a too familiar gown or modify its look." Rejuvenate meant covering worn patches or spots on fabrics that were not easily mended or cleaned. Ads assured potential customers that these items were "relatively easy to execute . . . and can be completed in a weekend." In the 1920s, the weeklies approved of sashes and flounces on skirts, and in the 1930s, collars on bodices and cuffs on sleeves, because home sewers or "little dressmakers" could attach them to existing dresses. But, the staffers insisted that additions had to be sleek and modern, not fussy or old-fashioned. For instance, cuffs and collars must be crisp linen, not the flimsy organdy "our grandmothers used." Sewing columns demonstrated how to remove old and attach new collars, cuffs, and sleeves. Although the columnists claimed that any reader could do this without wrecking the neckline or armholes, they assumed considerable sewing skill.[43]

All society, fashion, and women's magazines earned income from ads for accessories, and fashion and women's magazines also profited from ads for sewing supplies. Except for major milliners, who purchased full- and half-page ads and cross-marketed with couturiers and couturières, accessory makers placed smaller and less lucrative ads than couture and textile manufacturers did. Because many companies made each type of accessory and because some companies advertised constantly, their advertising contributed to the financial survival of magazines. *L'Officiel de la Couture,* which ran shopping columns specializing in accessories and trimmings, published a list of firms cooperating in the preparation of each issue.[44] The silk trade publication was less committed to transparency. As cashmere and paisley shawls became "passé" in the 1920s, the *Soierie de Lyon* reported that Lyonnais shawl makers had replaced cashmere with silk crepe and substituted Egyptian motifs for paisley prints. Although ads for these new shawls appeared in the same issue, the editors did not acknowledge any relationship between the ads and articles.[45]

Evidently fashion arbiters participated in economic campaigns to promote haute couture—and the Parisian look that included accessories made in and around Paris—as simultaneously French and international style. If all arbiters lobbied for international style, they were more divided about the controversial domestic subject of women's suffrage. This did not prevent many of them from discussing feminism.

## Hybrid Feminism

In theses and book on feminisms in France from 1914 to 1940, Christine Bard calls the decades before the Great War the "golden age" of suffrage feminism and the interwar decades a period of "hegemonic reformism." Although she records the activities of suffrage groups in the interwar years, she focuses on reformist feminist activities, specifically, pacifism and maternal feminist social reforms. She recognizes that militant reformists always insisted that their fight was "feminine" and traces this to a defensive reaction to antifeminist attacks on emancipated women as androgynous and frigid.[46] In these works, she cites no fashion magazines. In *La Garçonne,* Bard treats the cultural phenomenon of the garçonne, the boyish-looking woman who symbolized the "modern woman" in the mid-1920s, as an ambiguous figure of "words and images," part of a political discourse about liberation and depravity. Here she cites a few expensive fashion magazines that contributed to the popularization of the *garçonne.*[47]

But not all fashion magazines were elitist, and several of them articulated a kind of hybrid feminism. The fashion press provided space for a new mixture of cultural and consumer feminism, a hybrid feminism. In recent years, the combination of feminism and consumerism has been criticized as "lifestyle" feminism, but this early manifestation was emancipating insofar as it challenged women's economic and physical disabilities. Here I consider hybrid feminism's challenge to economic disabilities.

Mary Louise Roberts, who studied the fabled Marguerite Durand, editor of *La Fronde,* notes that Durand refused to call the newspaper feminist. Roberts considers Durand as part of a group of new women of the fin de siècle who were not dedicated to suffrage or maternal feminist reforms and who, in their refusal of motherhood or at least full-time motherhood, were "new women." As represented on stage, new women threatened to, and sometimes did, leave the confines of the marital home. As represented in press commentary, they were bluestockings or man-haters and in either case, unattractive. But as "performed" by Marguerite Durand, among others, the new woman tried out new behaviors, including greater independence, without abandoning fashionable clothes and other accoutrements of "femininity." Roberts calls this strategy of "disruptive acts a dialect of a new language of feminine resistance that comprised, but was not limited to, political, legal, and social feminism." Another, less spectacular dialect in this "language of resistance" might be the "everyday rebellions" of far more numerous modern women in the interwar years.[48] One guide to this subtle dialect is the fashion press.

In a speech, Marguerite Durand argued that the advent of women in journalism was "one of the conquests of which feminism is justly proud. It has pushed and will always push women toward this career because it is one of those careers that oblige women to leave their homes, to see, write, observe, comprehend and judge beyond the restrained circle of their family, relatives, class and customs." Because she knew that few women were assigned political or economic "beats," Durand would probably have included journalists in fashion and women's magazines.[49] She defined an economic and cultural feminism, while most contemporaries had a more narrowly political conception of feminism. If career fashion journalists fit Durand's definition, few of them identified themselves as suffrage or radical feminists. Rather than assuming that career *journalistes* were feminists, I show that some fashion journalists expressed sympathy with a vestimentary variant of cultural feminism. Nevertheless, some long-term fashion columnists who were initially sympathetic ceased to support suffrage feminism in the mid-1920s.

Their disengagement reflected disappointment after the Senate had defeated the female enfranchisement bill in 1922—part of postwar disillusionment.

Of the long-term editors and columnists, only the founder and director of *La Mode Pratique,* the Countess de Broutelles, openly participated in prewar campaigns for the vote.[50] In the immediate postwar period, *La Mode Pratique* ran articles on feminist legal and political issues, notably, the nationality of married women.[51] After the defeat of the female enfranchisement bill, the weekly invited Germaine Malaterre-Sellier (1889–?), a feminist pacifist and internationalist who had published a brochure on the franchise, to write a series of articles on the same subject.[52] In her articles as in her book, Malaterre-Sellier advocated the vote for nationalist, maternal feminist, and public health reasons, such as that women voters would boost the fight against depopulation, infant mortality, tuberculosis, and alcoholism.[53] After this, articles on suffrage ceased to appear in *La Mode Pratique.*

Prior to the war, *Femina* had covered campaigns for suffrage. Even after it was sold to Hachette Publishers, it remained sympathetic. Between 1917 and 1920, it published several articles about suffrage by Hélène Miropolsky, a supporter of suffrage feminism and the fifth woman to get a law degree in France.[54] Like many feminist activists, Miropolsky was not committed to either individualistic or maternal feminism but argued for the vote to attain equal rights and to enact maternal feminist reforms.[55] In a gesture toward unbiased coverage, *Femina* asked an infamous antifeminist to discuss the female franchise in 1918. Marthe Borely, author of a controversial recent book, *French Feminine Genius,* opposed feminism "as the bankruptcy of woman and the Frenchwoman is woman par excellence." She argued that feminism was "a foreign product that would pervert French feminine genius."[56] Closely aligned to the nationalist Charles Maurras, Borely rejected prewar feminist efforts to configure feminism as French by tracing its roots back to the French Revolution. In the article, she repeated prewar ethnic, religious, and biological criticisms of feminism as Anglo-Saxon, Protestant, and a drain on national energy, and she added medical and natalist metaphors about a feminist "germ" attacking "national life at vital points, the family and natality." She held that the war had finished off feminism in France but had revitalized antifeminism.[57] In the postwar context of angst about a low birth rate and of advocacy for the draconian bill against female-controlled birth control and abortion that passed in 1920, these arguments had some purchase.[58]

In the same issue of *Femina* as Borely's article, Miropolsky reviewed Borely's book. She refuted Borely's claim that feminism was finished on economic grounds, referencing the large number of young women seeking an occupation and independence through work. Focusing on economic opportunities and independence would be a recurring feminist theme in the fashion press between the wars. In subsequent columns, Miropolsky feted feminist political successes in England, citing the election of women to Parliament, and feminist legal successes in France, with juridical decisions giving women a role in the administration of the law on war orphans.[59] After publication of the Senate report decisively rejecting female suffrage in December 1919, rightly characterized as "a landmark of French anti-suffragism,"[60] Miropolsky wrote a final series of articles for *Femina* on what women needed to know about political and social life to avert apathy. The concluding article, "While Awaiting the Vote," recommended involvement in feminist social and legal reforms.[61] After this, *Femina* did not run features on suffrage feminism.[62] For a dozen years, Miropolsky continued to work for feminist legal reforms, in particular, the right to determine the paternity of illegitimate children.[63]

Like the Church itself, the Catholic weekly *Le Petit Echo de la Mode* supported female suffrage after the Vatican reversed its opposition to women's franchise in 1919. However, the weekly focused on getting the vote to pass maternal feminist reforms, whereas the Vatican was more interested in defeating republicans with the support of devout women voters. On the basis of church attendance, the Church calculated that Frenchwomen were more politically reliable than Frenchmen, too many of whom were secular and anticlerical.[64] On two occasions in the interwar period, the *Petit Echo* covered suffrage. In the lead-up to the Senate vote on women's vote, two "Pages féministes" columns supported women's suffrage in order to bring women's moral influence to bear on political life. The columnist Franceline tried to reassure opponents by insisting that women would complement, not supplant, men in the political arena.[65] In the spring of 1929, the meeting of an "Estates General of Feminism" revived public interest in women's suffrage, but the republican organizers, who emphasized individual rights, alienated the Vatican.[66] Only after the meeting of the Estates General did the morality column, "Jardin des âmes," make a case for women's political rights as "an equitable and inevitable consequence of the social duties imposed on them . . . in times of peace and war." The columnist Liselotte defended women from critics who claimed that their domestic lives disqualified them from politics:

> Modern life has created a radical revolution in the lives of women, it has demanded that they be educated and emancipated socially. Universal education for both sexes has

 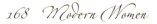

permitted women to have a greater understanding of their domestic role. But when women have been constrained to work, they have also demonstrated their professional abilities. The female doctor can heal, but she has no right to vote. A man charged with a crime and judged to be innocent has the right to vote, but his female lawyer does not.

Liselotte specified that the vote would give women "the power to save the family, which is constantly menaced" by alcoholism and a declining marital birth rate. In addition, women "will broach larger issues: day care, health care, schools. . . . The whole nation will benefit as women will choose candidates that will work toward the general good."[67]

Another woman's weekly raised the issue of women's suffrage but savaged suffrage feminists. In 1927 and 1928, *La Mode Illustrée* employed Camille Duguet, the only French fashion columnist who publicly self-identified as a feminist. Although she celebrated the accomplishments of English suffragettes, she had little regard for French suffragists, whom she described—in language redolent of antifeminist diatribes—as "a minority of women, single for the most part, having long ago renounced the charming weapon called coquetry."[68] General-interest magazines also alluded to the stereotype of the unattractive suffragette; reporters who interviewed political feminists praised their beauty and refinement, as if they had to assure readers that suffrage feminists were not plain and dowdy.[69]

Everything in Duguet's description but the term *minority* was grossly inaccurate, for most suffrage feminists were married and "kept up appearances."[70] Consider the avowedly feminist weekly *Minerva,* which filled its centerfold pages with drawings and photos of couture models under the heading "Feminism does not excuse women from their duty to be elegant." Or Mme. Cécile Brunshwig, President of the French Union for Women's Suffrage, who began her contribution to a book entitled "Emancipated Women" with the exhortation: "In emancipating herself, woman must lose nothing of her femininity." Like other feminists— and fashion journalists—Mme. Brunshwig associated femininity with fashion, cosmetics, and coquetry.[71] Feminists were defensive not only because critics associated feminism with masculinity and frigidity, as Bard contends, but also because in the public eye feminists were unfashionable, even ugly, as Roberts contends. Suffrage feminists interviewed by the fashion press distinguished "the stylish suffragist of 1931 from her predecessor of 1881, who disparaged beauty, fashion, and new fabrics."[72]

Only one fashion weekly had a public relationship to feminism—the same firm that published *Minerva* published *Eve,* the illustrated weekly supplement to regional newspapers.[73] Yet *Eve* did not openly advocate suffrage or feminism. The only time it spotlighted feminism was in a caption "Feminist Models" under sketches of female figures in tailored suits with slim, pleated skirts and jaunty caps, suggesting not a masculine but an androgynous look.[74] In 1921, a male contributor argued that the cost of living, women's work, and feminist ideas had made women's clothing more practical and masculine. "To work," René Degy explained, "you need an ample garment that does not impede movement."[75] The link between practical apparel and women's work was often repeated in *Eve;* the reference to feminist ideas was exceptional. Coded allusions to sartorial feminism through keywords—*practical* to describe modern styles and *independent* to describe modern women—appeared for a decade after this article appeared.[76] Even in the 1930s, *Eve* interpreted the new "feminine" styles as implicitly feminist by noting that they enabled independence and autonomy.[77]

Magazine attitudes toward economic feminism varied over time. Most society magazine only celebrated readers having paid employment in the early 1920s. One of the prewar columnists who remained at *Femina,* Claire Lausnay, wrote that many women "were launching themselves in business—a consequence of feminism and the high cost of living." Together with sports activities, participation in the work world favored the straighter, simpler, and more comfortable silhouette.[78] Thereafter direct links between paid work and feminism virtually disappeared from society magazines. In 1925, when *Vogue* published an article on a wardrobe for "women who collaborate with businessmen," there was no mention of feminism. Assuming that these women would work primarily with other office women, the staff writer recommended a "chic and sober" look in harmony with the clothes worn by the rest of the staff. The assumption about their work mates was correct, insofar as there was a massive movement of women into clerk-typist occupations in the 1920s.[79] The article recommended individual outfits "eclectic enough to meet the various obligations of the day and practical enough to adapt to changes in temperature."[80] The writer presumed that women needed to change their wardrobes to fit into the workplace, because *Vogue* readers had not previously done salaried work. The article was silent about why these women might enter the workforce and about such possible results as greater autonomy. Whatever the assumed motives and consequences, *Vogue* no longer raised the topic of independence.

Women's weeklies used the term *feminist* less frequently than society monthlies, though they were open to the concept of feminine liberation. After the lead article in a 1920 issue of *La Mode Illustrée* had expressed discomfort about discussing feminism, the editor insisted that "the strong woman of the twentieth century will not be exclusively a savant or a housewife." The modern woman "will no longer voluntarily accept the idea of consecrating all her life to a man."[81] Even if the author eschewed the label *feminist,* the notion of a women having more than a wifely and motherly role was subversive of bourgeois women's prescribed roles. A decade later Brigitte, a fashion writer for *La Mode,* asked what change "the liberated spirit of romanticism" (1830–1930) had brought women. She answered that Frenchwomen did not have full political rights only because "Frenchwomen have not unanimously consecrated their efforts to this." However, Frenchwomen had new rights to live independently, work, and live a better and more varied life, rights Brigitte correlated to fashion trends. "Women who wear long skirts cannot have the same mentality as those in short skirts. Constrained by long dresses, our movements inevitably had repercussions on our thoughts and sentiments."[82]

Women's weeklies acknowledged that their readers might have to work for wages. For several years after the First World War, *Le Petit Echo de la Mode* worried about the number of young widows who would have to work and the number of young women who would not have the opportunity to wed, given the loss of so many Frenchmen in the war. In addition to advising widowed mothers to take in boarders so that they could stay at home to care for their children, reporters urged all mothers to consider occupational training and careers for their daughters, since "it is no longer a shame to have to work."[83] In fact, 77 percent of the women born between 1917 and 1924 had an occupation as a young woman, and this included 69 percent of bourgeois daughters, presumably from the middle and lower echelons of the bourgeoisie.[84] *Le Petit Echo* directed readers to class- and gender-appropriate occupations like social service assistance or nursing and recommended Catholic social service and nursing schools. Given the expansion of social work and nursing between the wars and the influx of women into caring work, their advice was sensible, if sexist.[85]

The Baron de Clessy admonished them not to "overdress," because "ostentatious" clothes would arouse envy in their co-workers.[86] Generally, *Le Petit Echo* tried to sustain the distinction between their readers and regular workers. The Catholic weekly assumed that married women would work if they had to, not because they wanted to. By straddling the line between woman as worker and woman as wife and mother, the *Petit Echo* eased some of the tension in their relations with social Catholic groups that advocated a "return to the home" as a response to the economic downturn and to demographic fears.[87]

Other women's magazines changed their opinion about women working. In a 1931 article on working women's wardrobes, *La Mode Pratique* felt it had to justify women's employment. "In a time of a high cost of living, financial crises, material instability, and marriages difficult to conclude, young girls prepare for careers, and mothers themselves might work, in pink-collar jobs." The author recommended a small, practical wardrobe composed of a tweed coat, raincoat, navy or brown jersey or tweed dress trimmed with easy-care collar and cuffs, hat color-coordinated with the tweed coat, purse and shoes of calf leather, and warm, washable gloves.[88] By the mid-1930s, this weekly ran an unapologetic series, "Feminine Occupations," by Yvonne Ostroga, drawn from her book on occupations for "girls of today" entitled *Les Indépendantes*. Although the series treated many professions, it did not deal with masculine professions, like architecture or engineering, which were covered in the book. Nor did it extol independence, as the book did.[89] By the late 1930s, an article on work clothing plunged right into guiding principles for a work wardrobe. Now the office was "nearly a little home," where office workers should keep a supply of makeup and an extra pair of stockings so that they could "repair" any damage to their appearance during the day, and an umbrella, so that they could go directly to evening engagements.[90] Clearly, middle-class women working outside the home was being normalized.

Other women's weeklies were more conservative about women's paid labor. After reports on the economic crash, the *C'est la mode* fashion columnist argued that high (meaning high male) unemployment mandated that women stay home, where they could contribute to the family budget by sewing their own clothes. Another columnist explained that "real women" returned to a more conservative and less American (meaning slower-paced) way of life and "set themselves the task of getting by in hard times." These articles were part of an initial press reaction against married women engaging in paid work as the depression deepened. By comparison to governments in the United States, Great Britain, Germany, and many Western states, French governments pursued a moderate course on married women's employment. Although the government adopted quotas on hiring women in the civil service, they did not fire married women in public service.[91] Overall, the census recorded a drop of almost 600,000 women in the labor force between 1931 and 1936 (to 7,320,200), but the percentage of women in the labor force (34.2) remained higher than in other Western countries.[92]

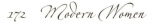

Gradually, women's weeklies recognized the reality of many married women working. As the desperate economic situation persisted in the mid-1930s, a series in *C'est la Mode* described job training, employment opportunities, working conditions, and wages of salesclerks, secretaries, librarians.[93] However, only *La Mode du Jour,* which addressed itself "to the mother of a family, a sportswoman, a worker, a housewife," ever featured a clerical worker on its cover and, on one occasion, a working-class woman inside the covers.[94]

These weeklies' position on women's work combined economic necessity with a not solely domestic ideal of bourgeois womanhood, as contemporary feminists did. Their position bridged the yawning gap between maternal feminist ideas and the image of the modern woman as single, independent, and childless. We will see how accurate the single and childless image was (chap. 10).

## Cross-Dressing

Antifeminists tried to link feminism with cross-dressing, by which they meant women wearing trousers with tailored jackets, shirts, and ties. Women in trousers can be considered a partial metaphor; women in trousers, tailored jackets, and shirts a total metaphor. Women engaged in sports like horseback riding had long donned masculine attire (jackets) above the waist, and feminine attire (skirts) below the waist. Although this "split sign" was acceptable by the 1920s, the reverse (feminine apparel above the belt, masculine apparel below the belt) was still transgressive.[95] In the previous five centuries, the most obvious gender division in European costume had been between pants and skirts. Dividing women's legs "with a layer of fabric seemed like a sexual sacrilege."[96] When a few female cyclists donned bloomers or culottes in the 1890s to avoid getting their skirts tangled in bicycle chains, journalists scoffed that bloomers and culottes, which allowed women to sit astride, made women "act like men," and bloomers, which exaggerated the hips and buttocks, made women look ugly. Note the double-edged criticism of bloomers. Women in bloomers were masculine in action (hence unfeminine) and overly feminine in appearance (hence ugly). In the 1890s, all the women interviewed for a book on women's views about cycling costumes considered bloomers "immodest and ridiculous," though some paid culottes the dubious compliment of no longer being disgusting.[97] Denigrating avant-garde styles and women who wore them as mannish and ugly would remain in the repertoire of critics of cross-dressing. This kind of ad feminum argument dissuaded some women from adopting mannish attire.

Designers who aligned themselves with modern women were either quiet about or critical of full cross-dressing and the mistakenly coupled subject of suffrage feminism. Elsa Schiaparelli, who appropriated many elements of menswear in the 1930s, wrote about wanting to be a man (or, more precisely, a flaneur): "Going out alone, at any time, anywhere, has always excited my envy. To wander aimlessly through the night, to sit in cafes and do nothing, are privileges that seem to be unimportant, but in reality they make the taste of living so much more pungent and complete." However, she disliked English suffragettes, whom she described as "mad masculine furies, collectively and individually hideous, screaming for the vote. . . . They got their vote and all their worries. Many men admire strong women, but they do not love them."[98] Her statement resembles Camille Duguet's put-down of French feminists.

In the early 1920s, male fashion commentators occasionally remarked upon city pants, though less in relation to feminists than to lesbians. In a *Gazette du Bon Ton* article entitled "Les Masculines," Roger Boutet de Monvel explained that he was not referring to "those who march in the streets demanding the vote for women," whom he characterized as "mischievous, mutinous, and gracious." He meant fashionable women, "feminists before the term existed," who appeared disguised as troubadours, little pages, or princes charming."[99] He was alluding to the lesbian circle around Natalie Barney.[100] In *The Pure and Impure*, published in 1932, Colette, who had briefly mingled but subsequently broken with that circle, dismissed the members as "timid snobs" who wore loose "Lady Bountiful" coats to cover their masculine attire when they went out. She mocked her own masculine apparel in that milieu, especially "male insignia" like shirtfronts, shirts, and starched collars.[101]

Most fashion reporters were silent about women wearing trousers in the city, Paris "lesbos," and the sexual underground. Although they did not as a matter of course review novels, it is noteworthy that they withheld comment upon the popular novels *La Garçonne* (1922), about which so many journalists discoursed, and *The Angel and the Perverts* (1930), written by Lucie Delarue-Mardrus, a contributor to the fashion press.[102] Both novels are cautionary tales about "new women" who cross-dressed. In *La Garçonne*, a new woman leaves home, cuts her hair, dons men's clothing, and lives a bohemian life, including lesbian romances, in the name of emancipation. When this lifestyle proves unsatisfying, a young man who believes in equality rescues her. *The Angel and the Perverts* tells the tale of an unhappy hermaphrodite who associates with gays and lesbians until she adopts a child and finds purpose for her "sterile existence." While the heroine is behaving like a woman, she wears a "tailored suit tight against her narrow hips" and a coat "cut like a man's overcoat." When she assumes a masculine persona, she simply replaced her skirts with pants and "became a man again, contemporary feminine fashion lending itself to this kind of transformation."[103]

In response to the outcry about city pants, designers and fashion columnists redefined pants as "elegant." Even before the Great War, women journalists made fun of men fretting about seeing women's calves.[104] Around this time, Poiret launched his harem pants, which combined puffed-out hips and upper thighs with calf-hugging lower legs and which evoked twice the anxiety, about confusing gender roles and about endorsing "racially marked exoticism." Poiret tried to deflect controversy over harem pants' potential to disrupt racial and gender categories by making them of rich materials and marketing them as loungewear for domestic use.[105] Later designers smoothed out the puffy upper legs and widened the clingy lower legs, which alleviated apprehension about exoticism, though straight legs aggravated angst about similarities to European men's trousers.

In the early 1920s, journalists redefined indoor pants as evening pajamas and interpreted them as feminine and even feminist. Martine Rénier's editorial "What feminine fashion has taken from masculine fashion?" contended that women only adopted attractive elements of trousers and shirts and wore them only indoors. Making ladies trousers of brightly colored silks and wearing them with tunics or blouses of lamé or muslin represented a feminization of masculine-looking garments. Rénier also praised pants as practical, comfortable, and loose enough to allow free movement—in short, she coded them as feminist. She understood that fashion, even cross-dressing, was multivalent. In the mid-1920s, anxiety about "the masculine allure" and liberating potential of loungewear briefly settled on smoking jackets worn with slim slacks, which even Rénier felt "lacked femininity." Camille Duguet agreed that smoking jackets looked "rather masculine" and felt that they "flattered some women's taste for emancipation."[106]

Throughout the 1920s, most women's and fashion weeklies either ignored the controversial subject of evening pants or timidly endorsed them.[107] Their reticence probably reflected the realities that few of their middle-class readers had occasions to wear evening pajamas and that their readers were more conservative about clothing than the elite—and elite wannabes—who subscribed to society magazines. However, by the late 1920s, when evening pajamas were worn with untailored jackets, there was no doubt about their femininity, even in the provinces. Evening pajamas were so respectable that a fashion columnist could defend outdoor pants—culottes—from charges of being "subversive" by calling them "the next logical step after the pajama."[108] Once again, the 1930s seem less conservative than they are often portrayed to be.

Columnists were more reserved about outdoor pants and jackets. In addition to being outdoor apparel, riding and hunting pants allowed horsewomen to sit astride and engage in vigorous and violent pursuits. One of the points of contention in the debate about women's riding apparel that had raged in the 1890s involved tailored riding jackets known as Amazons (other points of contention were tight corsets, which hygienists blasted for health reasons, and ballooning riding skirts, which hygienists considered unsafe).[109] By the end of the First World War, the covers of modest women's magazines and Belle Jardinière catalogs featured Amazons. In 1926 *Vogue* sponsored a competition to discover the "most beautiful Amazon," meaning both the rider and her riding habit. Critics, including the Duchess d'Uzes, an inveterate hunter, continued to query why women would want to dress like young men. Like many other lady riders, she preferred a more feminine jacket known as the *califouchon*.[110]

Ladies' riding and hunting breeches had long been made of lighter, softer woolens than those employed in their masculine counterparts, which might have established their suitability for women.[111] But light, soft fabric was insufficient to feminize riding and hunting pants; a skirt over the pants was required. When the couturière Amy Linker showed hunting breeches with overskirts in the early 1920s, Rosine opined in *Figaro* that, although "a little virile," the breeches were redeemed by "a short skirt draped at the sides that partly concealed the trouser legs." In addition, they were "very convenient and practical."[112] By 1928, Louise Boulanger was making breeches to be worn under skirts made of the same material—woolens for sports wear and chiffons for evening wear. The latter were beaded or embroidered, hence decorative and doubly feminine.[113] Despite growing approval, many fashion arbiters continued to prefer riding and hunting skirts.[114] Colette ridiculed mixed-sex hunt clothing. "The huntress of 1925 . . . will wear adorable little shoes and be covered from head to foot in a grid pattern that makes her look like a bathroom floor (or perhaps in chevrons that give her the appearance of a grizzled trooper). Beneath her masculine tie, she will wear a shirt made of white china crepe."[115]

Only one fashion columnist was ill disposed toward ladies hunting because it involved killing animals. Only Coline compared masculine riding and hunting attire to travesty costumes, not meaning costumes for travesty roles in the theater written for actresses playing young men or boys, but costumes for fancy-dress parties and Mardi Gras.[116] Fashion magazines featured Mardi Gras costumes every February, with society magazines focusing on adult costumes and women's magazines on children's costumes.[117] Most magazines concentrated on princess and fairy costumes, which were very attractive and not at all transgressive.

Culottes, with pleated legs that hung together to look like skirts, made skiing possible for respectable women in the 1920s. Although pleats obscured separated legs, a few fashion reporters called them "semi-masculine," and Ramon-Fernandez called them a "symbol of feminism."[118] By 1928, every major couture house showed sports culottes. In a short-lived journal called *La Femme, le Sport, la Mode,* Jane Saint-Roman proclaimed "this rather masculine outfit no longer frightens anyone." Although wearing "culotte skirts" to bicycle in the city was still associated with modern women, now women on bicycles were "an everyday feature of our life" (fig. 11).[119] In the 1930s, Norwegian ski pants, knickers, and "plus fours" borrowed from menswear were fashionable on the runways and the slopes. All were loose, unlike present-day, form-fitting ski pants. Beach pajamas—cotton, linen, or artificial silk slacks almost as light and flowing as evening pajamas—gained popularity in the early 1920s and respectability in the early 1930s.[120]

If it had become acceptable for modern Frenchwomen to wear pants for sports, French fashion magazines, and by inference their readers, did not consider tailored pants suitable for ladies to wear on city streets or in public. Not one article on wardrobes included city pants, and only a few articles on vacation attire included slacks of any kind. In the 1940s, it was still unusual for stylish women to wear pants in cities.[121]

Fashion magazines were not exactly apolitical, for they joined in campaigns to revitalize French couture and couture exports, and some addressed feminist political issues, including the vote. More importantly, fashion magazines defined modernity for women, meaning that women had more opportunities and independence than their predecessors. According to the fashion press, modern

927

FIGURE 11. A socialite in culottes beside a sporty car at the Concours d'élégance automobile, 1933. Séeberger Frères collection, Etampes, 0a381, no. M166236. Courtesy, Bibliothèque Nationale de France.

women wore Parisian clothes that combined mobility with elegance and put to-gether clothes and accessories in a total look. Both the clothes and the accessories were made in and around Paris but marketed, along with hybrid modernity, to women around the world. The fashion press articulated a new mix of commercial and cultural feminism, one that challenged women's economic and physical dis-abilities. Unlike cultural critics, fashion arbiters denied a direct link between com-fortable clothing and masculinity. Instead, they linked practical clothes to women's work and physical liberation, and hence to a covert and hybrid feminism.

*Chapter Nine*

# The Gender of the Modern

In the 1920s, many articles appeared in French journals about a new kind of woman wearing a new kind of dress with a low waistline, straight lines, and high—meaning mid-calf—hemline. Some critics drew disturbing conclusions from these modern women and styles. In an important book entitled *This Civilization Has No Sexes*—a phrase borrowed from one of these critics—Mary Louise Roberts shows how many male critics correlated the disappearance of the wasp-waist popular on Belle Epoque dresses (along with the popularity of short hair) with an apparent dwindling of sexual differences in post–World War I France. She attributed this discourse to postwar despair about the "ruin of civilization itself" and pronatalist anxieties about depopulation, which included angst about the large number of single women following the loss of 1,300,000 Frenchmen in the war.[1] Roberts did not explore fashion magazines to see how influential fashion arbiters defined the chemise dress and the new woman for their readers. She eschewed any effort to determine how individual Frenchwomen incorporated the image of the modern woman into their identities.[2] By focusing on fashion arbiters and fashionable women's attitudes about the gender of modernity, in this chapter I address some of the lacunae in our knowledge of what the chemise and new styles meant to Frenchwomen. I explore how designers, textile manufacturers, the fashion press, and bourgeois women diluted the impact of reputedly masculine styles by "feminizing" straight and "sober" lines with bright colors, soft fabrics, decorative details, and accessories, so that ladies could put together a "tasteful look" that mildly "disrupted" but ultimately reaffirmed the class and gender order.

## Cut and Color

Compared to the uproar about partial cross-dressing, cultural criticism of the straight lines of chemise dresses as masculine was muted. It rested on a misreading of vestimentary history as invariably curvilinear for women and rectilinear for men. As A. B. Young documented more than a generation ago, there had been a previous era of straight lines for women, in the late eighteenth and early nineteenth centuries.[3] And as Claudia Brush Kidwell demonstrated in the 1980s, the cut and padding of men's clothes in the 1840s had limned a figure-eight shape.[4] Still, the disappearance of the cinched waist—called by one student of dress "the appendage of Occidentalism" and by most other students of dress a potent marker of sexual difference—did evoke commentary.

Instead of seeking distant historical precedents, fashion arbiters traced the chemise dress back to styles developed during the First World War for volunteer nurses and simply noted the loss of a defined waistline as the nurses' uniform moved into general usage. Many journalists associated the popularity of the chemise to the increased number of women working outside the home, and they attributed shorter hemlines to the increased number of women who used public transport.[5] Most of them agreed with cultural critics that the straight line looked masculine and that it emancipated women.[6] Rather than lambaste the tubular look or lament its masculinizing effects, most fashion reporters described the new look as boyish, simple, and practical and defined emancipation as enabling bourgeois women to mount streetcars and walk city streets.[7] These adjectives and activities were not as threatening to the existing gender system as the terms *masculine* or *emancipating* implied. Boys were not yet men; and they were young at a time, after the massive loss of life during the war, when youth was prized. *Simple* and *practical* remained in the fashion magazine lexicon through the interwar years and took on new importance during the Vichy regime.[8] Mobility, a leitmotif of modernity, recurred in fashion reporting. Surely these themes would not have dominated the magazines if they had no resonance with the readers of fashion magazines.

In fact, fashion arbiters' reporting captured the spirit of the times. In 1923, Au Printemps department store conducted a poll among female customers about the new chemise style in the form of a contest with prizes of 500 francs for customers who answered the following questions: "What is the ideal fashion for woman of our day? Have you adopted the straight dress? Do you regret short skirts?" According to the public notice about the poll results, 203,351 customers responded, and the majority liked the new slim, straight dresses and shorter, pleated, skirts.[9] All department store catalogs showed large numbers of straight-lined dresses and pleated skirts during the 1920s, and their captions shared descriptors like "practical" and "youthful" with fashion magazines. Department stores would have reduced their stock of chemises and changed the captions if mail-order customers had not bought these items.

One of the mild flurries of criticism about the chemise occurred when Chanel showed her first "little black dress" in 1926, but some of the criticism was about the color, which had disquieting overtones. For many decades, black had signified mourning. During and after the war, the French observed stricter mourning customs than the British or Americans did.[10] Immediate family members practiced deep mourning, with widows wearing black; more distant relatives practiced demi-mourning, with female family members donning gray-colored clothing. In Jeanne Galzy's novel *La Cavalière,* the heroine, visiting Paris during the Great War, notices how many women in church are wearing gray, as if mourning distant relatives fallen in the war.[11] In addition, there were stages of mourning, with different sartorial rules. For a year, widows wore "austere" matte black dresses with thick English crepe veils and opaque black stockings. After a year, they could add discreet trim and a substitute a thinner black veil.

Because there were approximately 600,500 war widows and because they assembled on the many days memorializing the war dead, people, and young war widows in particular, found the landscape of black costumes bleak and depressing. Partly in response, the rules for deep mourning were relaxed in the early 1920s. Stockings could be transparent; lighter crepes and georgettes replaced English crepe; white collars and discreet jewelry could be worn.[12] Chanel introduced the little black dress with white cuffs at this propitious conjuncture. These innovations contributed to the trend of urban provincials donning less severe mourning attire.[13] They also adopted less dour and monotonous attire because the cult of remembrance of the war dead had become increasingly "incompatible with modern life." Nevertheless, the ideal of widows wearing "austerely cut" dresses made of black matte fabric, with a short veil and smoky gray stockings, lingered through the 1930s.[14] In small villages, widows and elderly women were still expected to wear black.[15]

Black had also been the color of men's suits, and as such, signified masculine authority,[16] and since the 1890s, black had been associated with naughty underwear and the demimonde, which unambiguously signaled sexual impropriety.

Chanel neatly sidestepped sex and gender controversies by adding white collars and trim. Raised as an orphan in a convent, Chanel was inspired by nuns' habits, and she publicized the sisters' influence on her design, thereby eliding masculine and immoral connotations yet rendering her dresses mildly transgressive in Catholic-raised but largely secular urban circles.[17] Over the next five years, black dresses with white trim became "the uniform of elegant ladies and entered the wardrobes of all but the most conservative bourgeois ladies."[18]

Cultural critics were not incensed about ladies' suits, which had hung in ladies' closets since the fin de siècle and had loose jackets and full skirts in the Après Guerre.[19] As designers made slimmer, straighter suits in the mid-1920s, many critics found their tailoring and cut masculine and, when accessorized with shirts and bowties, deviant.[20] Some critics, like Eugene Marsan, who called suits "virile," were being humorous. Marsan surely recognized that no one could fail to notice the gender of women wearing suits.[21] Fashion reporters offered more serious commentary. They insisted that suits were versatile and made from durable fabrics, hence practical, but also that they were "pretty" and "chic"—hence, feminine. They reported that well-cut suits in sturdy dark-hued woolens were the preferred city costume for spring and autumn walks in the park, shopping, and visiting.[22] Society and women's magazines alike recommended "morning suits" for travel on trains.[23] The color range extended from black in 1918, to black with white or beige trim in the early 1920s, to gray in the 1930s.[24] Long before that, a gray suit was de rigueur in the provinces. When the American Kay Boyle arrived at Le Havre in 1923, her French mother-in-law and two sisters-in-law wore identical gray suits. In the customs office, her mother-in-law inquired whether Boyle had a gray suit that she had, perhaps, forgotten to put on. Even though the family would be traveling in a private car, not a public conveyance, her mother-in-law felt that she should wear a gray suit because they would be eating in restaurants and sightseeing on the way home.[25] Boyle seems to have been unaware of the mourning customs that informed this question.

By the mid-1920s, some fashion arbiters simply recorded without further comment that many ladies were wearing "mannish cut" suits.[26] Those who remarked on the emancipatory implications of the suit insisted on its "coquetry" and reminded readers that coquetry in costume "is one of the most exquisite feminine qualities."[27] As the general-interest press welcomed the return of fitted bodices, natural waistlines, and fuller skirts, fashion writers pronounced the curvilinear line of the new dresses feminine and romantic.[28] Suit jackets were more fitted than previously, but the silhouette did not change as dramatically as it did in dresses. Yet *La Mode Illustrée* reported that women still favored suits because they were "easy and pleasant to wear [and] adaptable to many circumstances, thanks to substituting accessories, changing their appearance and character." As a male fashion columnist dryly observed, "the universal basis of the feminine wardrobe remains suits and sports dresses."[29] The sartorial reaction of the 1930s was not as definitive as cultural commentators and fashion historians have claimed.

When journalists described straight-cut ladies' jackets as masculine in the 1930s, they queried any direct links between ladies' and men's suits.[30] Even Schiaparelli's padded shoulders on suit jackets in the early 1930s and military-looking double-breasted jackets with epaulets on the shoulders in the mid-1930s aroused little controversy. In 1932, *La Mode Pratique* welcomed any accentuation of the shoulders that visually enhanced the slender waist.[31] Unusually, society magazines were slower to hail these innovations. A year later *Femina* condescendingly called the "geometrical mode, square shoulders, very straight skirts . . . an amusing adaptation from certain modern statues that only such a talented artist could carry off."[32] *Vogue* waited until Schiaparelli showed rounded shoulders, then welcomed "the end of the T-form silhouette."[33] As other designers took up the military look, *Vogue* praised it for being "well cut and rich in decoration.[34] The term *cut* referenced claims that the Parisian look was based upon a good cut; *decorative* implied feminine. The never intense debate over the gender of suits had dissipated.

Most fashion arbiters assumed that their readers were bourgeois women who did not normally work outside the home. Those who acknowledged that readers might work for pay explained that they or their daughters held jobs as clerk-typists in offices and retail clerks in shops. Wardrobe advice for these women tacitly acknowledged that office and retail workers did not earn enough to buy couture clothes but rather employed local dressmakers or sewed themselves. One of a handful of columns on proper attire for these occupations recommended either a "simple and practical" dress known as the "go-everywhere" or dresses made of solid tweed or jersey in a neutral color, such as navy blue or dark brown. In the 1930s, columnists promoted black dresses with collars and cuffs in a white or light-colored linen or lace, as long as the collars and cuffs were detachable and could be washed regularly.[35] English columnists also counseled office workers to wear detachable collars and cuffs.[36] This counsel accords with the number of "practical little dresses" in department store catalogs and the absence of the category of women's work clothes in all catalogs (women's work clothes were subsumed under generic work clothes, a category composed primarily of men's work clothes, in the Belle Jardinière catalog). This counsel also accounts for regular ads in stenographers' magazines for department stores and general clothing stores, both of which were much less expensive than ladies' wear shops. Long-running ads for sewing lessons in this organ are further proof of cost concerns among stenographers.[37]

Fashion arbiters' recommendation of sturdy fabrics in navy blue or black with lightweight, pale-colored collars for work clothing reminded contemporaries of the colors used in the uniforms of the armed forces during the war and the color combinations of the habits of the Sisters of Charity and other women's religious orders.[38] Both the military and the religious provenance indicate the importance of conformity and obedience. Lightweight and light-colored collars over plain dark dresses sent messages about sisterly chastity, messages that some fashion arbiters felt they had to spell out for readers.[39] In the shop and office, work clothes were not supposed to draw attention to women's presence in the newly integrated workplace, to imply gender equality, or to exacerbate sexual tensions.

Although fashion and society magazines were slow to include a suit in their wardrobes for employed women, some professional women were already wearing suits. In her 1929 book *Women of Today,* Colette Yver described a lady engineer on the worksite wearing a gray suit, black felt hat, and black leather shoes.[40] Today we might interpret her sartorial choice as adopting a uniform, or a "clothing metaphor to project an image of a social status or position."[41] As Yver described professional women, many in masculine professions followed dicta about durable fabrics in dark and neutral colors, though one lawyer had a cubist cravat—which she carefully tucked under her robes in the courtroom. A few women in more feminized professions, like civil servants, wore lighter- or brighter-colored silk dresses.[42]

Literary evidence suggest that many women who wore sober outfits at work to fit into the workplace liked to don more cheerful apparel in their domestic space. In her novel *Possession,* Raymonde Machard (editor of *Journal de la Femme*) described the scientist Claude Ambroise as "quietly dressed and restrained in manner." Ambroise changed from the tailored dress she wore at work into a colorful and "gracious" dress after work.[43] Schiaparelli exploited the day-time-nighttime dichotomy. She argued that workingwomen (really professional and business women, since service workers could not afford her clothes) needed to wear uniforms during the workday to protect themselves from the sexual advances of co-workers. In the evening, a woman became more seductive. If her women were defensively asexual by day, they were seductive at night. Schiaparelli's opinion must have been skewed by experience with her customers, who were hardly introverts, and by the fact that presenting dichotomous looks was good for business. But her opinion echoes other observations that workingwomen relieved some of the gender ambiguities of their position in the workforce by reverting to more traditionally feminine attire after work. Her opinion resembles the hypothesis of contemporary psychoanalyst Joan Rivière: new women engaged in professional work assumed the mask of femininity, at least insofar as the hypothesis discusses personal appearance.[44]

## Fabrics and Femininity

Because fashion "is ultimately determined by its materials,"[45] the texture, weight, colors, and motifs of fabrics are constituent parts of gender messages conveyed by any ensemble. Dani Cavallaro and Alexandra Warwick argue that materials "may be seen as embodiments of two distinct, albeit interacting, types of space: the smooth, as the locus of fluidity, fusion and boundlessness, and the striated, as that of order, classification and categorization." They submit that smooth fabric has a feminine inflection, ribbed fabric a masculine inflection.[46] In *The Fashion System,* Roland Barthes contends that all fabrics are classified by weight and that people who wear lightweight fabrics are imbued with a light, fine, and frivolous identity, while those in heavyweight fabrics are imbued with a heavy, authoritative, and solemn identity.[47] Although he did not impute gender differences to the weight of fabrics, interwar fashion arbiters did.

Initially, haute couture's flirtation with elements of menswear involved materials associated with lower-class men's clothing. Inspired by the striped jersey pullovers of English sailors, Chanel introduced very similar pullovers before the First World War, thereby leaping class and gender style barriers. Without denying her boldness, it is worth noting that sportswomen had already donned jersey tops and that sports or casual wear was more open to class and gender crossovers. Previously, jersey knits had been deemed too plebian and disreputable for ladies' outerwear, because of their use by sailors and in underwear. Jersey was also considered too clingy. When intrepid sportswomen donned jersey tops for sports activities, moralists deplored the public exposure of women's upper body (presumably the contours of their bosoms). Censure about revealing clothing was accompanied by condemnation of sportswomen as ugly and masculine—as with bloomers, condemning ladies' sport attire as overly feminine and therefore im-

 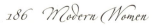

proper, yet simultaneously masculine and therefore ugly.[48] Something more than simple gender logic about feminine clothing and bodies was operating here. Nervousness about bourgeois women stepping out of their prescribed passivity and domestic confinement surely underlay this confused criticism. Using tightly knit jersey for pullovers, Chanel removed the cling and with it much of the stigma from jersey tops. During and after the war, she made the stripped-down sheaths and suits that became her signature styles in jerseys that neither sagged nor hugged the body. By the mid-1920s, tightly knit jerseys figured in many ladies' dresses.[49]

Stripes were also considered outré. Bold stripes had long been associated with convicts' uniforms. Discreet light-colored stripes on a white or pastel background had only recently become acceptable for underwear. In 1921, striped woolen tops worn by women were still considered "very sportsmanlike," though light-colored striped cottons were acceptable for women's summer dresses.[50] Presumably the different receptions occurred because cotton, unlike woolens, did not cling and because dresses had skirts. By the mid-1920s, the gender-bending innovation that attracted media attention was using the fine pale striped cottons initially used for men's shirts in women's sports costumes. The direct relationships with men's shirts and the practice of sports, also coded masculine, made these stripes more vulnerable to criticism than stripes in cotton frocks. By 1930, stripes combined with more obviously feminine motifs, like flowers, were appropriate in silk fabrics for formal wear.[51]

As commentators Henri Algoud, of *La Soierie de Lyon,* and Colette pointed out, plaids were based on geometric principles. Although the two authors remarked that plaids were now being used for ladies' coats and suits, neither discerned any masculine implications in these straight lines and sharp angles.[52] Why? At the end of the war, plaid woolens were commonly used in women's riding skirts, which were coded feminine—part of a well-developed system of "split signals" in women's sportswear, with masculine attire permitted above the waist and feminine attire prescribed below.[53] By the mid-1920s, textile manufacturers introduced more exotic plaids, such as a red "Chinese" plaid. Textile firms and couture houses sold muted plaids as backdrops for floral motifs for dresses, suits, and coats.[54] In addition to bright and soft colors being coded feminine, "plant life, with its eternal curves, its flowers, its leaves," had been considered feminine at least since the introduction of art nouveau.[55] By the 1930s, when plaids made a comeback, they were "*comme il faut,*" even in the provinces.[56]

In 1927, several designers adopted the homespun tweeds used in Englishmen's hunting jackets for suits. Chanel took credit for this, as for other innovations. Her personality, according to Cecil Beaton, was "a mingling of the masculine and the intensely feminine," and her designs were simultaneously elitist and democratic. She delighted in trespassing into masculine vestimentary territory and in publicizing her liaison with the duke of Westminster, from whom she borrowed the tweed jacket. Photographs of Chanel with the duke, both dressed in tweeds, added an aristocratic cachet to her suits.[57] In actuality, several designers encroached on two foreign sartorial realms by transferring traditionally thick and rough materials from men's into ladies' wear and by employing materials associated with sportswear in formal wear. Previously, homespun had been dismissed as too heavy and coarse for ladies' wear.[58]

Concurrently, French manufacturers were producing lighter and smoother tweeds and using softer colors, such as peach, apricot, or turquoise, to appeal to female consumers. They also made solid-colored fabrics in subdued complementary colors to coordinate with brightly colored checks and plaids. Provincial women committed to "harmonious and respectable" ensembles appreciated the opportunity to tone down the "loudness" of tweeds and plaids.[59] In less than a decade, fashion arbiters and fashionable women in Paris and the provinces no longer considered tweeds and plaids masculine.

In a reaction against wartime conventions of dark monotonal dress materials, textile producers took advantage of new dying processes to introduce lively new colors and expand production of prints.[60] They introduced bright new shades of green and purple and named new colors after fruits and vegetables, for example, "apricot" and "eggplant." They also produced many new floral prints set in far-away places and named them appropriately: "Persian Gardens," "Norwegian Flowers," "Harlem Tulips." During the Egyptian craze that followed the discovery of Tutankhamen's tomb, many fabrics set ancient Egyptian-style figures against floral prints.[61] Textile manufacturers and couturiers understood "a well-known principle in the fashion world: every era of simple and straight forms corresponds to an era of fantasy fabrics."[62]

A few years after the war, fashion arbiters reveled in the pleasure of colorful dress material and welcomed the drop in the high postwar price of textiles. Fashion reporters raved about unexpected colors and original prints, which brought "a new note to our wardrobes."[63] As the controversy over masculine styles came to a boil in the early 1920s, fashion arbiters labeled the new array of colors "exquisitely feminine."[64] These astute women not only acknowledged that color evoked a multitude of meanings but also rescued chemises and other clothing from their detractors' attempts to label them masculine. Conversely, when the waistline returned to its natural place in the early 1930s and was hailed by fashion arbiters as a revival of the feminine line, silk magnates added more checks and geometric designs to their repertoire of flowery prints.[65] Even though the silhouette signaled femininity, silk manufacturers obscured the masculinity of angular motifs by printing them on feminine materials like taffeta and on flowery backgrounds. *La Soierie de Lyon* publicized these fabrics as charming and "exquisitely feminine."[66]

Couturiers also tempered masculine-coded features by using light, soft, smooth, and supple materials for chemises and suits. As couturiers, dressmakers, savvy consumers, and home sewers understood, the body of material can ruin the fall of a relatively unfitted dress like a chemise.[67] Jeanne Ramon Fernandez reported as early as 1917 that the new straight-cut dress could "outline the shape of the body and free the body." The couturier who created that early chemise explained that the "fabric weds the contours of the body, not because of a . . . clingy quality, but because of the movement of the body." Ramon Fernandez drew further conclusions: "Supple attire, close to the body, allows a maximum liberty of movement and increases equality between the sexes."[68] In the aftermath of the war, designers made afternoon dresses for tea or cocktail parties out of silk crepe and silk georgette, materials that the fashion press described as "delicious to wear, light, fresh, and feminine."[69] Lightweight silks swayed with the movement of the body, revealing its curves. One fashion columnist found the light, delicate, and vaporous materials "excessively feminine."[70]

In the early 1930s, an advertising expert analyzed the language used in contemporary textile advertisements. In addition to appeals about good prices, selection, and novelty ("the latest thing"), Professor Klein discovered that the "principal argument was quality" and the secondary argument, practicality. Some typical adjectives and phrases were "pure," "fine," "supple," "easily cut," and "durable." With regard to clothing material, Klein identified a "psychological" pitch tapping into social insecurity, such as "one must be chic to be considered."[71] Because he did not focus on dress fabrics, he did not notice the prevalence of descriptors such as "smooth," "soft," and "delicate," usually in conjunction with "graceful," "elegant," and "feminine." Nor did he analyze the visual content of textile advertisements, including the frequent use of feminine figures to advertise dress and ladies suit fabrics (fig. 12).

FIGURE 12. Advertisement for Les Reps woolens in *Vogue*, 1923. Photographed and reproduced by kind permission of the Bibliothèque Nationale de France.

## Accessorizing Femininity

The gradual acceptance of supposedly masculine features in women's wardrobes was also due to reinterpretations of these features as essentially feminine and redirection of the gaze to more feminine features. Reinterpreting entailed more than critics becoming accustomed to women's wearing tubular dresses and tailored suits. Fashion arbiters accomplished this rhetorically. As early as 1917, one columnist argued that straight, slim skirts prevented "the overly masculine walk that wide skirts encourage."[72] Soon consumer interest in mobility persuaded designers to show finely pleated skirts, or skirts with pleats sewn together to the hips and opening below the hips, which maintained an impression of slimness while allowing longer strides. Improvements in pleating machinery made new kinds of pleats possible. *Le Jardin des Modes* offered home sewers the use of a mechanical pleating service that made simple pleats less than a centimeter wide, different-sized pleats, and clusters of four pleats alternating with a single layer of material.[73] By the mid-1920s, pleats were popular on the skirts of thin woolen and silk dresses, inserted in spirals around the skirt or in panels at the side or front.[74] Journalists welcomed the sway of pleats as practical, gracious, modern, and feminine.[75] A 1923 *Vogue* feature on Chanel claimed that she "expresses the very soul of the modern woman. Coats with straight lines cover loose-fitting dresses with a youthful look. . . . The dresses are feminine in their details, often composed of very thin pleats, with draped panels falling from the shoulder or the hips, making walking seem like gracious flight."[76] Journalists asserted that pleated skirts as part of a suit feminized these otherwise strict and severe outfits.[77] As the survey of Au Printemps customers revealed, customers agreed. Based on the number of pleated skirts and suits with pleated skirts in other department store catalogs, customers of other department stores concurred.

Couturiers' devotion to detail could divert attention from masculine features of chemises, suits, and slacks. Design details distinguished haute couture models from otherwise similar ready-made items. Though the details were subtle, fashion arbiters ensured that socialites recognized them. Employed by a fashion reporter in the mid-1920s, when the silhouette did not vary significantly, Elizabeth Hayes was instructed to "concentrate on details" such as newly fashionable pleats and floating panels. While a few designers pursued the burgeoning number of copy houses in court, most incorporated details that distinguished haute couture from cheap copies, and the fashion press promoted the doctrine that real distinction meant combining the details and accessories into a "look."[78] In his 1979 work on the importance of social and symbolic capital, Pierre Bourdieu demonstrated how making fine distinctions between similar items signals social *distinction*. In her ethnography of the French bourgeoisie in the 1980s, Beatrix La Wita applied Bourdieu's insights to bourgeois women's clothing, identifying the importance of subtle details to establish the wearer's taste and social standing.[79] Bourdieu and La Wita's insights certainly applied to ladies' wear in the 1920s and 1930s, when brand names and logos were not emblazoned on clothing.

Designers obscured masculine elements in their models through "finishing touches"—embroidery and lace collars, cuffs, and trim. While these touches had been decorative elements for both men and women's clothing well into the eighteenth century, they were all considered feminine by the twentieth century.[80] Embroidering was a stereotypically feminine activity. In the difficult postwar years, even society magazines advised readers to embroider to update a dress.[81] As lace became lighter and more delicate in the nineteenth century, it took on a feminine inflection. One fashion weekly called lace "femininity incarnate . . . It evokes . . . the vision of light, gracious, delicate things that we touch carefully with one finger."[82] Generally, fashion writers contended that all the trimmings known as "*fanfreluches*"—embroidery, lace, linen cuffs and collars, bows, inserts, etc.—"soften the sharpness of the chemise line and, indeed, represent femininity itself."[83]

Accessories played a pivotal role in the redefinition of masculine attire as feminine. One way of feminizing masculine-coded features like a suit made of sturdy, dark-colored material was adding soft-textured and bright-colored scarves or shawls. In 1924, *La Soierie* proclaimed that colorful silk scarves and shawls had never been more popular "to brighten up a plain tailored suit or a khaki coat."[84] Similarly, one could cancel out the masculine connotations of severe, dark suits by wearing frilly blouses in a bright hue and arranging for the frills to spill out over the jacket lapels. In 1930, *Excelsior-Modes* described this effect as "femininity refound."[85] Chanel showed her collection of "slightly masculine" tailored suits with brightly dyed print blouses.[86] Multihued silk print scarves added a flamboyant note to ski or tennis outfits made of practical fabrics like wool or cotton. A sewing magazine explained that "these happy accessories" gave the sport silhouette "an entirely feminine grace."[87]

Some accessories mediated the simplicity and severity of chemise dresses without any fanfare about their femininity. In 1922, Jenny and Chanel added fichus to their chemises. Fichus were squares of silk muslin with borders in different colors that were draped around the shoulders, tied in front, and fell in a point down the upper back. Journalists did not need to proclaim the fichu feminine because it had traditionally been part of feminine costume and because it pulled the viewer's eyes to the upper body, away from the low waistline that evoked so much controversy.[88]

Columnists and couturiers also redefined masculine features as feminine by insisting that womanly gestures reasserted their essential femininity and bodily charms peeked through straight lines. Juliette Lancret noted "a feminine gesture"— a woman putting her hands on her hips—that revealed waist and hip curvature despite the straight line of chemise dresses.[89] In an article entitled "The Dress and the Woman," Pierre Drecoll of the House of Drecoll wrote: "Dressing up is a primordial instinct for women. . . . To create a dress for today, one must know the era, feel its acute modernism, and understand the evolution of women, who have become sportier. . . . Her body is transformed, its lines are leaner, neater, virile some say, and yet her charm has never been more perfectly feminine."[90] Speakers at fashion galas, where many couturiers displayed their designs, spoke of a "renewal" of coquetry.[91]

Finally, couturiers counterbalanced their understated morning or sports dress with fancier afternoon (tea and cocktail) frocks and evening gowns. Immediately after the war, many designers compensated for the penury of the war years by showing evening gowns of shiny lamé glittering with sequins and embellished with braid, ribbons, and fringes.[92] Following a brief vogue for evening sheaths in the mid-1920s, gathered or flared skirts, flounces, and floating panels reappeared on evening gowns. In 1929, Martine Rénier asserted that "in the evening, women are truly feminine, truly themselves."[93]

## Gender and Fashion

Comparing fashion commentary by Frenchmen and Frenchwomen exposes not only differences but also similarities in attitudes toward new styles and modern women. Comparing trends in men's and ladies' wear modifies the impression that women's fashion was the only kind of clothing undergoing change.

During the war, both men and women wrote favorably about dramatic changes in ladies' wear. A 1917 *L'Opinion* article subtitled "The Little Amazons" described Parisiennes "successively appropriating" elements of military uniforms, meaning belts, metal buttons, and pockets with visible stitching on jackets, rather than the cut of the jackets. Gustave Fréjeville conceded that these "encroachments" might be evidence of women's emancipation or their pursuit of "forbidden fruit," but he interpreted them, condescendingly and reassuringly, as touching demonstrations that "our weak and gracious companions" encourage "the regeneration of virile virtues, notably courage and daring."[94] In the "Women's Words" column of the daily newspaper *Figaro,* Camille Duguet found the number of pockets on women's clothing "vaguely masculine," but more definitively boyish.[95] The shift from the adjective *"masculine"* to *"boyish"* would be a staple in fashion reporting. The following year, Jeanne Farmant and Claire de Monclos of *Femina* ignored the fact that the chemise dress had been named after its collar, borrowed from men's shirts, and focused on its having been modeled on nurses' uniforms. They noted that the new slim-line skirts "gave the impression one was wearing trousers" but did not draw any masculine implications from that impression. Rather than extolling women's tribute to virility or military virtues, the two journalists explained that the new styles were sober and pragmatic responses to women's wartime exigencies.[96] Although adjectives like "sober" would soon lose appeal, "pragmatic," like "practical," would become staples in fashion magazine reporting on the new styles.

What does a historian make of these observations? A glance at fashion illustrations in the latter years of the war confirms that military details were present in the uniforms of women tram conductors, taxi drivers, and postal workers, but only the ubiquitous blue color of these uniforms was widely adopted by nonworking women. (The textile industry, largely converted to wartime production, produced mainly blue-colored fabrics for military personnel.) Conversely, nurse's uniforms, a loose chemise dress, buttoned up the front down to the upper hips, and belted, had already influenced ladies' dress. Although collars, buttons, and belts would nearly disappear from chemise dresses in the 1920s, the term *chemise* would continue to be used for simple, straight-lined dresses.[97]

During the pinnacle of the straight silhouette in the mid-1920s, not all men who wrote about fashion fixated on gender dissonance. In 1927, a special issue of *Les Cahiers de la République des lettres, des sciences et des arts* called *On Fashion: Yesterday, Today, Tomorrow* presented opinion pieces by men of letters and interviews with seven designers. Although many of the literati agreed that fashion was irrational and impractical, one insisted that modern styles were rational and pragmatic. Paul Reboux, who often wrote about women's issues, claimed that the new "restrained" styles harmonized with the necessities of modern life. He repeated feminist claims about the bob hairdo as being "the clearest symbol of feminine enfranchisement" and looser dresses signifying bodily comfort, a necessary complement to "the age that liberated the individual." To the extent that designers addressed the meaning of new styles (they mainly used the occasion to promote their latest creations), they used buzzwords like "simple," "practical," and "youthful."[98]

Two new men's magazines, *Monsieur* (1920–25) and *Adam* (1925–40), fall in the genre of society magazines. Like *Vogue* and *Femina,* they were semiglossy monthlies, hired art deco illustrators, cross-promoted fine clothing, textiles, the theater, and the races. *Adam* added automobiles to the marketing mix. Following art deco conventions for drawing figures, the silhouettes of male figures on their covers look almost as slim and asexual as those of female figures on women's fashion magazines. Of course, *Adam* and *Monsieur* also differed from *Vogue* and *Femina.* They claimed to be councilors of "men of taste" and they collaborated with "the principal tailors [and] shirt makers . . . of Paris," rather than with couturiers.[99] They had a defensive tone, which was their response to prejudices that fashion-consciousness was effeminate,[100] and the most frequent descriptors in advertisements and article were "quality" and "durability," not "elegant" or "chic."

Ever since the 1860s, when the plain dark lounge suit and white or striped shirt became a virtual uniform for bourgeois men, men had had few opportunities for sartorial display, and then primarily through bright colors and exuberant and exotic patterns in ties, vests, and (in the privacy of the home or club) dressing gowns.[101] Ten years before the Great War, there had been a break with the monotonous profile of the waistless "sack" suit of 1900, as more form-fitting jackets with high but defined waistlines came into fashion. In his *History of Men's Fashion,* Farid Chenouine notes the similarity between these jackets and the new high waistline introduced by Paul Poiret.[102] In 1920, *Monsieur* commented on the "femininity" of the prewar and immediate postwar jackets, remarking that they had been replaced by longer, looser jackets "that pay homage to our muscular system."[103]

Conversely, *Adam* and *Monsieur* welcomed the adoption both of colors like mauve and rose from the palette of ladies' dress materials and of the lighter wools used in ladies' wear into men's casual wear. In men's as in ladies' clothing lines, casual wear and sportswear were more open to gender crossovers than formal wear. When *Adam* and *Monsieur* lauded women for accepting artificial silk, they urged men to consider artificial woolens—and soon added artificial silk for men's dressing gowns.[104] *Adam* also published pieces on women adopting masculine sports pants, suits, and ties that were dispassionate, even positive, about "reciprocal influences" between masculine and feminine fashion.[105] Aside from this sort

*The Gender of the Modern* 195

of observation, *Monsieur* and *Adam* were unconcerned about women cross-dressing, which was, in any case, only partial cross-dressing or androgynous attire. They were far more anxious about competition from British tailors and shirtmakers (all the while advertising British woolens and cottons for suits and shirts). They worried that French suits and shirts did not have the cachet of their English counterparts, even in France.

In the postwar period, when all fashion magazines supported the revival of French fashion, Fernand Gregh wrote in *Monsieur* that elegance was "a bastion against barbarism" that "implies reflection, will power, refinement, morality almost."[106] A decade later, a staff writer for *Adam* praised the French woolen industry for developing more supple woolens, "the primordial element of our elegance."[107] As the depression unfolded, *Adam* exhorted Frenchmen to dress well and made exorbitant claims about the meaning of sartorial display. The president of the Shirtmakers' Syndicate urged Frenchmen to raise themselves to the vestimentary level of Frenchwomen, who are "envied by the entire world for their elegance and distinction." André de Fouquières argued that being well dressed was "an expression of optimism, a courageous way to fight against the crisis. . . . Façade, you say?—but of the kind to give confidence to others, to brighten and embellish the atmosphere."[108]

Aside from the occasional article proclaiming the elegant Frenchwomen the representative of "the soul of France . . . all harmony and grace," ladies' fashion magazines did not make grandiose claims about the meaning of ladies' fashion.[109] These magazines avoided sweeping statements about ladies' wear as expressions of morality because the subject was fraught with religious, sexual, antifamily, and even more implausibly, racist and anti-Semitic implications.[110] Catholic critics published diatribes about low décolletage and bared calves undermining decency and new styles encouraging feminine independence, removing women from their homes, and destroying the family and social order. They railed against the dance craze, indicting body-hugging dresses as well as "the invasion of lascivious . . . African" dances. Their real targets were general moral decline or "that revolutionary error, individualism." Mlle. De Saint-Seine, a member of the Christian Association for the Protection of the Young Girl, called fashion "merely an episode or chapter in the great drama of the dechristianization of the women and through her, Society." Already "perverted women" who recoiled from "the maternal burden" and practiced birth control had become "the playthings of foreign and Jewish couturiers and of an entire international underground." The remedy was not raising necklines or lowering hemlines but "remaking consciences."[111]

While individual fashion columnists criticized low décolletage, high hemlines, or sheer fabrics, only one woman's magazine publicized any moralistic clothing campaign.[112] In 1920, *La Mode Illustrée,* which supported the Maison de la Vie Sociale (an organization similar to the YWCA), ran an appeal from the Women's Social Action group to departments stores, tailors, lingerie stores, and couturiers and couturières to "help end the inconvenience and immodesty of present-day fashion . . . by abolishing the use of misplaced décolleté and exaggeratedly short and narrow skirts, and by prohibiting the abusive use of transparent textiles." The appeal put "young women on guard against the grave danger of displeasing their husbands" by wearing scandalous attire.[113] *La Mode Illustrée* was not very sympathetic to the crusade, for they never again referred to it. Otherwise, most fashion writers ignored moralistic reactions to modern style. The editor of *Chiffons,* Mme. Guilbert, joined general-interest journalists in mocking "anathemas and threats of interdiction" issued by the Church.[114]

Instead, ladies' fashion journalists wrote about how ladies' fashion reflected bourgeois women's lifestyles. In 1920, Henri Bidou contended that "all the life of a woman is reflected in the outfits they wear. A fashion magazine is the hourly history of women's lives."[115] However, the custom of changing many times a day was contested. On the one hand, *Chiffons* ran articles with titles like "The Transformation of the Parisienne According to the Hour" and "How We Dress Hour by Hour" until its demise in 1932. These articles suggested three or four changes per day for activities like a morning walk, a luncheon, a tea, and a play.[116] On the other hand, many fashion arbiters acknowledged that so many changes of clothing were costly in the difficult years of the early 1920s or that modern women were too busy for "fastidious changes of costume." These reporters recommended simple dresses, suits, or ensembles (three color-coordinated pieces, including a coat) that could be worn for several daytime activities. They agreed that "modern Parisiennes" always changed for evening events.[117] Even modest fashion magazines like *La Mode Pratique,* which encouraged a reduction in the wardrobe for budgetary reasons and promoted coat-dresses "for all day," felt that that a plain day dress, suit, or ensemble was unacceptable for afternoon tea or cocktails.[118]

Designers and marketers maintained the fundamental divisions of ladies' wardrobes by time of day: morning dresses and suits, late-afternoon frocks and ensembles, and evening gowns and suits.[119] As Jeanne Ramon Fernandez explained, women of the world, "obliged to dress three or four times a day, are not satisfied with a suit, even a very elegant one; they need a suite of dresses, . . .

we have even revived the 'five o'clock toilette' to receive guests, a style that has been completely abandoned since the war."[120] In addition, designers created new genres of dresses for new activities, such as the glamorous cocktail dress in chiffon or satin, sometimes with beading, embroidery, and lace trim.[121] One columnist wrote about different silhouettes for different hours of the day, with straighter lines in the daytime, curvier ones in the evening. Even women's magazines and pattern books accepted some further subdivision of the basic day and night categories of clothing.[122]

Neither marketers nor journalists were prepared to abandon the lucrative nineteenth-century custom of organizing ladies' wardrobes on "temporal and spatial oppositions (night/day, morning/evening, winter/summer, interior/exterior, town/country)."[123] Seasonal variations were central to the system of quarterly collections, but the essential dichotomy was winter/summer, which overlapped with the city/country dichotomy. The most obvious differences were the materials used, with cottons, linens, and prints in white, pale, or bright colors more common in the summer and in the countryside. Suits and dress styles did not vary as much, though sporty versions were preferred in the summer. Slacks were more prevalent in the summer, albeit more on the beach than in the country house.[124] We have already discussed many internal/external variations in ladies' wear. *Vogue* noted another variation in 1930, when it distinguished day dresses for outdoor sports activities like golf, which were made of wool or cotton and had pleated skirts, from day dresses for indoor leisure activities like bridge, which were made of silk and had gathered skirts.[125]

One salutary correction to the recent scholarly attention to the cultural commotion about the straight silhouette is more knowledge of developments in and reactions to developments in menswear. While military uniforms were universally acclaimed as masculine, wartime trends in civilian menswear, such as trousers suggesting rounded hips, raised doubts about the gender of their wearers, especially in conjunction with the trend toward a rectilinear line in women's wear. It was with some relief that fashion magazines welcomed the revival of more masculine lines after the war.[126] A mildly androgynous style in the mid-1920s, in the form of simpler, slimmer jackets, was followed by a hypermasculine style epitomized by exaggerated shoulders in the 1930s. Broad pleated trousers, similar to women's slacks, and softer-colored glen plaids, like those used in ladies' garments, were innovative features of interwar menswear. The futurist avant-garde proposed and donned colors as bright, and even brighter, than those of women's dress fabrics.[127] Men's fashion magazines became comfortable noting the "reciprocal influences of feminine and masculine fashion."[128] Perhaps the interwar era should be regarded as one of experimentation in men's and women's clothing, not of women adopting elements of menswear or of ladies' fashion undermining the gender order.

# Chapter Ten

# /The Modern Woman?

Recent studies of the modern girl in the 1920s represent her as a young, single, urban woman. As depicted in the media, she spent little time in the home, because she had a job and a full leisure life going to cafes, movies, and dances. As Birgitte Søland underscores, her slender and agile body was a primary site for displaying her modernity. She wore the new, straight-lined chemise with hemlines at mid-calf, higher than ever before, and she cut her hair in a bob, shorter than ever before. Only a minority of women could aspire to the full package. Modern clothing, salon haircuts, automobiles, and most leisure activities—except dancing and the movies—were too expensive for working-class or petit bourgeois women to indulge in regularly. The more complicated question is whether middle-class women were seduced by this media representation.

French fashion magazines and marketers present a contradictory view of modern femininity and modern girls. For instance, media and public alike considered smoking cigarettes in public to be a sign of a modern woman. The one survey about why women smoked, conducted by a fashion columnist for *L'Echo du Nord*, found that all the respondents associated women smoking with modernity. One reader compared smoking to short hair as a signifier of feminine modernity. She explained that, being "a bit coquette," she liked how smoking "permits me to adopt poses." Another who smoked as a "convinced feminist" claimed smoking as a right.[2] Yet only 5 of 240 female figures on *Vogue* and *Femina* covers held cigarettes, and barely 3 percent of the hundreds of photographs of *les élégantes* at showcase fashion events between 1920 and 1936 held cigarettes.[3] Even ads for and articles about cigarettes were diffident; most cigarette ads did not display women smoking and most articles stressed that smoking showed off "your beautiful hands and graceful gestures" or "marvelous cigarette case," rather than any physiological gratification. Recommendations that women only smoke in the privacy of their home, especially in studio rooms (informal rooms that accommodated a few intimate friends) was another sign of uneasiness about women smoking.[4] Journalists were not worried about health risks, which were mainly unidentified at that time, but about women trying out new behaviors in public. Here, as elsewhere, they compromised on hybrid modernity.

Other representations of modern femininity were equally qualified. Cover drawings exhibit dozens of automobiles, but few women drivers. Inside issues, journalists informed readers that Parisiennes, role models in modernity, were driving, initially as sportswomen and later for everyday activities.[5] As the closed sedan became more popular, fashion columnists abandoned the idea of wearing special clothing, especially veils to protect women's complexion from the wind. (In general, veils were fading from public sight; only widows and older provincial women wore them.)[6] *Femina* continued to engage in cross-promotion of automobiles and clothes by cosponsoring an annual contest to select the most elegantly dressed women driver and lauded women drivers and passengers who coordinated their clothes with the upholstery in their cars.[7] Here too, there were limits to the modernity of the women promoted by fashion magazines. The emphasis was on their appearance, not their activity.

While magazine covers, fashion spreads, and advertisements were full of images of youthful women, articles and advertising texts paid more attention to the modern woman ( *femme moderne*) than the modern girl ( *fille moderne* or *grande jeune fille moderne*). Journalists did not specify the age of the modern woman, only her activities, her slim and supple physique, and, of course, the products and services "needed" for her to be, to seem to be, modern. Systematic reading of magazine contents leaves the impression that many readers were not young, agile, and slender, though they must have wanted to be, to subscribe to magazines that glorified youth, agility, and thinness. Although these magazines were swayed by the infinite marketing possibilities of products to help women stay young and slim, their position was also an expression of a new cultural preference for youthful, lean, and limber female bodies. This preference survived the clamor about the return of the natural waistline, tighter bodices, and fuller skirts in 1929–30, indicating that the penchant for youthful-looking women was more than a response to new clothing or to the loss of so many young men during the Great War.

## Young and Single?

Because French fashion magazines rarely specified the age, marital status, or occupations of modern women, we must guess their age, status, and pastimes. On the rare occasion that these magazines focused on the modern girl as opposed to the modern woman, they defined *jeunes filles* as single women between the ages of eighteen and twenty-five, with a subcategory of *grandes jeunes filles,* aged twenty to twenty-five years. Only the subcategory of *grandes jeunes filles* was labeled modern.[8]

Most *grandes jeunes filles* had finished their schooling. Although an increasing number of young bourgeoises attended university after 1924 (when a decree making the baccalaureate identical in boys and girls *lycées* facilitated young women's access to university), this privileged minority attracted far less attention from *Vogue* Paris than *Vogue* New York paid to coeds in the United States. A *Vogue* Paris contributor complained that there were "too many young women, young girls, who think of nothing but amusing themselves."[9] *Femina* was more interested and positive. An article entitled "The Young Woman of 1930" praised her as "studious, simple in appearance, yet quite elegant. She is enrolled at the [Ecole des Hautes Etudes en] Sciences Politiques but does not neglect dancing or bridge."[10] Fashion weeklies took a position closer to *Vogue*'s. When monthlies arranged social or charitable events other than balls, they chose golf or bridge tournaments, which attracted few young women.[11] One reason for these editorial choices was that these magazines did not target young women as opposed to their mothers. Most were interested only in young single women who remained at home until marriage.

Although the message about staying home until marriage was moral, magazines had a material interest in promoting wedding apparel and accessories. In the 1920s, *La Mode, La Mode Illustrée,* and *Le Petit Echo de la Mode* advised mothers to keep their daughters at school and safely in the family setting past the age of sixteen, so that they could protect their "innocence" and teach them to manage a household. One article acknowledged that this period of time together developed strong mother-daughter bonds and warned that the marriage of an only daughter or of the last daughter in the family was emotionally wrenching for a mother, leaving her in "an empty void."[12] Materially, entire issues on weddings were devoted to mothers' preparations for their daughters' weddings. Reading between the lines, one can infer that these preparations diverted maternal attention from the impending departure of the daughters.

In 1926, the "Spring Weddings" issue of *La Mode Pratique* began with compiling the trousseau. Another article describing the seating plan, courses, and attire for the dinner party hosted by the parents of the new fiancée after the marriage contract had been signed. This article devoted as many lines to the afternoon dress of the mother of the bride as it did to the afternoon dress worn by the bride-to-be. For family gatherings preceding the wedding, mothers could wear dresses they had previously worn; for the ceremony, they needed a new afternoon dress in a neutral gray or even black, which was "not the least sad for a wedding." Not incidentally, given a middle-class readership, this dress could serve for other extended family dinners. The bride-to-be should have at least one new afternoon frock for these preliminaries and a new white gown for the wedding.[13] The clothes worn by the bride, the mother of the bride, and the female attendants displayed the bride's family's social capital. If bridal gowns served a constant social purpose, styles varied. In the early 1920s, they were not supposed to be "too fashionable" or "too modern," but by mid-decade, they had become modern, which is to say that they were simpler, straighter, and sometimes shorter than earlier in the decade. By 1930, one could purchase bridal attire consisting of white pleated skirts and white silk pullovers with racquets embroidered on them, accessorized with a headband made famous by the tennis diva Suzanne Lenglen. Even in the countryside, brides wore modern gowns.[14] In the 1930s, bridal gowns reverted to longer, full-skirted styles.[15]

When these magazines acknowledged that some young women had to study or work away from home in the 1920s, they expressed admiration and sympathy for them, because "young women are made for family life."[16] Although society magazines virtually ignored husbands, they did not, in compensation, validate single women. For a few years after the armistice, women's magazines worried about the large number of war widows and daughters of bourgeois families that could no longer afford to provide a dowry.[17] The spiritual columnist in *Le Petit Echo de la Mode* urged readers to show kindness to spinsters, but only Aline Raymond, director of *La Mode Illustrée,* condemned negative attitudes toward them and advocated retiring the term *spinster*.[18] Given societal concern about the surplus of young women and the phenomenon of 40 percent of war widows remarrying, surprisingly few articles dealt with the marriages of war widows—evidence that fashion magazines "avoided" some real situations in women's lives that caused discomfort. One article strongly recommended that widows not marry in white.[19] The phrase "white widows" referred to war widows who did not remarry. The color-coded message about the desirability of remarriage of war widows was unmistakable.[20]

Fashion magazines dealt with young women's and girls' clothing in occasional features and annual issues on these topics.[21] Some spring issues considered children's beach or country clothing; fall issues provided guides to shopping for the *rentrée*, or return to school after the summer vacation. *Rentrée* issues concentrated on mothers' wardrobes, partly because children's school clothes changed less than women's wear and some students wore school uniforms, but mainly because editors knew who subscribed to their magazines.[22] Despite a small but growing number of French girl-guide troops, there were no articles like *Vogue* New York's "Outfitting the Modern Girl for Camp" in *Vogue* Paris.[23] Instead, French society and fashion magazines promoted a few couturiers' lines for "mademoiselle" and Lanvin's mother-daughter outfits. Women's weeklies explained to their middle-class readers how to "turn last year's coat into a coat for your daughter."[24]

From the first, society magazines gushed that young Parisiennes "adored" modern costumes and that the new simple styles and floral and geometric print fabrics suited their slim bodies.[25] Fashion magazines were slower to accept that young women wore chemise dresses. Initially, they thought young single women ought to have higher necklines and fewer accessories than young married women and that young singles should avoid black, gray, bright violet, or shiny green colors. Although they explained that these bright, shiny colors were not flattering to young women, their attitude reflected disdain for gaudy clothing and bold fashion statements in general and for young women in particular.[26] These magazines, and presumably their readers, had anxieties about young single women "flaunting" themselves. Nevertheless, fashion writers did not uphold the stringent prewar distinctions between clothing for young single women and young married women whereby single women wore looser-fitting dresses in pastel-colored material. Prim styles and muted colors signaled purity and chastity, which were valuable qualities in a potential bride before the war. After the license of wartime, these qualities were less obsessively broadcast in young women's clothing.[27]

Once fitted clothing reappeared in the 1930s, society magazine features "Fashion for Those under Twenty" and "For Twenty-Year-Olds" recommended dresses with large collars, floppy bow ties, and bouffant sleeves, which they now found "suitable for their slender figures." Because there were fewer articles on young women's clothing, these articles most clearly exhibit what Roland Barthes calls the rhetoric of fashion, or setting up "arbitrary oppositions between what is to be approved and what is not, while appearing to make this sound natural."[28] At the beginning of the 1930s, the fashion columnist for *La Mode du Jour* expressed a nostalgic desire for young women to resume wearing traditional white or pale-colored evening frocks, but neither she nor her successor repeated that wish as the decade unfolded.[29] Photo collections show very few women wearing white or pastel frocks, except at the seashore. Even those who wanted a revival of prewar styles accepted that any revival should be selective, not all-encompassing.

In the course of the 1930s, fashion and women's magazines recognized that young bourgeois women would work. They approved of suits for young workingwomen, even though suits were "severe." Many columnists noted that young women expressed their new independence in "strict" and sober outfits for daytime and more exuberant cocktail dresses—or black dinner dresses "softened by lace trim or flowers"—in the evening.[30] So, we have seen, did older bourgeois women.

Compared to the Belle Epoque, when society magazines addressed older women, postwar society magazines ran few articles openly intended for women past the age of forty.[31] Most of these articles appeared in the 1920s, when the admiration of youth was at its apogee. Not surprisingly, their attitude toward aging was negative. Titles like "When Youth Leaves" and "For Women Who Are No Longer Young" express discomfort with aging, and the contents contend that the aging body—being fat, sagging, and unattractive—should be camouflaged by straight dresses to conceal thickened waists and tummies, long sleeves to cover arm flab, and scarves to hide wrinkled necks. Fashion arbiters further prohibited tight sweaters, which revealed drooping bosoms and rolls of upper body fat, any skirt that accentuated hefty hips, and bright colors and loud patterns, which drew attention to corpulent or curvy torsos.[32] At least Claire Lausnay of *Femina* recognized that some "mothers nearing their forties" and "grandmothers with white hair" liked "modern dresses, so svelte, so supple and so elegantly simple." Ten pages later in that issue, a fashion spread was entitled "To Remain Young."[33] As always in the fashion press, looking like something was conflated with being something. Ultimately, the appeal about looking and acting young prevailed because it generated more advertising revenue.

Fashion and women's weeklies did publish articles on sartorial strategies for older women, presumably because their middle-class readership wanted this. After being reproached by a reader for ignoring "older women who also like to be elegant," Alice de Linières penned a column subtitled "Fashion for the Good Mother." Her recommendation of hemlines down to the ankles, at a time when hemlines were rising to mid-calf, was another sign of aversion to almost all parts of matronly bodies.[34] Although columnists initially referred to prewar notions of matronly styles, they soon refocused on how to look younger and slimmer by donning "an outfit that lengthens and slims the body, makes the neck and arms appear longer and leaner, the waist seem supple." They liked bias-cut skirts, which "effaced" the hips, and abhorred wide belts, which "cut horizontally across a dress, thickening the waist disagreeably."[35] Soon titles of articles, for example, "Women who are no longer twenty years old," only indirectly referred to aging.

Ads in the fashion media promised to prevent or conceal signs of aging. Ads for facial creams had simultaneously the most demeaning and most consoling messages. Slogans for Tokalon, a cosmetics company that claimed to exploit "An Astonishing Discovery by a Doctor That Restores Youth to Old and Wrinkled Skin," claimed that their cream would "bring back youth" and that faithful users would "have a youthful air at forty." Some of Tokalon's advertising was more age-inclusive, in order to expand its market. Thus, Tokalon informed readers that "it is not age that causes wrinkles but the skin's lack of nourishment," a claim intended to appeal to younger women who feared the onset of wrinkles. By comparison, there were few ads intended for girls and young women, such as potions to stop pimples and blackheads, in the fashion press. Even without demographic data, advertisers knew who read these magazines.[36]

Although society magazines and columnists extended fashion-type marketing to young women, another tendency prevailed in the 1930s. The marketing catchphrase "young woman's dress" gave way to pitches about clothing with "a young effect" or young-looking features.[37] In the same decade, society and fashion magazines began to incorporate advice for older women in general articles, although they did not abandon the theme of concealing thickening figures. Journalists revived the honorific "Madame," which signified a mature, not simply a married, women.[38] These developments were part of what would become known as age-compression advertising. Department store catalogs also made less distinction between young women's and older women's attire. In the 1920s, these catalogs had separate sections for dresses for *jeunes filles* and for *dames*.[39] In the 1930s, dresses in the two sections began to resemble one another, and sections of dresses for *dames et jeunes filles* appeared.[40] A Galeries Lafayette date book declared that modern mothers looked as young as their daughters.[41] The concept of a separate wardrobe for young single women was fading as youthful-looking garments became the norm.

Do these marketing trends reflect changes in the readership and buying public, a decline in the proportion of young women, or developments in advertising? The answer is not simple. In the absence of circulation breakdowns, we have to rely upon population statistics, which are suggestive but hardly conclusive. In 1921, the largest cohort of women was twenty to twenty-four years of age; in 1931 the largest cohort was twenty-five to thirty years of age. (In 1936, teenagers formed the largest cohort.) However, the difference between the number of women in their twenties and in their thirties was never great. A more significant change occurred in the percentage of women in their forties and fifties: both of these cohorts were larger in the 1930s than in the 1920s. In short, there was an aging of the adult female population.[42] The proportion of young women in employment—and therefore able to buy magazines—also changed. Between 1921 and 1936, the percentage of twenty- to twenty-four-year-old women in employment fell from 60.6 to 55.[43]

While fashion arbiters likely responded to these demographic changes, they certainly responded to changing attitudes toward youth. The concept of the youth of modern women was as adaptable and commercial a concept as that of modernity itself. Don Slater argues that modernity was transformed into a commodity and an advertising slogan in this era.[44] Fashion and cosmetics publicity commodified youthfulness, using and reusing it as an adjective to sell products. Simultaneously, women's self-gratifying consumption of fashion, cosmetics, sports, and entertainments was promoted. In France, as in America, marketers discovered the youth and female market in the 1920s but did not restrict themselves to youth or youthful rebellion, as marketers in the 1960s did. Like the famous "Pepsi generation" campaigns of the 1960s, their promotions encouraged the emergence of a new market segment.[45] As far as this study can ascertain, the new demographic was only feminine, though the subject of masculine consumption deserves more attention. As the 1920s gave way to the 1930s, fashion magazines promoted more and more products to keep women looking—and, as always in fashion lingo, being—youthful.

## Active?

French fashion magazines defined the modern woman by behaviors that implied a youthful vitality, agility, and appearance. Covers portrayed the ideal modern woman as active, and between the covers, journalists described her typical activities as sports, visiting, and other leisure pursuits.[46] Surprisingly few journalists wrote about the dancing fad in the 1920s, which may reflect their discomfort with new, sensuous dances. Columnists who did notice remarked on young women's desire for freer movement and young people's pleasure in the dynamic movements of African-American dances like the Blackbottom.[47]

After early warnings that women should not "abuse" sports on the grounds that they would lose too much weight and age too rapidly, most fashion magazines became more positive about women's sports.[48] Even *Le Petit Echo de la Mode* agreed that being in good physical condition facilitated doing "one's virtuous activities," though sports were not to distract women from domestic duties.[49] Almost all society and fashion magazines interviewed famous sportswomen, though few covered their sports events (likely because it made little sense in weeklies and monthlies). *Femina,* which had approved of sports before the war, funded a women's golf trophy between the wars. Department stores advertised tennis rackets and equipment for other socially approved sports, such as skiing, in *Femina* and the daily newspapers.[50]

One reason for changing attitudes toward women's sports was the popularity of certain sports. As early as 1921, Alice de Linière informed readers about the multiplication of women's tennis, golf, grass hockey, and soccer clubs. Her attitude toward these sports wavered between the old anxiety about the deleterious effect of excessive exertion on women's reproductive organs and the new ideal of a flexible, youthful body. She resolved the conflict by concluding that "only rationally practiced sports can develop and maintain the suppleness and elegance of the figure and the youth of the body." Four years later, Juliette Lancret reported that "the intensified practice of sports" accounted for "the prolonged youth of the modern woman. . . . Hardly fifty years ago, a coquette past the age of thirty would in effect be relegated to the rank of old woman. Today, at forty, she is still considered a young woman! And even better, she has all the appearance of youth: her waist is svelte, her leg supple, her silhouette has an adolescent's smooth curves."[51]

There were dissenting voices. In 1920, the fashion correspondent for *Le Progrès de Lyon* rightly questioned generalizations about all women playing sports, noting that horseback riding and automobile driving were only for "the privileged." But even this columnist agreed that most women were interested in sports because they knew people who played them. "Additionally, sports have their fashions, their specialized, slightly boyish fashion."[52] The addendum identifies the main reason for fashion magazines' interest in women's sports: haute couture and confection were promoting a whole new line of women's clothing called sports clothes.

Some sports clothes migrated directly from sports activities. Like their counterparts in other countries, French gymnasts sought looser apparel for easier movement.[53] By 1920, French girls had won the right to wear tunics (loose shifts) in gym classes and gym fêtes. At the same time, long overblouses known as tunics entered haute couture, to be worn over the new chemise dresses or evening pajamas.[54]

Professional tennis player Suzanne Lenglen (1899–1938) affected clothing styles. Lenglen is widely recognized as "the best woman tennis player ever." She won several Wimbledon championships between 1919 and 1926 and became a professional in 1927. Her international success brought her national recognition as a "Sports Diva," because she had a forceful forehand and accurate backhand and because she beat the English on their own turf.[55] Yet all reporters paid as much attention to her chic as to her techniques. Women's magazines in particular commented upon her mid-calf and short-sleeved outfits and her collaboration with the couturier Jean Patou.[56] When ladies took up tennis after 1874, they wore garden-party frocks with long, full skirts and big, floppy hats. Until Suzanne Lenglen arrived at Wimbledon after the Great War, the major innovations in ladies' tennis wear had been the elimination of bustles and hats. Lenglen's appearance at Wimbledon in a Patou chemise dress, without a corset or petticoat, "influenced all future tennis fashion"[57] As director of the sports department at Patou's house, Lenglen proposed a knee-length, pleated tennis skirt, which became the prototype for sports skirts. Another well-known tennis player, Jane Regny, opened a couture house dedicated to sports and travel outfits. Four other sportswomen followed in their footsteps. Other women without sports experience specialized in sports attire that was actually smart casual wear (not sweat suits).[58] Ads for sports clothes featured drawings and later photographs of the most active female figures in fashion magazines. Captions interpreted the illustrations: "All movements are possible thanks to the Olympic skirt created by Amy Linker."[59]

Older sports clothes, such as "the classic Amazon" jacket, were intended for specific sports. Couturiers and couturières initially made sports clothes because "each sport was the pretext for an adequate toilette, made to serve coquetry, elegance, and comfort."[60] Realizing that the market for any particular type of sports clothing was limited, designers soon developed generic sportswear, which we would call casual wear. *Vogue* extolled Chanel's "charming" knit woolen tops of many colors paired with short, slim skirts. It lauded sports tunics and pleated skirts designed by Jean Patou and Jenny. By 1925, Patou, Premet, Lucien Lelong, and two other couture houses had developed special sports lines.[61] Although Patou was subsequently associated with dresses with natural waistlines, fuller skirts, and longer hemlines, he opened the first sports boutique. Similarly, Lanvin,

Lecomte, Vionnet, and Schiaparelli, remembered today for other kinds of clothing, showed many sports outfits in the late 1920s and early 1930s. The couturières best known for their sportswear—Amy Linker, Jenny, and Jane Regny—are less well known today.[62] One reason is that the American garment industry became the industry leader in casual clothing.

As couturiers began to show simple sports dresses, arbiters explained that one did not need to engage in sports to wear them. Initially, society magazines argued that sports costumes were ideal for spectators but soon added that they were ideal for country or beach vacations and then maintained that they were practical for walking and other urban activities.[63] In the late 1920s, Rosine reported that wearing sports dress for breakfast was now "very chic"; by 1934, she contended that "distinguished and discrete" sports dresses were now acceptable for daytime social activities, and one year later, she added that some sports dresses functioned as "transitional" dresses, passing from day into evening wear and eliminating tiresome changes of costume. Another *Figaro* fashion columnist wrote that all day dresses were conceived for "sports, comfort, and liberty." Loose bodices and pleated skirts permitted "all the coming and goings and various movements of an alert sportswoman."[64]

Women's weeklies were slower to welcome sports clothing into general usage, perhaps because their readers did not take country or beach vacations. When these weeklies did accept sportswear as everyday wear, they stressed its practicality for errands, with no mention of saving the wearer from frequent changes of costume—suggesting that they never had changed costume that often. By 1937, Lucy called sports outfits "the most practical and chic solution for doing everything. There is no need to be an outdoor sports specialist to wear clothing of this type, which is admitted everywhere when it is correct and elegant." Her *Mode du Jour* column explained that there were two categories of sports apparel: one for sports themselves and another for the city. The latter were "simple and proper models comfortable for walking, driving, and shopping."[65]

The best evidence that fashion reporting on sportswear was generally realistic is that department stores opened sportswear departments that sold casual wear and vacation clothing as well as actual sports clothes and gear.[66]

## Sportive?

As simple, loose day dresses became known as sports dresses, fashion journalists credited their introduction to the influence of sports.[67] As a student of dress behavior, Agatha Young did not privilege sports per se in her interpretation of the second cycle of tubular silhouettes. She pointed to developments in technology, such as the invention of pneumatic tires, and accordingly in women's lives, as bicycles enabled greater mobility for women and required reduction of big, billowy skirts.[68] Her approach is an antidote to the literature focusing exclusively on the "genius" of individual couturiers or on the impact of sports divas to explain sports clothing. However, technological and sports determinism underestimates cultural influences, such as the modernist predilection for clean lines and mobility. A more convincing approach examines the wider phenomenon of more women engaging in physical activity, not just sports, and the impact of artistic and fashionable partiality to thin, taut bodies.

To understand the significance of physical activity for women, it is necessary to understand that numerous obstacles stood in the way of women being physically active. One obstacle was biomedical and popular opinion about women's bodily weakness, especially the vulnerability of their reproductive organs; another was the association of exercise with the vigorous and some said virile movements of acrobatics. Lingering beliefs that women's reproductive organs could easily be dislocated resulted in parental objections to schoolgirls straddling or doing routines on the wooden horse. This antiquated kind of thinking kept certain kinds of gymnastics and all acrobatics out of girls physical education programs. In the 1890s, the public school system adopted a type of Swedish gymnastics, a set of repetitive exercises devised to isolate and strengthen muscles, which bored girls and ensured that they did not continue these exercises as adults. After curricular revisions in 1908, girls' schools added rhythmic gymnastics—dancelike movements to music—that schoolgirls and their parents found more engaging. After the war, an International Physical Education Congress convened to advise on physical training approved a mix of aerobics, acrobatics, and orthopedic gymnastics for girls' physical education.[69] When the Ministry of Education adopted new rules in 1929, it still did not include most acrobatics, athletics, and sports in the girls program. While authorizing short-term suspensions from bars, two-handed fencing, and racket ball, the physical education manual prohibited all contact sports as dangerous to the uterus. Public girls schools used this manual, with minor modifications, until the end of the Third Republic.[70]

In the 1920s and 1930s, French advocates of women's sports tried to define racket ball and field hockey as feminine to persuade girls and women to play these sports. When postwar anxiety about low birth rates revitalized aversion to women in competitive sports, feminist sports enthusiasts, including Nellie Roussel, responded that non-competitive sports prepared women for their dual role as mothers and paid workers.[71] In *Sports and Women* (1931), Dr. Yvonne Legrand of Femina-Sport catalogued the benefits of noncompetitive sports and tracked the effect of playing sports on her own pregnancy and those of twenty-four other sportswomen. All twenty-five subjects reported that toned abdominal muscles facilitated normal deliveries, postpartum recoveries, and a rapid return to flatter stomachs.[72] Only Dr. Marie Houdré-Boursin, president of Fémina Sports, encouraged women to play sports because they would enjoy them.[73] The medical and maternal arguments no doubt appealed to policy-makers; appeals to pleasure, had they prevailed, might have persuaded more women to exercise.

Frenchwomen had little access to competitive sports and little support if they did compete, except in tennis, skating, and other "gender-appropriate" athletic activities. Acquiring practice and playing space was a serious problem. In 1929, just one of the eight stadiums in the Paris region was open to Femina-Sport to hold track meets. Only 10 percent of state support for amateur gymnastics and sports went to feminine societies, and most of this went to gym societies. With 565 affiliates and 25,000 members in the mid-1930s, the Federation of Feminine Gym and Physical Education Societies was the largest of the women's federations in France. This federation, which was dominated by male enthusiasts, was ambivalent about women's sports. Several affiliates that wanted to play mixed sports seceded in the mid 1920s; thereafter the federation only sponsored single-sex track and field meets. After disappointing results at the Women's Olympic Games of 1928, the federation eliminated several track and field events from their meets.[74]

Some non-team sports became more accessible to middle-class women. In 1934, the fashion columnist for *La Mode du Jour* insisted that winter sports were no longer "distractions reserved for the elite. . . . Not in our era of movement and desire to live and to profit from all that is good." Lucy mentioned new skiing packages that included bus fares to ski sites as well as the cost of accommodations in ski chalets.[75] While these packages hardly compare to the development of mass vacations after the Popular Front's law on paid vacations in June 1936, they did represent a modest democratization of sports vacations. These ski packages offered greater accessibility with some exclusiveness, a sense of "social distinction and cultural difference."[76]

In the late 1930s, the biomedical and the wider community remained divided on the subject of women in competitive sports. After summarizing research on women's pulmonary capacity, bone density, and muscle elasticity, Dr. Martinie-Doubousquet concluded that athletic events requiring intense or prolonged effort, like sprints or long-distance running, exceeded women's respiratory capacities. "Normal" women who engaged in competitive sports lost subcutaneous fat; their shoulders enlarged, and their breasts and hips shriveled. In a typical rhetorical shift from verifiable physical tests to psychological speculation, Martinie-Doubousquet claimed that sportswomen "too often forget the condition of their sex. The ambiance in which they live is charged with an extreme *masculinisme.*" Some were lesbians. At the Congress on Medicine Applied to Physical Education and Sports, Robert Jeudon retorted that sports did not alter biotypes and had good gynecological effects. He did not respond to the accusation—for it was an accusation—about lesbianism.[77] Not surprisingly, public opinion was mixed. An article in a 1933 *Figaro* supplement, "Today's Women," admired women in sports "that are less tests of strength and prowess than ceremonies" (e.g., rhythmic gym displays). Asserting that sports encouraged a new camaraderie between the sexes, *Vogue* editor Jeanne Ramon Fernandez warned that a sportswoman "risks a lot. By adopting men's ways, she will find herself without defenses when the other woman, the one they call eternal, resumes her rights." The other woman, apparently a femme fatale, was "distant, mysterious, supine."[78] A year later, a Catholic newspaper reported that girls and woman's "special functions . . . are incompatible with intense muscular efforts."[79]

Meanwhile, private physical fitness programs proliferated. In the first decade of the twentieth century, the Feminine League for Physical Culture' founded by a militant suffragist, Caroline Kauffmann, favored Swedish gymnastics.[80] This rigorous exercise regimen did not attract many adult women, but the public continued to link women's physical exercise and sports clothes to feminism. *Vogue*'s Jeanne Ramon-Fernandez associated masculine elements in ladies' sportswear with modernity and ease of movement and hence, indirectly, with feminism.[81] During the transition to more fitted, "feminine" sports dresses, Ramon-Fernandez replaced adjectives like "boyish" and "active" with claims that the new styles expressed modern femininity and individuality—the latter, in conjunction with the former, a feminist quality.[82] Recall that the terms "individuality" and "individualism" were so loaded that women's weeklies avoided them.

After the Great War, Naval Lieutenant Georges Hébert slightly adapted his system of fresh-air aerobics for young men to suit young women. Outdoor aerobics attracted many young women to his colleges.[83] Graduates went into the public school system and set up private physical education programs. A popular health and beauty manual prescribed a variant of the Hébert system: daily walks and exercise outdoors or by an open window.[84] Irene Popard and other women held rhythmic gymnastics courses for adult women that fashion and women's magazines promoted. Magazines engaged in cross-promotions of sports and physical culture institutes. An article on how sports made one svelte, supple, and "perfectly equilibrated" concluded with a plug for an institute that "offered scientific means to combat generalized or localized obesity."[85]

By the late 1920s, fashion magazine promotion was shifting from sports signifying youth to sports keeping one youthful looking—and, being fashion magazines, sports clothes making one seem youthful. Lucie Neumeyer averred that "there are no longer old women, no more women of a certain age, not even women of an uncertain age. All women are . . . thirty years old, in the splendid summer of life." Sports "has rejuvenated, harmonized, fortified, and made the body flexible." But fashion was "the good fairy that sprinkled a source of youth on modern femininity, and along with sports has made the miracle of eternal charm and durable beauty."[86] Articles in society and fashion magazines asserted that straight lines, soft fabrics, and bright colors made the wearer appear to be young and vital.[87] As natural waistlines reappeared, hemlines fell and decorative touches multiplied, journalists replaced adjectives like "simple" and "boyish" with "individuality" and "femininity."[88] Longer, fuller skirts were redefined as sporty—because they allowed longer strides—and modern women were still described as active and youthful looking.[89]

## Slim and Supple?

Analysis of more than six hundred cover drawings of female figures on *Femina, Vogue, Chiffons, La Mode Pratique, La Mode,* and *C'est la Mode* found that almost every one was slender and many were skinny (though not one was as emaciated as "top models" in the 1970s). In the 1920s, cover and internal drawings privileged nearly straight figures, and after 1930, the tall, slim figures took on a subtle, smooth curvature. Botanic metaphors like "string bean" or "vine" replaced the geometric terms used to describe these images in the 1920s. While photographs of famous women presented a greater variety of body types, the overall message was that the ideal reader was lanky. Photos of women athletes and the discourse about sports clothes implied that the modern woman was also limber.

Internally, articles and advertisements reinforced the messages about the desirability of being slim and flexible.

Department store mannequins repeated the messages. In 1922, the administrator of Galeries Lafayette, Jerome Le Marechal, asked mannequin makers to sculpt, not from living models, but from drawings by art deco artists. At the 1925 international exhibition, another firm introduced extremely tall and thin mannequins, and afterward their popularity spread rapidly throughout France. The major supplier, Victor-Napoleon Siegel, owned sixty-seven plants and employed more than two thousand workers in 1927. In the language of a contemporary fashion reviewer, his mannequins represented "Dianas in love with fresh air and with sport." In other words, they combined ancient and modern ideals of feminine physique. Another example of artistic influence can be seen in the "*style moderne*" mannequins of the 1930s. In its ultimate expression at the international exhibition of 1937, this fad produced display models all in white, with blank eyes, resembling ancient Greek statues. According to Tag Gronberg, the effacement of display models displaces desire from the female body to the commodity on display.[90] But surely these display models conveyed something about the desirability of the slender body under the clothing?

Given the ubiquity and uniformity of art deco representations of women's bodies on the covers of fashion magazines, mail-order catalogs, department store flyers, department store and ladies' wear shop window and floor displays, they must have influenced bodily aspirations among their subscribers and customers. Moreover, the art deco predilection for bodies without bulges merely exaggerated earlier ideals of feminine beauty. Nineteenth-century French artists depicted little fat on female nudes. With the exception of the Courbet's painting *The Source,* French nudes were not pear-shaped. In her study of the female nude, Linda Nead posits that the fleshiness and fuzzy outlines of Toulouse-Lautrec's paintings of prostitutes' bodies reflect a fear of fat as excess, a false boundary, in the artistic aesthetic.[91] Modern fashion design and plates exhibited a similar aversion toward fleshy, flabby bodies. Both clothing and illustrations communicated this aversion to consumers of fashion.

In turn, physical fitness advocates who promised to deliver the small breasts, flat stomachs, and slightly rounded hips of the Venus de Milo evoked artistic ideals. When naval lieutenant Georges Hébert advertised feminine aerobics, he argued that his natural program enhanced true beauty, defined classically as harmonious proportions and graceful movements. His illustration was a photo of the moderately curved torso of an ancient statue.[92] Into the 1930s, purveyors of physical culture claimed that they could sculpt women's bodies to meet the classical canons for beauty.[93]

## Corsets?

Fashion discourse about foundation garments demonstrates that the switch from a curvilinear to a rectilinear line in women's apparel altered assumptions about the ideal shape of the female body. From the mid 1880s through 1908, the fashion press linked the desired hourglass figure with a stayed and laced corset (fig. 13). After 1908, Poiret and Vionnet claimed to have "liberated" women from the corset. Poiret ridiculed the undergarment for dividing women's body "into two lobes, like tugboats pulling barges." More positively, if equally imperially, Vionnet told an interviewer that she "wanted to impose on my clients a respect for their bodies, the practice of exercise and rigorous hygiene that would forever rid them of the artificial armor that had deformed them."[94] Criticisms of cinched waists and overflowing breasts and hips and praise for thin, taut, and straight bodies were common in women's magazines.

Discarding or reforming corsets was part of a larger process of streamlining ladies underwear in tandem with their outerwear. Under the new, slimmer dresses, women could not wear cumbersome items of underwear, such as crinolines, which survived only for *robes de style* and other full-skirted evening gowns. With encouragement from the lingerie industry, women replaced full-length slips with combination panty-slips, which molded to the body. Other changes included the substitution of cheaper, more easily washed fabrics, like thin cotton or rayon for linen and silk, which improved personal hygiene as well as reducing costs and easing maintenance.[95] Note the familiar modernist litany of sleeker lines, greater mobility, and practicality combined with an equally modernist quality: hygiene. Although magazine and catalog descriptions praised the delicate fabrics and lace insets, they did not mention the possibilities of women enjoying the sensual pleasure of silky material sliding over the skin or of women feeling feminine and respectably—because quite privately—seductive.

Although fashion arbiters seldom cited medical criticism about corsets, their disdain for corsets built upon a century-long hygienic campaign against corsets. By the Belle Epoque, medical popularizers had accepted that mature—meaning portly—women refused to abandon corsets, which these hygienists attributed more to coquetry than to the medically acceptable reason of stabilizing internal

FIGURE 13. Corset, Fourreau Berthe Sauvigny, 1905. C1. Photograph
by Françoise Rivière. Courtesy, Archives de Paris.

organs. Hygienists targeted metal stays and tight lacing for adolescent girls and
pregnant women. Without presenting any evidence of debility from corsets or stays,
they raised doubts about corsets' deforming girls and fetuses.[96] In the prewar
decade, the number of adolescent girls and pregnant women wearing stiff, back-
laced corsets fell. Many girls and young women turned to garter belts to hold up

stockings.[97] As they matured, they were unaccustomed to corsets and averse to wearing them as long as their figures remained acceptably lean. Pregnant women wore expandable pregnancy belts to support their distended abdomens; physicians and midwives endorsed these as "rational" girdles.[98]

Even before the war, enterprising doctors responded to condemnations of corsets by inventing and marketing "reformed"—meaning pliant—corsets.[99] After the war, corset manufacturers, often in concert with doctors, produced wide rubberized and later elasticized sports bands to protect the pelvic organs, which, they cautioned, would otherwise be jostled when modern girls played sports. At least one sports corset with flexible stays and several sports girdles— rubberized or elasticized garments similar to corsets, but without stays—were manufactured through the 1930s.[100]

In the 1920s, some fashion commentators declared the corset "passé" except for "older . . . no-longer svelte" women, either because low-waisted styles hid the waist or because women's employment and sports made corsets impractical.[101] Others complained that couturiers treated the female body as putty to be molded and that women responded by using formidable will power, even sickening themselves, to trim their bodies.[102] Articles in upscale magazines claimed that "trained, slender bodies . . . fit the scheme of life led by active society women."[103] Such claims are exaggerated. Only a minority of young women engaged in gymnastics or sports and only mannequins took pills to stay thin.[104]

Although ordinary women dieted to lose weight, dieting was seldom effective. At the turn of the century, some so-called experts revised diets to reflect new concerns about fat and carbohydrates, but as many prescribed alarmingly high doses of thyroid extracts and iodine for weight loss.[105] These experts made contact with the home economics movement led by Mme. Moll-Weiss, author of several books on home economics and, under the pseudonym Lucie-Laure, a columnist in women's magazines.[106] New and questionable techniques for reducing weight infiltrated women's health manuals and medical advice columns in women's magazines.[107] Women's health manuals denounced thyroid extracts but endorsed dubious techniques like fasting and cold showers.[108] The number of ads for slimming bath salts, creams, and thyroid and iodine pills soared. Unlike most ads, diet ads shunned graphics for text promising that the product would produce "the silhouette of a vine, without apparent contours" required for "la mode."[109] By the 1930s, a book entitled *Stay Slim* advocated dieting primarily for aesthetic reasons. The author approved herbal and iodine compresses to spot reduce and wearing "very tight corsets in the daytime, and an elastic belt around the stomach at night."[110] The probability of these diets or devices having anything but temporary results is very tiny.

In addition to and often instead of exercising, playing sports, and dieting, most Frenchwomen kept their foundation garments. In the 1920s, shopping guides for Americans visiting Paris explained that Frenchwomen endorsed "the fundamental art of corseting . . . in spite of the simplification of line in clothes." Couturiers and couturières demand "an elasticized girdle if nothing else. Even chez Vionnet, who advocates freedom in movement and unrestrained lines . . . you might be told to go to a *corsetière.* "Guides gave addresses for ten to twelve corset shops and telephone numbers for *corsetières* who brought samples to hotels to fit customers privately.[111] Fitting was a problem because women indoctrinated about the value of lithe bodies tended to "underestimate" their measurements. Mme. Coullaud-Minier, president of the Corset Employers Syndicate, who taught courses for corset salesclerks, recommended ignoring customers' orders: "If she says she takes a little size 66, bring her a size 68."[112]

Frenchwomen may have preferred made-to-measure corsets, but corset manufacturers had developed and marketed standard-sized corsets and girdles. One of Colette's vignettes reveals the progress made by foundation garments. In it, a *corsetière* warns the protagonist that women who wear ready-made corsets, like her, will end up with flabby stomachs. She would rearrange the flab into "a divine silhouette; no more hips, stomach, or rear than a bottle of Rhine wine, and especially, the chest of a youth."[113]

The corset industry reacted to changes in silhouette. For a few years, the Corset Employers Syndicate and American companies like Lily of France waged war on chemise dresses with loose-fitting skirts. When tighter skirts returned around 1924, there was a rapprochement. Many designers now reported that they expected their customers to wear girdles. Later in the decade, leading manufacturers welcomed the reappearance of the natural waistline.[114] Meanwhile, most corset makers adapted their products. Technical changes like knitting rayon with rubber and later with elastic produced lighter and washable corsets and girdles, which were therefore more comfortable and easier to clean.[115] Because the new, slimmer skirts revealed the contours of the hips and upper thighs, manufacturers developed girdles that molded the torso from the bust down the thighs (fig. 14). Corset companies also adapted sales pitches to the new reality. Dr. Clarins marketed a girdle "without stays, straps, or buckles[;] it adds no thickness, causes no dis-

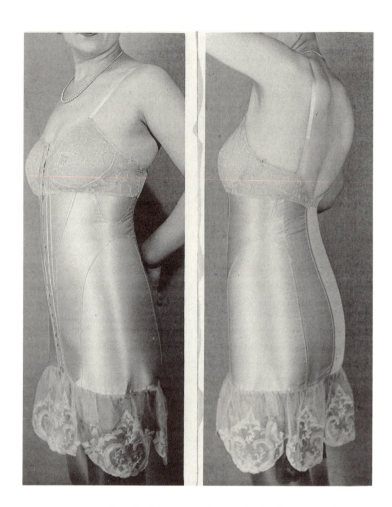

FIGURE 14. Cadolle girdle, 1934. Photographed and reproduced
by kind permission of the Archives de Paris.

comfort." With the advertising slogan "To be beautiful with pleasure, follow fashion with ease," Claverie Company launched its "Thousandth Creation, the Easter
Flowers Corset." Ads for corsets appealed directly to the modern woman, who
"will not accept losing her habits of suppleness, well-being, and sinuous grace." [116]

Far from falling, corset and girdle production and retailing rose. In 1926, Paris
counted forty wholesale corset firms, most of which also sold girdles, as well as
thirty made-to-measure corset shops. Even then, when the waistline was low, seven firms specialized in stays for corsets. [117] By 1933, there were sixty-nine corset
companies in the capital. Claverie, a large company founded in 1880, had two large

factories and three provincial branches that together employed eight hundred work-ers.[118] In the winter of 1918–19, the Au Printemps catalog offered seven corsets costing between 12 and 33 francs; in 1925–26, the same catalog carried twice as many corsets and girdles priced from 14 to 95 francs. Stretchy corsets (with stays) and girdles (without stays) helped most *bourgeoises* adapt to new body standards; silk stockings were not as widely adopted. Corsets and girdles were the most ex-pensive items of lingerie in catalogs, but silk stockings came a close second. Prices for stockings reached 55 francs for "our Printemps brand stockings in pure silk from the Cevennes, our most elegant and solid stocking."[119] At a special hosiery shop in Paris, the prices were higher, topping 100 francs for hand-sewn, fine mesh, flesh-colored silk stockings.[120] Cotton, woolen, and rayon stockings cost be-tween 2.95 to 19.50 in the late 1920s and early 1930s. The Belle Jardinière cata-log sold cotton, woolen, and rayon stockings at slightly lower prices.[121]

Fashion magazines themselves reveal the fallacy of premature announce-ments of the demise of the corset. In 1921, *La Mode Pratique* explained that the new lightweight dress fabrics clung to the body, so even gathered skirts required a long foundation garment to constrict the hips and thighs. Questioned by readers who thought they were rid of corsets, the editors answered that the "new undergarment gave the silhouette a . . . purity of line that 99 women out of 100 cannot attain without it."[122] In 1922, *La Mode Illustrée* reported that low-waisted dress styles meant "nearly flat and unadorned bodices, which are not attractive without a corset of impeccable cut." Captions for the illustrations that accompanied this article indicated pattern numbers so that readers could make the corsets. Other women's magazines also published and publicized corset patterns through the 1920s.[123] No doubt the cost of ready-made corsets encouraged home production.

Society magazines also insisted on a corset under the new line.[124] Regular columns on corsets in *L'Officiel de la Couture* praised luxury items "that give the silhouette the extreme slenderness and suppleness without which there can be no real elegance."[125] Journalists explained that the return of the natural waist-line in the late 1920s meant a return to corsets, complete with stays and laces (though the laces might be on the sides of the garment and hooks and eyes played as important a role as laces did).[126]

Of course there were back shots of women in corsets with partly undone laces trailing down their backs, looking like voluptuous presents being opened, as in Horst P. Horst's photograph entitled "Mainbocher Corset." There were also fa-mous shots of woman in partly unlaced corsets reclining seductively, like Brassai's photograph of a black-lace corset. These iconic photographs resemble the nostalgic and erotic representations of corsets in *Victoria's Secret* today.[127] Generally, fashion photographers, journalists, advertisers, and consumers promoted reformed corsets and girdles and associated them with the smooth lines of modernity.

Although French fashion marketers paid homage to the modern girl, their notion of who she was deviated from the widespread image of the young, single, lean, and limber woman. Their ideal readers were clearly mature, married women, many of them mothers, who wanted to look young, slim, and active. After some flirtation with the modern girl in the 1920s, these magazines addressed adult women whose numbers were growing and whose disposable income attracted advertisers. Their relentless promotion of products to look and (they implied) stay young, thin, and agile expressed more than advertisers' desires. Attention to youthful appearance echoed a postwar disposition to value youth, a disposition that lasted for at least two decades and more. Illustrations and articles alike articulated an aversion toward aging and especially thickening bodies or sagging body parts. As magazines and marketers worked out the particulars of this repugnance, they replaced entire categories like "young women's dresses" with dresses with "a young effect" or "young-looking features."

Although fashion arbiters expressed some anxieties about women's sports, they approved of ladies' sports, that is to say, a limited number of single and team sports with little bodily contact. Their stated reason for approval was that sports kept women youthful and agile; their unstated reason was profit from sports or casual clothes advertising. Moving quickly beyond promoting sports clothes designed for particular sports, fashion arbiters followed haute couture and confection in publicizing sports clothes for spectators at sports events, then for walking or shopping, and finally for almost all daytime activities. By the late 1920s, fashion magazine slogans had shifted from sports and sports clothes that signified youth to sports and sports clothes that made the wearer look youthful.

The penchant for tall, straight physiques can be traced to the ubiquitous art deco representations of women's bodies on the covers of fashion magazines, mail-order catalogs, department store flyers, department store and ladies' wear shop window and floor displays. Ridicule of the cinched waists with bulging breasts and hips of earlier generations of women and acclaim for slimmer, firmer bodies were leitmotifs in women's magazines. Reading between the lines or perusing advertisements undermines these leitmotifs. Despite proclaiming the corset dead—except for older, plumper women—fashion columnists and advertisers recommended expandable corsets or elasticized girdles, albeit to compress the hips and thighs, rather than the waist. Corset and girdle production and retailing expanded, rather than shrank. On this subject, the press both misrepresented and accurately represented the realities of women's bodies and activities.

# Epilogue

I n September 1939, France and Great Britain declared war on Germany and, after several months of "phony war," Germany invaded and occupied northern and eastern France. The remnants of the French government that had retreated to Vichy capitulated. From June of 1940 through June of 1944, France was divided into a successively enlarged occupied zone in northern France and a shrinking free zone in the south. The war, the Occupation, and the collaborationist Vichy regime had deleterious consequences for haute couture, clothing, and textiles, as well as for other industrial sectors. Christian Dior and Pierre Balmain, young couturiers, were called up, and Vionnet's, Schiaparelli's, and other long-established houses closed or ceased part of their operations. Some did not reopen until the Liberation, and Vionnet never reopened her atelier. Chanel shut down her couture house and handed her perfume company over to the Wertheimer brothers, who had invested heavily in her brand. When the laws to eliminate Jews from business were promulgated, she tried, with German support, to regain her perfume company. Supplies dwindled, due to the diversion of material to the Third Reich and shrinking allotments of stock by German and Vichy officials. In 1941, rationing cards issued to Frenchwomen only allowed them to buy two dresses, two aprons or overalls, a raincoat, a winter coat, two slips, three pairs of panties, six pairs of stockings, and two pairs of winter gloves. As reported by the eminent historian of fashion under the Occupation, Dominique Veillon, the Third Reich "wanted to appropriate French fashion arts" and "crush its rival."[1] Although the Nazi regime abandoned its plan to move couture to Vienna and Berlin, it tried to forbid the forty-seven houses still operating in 1943 to engage in any publicity.

But, as demonstrated in Veillon's germinal book *Fashion under the Occupation,* haute couture and fashion survived, albeit in attenuated forms. Lucien Lelong, president of the Syndical Chamber, assumed leadership of the couture group within the new corporative structure imposed on clothing. He and Daniel Gorin, secretary of the Syndical Chamber, used their administrative and promotional skills (discussed in chap. 6) to negotiate with Nazi officials for the continued existence of haute couture in Paris. Aside from their commonsensical case that skilled workers would not respond well to removal from their families, they made the classic argument that "luxury and quality are national industries. They bring millions of foreign currency into state coffers."[2] Lelong, who evaded proscriptions on advertising by publishing albums in Monte Carlo, later persuaded German authorities in Paris to allow some advertising. The Nazis failed to decimate French couture. On the contrary, the Holocaust essentially destroyed the German fashion industry through the closure of important Jewish garment and textile businesses and the persecution of Jews in these sectors.[3]

Individual couturiers actually opened new houses during the Occupation. Several designers who had worked as premières in the interwar period, notably in Vionnet's house, established their own houses, initially in the Free Zone but ultimately in Paris. Mme. Grès exasperated the Occupation officials with her red, white, and blue patriotic dresses and her indifference to restrictions. After her house was shut down, it was reopened on condition that she abandon her signature style. A few new couturiers, like Jacques Fath, who started his house in 1939, cooperated with the Occupiers to build their businesses. Other couturiers cooperated with the Nazis to save as much as possible of the threatened industry. The notable example is Lucien Lelong. Nevertheless, charges that he collaborated with the Nazis—arising from his participation in luncheons with Nazi and Vichy officials—were dismissed during the Liberation. As in other industries, there were degrees of accommodation to the Nazi occupiers and degrees of punishment during the Liberation.[4]

In textiles, German and Vichy officials promoted development of artificial fibers and fabrics. Bianchini-Férier and nineteen silk industrialists who had already invested in rayon production formed a cartel to produce rayon. Beginning in 1941, ersatz fabrics became fashionable. In silk and woolens, the leading producers,

Rodier and Coudurier, Fructus et Descher, produced more of the woolen and silk blends that they had introduced in the 1920s and 1930s.

The Germans continued to publish fashion magazines that brazenly plagiarized French styles. A system of press permissions reduced the number of French society, fashion, and women's magazines to eleven, including *L'Officiel de la Couture, La Mode du Jour, Le Petit Echo de la Mode,* and *Modes et Travaux*.[5] *L'Officiel de la Couture* and other high-end magazines were suspended two or more times. Even the usually anodyne *Modes et Travaux* experienced routine persecution. A few magazines, though none of those analyzed in this book, came under direct German control.

As for fashionable Parisiennes, they still dressed up, especially when the Auteuil races resumed in October 1940. Nearly twenty thousand ration cards for couture were in circulation in 1943, the same number as the average number of subscribers to *Vogue* or *Femina* in the interwar decades. If these coupons were distributed to some of the remaining *élégantes,* including rich foreigners, they were also allocated to new style setters: wives of collaborators and businessmen who profited from the Vichy regime and the Occupation. Curiously, given Nazi interest in haute couture, wives of Nazi officials were not numerous among the cardholders. Some Parisiennes wore the red, white, and blue dress styles that were understood to be manifestations of continued loyalty to republican France. More wore elaborate hats that defied the restrictions on clothing or scarves celebrating the glories of France. But most Frenchwomen had to make do with fewer items of clothing made of artificial fabrics and less comfortable accoutrements, like wooden shoes, than they had been accustomed to, even at the lowest points of the Great Depression.[6]

Although Veillon is persuasive about the survival of fashion under Vichy, she emphasizes the gulf between fashion, fashion magazines, marketing, and clothing behavior in the Third Republic and in the Vichy regime. In addition to the rationing of material and clothing and the closures of couture houses and fashion magazines, she mentions the introduction of French regional costumes—the very costumes resisted by consumers in the aftermath of World War I—and short peasant skirts—fuller than the short, looser skirts donned during the Great War and far removed from the long, slightly flared skirts of the 1930s. She records that some Vichy officials (briefly) forbade women to wear masculine apparel, notably slacks. She contrasts fashion magazines' new ideals of women as maternal, serious, and ready to sacrifice to the frivolous and leisurely image of women in interwar fashion magazines.[7]

Of course, Veillon had no serious study of the relationships between haute couture, fashion, and women between the two world wars to which to compare the situation in the 1940s. The present study suggests that there were parallels between fashion trends and feminine behaviors under Vichy and in the preceding thirty years.

The parallels begin with reactions of haute couture and textiles during the First and Second World War and the Occupation. Military features, for example, navy blue colors in both periods and airplane gray in the latter period, were added to women's apparel. In both periods, couture adopted and adapted more plebian materials, although both the heavier and lighter materials introduced during the First World War had a more lasting impact on haute couture in the 1920s than the artificial fabrics of the 1940s had on haute couture in the 1950s. A related parallel is that French textile magnates increased investment in technological innovation to circumvent the loss of supplies and advance the production of artificial fabrics during both world wars.

Other responses to the phony war and the Occupation resemble responses to privation in the waning days and immediate aftermath of World War I. In the 1940s, couture spokesmen and fashion arbiters argued that wearing couture and fashionable clothing was a contribution to the war effort and economic recovery after the debacle of the Occupation and that dressing stylishly was a form of propaganda for the industry and the nation. Between 1917 and 1919, fashion magazines made the same kind of appeal to hard-pressed bourgeois women: dress up as their contribution to the war effort; to be well dressed was "homage publicly rendered to the courage and heroism of our soldiers." Women wore black outfits, decorated with embroidery, in the early 1920s and again in the early 1940s. Just as fashion magazines ran columns on how to mend silk stocking in 1917, 1918, and 1919, shops that mended laddered stockings operated in the mid 1940s. Furthermore, fashion magazines supported the campaigns of haute couture and French textiles to reclaim the international market in the early 1920s and again in the Great Depression, just as fashion arbiters did during the Occupation and the Liberation.[8] These campaigns had serious implications, not only for a few hundred couturiers/couturières and textile manufacturers but also for a major export sector and hundreds of thousands of workers employed in the garment and textile sector. Finally, there are parallels between the reception of Christian Dior's "New Look" in 1947 and of the *garçonne* look in the 1920s, including women's desire to move beyond the drabness of wartime clothing, and the controversy, though the latter controversy focused on extravagance, the former on gender implications.[9]

*Epilogue* 227

*Fashion under the Occupation* is very critical of the trivial and unrealistic quality of fashion discourse in the late 1930s, although it cites only one society magazine, *Votre Beauté*, in support of this position. Veillon is more positive about the practical tips on fashion in magazines that survived German closures in 1940 and 1941. Wider reading of interwar fashion magazines, over a longer span of years, would have modified her judgments. As I show in chapter 3, even society magazines offered practical advice, such as maintaining a limited wardrobe, mixing and matching individual outfits, and building a wardrobe around a basic piece. Magazines ostensibly devoted to leisurely and aesthetic pleasures offered useful advice about how to get neighborhood dressmakers to copy couture styles. Society monthlies offered tips on how to resist the blandishments of couture salesladies, which may seem unimportant but which nonetheless met the needs of their privileged readership. Attention to interwar fashion and women's weeklies, which were service magazines, alter any lingering assumptions that all fashion magazines were relentlessly frivolous. Although these weeklies covered haute couture, which most of their readers could not afford, they also ran columns about how dressmakers and home sewers might replicate couture styles. The prevalence of sewing advice and services in interwar magazines and other publications suggest that more attention might be paid to home sewing during the Vichy regime—and the difficult years of the postwar period—as well.

Comparing fashion discourse in the two periods identifies continuities worthy of study. For instance, the argument that elegant ladies no longer had the time to change dresses three or four times a day was hardly new to Vichy. This line of argument had been a mainstay in fashion magazines representing the modern woman as busy and active. Another example is how many of the interwar fashion and women's weeklies advertised new styles as practical and comfortable, enabling movement and mobility. Although the Vichy fashion press put more emphasis on unostentatious and pragmatic fashions, it built upon interwar designers and fashion arbiters' claims of simple and practical attire and how it facilitated mobility.

Veillon's statement, "Whereas the misogynous discourse current in the interwar period depicted women as capricious children, Vichy wanted France to be populated by women who were rational, serious, and ready to make every sacrifice" exaggerates the rupture between the rhetoric about Frenchwomen in the fashion press of the two regimes. As my study indicates, the interwar fashion press did not treat Frenchwomen like capricious children. Quite the contrary! The fashion press flattered Parisiennes and Frenchwomen as more tasteful and tactful, as having more discretion and distinction, than other women. If society magazines depicted their ideal readers as leisured women pursuing pleasures, they also insisted that these readers were independent and active. *Femina* and several women's magazines suggested that readers were devoted to charity work. Conversely, fashion and women's weeklies were aware that their readers had familial and housekeeping duties and that many of them worked for pay. Both types of magazine assumed that readers wanted rational advice about clothing for social events and social display, whether of individual style (in society monthlies) or of family or work status (in women's weeklies). Readiness to sacrifice was not a consistent theme in the interwar decades, but it certainly appeared in all these magazines in years of economic privation, such as the immediate post–World War I period and the low points of the Depression.

Two misconceptions about interwar fashion and femininity explain why historians of Vichy fashion and representations of women overstate the contrast between fashions and images of femininity in the interwar years and under Vichy.[10] One misconception derives from underestimating the democratization of haute couture styles in the interwar decades; the other involves ignorance about the modern woman throughout that period.

Until now, no scholarly study of the connections among interwar haute couture, confection, and textiles has been available. As several of my chapters document, confection and their major outlets, department stores, imitated haute couture styles and marketing, while textile producers supplied both branches of clothing and department stores. Textile producers therefore had an interest in marketing luxury fabrics and less expensive variations of them to a broader market. They facilitated democratization by remaindering returned "exclusive" couture fabrics and marketing shadow brand fabrics similar to exclusive fabrics at lower prices. Chapter 6 demonstrates that couturiers and couturières facilitated democratization through the simplification of styles and the development of sports lines that favored copying. Even before the Great Depression, they established ready-to-wear outlets, and during the depression, some leading designers made limited-edition dresses and sold dresses made after few fittings at drastically lower prices than true couture dresses.

Studies of the modern woman have focused on the image of the young, slim, and athletic icon projected by the popular press and condemned by cultural critics in the 1920s. By tracking the transmission of the image of modern women to women through the fashion press, this book has complicated the notion of "the modern woman" and extended the chronological scope of its sway. Although there were certainly monolithic elements in representations of modern women as active and slim, there were also variations that reflected the social status of readers and changes over time. If society magazines briefly celebrated a transgressive version of modernity, popular magazines advocated a more moderate version for their modest middle-class readership. One disparity was between encouraging dressing and acting as individuals in society monthlies versus older prescriptions about dressing and acting as representatives of one's family. Another disparity was between the monthlies' stress on leisure versus the weeklies' growing recognition that middle-class women had household obligations that had to be fulfilled before they found time for leisure activities. Although labeling clothing "modern" and "youthful" remained in the couture-marketing lexicon throughout the 1930s, the term "youthful" was more often (and more realistically) applied as an adjective in the phrase "youthful-looking," as the population and the readership of fashion magazines aged. In this as in many other instances, haute couture promotion introduced a marketing tool that had a widespread and enduring market appeal.

The treatment of allegedly masculine features of the new styles differed less in the two types of magazine than they differed from Vichy attitudes. Both interwar monthlies and weeklies were hostile to the extreme manifestations of masculine attire and behavior, such as trousers worn in the city. But neither set of fashion arbiters proscribed slacks or culottes, as Vichy officials tried to do. Instead, society and fashion magazines described how to "feminize" putatively masculine features by adding feminine touches, such as softly textured, brightly colored blouses and scarves. The process rescripted new styles to reaffirm the existing social and gender order. This combination of new and old, masculine and feminine features into a socially and sexually acceptable ensemble was one of many ways that interwar couture—and Frenchwomen—blended the modern and the traditional.

*Hybrid modern* is the term I use to describe the ways that clothing manufacturers, marketers, and advertisers sold haute couture styles (if not necessarily haute couture models) to Frenchwomen. This kind of hybridity was expressed in designers' artistic influences, which drew upon the statues of antiquity in the Louvre and modern, though not necessarily avant-garde, artistic movements; in the equally eclectic mixture of traditional and modern architecture and décor in interwar couture houses; and in the joint efforts of couturiers/couturières and other designers to gain recognition as artists, or creators, culminating in the International Exhibition of the Decorative Arts in 1925. Common to these creators'

products was a commitment to straighter lines, greater simplicity, and less ornamentation. If couturiers/couturières revived curves and decorative details in 1930s
dresses, they did not revert to the S–shaped silhouette, flowing skirts, elaborate
bodices, and ostentatious display of Belle Epoque couture. "Simple" and "practical" remained bywords for modern women. But the term *hybrid modern* has also
been applied to the phenomenon of the new woman or, more appropriately, to
modern women.[11] Haute couture's advertising strategies, and notably their appeals to modernity, activity, and youthfulness, would not have been so successful
without customer receptivity. As several chapters indicate, Frenchwomen did buy
the new styles, albeit selectively, and they developed a taste for modern, meaning
simpler and more comfortable clothing, as the long resistance to the return of the
natural waistline and longer, fuller skirts revealed in the late 1920s and the insistence on shorter hems and slimmer skirts confirmed in the early 1930s.

Moreover, the often-maligned interwar fashion press included references to
hybrid feminism. Although much of this feminism was coded as "practical" or
"liberated," these words were understood to mean that women engaged in paid
labor and enjoyed greater mobility. Of course, it is difficult to extrapolate from
fashion writing to experience, given fashion arbiters' habit of conflating appearance with experience. However, independent evidence cited throughout my final
chapters substantiates the idea that Frenchwomen were more frequently employed
outside the home than most Western women.

Two elements of the Vichy message in fashion magazines, but also in official
propaganda, differed dramatically from fashion discourse in the 1920s and 1930s.
One was the appeal to naturalness, which was not present in interwar fashion discourse, though it was occasionally mentioned in cosmetics advertisements. The
other was the relentless exhortation to become mothers, which was largely absent
from interwar fashion magazines other than the Catholic organ, *Le Petit Echo de
la Mode*. At most, interwar women's magazines occasionally proffered advice on
maternity clothes and child rearing. Interwar fashion discourse did not define or
confine women to their biological, maternal role. Once again, independent evidence, in this case demographic statistics, verify that this accorded with bourgeois
and other Frenchwomen's avoidance of repeated pregnancies and lifelong maternal devotion. Surely this is not a frivolous or trivial observation of the realities
of interwar French society.

# Notes

1. Gini Stephens Frings, *Fashion from Concept to Consumer,* 2nd ed. (Englewood Cliffs, NJ: Prentice Hall, 1987), 6.

2. Daniel Roche, *The Culture of Clothing: Dress and Fashion in the "Ancien Regime,"* trans. Jean Birrell (Cambridge: Cambridge University Press, 1994), 41, and Joanne Finkelstein, *The Fashioned Self* (Cambridge: Polity Press, 1991), 130.

3. Recent examples are Dylis E. Blum, *Shocking! The Art and Fashion of Elsa Schiaparelli* (New Haven: Yale University Press, 2003), Xavier Chaumette, *Tissus pour un siècle de mode: Les textiles et les modes féminines en France au XXème siècle* (Neuilly-sur-Seine: Michel Lafon, 2002), Alain-René Hardy, *Art Deco Textiles: The French Designers,* trans. Ian Monk and Harriet Mason (London: Thames & Hudson, 2003), and Betty Kirke, *Madeleine Vionnet* (San Francisco: Chronicle Books, 1998).

4. Valerie Steel, *Paris Fashion: A Cultural History,* 2nd ed. (Oxford: Berg, 1998), and Nancy J. Troy, *Couture Culture: A Study in Modern Art and Fashion* (Cambridge, MA: MIT Press, 2003).

5. Elizabeth Hawes, *Fashion Is Spinach* (New York: Random House, 1938), 70–73, and Finkelstein, *The Fashioned Self,* 135.

6. David Frisby, *Fragments of Modernity* (Cambridge, MA: MIT Press, 1986), 4.

7. Charles Baudelaire, *The Painter of Modern Life and Other Essays,* trans. and ed. Jonathan Mayne (London: Phaidon Press, 1964), 13 and 30–31.

8. Rita Felski, *The Gender of Modernity* (Cambridge, MA: Harvard University Press, 1995).

9. Judith Butler, *Undoing Gender* (New York: Routledge, 2004).

10. Ann Heilmann and Margaret Beetham, eds., *New Woman Hybridities: Femininity, Feminism, and International Consumer Culture, 1880–1930* (London: Routledge, 2004), 2–9.

11. Paul Jobling, *Fashion Spreads: Word and Image in Fashion Photography since 1980* (Oxford: Berg, 1999), 90–91.

12. Leora Auslander, *Taste and Power: Furnishing Modern France* (Berkeley: University of California Press, 1998), 142ff.

13. Contemporary sociologists, including Louise-Marie Ferré, in *Les Classes sociales dans la France contemporaine* (Paris: A. Vrin, 1936), differentiate the *grande bourgeoisie* from the *classes moyennes* and the *petit bourgeoisie.* So do I.

14. E.g., "Comment habiller nos femmes de chambre," *Vogue,* 1 June 1922; "Les Devoirs d'une maitresse de maison," *La Mode Illustrée,* 7 Mar. 1920; and Marthe Pattez, "Le Foyer sans servant" and "L'Organisation du travail ménagère," *Nos Loisirs,* 1 Dec. 1921 and 1 Mar. 1923.

15. Guillaume Garnier, *Paris-Couture-Années trente* (Paris: Musée de la Mode, 1987), stresses differences between styles in the 1920s and 1930s.

16. Ben Fine and Ellen Leopold, *The World of Consumption* (London: Routledge, 1993).

17. Mark Tungate, *Fashioning Brands: Branding Style from Armani to Zara* (Sterling, VA: Kogan Page, 2005).

18. My understanding of wardrobes draws on *Garde-robes: Intimités dévoilées, de*

*Cléo de Mérode à . . .* (Paris: Musée de la Mode, 1999) and features on wardrobes in the fashion press.

19. Lou Taylor, "Doing the Laundry? A Reassessment of Object-based Dress History," *Fashion Theory* 2, 4 (1998): 337–58.

20. Randall Johnson, ed., *The Field of Cultural Production: Essays on Art and Literature* (Cambridge: Polity Press, 1993); "Haute Couture and Haute Culture," in *Sociology in Question,* trans. Richard Nice (London: Sage, 1993); and Pierre Bourdieu and Yvette Delsaut, "Le Couturier et sa griffe: Contribution à un théorie de la magie," *Actes de la recherche en sciences sociales* 1 (Jan. 1975).

21. *The Logic of Practice,* trans. Richard Nice (Cambridge: Polity Press, 1991), 52.

22. Pierre Bourdieu, *La Distinction: Critique social du jugement* (Paris: Editions du Minuit, 1979).

23. Beverley Skeggs, "Context and Background," in *Feminism after Bourdieu,* ed. Lisa Adkins and Beverley Skeggs (London: Blackwell, 2004).

24. Beatrix Le Wita, *French Bourgeois Culture,* trans. J. A. Underwood (Cambridge, Cambridge University Press, 1994).

25. Gilles Lipovetsky, *The Empire of Fashion: Dressing Modern Democracy,* trans. Catherine Porter (Princeton: Princeton University Press, 1994), 5 and 16.

26. E.g., Christine Bard, *Les Femmes dans la société française au 20e siècle* (Paris: Armand Colin, 2001), Linda L. Clark, *The Rise of Professional Women in France: Gender and Public Administration since 1830* (Cambridge: Cambridge University Press, 2000), and Siân Reynolds, *France between the Wars: Gender and Politics* (London: Routledge, 1996).

27. "1904/1924," *Vogue,* 1 Sept. 1924.

28. "Deux gestes féminines," *L'Illustration,* 1920–25; quotation, 1921, 102.

29. Preface to Judith Butler, *Gender Trouble: Feminism and the Subversion of Identity* (New York: Routledge, 1999), xv–xvi.

30. "Bridging the Gap: Feminism, Fashion, and Consumption," in Angela McRobbie, *In the Culture Society: Art, Fashion, and Popular Music* (London: Routledge, 1999).

31. My guides are Jennifer E. Milligan, *The Forgotten Generation: French Women Writers of the Inter-war Period* (Oxford: Berg, 1996), Anna Favrichon, *Toilettes et silhouettes féminines chez Marcel Proust* (Lyon: PUL, 1987), and Rose Fortassier, *Les Ecrivains français et la mode de Balzac à nos jours* (Paris: PUF, 1988).

32. Serge Tisseron, *Comment l'esprit vient aux objets* (Paris: Aubier, 1999).

33. On ideal readers, see Linda McLoughlin, *The Language of Magazines* (London: Routledge, 2000), 5ff. On art deco drawing, see *Erté (Romain de Tirtoff),* text by Roland Barthes, trans. W. Weaver (Parma: Franco Maria Ricci, 1972), and Lucy Fischer, *Designing Women: Cinema, Art Deco, and the Female Form* (New York: Columbia University Press, 2003).

34. Erving Goffman, *Gender Advertisements* (Cambridge, MA: Harvard University Press, 1978), and Mee-Eun Kang, "The Portrayal of Women's Images in Magazine Advertisements: Goffman's Gender Analysis Revisited," *Sex Roles* 37 (1997): 11–12.

35. A.-M. Dardigna, *La Presse féminine: Fonction idéologique* (Paris: François Maspero, 1979), Blanche Grunig, *Les Mots de la publicité* (Paris: PUF, 1990), Joke Hermes, *Reading Women's Magazines: An Analysis of Everyday Media Use* (London:

Polity Press, 1995), and Judith Williamson, *Decoding Advertisements* (London: Marion Boyars, 1978).

## CHAPTER ONE. COUTURIERS/COUTURIÈRES

1. Leora Auslander, *Taste and Power: Furnishing Modern France* (Berkeley: University of California Press, 1998), 1, 20, 58, 261–62, 290, and 321, and "National Taste? Citizenship Law, State Form, and Everyday Aesthetics," in *The Politics of Consumption: Material Culture and Citizenship in Europe and America,* ed. M. Daunton and M. Hilton (Oxford: Berg, 2001), 109–28, and Whitney Walton, *France at the Crystal Palace: Bourgeois Taste and Artisan Manufacture in the Nineteenth Century* (Berkeley: University of California Press, 1992).

2. Jennifer M. Jones, *Sexing la Mode: Gender, Fashion, and Commercial Culture in Old Regime France* (Oxford: Berg, 2004), 118.

3. "A la recherche de l'âme française" and "Une Parisienne a choisi," *Vogue,* 1 Dec. 1922 and June 1933.

4. Mag Olivier, "Du Choix d'un costume sportive," *Nos Loisirs,* 3 Jan. 1926; "De la distinction et de la mode," *Vogue,* 1 Nov. 1920; and M.R., "Le Dernier cri de la mode?," *Femina,* Feb. 1938.

5. "La Mode nouvelle s'inspire de plusieurs époques mais n'en copie aucune," *Femina,* Oct. 1931.

6. Nancy J. Troy, *Couture Culture: A Study in Modern Art and Fashion* (Cambridge, MA: MIT Press, 2003), 6 and 9.

7. Diana De Marly, *The History of Haute Couture* (London: B. T. Batsford, 1980), 14ff.

8. Elizabeth Ann Coleman, *The Opulent Era: Fashion of Worth, Doucet, and Pignat* (Brooklyn: Brooklyn Museum, 1989), 9–12, 29, 44–48, 69–85, and 137ff.

9. Clare Haru Crowston, *Fabricating Women: The Seamstresses of Old Regime France, 1675–1791* (Durham, NC: Duke University Press, 2001), 1–2, 11–12, and passim.

10. Coleman, *The Opulent Era,* 15.

11. Gill Perry, "The Parisian Avant-Garde and 'Feminine' Art in the Early Twentieth Century," in *Gender and Art,* ed. Gill Perry (New Haven: Yale University Press, 1999), 108–28 and 199–228.

12. Germano Delant, "To Cut Is to Think," in Biennale di Firenze, *Art/Fashion* (Florence: Skira, 1997), 21–24.

13. Richard Martin, *Cubism and Fashion* (New York: Metropolitan Museum of Art, 1998), 16 and 37.

14. Paul Poiret, *En Habillant l'époque* (Paris: Bernard Grasset, 1930), 62–63 and 78.

15. Diane Vreeland, *Inventive Paris Clothes, 1909–1939* (New York: Viking Press, 1977), 14, and Valerie Steel, *Paris Fashion: A Cultural History* (New York: Oxford University Press, 1988), 219ff.

16. Agatha Brooks Young, *Recurring Cycles of Fashion, 1760–1937* (New York: Cooper Square Publishers, 1966).

17. Alice Mackrell, *Paul Poiret* (London: B. T. Batsford, 1990), 15 and 29ff. She cites Poiret's *My First Fifty Years* (1937) on page 20.

18. Herbert Blau, *Nothing in Itself: Complexions of Fashion* (Bloomington: Indiana University Press, 1999), 119.

19. E.g., M.R., "Histoire et géographie de la mode d'hiver," *Femina*, Oct. 1935.

20. Guillaume Garnier, "Quelques robes de Paul Poiret," in *Paul Poiret et Nicole Groult: Maîtres de la mode art déco* (Paris: Musée de la Mode et du Costume, 1986), 12–24, and notice about the Passy Couture House in "The Summer Collections 1932," *La Soierie de Lyon*, Mar. 1932.

21. *Paquin: Une rétrospective de 10 ans de haute couture* (Lyon: Musée des Tissus, 1989), 9.

22. Dominique Sirop, *Paquin* (Paris: Adam Biro, 1989), 10 and 39ff, and "Jeanne Paquin, la haute couture oubliée," *Journal du Textile*, 27 Nov. 1989.

23. Sirop, *Paquin*, 25.

24. Musée du Mode de la Ville de Paris, *Grands Couturiers parisiens, 1910–1939* (Paris, 1966), no pagination, and Musée Richard-Anacreon, *Femmes créatrices des années vingt* (Paris: Editions Arts et Culture, 1988), 44 and 48.

25. Martin, *Cubism and Fashion*, 51, 70, and 74, and Betty Kirke, *Madeleine Vionnet* (San Francisco: Chronicle Books, 1998), 46 and 53.

26. "Une Coupe savante sous une apparente simplicité," *Vogue*, 1 Feb. 1924, and "L'Elégant simplicité de Madeleine Vionnet," *Femina*, July 1924.

27. "Une Artiste éprise de la beauté antique et de l'harmonie du corps féminin," *Vogue*, 1 Mar. 1926.

28. Georges Le Fèvre, *Au Secours de la couture (Industrie française)* (Paris: Editions Baudinière, 1929), 33, and "La vie et le secret de Madeleine Vionnet," *Marie Claire*, 28 May 1937.

29. Valerie Steele, *Women of Fashion: Twentieth-Century Designers* (New York: Rizzoli, 1991), 13–14.

30. Cecil Beaton, *The Glass of Fashion* (London: Wiedenfeld & Nicolson, 1954), 183.

31. Vreeland, *Inventive Paris Clothes*, 36.

32. E.g., Comtesse Jacqueline de Monbrison Rehbinder, *12 Articles de mode, 1924–1925* (Paris: n.p., 1926), 34.

33. Axel Madsen, *Chanel: A Woman of Her Own* (New York: Henry Holt, 1990), 64, 69, and 118.

34. M.R., "Des Jerseys à profusion," *Femina*, Oct. 1927, and "La Vie féminine," *Le Progrès de Lyon*, 29 Jan. 1929.

35. Beaton, *The Glass of Fashion*, 184.

36. Quotations from Claude Bailen, *Chanel Solitaire*, trans. Barbara Bray (London: Collins, 1973), 62 and 64. On sleeves, see Amy de la Haye, *Chanel: The Couturière at Work* (London: Victoria & Albert Museum, 1975), 31.

37. Untitled review of the collections in *Vogue*, 1 Oct. 1923.

38. Beaton, *The Glass of Fashion*, 162–63 and 168.

39. Gilles Lipovetsky, *The Empire of Fashion: Dressing Modern Democracy*, trans. Catherine Porter (Princeton: Princeton University Press, 1994), 60, and Carolyn Evans and Minna Thornton, *Women and Fashion* (London: Quartet, 1989), 121–24.

40. Palmer White, *Elsa Schiaparelli: Empress of Paris Fashion* (New York: Rizzoli, 1986), 86–87.

41. Elsa Schiaparelli, *Shocking Life* (New York: Dutton, 1954), 64.

42. Ibid.

43. M.R., "Histoire et Géographie de la Mode d'Hiver," *Femina,* Oct. 1935.

44. James D. Herbert, *Paris 1937: Worlds on Exhibition* (Ithaca, NY: Cornell University Press, 1998), 72.

45. E.g., Béatrice, "Propos sur la mode," *La Mode,* 9 Feb. 1930.

46. Evans and Thornton, *Women and Fashion,* 134–41.

47. "Madame Schiaparelli," *L'Officiel de la Couture,* Mar. 1929, "Métamorphoses," and "La Mode du jour," *Vogue,* Oct. 1933 and Oct. 1935. See also Dylis E. Blum, *Shocking! The Art and Fashion of Elsa Schiaparelli* (New Haven: Yale University Press, 2003), 15, and photographs on 38, 40, 43, and 44.

48. M.R., "La Mode est surtout intéressante par la nouveauté de ses détails," *Femina,* Apr. 1933.

49. M.R., "La Mode nouvelle: Ligne simple—tissus fantaisistes— . . . contrastes de coloris," *Femina,* Apr. 1931.

50. E.g., "Toute la mode," *Eve,* 15 Mar. 1925.

51. Sonia Delaunay, *Nous irons jusqu'au soleil* (Paris: Robert Lafont, 1978), 11, 35, 45, and 98, and Elizabeth Morano, "Introduction" to *Sonia Delaunay: Art into Fashion* (New York: George Braziller, 1986), 11 and 21.

52. Marsha Meskimmon, *We Weren't Modern Enough: Women Artists and the Limits of German Modernism* (New York: I. B. Taurus, 1999).

53. Morano, *Sonia Delaunay,* 21–23, and Monique Schneider Maumoury, "Sonia Delaunay: The Clothing of Modernity," in Biennale di Firenze, *Art/Fashion,* 59–65.

54. Steele, *Women of Fashion,* 15.

55. Musée Richard-Anacreon, *Femmes créatrices des années vingt,* 44–55, Steele, *Women of Fashion,* 15, and Thérèse and Louise Bonney, *A Shopping Guide to Paris* (New York: Robert M. McBride, 1929), 29–36.

56. "La Taille basse pourrait bien ne pas survivre la saison qui commence," *Vogue,* 1 Apr. 1925; Luce, "L'Orientation nouvelle," *Les Modes de la Femme de France,* 6 Sept. 1925; "Toute la mode," *Eve,* 8 Nov. 1925; M.R., "Les Caractéristiques de la mode nouvelle," *Femina,* Mar. 1929; and "Le Courrier de la mode," *La Mode Illustrée,* 14 Apr. 1929 and 16 May 1930.

57. Bailen, *Chanel Solitaire,* 57 and 62.

58. Lydia Kamitsis, *Madeleine Vionnet* (Paris: Assouline, 1996).

59. Frances Kennett, *Coco: The Life and Loves of Gabrielle Chanel* (London: Victor Gollancz, 1989), 10 and 42.

60. Paul Morand, *L'Allure de Chanel* (Paris: Hermann, 1976), 20 and 46–47.

61. Kennett, *Coco,* 70.

62. Odile Valenset, "Madeleine Vionnet et la Texture des Tissus," in *Madeleine Vionnet, Les Années d'innovation* (Lyon: Musée des Tissus, 1994), 23ff.

63. Kamitsis, *Madeleine Vionnet,* 14.

64. Morand, *L'Allure de Chanel,* 45, and Kennett, *Coco,* 23.

65. Garnier, "Les Soeurs Poiret et la mode," in *Paul Poiret et Nicole Groult,* 33;

"Le Noir et le rouge," *Le Jardin des Modes*, 24 Nov. 1931; and "Des Robes pour le bridge," *Femina*, June 1930.

66. Ad in *Vogue*, 1 Oct. 1924, and pages on Louiseboulanger in *L'Officiel de la Couture*, Mar. and Apr. 1928.

67. "Robes de studio," *Femina*, Nov. 1929, and "Les Pyjamas et les robes de studio," *Vogue*, June 1930.

68. Nancy J. Troy, "Domesticity, Decoration, and Consumer Culture: Selling Art and Design in Pre–World War I France," in *Not at Home: The Suppression of Domesticity in Modern Art and Architecture*, ed. Christopher Reed (London: Thames & Hudson, 1996), 114–16.

69. J.L., "Toute la mode," *Eve*, 10 Feb. 1924.

70. "Pour Mademoiselle, Pour Madame," *Nos Loisirs*, Aug. 1921; "Une Romantisme savamment discipliné inspire le talent de Jeanne Lanvin," *Vogue*, 1 Mar. 1923; "La Grâce des robes de style," *La Mode Pratique*, 16 Apr. 1927; "Robes pour le bridge," *Femina*, Jan. 1930; and page on "Jeanne Lanvin," *L'Officiel de la Couture*, June 1935.

71. *Grands couturiers parisiens*, no pagination.

72. Regis-Leroi, "Mme Jeanne Lanvin, Princesse de la Couture," *Miranda*, 3 Mar. 1929.

73. Steele, *Women of Fashion*, 34–35.

74. The only illustrations of nanny's uniforms or baby outfits were in Henri Clouzot, "La Parure à l'exposition des arts décoratifs," *La Renaissance de l'art français et des industries de luxe* 9, 1 (1926): 19.

75. On pronatalism, see M. M. Huss, "Pronatalism in the Inter-war Period in France," *Journal of Contemporary History* 25 (Jan. 1990), and on Frenchwomen's reactions, see Mary Lynn Stewart, *For Health and Beauty: Physical Culture for Frenchwomen, 1880s–1930s* (Baltimore: Johns Hopkins University Press, 2000).

76. Figures on live births in 1901, 1913, 1925, 1930, and 1933 in Achille Viallate, *L'Activité économique en France de la fin du XVIIIe siècle à nos jours* (Paris: Marcel Rivière, 1937), 450.

77. "Courrier de la mode," *La Mode Illustrée*, 12 Apr. 1931.

78. Poiret, *En Habillent*, 78.

79. "Mondanités," *L'Officiel de la Couture*, 20 Aug. 1921.

80. Cheryl Buckley and Hilary Fawcett, *Fashioning the Feminine: Representation and Women's Fashion from the Fin de Siècle to the Present* (London: I. B. Taurus, 2000), 11, 13, and 22–25, and Didier Grumbach, *La Haute Couture* (Paris: Editions de Seuil, 1993).

81. Bianchini-Férier produced a blue-colored silk called "cornflower" through the interwar period. See ADR, 67J 363, Archives Bianchini-Férier, Marques déposés, Noms déposés.

82. Rebecca Arnold, *Fashion, Desire, and Anxiety: Image and Morality in the Twentieth Century* (New Brunswick, NJ: Rutgers University Press, 2001).

83. *Ouverture des nouveaux Salons de Boué Soeurs* (n.p., n.p., 1930) and AP, DEM 11, Maison Bernard, Dépots, 1926.

84. Sarah Berry, *Screen Style: Fashion and Femininity in 1930s Hollywood* (Minneapolis: University of Minnesota Press, 2000), 6.

85. ADR, 67J 368, Archives Bianchini-Férier, Marques déposés, Noms déposés binder.

86. F.A., "Romantisme ou Lointains voyages inspirent les tissus imprimes," *Femina,* Mar. 1936.

87. Ads in Théâtre Femina programs in 1921 and 1926, in Bibliothèque de l'Opéra, Programmes for Théâtre Femina, Pro. B. 168.

88. Sirop, *Paquin,* 10, and *L'Elégance de Jacqueline Delubac* (Paris: Biro, n.d.).

89. "La Mode au théâtre," *L'Officiel de la Couture,* 15 Apr. 1922. The other three designers were Lanvin, Patou, and the house of Martial et Armand.

90. Georges-Armand Masson, *Tableau de la mode* (Paris: Editions de la *Nouvelle Revue française,* 1926), 71, and "Entretien avec Arletty," *Hommage à Elsa Schiaparelli* (Paris: Musée de la Mode et du Costume, 1984), 126–29.

91. "Sur la simplicité," *Vogue,* 1 Jan. 1923, and "Chez Marie-Louise, rue de la Paix," in "Une Nuit de Mistinguette," in Michel Georges-Michel, *Nuits d'actrices* (Paris: Editions de France, 1933).

92. "Comment habiller nos femmes de chambre," *Vogue,* 1 June 1922.

93. Diana Vreeland, "Foreword" to *Sonia Delaunay,* 7, and Jacques Demase, with Sonia Delaunay, *Sonia Delaunay: Rythmes et couleurs* (Paris: Hermann, 1971), 131–53, and Axel Madsen, *Sonia Delaunay: Artist of the Lost Generation* (New York: McGraw-Hill, 1989), 178–88.

94. Gérard Bauer, "Preface" to Andral, *Au dela du rideau,* 6, and Regis Leroi, "Les Vedettes de la scène: Suzy Prim," *Minerva,* 10 Mar. 1933.

95. Y.-Georges Prade, "La Mode à l'écran: Ce qu'en pense Dolly Davis," *L'Officiel de la Couture,* Sept. 1925.

96. Photo of Brigitte Helm, *Femina,* Jan. 1929; photo spreads entitled "Vedettes de l'écran," *Vogue,* Aug. 1929, and "L'Elégance féminine à l'écran," *Excelsior-Modes,* spring 1931.

97. Berry, *Screen Style,* 24, 106, and 107. See photo spread in *Excelsior-Modes,* winter 1930, and "Pitié pour les vedettes," *Vogue,* May 1939.

98. Marcelle Auclair, *Anne Fauvet ou l'assortiment difficile* (Paris: Gallimard, 1931), 15.

99. BNF, Rondell Collection, 8 Rk 6096 and 6097, Receuil des documents concernant "Mannequins," 1938, and "Mannequin de Paris," 1929.

100. Chanel quote in Dominique Lebrun, "Les Couturiers français dans le cinéma étranger," in *L'Elégance française au cinéma,* ed. Madeleine Delpierre, Marianne de Fleury, and Dominique Lebrun (Paris: Palais Galliera, 1988), 111. Lelong quote in Berry, *Screen Style,* 83. See also Prade, "La Mode à l'écran," *L'Officiel de la Couture,* Sept. 1925.

101. Madsen, *Chanel,* 205. For an American perspective on Chanel and other French designers' efforts, see Laura Mount, "Designs on Hollywood," *Colliers,* 4 Apr, 1931.

102. Berry, *Screen Style,* 84 and 89, and "Le Style 'Schiap' à l'écran," in *Hommage à Elsa Schiaparelli*, 108.

103. Dominique Lebrun, "Pionniers et artistes française créateurs de costumes à Hollywood" and "Index des Costumiers de Cinéma," in Delpierre, Fleury, and Lebrun, *L'Elégance française au cinéma.*

1. Jennifer M Jones, *Sexing la Mode: Gender, Fashion, and Commercial Culture in Old Regime France* (Oxford: Berg, 2004), 118 and 128.

2. Ghislaine Wood, *Essential Art Deco* (London: Victoria & Albert Publications, 2003),15ff., and Bevis Hellier and Stephen Escritt, *Art Deco Style* (London: Phaedon, n.d.), 8ff.

3. Diane De Marly, *The History of Haute Couture, 1850–1950* (London: B. T. Batsford, 1980), 2.

4. Radu Stero, *Against Fashion: Clothing as Art, 1850–1930* (Cambridge, MA: MIT Press, 2004), 5, and Marilyn R. Brown, *Gypsies and Other Bohemians: The Myth of the Artist in Nineteenth-Century France* (Ann Arbor, MI: UMI Research Press, 1985), 93.

5. Alicia Foster, "Dressing for Art's Sake: Gwen John, the Bon Marché, and the Spectacle of the Woman Artist in Paris," in *Defining Dress: Dress as Object, Meaning, and Identity,* ed. Amy de la Haye and Elizabeth Wilson (Manchester: Manchester University Press, 1999), 114–20.

6. Valérie Guillaume, "Les Artistes russes à Paris et en la mode," *Europe, 1910–1939: Quand l'Art habillait le vêtement* (Paris: Musée de la Mode et du Costume, 1997).

7. Valérie Guillaume, "La Couture, une culture," in *Mille ans de costume français, 950–1950* (Thionville: Gerard Klop, 1991), 124, and Robert Jensen, *Marketing Modernism in Fin-de-siècle Europe* (Princeton: Princeton University Press, 1994), 264.

8. Guillaume Garnier, "Les Soeurs Poiret et la mode," in *Paul Poiret et Nicole Groult: Maîtres de la mode art déco* (Paris: Musée de la Mode et du Costume, 1986), 33–38.

9. "Une Mode très diverse," *Femina,* Sept. 1931.

10. "Schiaparelli," *L'Officiel de la Couture et de la Mode,* Sept. 1929.

11. Palmer White, *Elsa Schiaparelli: Empress of Paris Fashion* (New York: Rizzoli, 1986), 17–18 and 63, and *Hommage à Elsa Schiaparelli* (Paris: Musée de la Mode et du Costume, 1984), 40.

12. Elsa Schiaparelli, *Shocking Life* (New York: Dutton, 1954), 114.

13. Valérie de Givry, *Art et Mode: L'Inspiration artistique des créateurs de mode* (Paris: Regard, 1998), 38–39.

14. Untitled feature in *Vogue,* 1 Jan. 1921, and L.d.L., "La Mode" and "Silk and Fashion at the Races," *La Soierie de Lyon,* 1 Mar. 1925, and 16 July 1925.

15. Claude Silvère, "Au Salon d'automne: Portraits de femmes," *L'Art et la Mode,* 20 Nov. 1920, and Jean-Louis Vaudoyer, "Kees Van Dongen, le dernier peintre de la femme," *La Gazette du Bon Ton,* Apr. 1920.

16. "Un Journal de modes masculines? Pourquoi pas?," *Adam,* 25 Jan. 1926. See also "Une Revolution dans la mode," *Excelsior-Modes,* Oct. 1926.

17. *L'Officiel de la Couture et de la Mode,* esp. "Dans la confection," 15 Jan. 1922.

18. See the 1927 issue of *Les Idées Nouvelles de la Mode et de l'Art* or the 6 Nov.1926 issue of *La Mode Pratique.*

19. E.g., "Avis à nos lectrices," in *Eve,* 12 Mar. 1920, and ad for "Dernières créations au Louvre," *Femina,* June 1933.

20. Schiaparelli, *Shocking Life,* 59 and 71.

21. "La Despotique et séduisante souveraineté de la mode vue par la Princesse

Bibesco," *Excelsior-Modes,* spring 1930, and Princesse Bibesco, *Noblesse de robe* (Paris: Grasset, 1928), 24.

22. "Coup d'oeil général sur La Mode," *Vogue,* 1 June 1925.

23. "Bien choisir robe ou manteau Madame, c'est un art," *La Mode Pratique,* 5 Dec. 1936.

24. Daniel Gorin, "L'Art et la couture," *La Grande Revue,* June 1934, 609–18.

25. David Guillon, "Raoul Dufy, Paul Poiret: Une collaboration heureuse," *Dufy-Poiret.* (London: Neffe-Degandt, 1999), 2–9, and Mackrell, *Paul Poiret,* 49–56.

26. Sarah Wilson, "Raoul Dufy: Tradition, Innovation, Decoration, 1900–1925," and René Simon Levy, "The Fabrics of Raoul Dufy: Genesis and Context," in *Raoul Dufy, 1877–1953* (London: Arts Council, n.d.), 71–89 and 97–107.

27. Pierre Vernus, *Bianchini-Férier, fabricant de soieries à Lyon (1888–1973)* (Thèse, Université Lyon II, 1997), 60–63, 73–80, and 89–96.

28. Rene Simon Levy, "The Fabrics of Raoul Dufy," 99–193.

29. ADR, 67J 14, Journal général, 1919, Report, 31 Dec. 1919, and 67J 364, Dépots dessins, note dated 18 Aug. 1920,

30. Vernus, *Bianchini-Férier,* 190.

31. Georges Cornille, *Exposition de l'art de la soie (juin–octobre 1927)* (Paris: Musée Galliera, 1928).

32. "Nomenclature des cours se rattachant au tissage et a la soierie à Lyon," and L.deL., "De la formation des jeunes dessinateurs en soieries," *La Soierie de Lyon,* 1 Nov. 1918 and 16 Aug. 1921.

33. Luc Benoist, "Un Atelier moderne de décor textile," *Art et Décoration,* Jan. 1925, 23–28; *Les Folles années de la soie* (Lyon: Musée des Tissus, 1975).

34. Valérie Tello, "Les Dessinateurs textiles dans les années 1910 à 1930 à Lyon" (Mémoire de Maîtrise, Université d'Aix-Marseille, 1989), 13–23 and 39–53; *28 Compositions de Michel Dubost pour des tissus de soie realiseé par les Soieires F. Ducharne* (Lyon: Marius Audin, 1930), and *Fleurs de Lyon, 1807–1917* (Lyon: Musée des Beaux-Arts, 1928).

35. P.A., "L'Ecole des Beaux-Arts de Lyon," and J.T., "The Lyons School of Fine Arts and the Lyonnais Silk Guide," *La Soierie de Lyon,* 16 Aug. 1923 and 16 Aug. 1924.

36. Grazietta Butazzi, "Chromatic Contrasts and Harmonies from 1900 to the 1930s," in *Silk and Color,* ed. Chiara Buss (Como: Ratti, 1997), 83.

37. In the Coudurier, Fructus, et Descher collections, 1920 to 1931, in the Banque d'images at the Musée de Tissus de Lyon, there are twice as many floral motifs as any other. Stripes, often for scarves and ties, come second. In 1931 alone, there were forty-three floral prints, seven flowering branch prints, twenty-five leaves and nonflowering plant motifs, and twenty geometrical, check, polka dot, or other patterns.

38. Alain-René Hardy, *Art Deco Textiles: The French Designers,* trans. Ian Monk and Harriet Mason (London: Thames & Hudson, 2003), 48–216; F. Hinchcliffe, *Thirties Floral Fabrics* (London: Webb & Bower, 1988); L.deL., "Silks and Fashion at the Races," *La Soierie de Lyon,* 1 July 1926; and MEIM, Abonnement Séide, Soies imprimés, 1923–26.

39. Jean Gallotti, "Les Arts indigenes à l'exposition coloniale," *Art et Décoration* 30 (July 1931): 90–92.

40. Elizabeth Ezra, *The Colonial Unconscious: Race and Culture in Interwar France* (Ithaca, NY: Cornell University Press, 2000), 2–22.

41. "Articles pour l'Orient, le Levant, et les Indes," *La Soierie de Lyon,* 1 Nov. 1919.

42. John F. Laffey, "The Lyon Chamber of Commerce and Indochina during the Third Republic," *Canadian Journal of History* 10, 3 (1975): 340 and 345.

43. Adrien Artaud, "L'Exposition national coloniale de 1922 et son album"; X. Loisy, "Les Enseignements de l'Exposition de Marseille"; J. de la Mezière, Délégué du Commissaire Général pour les Arts indigènes, "Les Artisans et les industries d'art indigènes," and J. d'Allest, "La Section métropolitaine," in *L'Exposition nationale coloniale de Marseille* (Marseille: Commissariat Général de l'Exposition, 1922), 10, 14, 112, 218, and 234–38. On the exhibitionary complex and myth of progress, see Ezra, *The Colonial Unconscious,* 32.

44. M.T., "Sylviac et les belles étoffes ou de l'utilité des colonies: Tissus de Rodier" and "Rosine rêve des nouveaux tissus," *Vogue,* 1 Feb. and Oct. 1923; "Les Tissus nouveaux de Rodier," *Femina,* 15 Apr. 1923; and "Toute la mode," *Eve,* 11 Mar. 1923.

45. "Les Tissus de Rodier," *L'Officiel de la Couture,* 15 Jan. 1922, and "Les Belles étoffes de soie chez Bianchini," *Vogue,* 1 Nov. 1922.

46. Patricia A. Morton, *Hybrid Modernities: Architecture and Representation at the 1931 Colonial Exposition, Paris* (Cambridge, MA: MIT Press, 2004), 4, 6, 20, 91, 112–13, and 131 (quotation).

47. F.A., "Nos Lainages se ressentent de l'influence coloniale," and M.T., "A l'Exposition coloniale: Le Nouveau 'climat' de Paris," *Femina,* Apr. and June 1931; and "Entre nous" and "A Travers la Mode," *La Mode Illustrée,* 7 and 28 June 1931.

48. "Les Tissus nouveaux: Tissus coloniaux" and "L'Imprimé dans les Collections, *Vogue,* Sept. 1931 and Apr. 1937.

49. Paul Leon, *Exposition internationale des arts décoratifs et industriels modernes: Paris 1925* (Paris: Larousse, 1927), Classe 20, Vêtement Section Française, 23ff.

50. P. Drecoll, "La Robe et la femme," *La Nouvelle Revue,* 4th ser., 77 (1925): 188–89.

51. Tag Gronberg, *Designs on Modernity: Exhibiting the City in 1920s Paris* (Manchester: Manchester University Press, 1998), 31 and 41–42.

52. Rosalind H. Williams, *Dream Worlds: Mass Consumption in Late Nineteenth-Century France* (Berkeley: University of California Press, 1982), 90.

53. Lucy Fischer, *Designing Women: Cinema, Art Deco, and the Female Form* (New York: Columbia University Press, 2003), 76.

54. Kirke, *Madeleine Vionnet,* 119–21. See also Karen D. Stein, "Fashion Statement," *Architectural Record* 181 (Sept. 1993): 9.

55. "Jean Latour," *L'Officiel de la Couture,* Feb. 1928.

56. Florence Camard, *Ruhlmann: Master of Art Deco* (New York: Harry N. Abrams, 1983), 11, 37, and 210.

57. Guillaume Janneau, "Introduction à l'Exposition des arts décoratifs: Considerations sur l'esprit moderne," *Art et Décoration,* Feb. 1925, 149ff.

58. "La Mode au Pavillon de l'Elégance s'affirme très féminine," *Vogue,* 1 Aug. 1925, and Gerard Bauer, "Des Analogies et des contrastes entre la femme moderne et l'art décoratif," *Femina,* Sept. 1925.

59. Pierre-Marie Lannou, "L'Exposition de la Mode aux Arts Décoratifs," *L'Officiel de la Couture,* June 1925, and M.P.B., "Decorative Art at the Paris Exhibition," *Vogue* (London), Aug. 1925.

60. Raymond Isay, "Costumes d'hier et d'aujourd'hui," *Revue des Deux Mondes,* 15 Nov. 1937, 187–88; L.N., "Les Pavillons de l'Elégance," *L'Illustration,* 6 Aug. 1925; and Leon, *Exposition internationale des arts décoratifs,* Classe 20, Vêtement Section Française, 23.

61. Gronberg, *Designs on Modernity,* 33, 42, 72–73.

62. Ghislaine Wood, *Essential Art Deco* (London: Victoria & Albert Publications, 2003), 11.

63. Jean-Gabriel Lemoine, "Boutiques modernes," *Les Arts Françaises,* no. 35, 1919, 173–78; *Présentation 1927: Le décor de la rue, les magasins, les étalages, les stands d'exposition, les éclairages* (Paris: Editions de Parade, 1927), 185; and *Paris: Boutiques d'hier* (Paris: Editions des Musées Nationaux, 1977), 15 and 16.

64. *Présentation 1927,* 31–38, and René Herbst, *Nouvelles devantures et agencements de magasins,* 4th ser. (Paris: Editions d'Art Charles Moreau, ca. 1930).

65. Henry Delacroix, *Boutiques* (Paris: Editions S. de Bonadona, ca. 1930), Introduction, unpaginated.

66. "At Cyber's," *L'Officiel de la Couture,* Aug. 1936.

67. René Chevallier, "Architecture et publicité," *Publicité,* June 1931, 347–48.

68. Inventaire, 13 July 1935, in AP, 1049WC, 100 23655, Liquidations judiciaires, Jean Patou; and "Le thé chez Drecoll," *Femina,* Feb. 1926.

69. Mackrell, *Paul Poiret,* 9, and Valerie Steele, *Paris Fashion: A Cultural History,* 2nd ed. (Oxford: Berg, 1998), 25–26.

70. Marcus Osterwalder, *Dictionnaire des illustrateurs, 1890–1945* (Neuchâtel: Ides et Calendes, 1992).

71. Françoise Tétart-Vittu, "Presse de mode et dessin," in *Le Dessin sous toutes ses coutures: Croquis, illustrations, modèles, 1760–1994* (Paris: Palais Galliera, 1995), 102–3.

72. Julian Robinson, *The Golden Age of Style* (New York: Gallery Books, 1976), 17–36, and Martin Battersby, *Art Deco Fashion: French Designers, 1908–1925* (London: St. Martin's Press, 1974), 50 and 68.

73. *Farbalas et fanfreluches, 1925, aquarelles par G. Barbier* (Paris: Menial, 1925) and *Les Modes d'Erté par Erté* (Paris: Flammarion, 1972).

74. *Page d'or de l'édition publicitaire* (Paris: Bibliothèque Forney, 1982).

75. *Ouverture des nouveaux Salons de Boué Sœurs* (n.p., n.p., 1930), at the BHVP.

76. Tétart-Vittu, "L'Art de la mode, une idée du XIXe siècle," in *Le Dessin sous toutes les coutures,* 114–15. Because these illustrations were not signed, we do not know the names of these illustrators.

77. Lisa Tiersten, *Marianne in the Market: Envisioning Consumer Society in Fin-de-Siècle France* (Berkeley: University of California Press, 2001), 140–41.

78. Barbara Baines, "Introduction: The Artists and the Illustrations," in Robinson, *The Golden Age of Style,* 9–10.

79. *Femina,* 1 Feb. 1910; Samra-Martine Bonvoisin and Michele Maignien, *La Presse féminine,* 2nd ed. (Paris: PUF, Que sais-je?, 1996), 16; Pamela Francis Stent Langlois, *The Feminine Press in England and France* (Ph.D. diss., University of Michi-

gan, 1979), 55, 64, 69, 76, and 227–29; and Gilles Feyel, "Naissance, Constitution progressive et épanouissement d'un genre de presse aux limites loués: Le Magazine," in *Réseaux: La presse magazine,* ed. Jean-Marie Charon and Rémy Rieffel (Paris: Hermès Sciences Publications, 2001), 26–30.

80. Sylvie Aubenas et Xavier Demange, "Les Séeberger, photographes de l'élégance," *Chroniques de la Bibliothèque Nationale de France* 35 (summer 2006): 16.

81. Alain Weill, "Préface," *La Mode Parisienne: La Gazette du Bon Ton, 1912–1925* (Paris: Bibliothèque de l'Image, 2000).

82. Circulation figures from *Annuaire de la Presse,* 1924; and AP, D10/3 Registres des faillites, no. 97, 3 Feb. 1931; *Revue de la Femme;* et *Gazette du Bon Ton.*

83. *Le Jardin des Modes, ou L'Illustration des Modes,* 15 Aug. 1922.

84. William Packer, *Dessins de mode Vogue, 1923–1983* (London: Condé Nast, 1983), 36 and 38.

85. "Les Animateurs de *Vogue* en Amerique, en Angleterre, en France," *Vogue* (Paris), 1 Mar. 1923.

86. See the August 1922 issues of the three editions.

87. "Nos artistes français," *Vogue,* 1 Mar. 1923.

88. *Art et publicité,* special issue of *The Studio,* 1925, with French translation (Paris: Flammarion, 1925), 20. The list should include *Monsieur,* who regularly employed artists like Benito, Brissaud, and Marty.

89. *Illustrateurs des modes et manières en 1925* (Paris: Galerie du Luxembourg, 1972).

90. *Art et publicité,* special issue of *The Studio,* 20.

91. A. Fried, "Dans la mode: Photo ou dessin?," and Jacques Fontenay, "L'Influence de l'illustration, du texte et du titre sur le rendement d'une annonce," *Vendre,* Dec. 1931 and Aug. 1936.

92. Osterwalder, *Dictionnaire des illustrateurs.*

93. *Vogue* (New York), 15 Jan. 1921.

94. Patrine Archer-Straw, *Negrophilia: Avant-Garde Paris and Black Culture in the 1920s* (London: Thames & Hudson, 2000), 34–38.

95. Ibid., 9 and 94–97. See "L'Art nègre," *Femina,* 1 Sept. 1919, and "L'Humour nègre personnifié par une artiste," *Vogue,* 1 Dec. 1925; "A Paris on voit," *L'Officiel de la Couture,* May 1926; and "Josephine Baker sur les pointes," *Femina,* Jan. 1933.

96. Mark B. Sandburg, *Living Pictures, Missing Persons: Mannequins, Museums, and Modernity* (Princeton: Princeton University Press, 2003).

97. Lucy Fischer, *Designing Women: Cinema, Art Deco, and the Female Form* (New York: Columbia University Press, 2003), 13–36, and Roland Barthes, "Literally," in *Erté (Romain de Tirtoff),* trans. W. Weaver (Parma: Franco Maria Ricci, 1972).

98. Analysis of 480 covers of *Femina* and *Vogue* between 1920 and 1939 done by Sean Richards, who also analyzed one cover per month for six years of *C'est la Mode.* I analyzed one cover a month over ten years of *Chiffons, La Mode Pratique,* and *La Mode.*

99. On ideal readers, see Linda McLoughlin, *The Language of Magazines* (London: Routledge, 2000), 5ff.

100. Gronberg, *Designs on Modernity,* 82–83.

101. Erving Goffman, *Gender Advertisements* (Cambridge, MA: Harvard Univer-

sity Press, 1979), and Geneviève Calbris, *The Semiotics of French Gestures* (Bloomington: Indiana University Press, 1990).

102. For interpretation of these images as representations of feminine pleasures, not as expressions of lesbian desire, see Molly Anne Rothenberg and Joseph Valent, "Fashionable Theory and Fashionable Women: Returning Fuss's Homospectatorial Look," *Critical Inquiry* 22 (winter 1996): 140.

103. *Oxford English Dictionary Online* (Oxford: Oxford University Press, 2001).

104. See, e.g., Rudy Koshar, ed., *Histories of Leisure* (Oxford: Berg, 2002).

105. Gianni Clerici, *Suzanne Lenglen: La diva du tennis* (Paris: Rochevignes, 1984), and Maggio Rosalie and Marcel Cordier, *Marie Marvingt: La femme d'un siècle* (Sarreguemines: Editions Pierron, 1991).

106. E.g., covers, captions, and interviews of Mlle. Fanny Heldy, *Femina*, Mar. 1924, and of Suzanne Lenglen, *Eve*, 31 Oct. 1926.

107. Carmine, "L'Activité féminine dans la vie moderne," *C'est la Mode*, 18 July 1937.

108. Siân Reynolds, *France between the Wars: Gender and Politics* (London: Routledge, 1996), chap. 3.

109. Roland Barthes, *The Fashion System*, trans. Matthew Ward and Richard Howard (London: J. Cape, 1985), 153–54.

110. The distinction is from Orvar Löfgren, *On Holiday: A History of Vacationing* (Berkeley: University of California Press, 1999).

111. Four covers with women engaged in tennis, golf, boating, or punting in *Vogue* versus fifteen covers with women doing sports (skating, riding, and hiking) in *Femina*.

112. Lisa Tiersten, *Marianne in the Market: Envisioning Consumer Society in Fin-de-Siècle France* (Berkeley: University of California Press, 2001).

113. See Mee-Eun Kang, "The Portrayal of Women's Images in Magazine Advertisement: Goffman's Gender Analysis Revisited," *Sex Roles* 37 (1997): 11–12.

114. Diana Crane, "Gender and Hegemony in Fashion Magazines: Women's Interpretations of Fashion Photographs," *Sociological Quarterly* 40, 4 (1999): 555, re *Vogue* New York in the 1940s.

115. E.g., Claire Lausnay, "Le Style c'est la jeune fille" and "La Mode des moins de vingt ans," *Femina*, 1 May 1921 and Feb. 1935; Colette "Cadeaux de Noel" and "Le Problème de l'âge ingrate," *Vogue*, 1 Dec. 1924 and 1 Jan. 1929; J. S. Taylor, L. L. Layne, and D. F. Wozniak, eds., *Consuming Motherhood* (New Brunswick, NJ: Rutgers University Press, 2004), informed my interpretation.

116. Christine Bard, *Les Femmes dans la société française au 20e siècle* (Paris: Armand Colin, 2001), 44–47, and Ann Taylor Allen, *Feminism and Motherhood in Western Europe, 1890–1970: The Maternal Dilemma* (New York: Palgrave, 2005), 166.

117. E.g., "Les Enfants et les terrrains de jeu" and "Sport," *La Mode Illustrée*, 18 May 1919 and 13 Mar. 1927; "Soignez-vous bien" and "La Page des jeunes filles," *La Mode Pratique*, 28 July 1934.

118. "L'Elégance chez soi," *La Mode Illustrée*, 17 July 1927, and "Pour nos instants de loisir," *C'est la Mode*, 7 Feb. 1932.

119. "Robes d'interieur," *La Mode*, 5 Jan. 1930, and Lucy, "Quand on est chez soi," *La Mode du Jour*, 17 Aug. 1932.

120. C.M., "Conseils aux futures mamans," *Le Petit Echo de la Mode*, 7 Mar. 1926;

"Futures Mamans," in *La Mode Pratique,* 8 Aug. 1928; and "Pour les futures mamans," *La Mode du Jour,* 28 Nov. 1929, 12 May 1932, and 16 Feb. 1933.

121. Mme. Georges Regnal, "Entre Françaises," *La Mode,* 19 May 1919.

122. Tétart-Vittu, "Presse de mode et dessin," 94 and 99, and Michael Peppiatt, "Catherine Marioton Remembers," *Architectural Digest* 52 (Oct. 1994): 82, 86, and 88.

### CHAPTER THREE. PUBLICITY

1. Fred Davis, *Fashion, Culture, and Identity* (Chicago: University of Chicago Press, 1992), 17, 103, and 123.

2. Quoted in Henri Clouzot, "La Parure à l'exposition des arts décoratifs," *La Renaissance de l'art français et des industries de luxe* 9, 1 (1926): 20.

3. Pascale Saisset, "La Vie féminine," *La Grande Revue,* Nov. 1922, 159; Jean Fayard, "Mode 1931," *Figaro Illustré,* Apr. 1931; and Eve et Lucie Paul-Margueritte, "La femme, l'amour et la mode," in *Histoire de la 3me République* (Paris: Librairie de France, ca. 1933), 1:89.

4. Jennifer M. Jones, *Sexing la Mode: Gender, Fashion, and Commercial Culture in Old Regime France* (Oxford: Berg, 2004), 148ff.

5. Jean Ravennes, "Aux Sanctuaires mystérieux de l'élégance et de la mode," *La Revue française hebdomadaire,* 9 Apr. 1922; "Chanel exprime toute l'âme de la femme moderne," *Vogue,* 1 Oct. 1923; and Axel Madsen, *Chanel: A Woman of Her Own* (New York: Henry Holt, 1990), 117–18.

6. Lilou Marquand, *Chanel m'a dit* (Paris: J. Clattès, 1990), 37 and 103.

7. *Prisons et Paradis* (1932) in *Colette: Romans-Récits-Souvenirs (1920–1940)* (Paris: Robert Laffont, 1989), 2: 1023.

8. Edna Woolman Chase and Ilka Chase, *Always in Vogue* (London: Victor Gollancz, 1954), 159 and 229.

9. Jean Charles Worth, "La Mode est Fleur de France," *L'Officiel de la Couture,* 15 July 1922.

10. Quoted in Clouzot, "La Parure à l'Exposition des arts décoratifs," 20–21; "Impressions sur les Modes à venir pour le Printemps 1924" and "L'Individualité se traduit par des nouveaux détails," *Vogue,* 1 Feb. 1924 and Feb. 1931.

11. C.D., "Visions élégantes," *Chiffons,* 20 Apr. 1925.

12. "Les Grandes enquêtes d'*Eve:* La tyrannie de la Mode," *Eve,* 3 Jan. 1926.

13. Comtesse Jean de Pange, "La Courbe de la mode est une spirale," *Excelsior-Modes,* winter 1930.

14. Paul Léon, *Exposition internationale des arts décoratifs et industriels modernes. Paris 1925. Section artistique et technique. Parure* (Paris: Larousse, 1927), 13, and Mag Olivier, "Du Choix d'un Costume sportif" and "Pour la rue, pour les visites, pour le soir," *Eve,* 14 Mar. 1920 and 31 Oct. 1926.

15. Catherine Horwood, *Keeping Up Appearances: Fashion and Class between the Wars* (Thrupp-Stroud, UK: Sutton, 2005), chap. 1.

16. Stuart Ewen, *All Consuming Images: The Politics of Style in Contemporary Culture* (New York: Doubleday, 1999), 57.

17. Sarah Berry, *Screen Style: Fashion and Femininity in 1930s Hollywood* (Min-

neapolis: University of Minnesota Press, 2000), 47–48; "Le Point de vue de Vogue" and "Métamorphoses," *Vogue,* Nov. 1930 and Oct. 1933.

18. J.F., "Les Modes de janvier," *Femina,* 1 Jan. 1920, and "Une Robe. Six transformations," *La Mode Illustrée,* 25 Sept. 1932.

19. Maggy-Rouff, "Un Peu de psychologie vestimentaire," *Femina,* Feb. 1937.

20. Magdeleine Chaumont, "Le Monde et la Mode," *Figaro,* 21 Feb. 1934, and Christine Bard, *Le Mouvement féministe en France, 1914–1939* (D.E.A., Université de Paris VII, 1989), 899.

21. Georges-Armand Masson, "Psychologie de la parure," *Gazette du Bon Ton* 4, 3 (1920).

22. Compare Estelle De Young Barr, *A Psychological Analysis of Fashion Motivation* (New York: Archives of Psychology, June 1934), to Edith Weiler, *La Publicité: Sa psychologie* (Paris: Recueil Sirey, 1932), 14.

23. Marjorie A. Beale, *The Modernist Enterprise: French Elites and the Threat of Modernity, 1900–1940* (Stanford, CA: Stanford University Press, 1999), 16ff.

24. E.g., Charles Lalo, *La Beauté et l'instinct sexuel* (Paris: Flammarion, 1922).

25. Mike Easey, ed., *Fashion Marketing,* 2nd ed. (Oxford: Blackwell Science, 2002), 5–6.

26. "Toute la Mode: La séduction des robes longues et des grands chapeaux," *Eve,* 29 June 1930, and "Tendances," *Vogue,* Sept. 1937.

27. Claire Launay, "Pour qui une femme s'habille t'elle?," *Femina,* 1 Mar. 1920.

28. "Six leçons de mode par six femme de goût," "Les Observation de la comtesse Elie de Ganay," and "Les Preceptes de Mrs Reginald Fellowes," *Femina,* Feb. 1938.

29. Cecil Beaton, *The Glass of Fashion* (London: Wiedenfeld & Nicolson, 1954), 138, and Elsa Schiaparelli, *Shocking Life* (New York: Dutton, 1954), 114.

30. Maurice Hamel, "La Parure et la femme," *La Revue française hebdomadaire,* 9 Apr. 1922, and Francis De Miomandre, *La Mode* (Paris: Hachette, 1927), 24 and 26.

31. Nada, "Habillez-vous suivant les exigences de votre silhouette," *Femina,* Mar. 1917, and "Le Trousseau de robes d'une femme de cinquante ans," *La Mode Pratique,* 8 Sept. 1923.

32. Catherine Pozzi, *Journal* (Paris: Ramsay, 1987), 129, entry for 12 June 1920, and 541, entry for 17 May 1930.

33. Alexandra Palmer, *Culture and Commerce: The Transatlantic Fashion Trade in the 1950s* (Vancouver: University of British Columbia Press, 2001).

34. The exception is Alice Piguet, "Soyez coquettes," *La Mode Pratique,* 17 Feb. 1934.

35. M.H., "Les Couturiers proposent, la Parisienne dispose," and J.R.-F., "Paris: L'Ecole des femmes," *Vogue,* Feb. 1922 and Jan. 1929.

36. M.R., "Quelle surprises nous réserve la mode nouvelle?" *Femina,* Sept. 1922.

37. Philippe Simon, *Monographie d'une industrie de luxe: La Haute couture* (Paris: PUF, 1931), 77–85.

38. BHVP, Fonds Vionnet, Croquis, 1926.

39. M.R., "La Mode dans les réunions élégantes," *Femina,* Feb. 1929.

40. "La Taille basse pourrait bien ne pas survivre à la saison qui commence," *Vogue,* Apr. 1925; M.R., "La robe droite a vécu," *Femina,* Sept. 1925; C.D., "Visions élégantes," *Chiffons,* 5 Oct. 1925; and "Toute la mode," *Eve,* 8 Nov. 1925.

41. "Courrier de la mode," *La Mode Illustrée,* 17 July 1927, and "La Vie féminine," *Le Progrès de Lyon,* 29 Nov. 1928; and Coline, "Laquelle des deux? Ligne droite ou ligne évasée?," *Les Modes de la Femme de France,* 7 Apr. 1929.

42. "La Vie féminine," *Le Progrès de Lyon,* 18 Apr. 1929.

43. J.L., "Des Robes longues et des robes courtes," *Minerva,* 5 Dec. 1929, and "La Vie féminine, *Le Progrès de Lyon,* 31 Oct. and 12 Dec. 1929. The latter refers to a Lancret article in *Le Journal* and the syndical reaction.

44. "Le Point de vue de Vogue," *Vogue,* Feb. 1930; "Toute la Mode," *Eve,* 23 Mar. and 29 June 1930 and 10 May 1931; and M.R., "La Mode de la demi-saison marque un retour très net vers la sobriété," *Femina,* Jan. 1931.

45. Chef de publicité, in Yvonne Ostroga, *Les Indépendantes: Vingt-cinq professions pour les jeunes filles d'aujourd'hui* (Paris: Plon, 1932), 1–10.

46. Marie-Emmanuelle Chessel, *La Publicité: Naissance d'une profession, 1900–1940* (Paris: CNRS, 1998), and Léon Jones, "La Couture française perd-elle le marché américain?," *Vendre,* Aug. 1931.

47. *Cours pratique de publicité appliquée au commerce, à l'industrie et aux affaires en général* (Paris: Librairie comptable Pigier, 1928), 17ff.

48. André Aubrespin, "L'Affiche vend"; "Ce que coute un affichage à Paris" and André Carriez, "Parlons d'affichage," *Vendre,* Mar. 1927, Jan. 1928, and Apr. 1935.

49. Marc Martin, *Trois siècles de publicité en France* (Paris: Editions Odile Jacob, 1992), 201–2, Musée Nationale des Arts et Traditions Populaires, *Quand l'affiche faisait de la réclame! L'Affiche française de 1920 à 1940* (Paris: Editions de la Réunion des musées nationaux, 1991), 16–21, and *1930s Commercial Art: Illustration, Advertising, Decorative Patterns, and Designs for Packaging* (Amsterdam: Pepin Press, 1998).

50. Henri Lièvre, *Une Forme de la concentration commerciale: Les entreprises à succursales multiples dans l'industrie et le commerce du vêtement* (Paris: Villain et Bar 1934), 121.

51. The exceptions were ads for couturiers' perfumes and a few interviews in the daily press.

52. "La Mode" and "Toilettes de Printemps," on front pages of *L'Echo du Nord,* 30 Jan. 1920 and 29 Apr. 1930, and "Le Mode" and "L'Actualité photographique," in *L'Echo Illustré du Nord,* 18 Oct. 1923.

53. *Annuaire de la Presse,* 1924, Jean-Marie Charon, *La Presse quotidienne,* new ed. (Paris: La Découverte, 1996), 14, and Samra-Martine Bonvoisin and Michele Maignien, *La Presse féminine,* 2nd ed. (Paris: PUF, Que sais-je? 1996), 19.

54. Claude Bellanger, Jacques Godechot, Pierre Guiral, and Fernand Terrou, eds., *Histoire générale de la presse française,* vol 3, *De 1871 à 1940* (Paris: PUF, 1972), 481.

55. Advertising rates in *Annuaire de la Presse,* 1923 and 1926.

56. MTL, Procès-verbaux, Comité syndical, 18 May 1933.

57. "House-Organs, *Art-Goût-Beauté,*" *Vendre,* July 1927. See *Art-Goût-Beauté,* 1921–33, and *Le Sucès d'Art-Goût-Bon Ton,* which lasted less than six months.

58. MTL, Procès-verbaux, Comité syndical, 14 Nov. 1927 and 13 Mar. 1935.

59. Columns from Parisian correspondent Mme. L.deL., *La Soierie de Lyon,* 1919–29.

60. MTL, Procès-verbaux, Comité syndical, Bureau, 17 Sept. 1919.

61. Ibid.

62. MTL, Procès-verbaux, Comité syndical, 3 and 20 Mar. 1933.

63. "Bond Street contre la Rue de la Paix," *Vendre,* Feb. 1925, 89.

64. *Les Elégances parisiennes: Publication officielle des Industries françaises de la mode* (Paris: Hachette, 1918–22).

65. *Bulletin Officiel de la Chambre Syndicale de la Couture Parisienne,* June 1930–Dec. 1932.

66. E.g., *La Mode Parisienne,* 1900–37, *Costumes Tailleur: Précurseur de la Mode* (1895–?), and *Paris Couture: Review of Dress Openings* (1928).

67. Ad for Librairie H. Gauthier, *Annuaire de la Presse,* 1920.

68. Fashion magazine section of *Annuaire de la Presse,* 1920–39; and René Dubois, "La Presse féminine," *Vendre,* Feb. 1939.

69. *Chiffons* changed its name to *Françoise,* which appeared in a smaller, glossier format late in 1932. *La Mode du Jour* absorbed *La Mode.* AP, D10/U3, Registres des faillites, 107, 113, 116, and 124 (1933–35).

70. Jules Piteraerens, "Publicité et suggestion," and O. Luttringer, "La Publicité pour l'article de luxe," *Publicité,* Nov. 1919 and July 1925; Paul de Gironde, "La Publicité française commence à utiliser la photographie"; and Jacques Fontenay, "L'Influence de l'illustration, du texte et du titre sur le rendement d'une annonce," *Vendre,* Apr. 1929 and Aug. 1936.

71. D. C. A. Hémet, *Traité pratique de Publicité commerciale et industrielle,* new ed. (Paris: Bureau Technique de *"La Publicité,"* 1922), 156 and 159; Françoise, "Quelques opinions féminines sur la quatrième page du journal," *Publicité,* Mar. 1921, and André Vauglin, "Quels journaux choisir pour toucher une clientèle déterminée?," *Vendre,* Apr. 1928.

72. *Femina* used la Société Nouvelle de Publicité and provincial agencies; *La Mode du Jour* relied upon Société Européen de Publicité. Both Paris agencies were located in the haute couture district.

73. Advertising costs are from individual publication's notices in *Annuaire de la Presse.*

74. AP, 1049w, 43119, Faillite Sté A. Premet, Bilan M. Boisseraud, Sommes dues aux fournisseurs au 12 Sept. 1931.

75. E.g., *L'Officiel de la Mode,* Feb. 1926, or M.R., "Tissus à la mode," *Femina,* Sept. 1936.

76. See ad for *Nos Loisirs* in the Mar. 1923 issue, as well as their ads in the *Annaire de la Presse,* 1928 and 1929. On contemporary studies, see Joke Hermes, *Reading Women's Magazines: An Analysis of Everyday Media Use* (Oxford: Polity Press, 1995), chap. 2.

77. *Marie Claire,* 28 Jan. 1938.

78. Bellanger et al., *Histoire générale de la presse,* 601.

79. "Chères lectrices" and "Les Patrons de Marie Claire," *Marie Claire,* 25 Mar. and 13 May 1938.

80. Directors of fashion magazines also remained in their jobs for a long time; witness the Comtesse de Broutelles, director of *La Mode Pratique* from 1891 to 1936.

81. Camille Duguet also wrote for *La Mode Illustrée* in 1927–28. Juliette Lancret

and Lucie Neumayer, who successively wrote "Toute la mode" columns in *Eve* for more than a decade, contributed to *La Femme Chic* and *Art-Goût-Beauté*. Marcey Ducray first wrote for *Nos Loisirs* and then for *Excelsior-Modes*.

82. See offers to readers in *Eve*, 12 Mar. 1920, *Chiffons*, 5 Apr. 1926, *La Mode Illustrée*, 12 Jan. 1930, *La Mode du Jour*, 10 Jan. 1935, and *Femina*, Dec. 1936.

83. Jennifer E. Milligan, *The Forgotten Generation: French Women Writers of the Interwar Period* (Oxford: Berg, 1996), 150, and "La Dernière Mode and Its Pre-history," in *Mallarmé on Fashion*, ed. P. N. Furbank and A. M. Cain (London: Berg, 2004), 5.

84. Vogue's Information Bureau offered counsel on "the choice of a dress as well as a perfume, a hotel, even a restaurant"; the Académie de la Femme de France offered sewing, knitting, crochet, and cutting courses.

85. Full-page ad for the *Almanach* in *Eve*, 22 Aug. 1926.

86. Simone Weil Davis, *Living Up to the Ads: Gender Fictions of the 1920s* (Durham, NC: Duke University Press, 2000), 96.

87. E.g., C. de Monclos "Conseils de guerre," *Femina*, June 1918; "Lettre à une amie," *Vogue*, Dec. 1928; and "Chronique parisienne," *La Mode Pratique*, 1922–23. On synthetic personalization, see Linda McLoughlin, *The Language of Magazines* (London: Routledge, 2000), 68–73.

88. Columns with reporters responding to readers' inquiries about "sentimental questions" appeared in the late 1930s, about the same time as *Confidences*, the first true-stories-type publication. See *La Mode du Jour*, 15 Dec.1938.

89. "L'Individualité se traduit par de nouveaux détails" and "La Mode de jour," *Vogue*, 1 July 1927 and Apr. 1936.

90. *Garde-robes: Intimités dévoilées, de Cléo de Mérode à ...* (Paris: Musée de la Mode et du Textile, 1999), 82–83, 96–97, and 120–21.

91. "Madame, votre plus grand désir est d'être conseillée" and "Les Animateurs de Vogue en Amérique, en Angleterre, en France," *Vogue*, 1 Mar. and 1 May 1923.

92. "En plein succès," *Femina*, Mar. 1935, and ad in *Annuaire de la Presse*, 1936, where *Femina* announced its new formula: "Fashion yes . . . but also life."

93. E.g., "Une Garde-robe complète pour la voyageuse," *Vogue*, 1 June 1924, and "L'Armoire à robes des Parisiennes à la mode," *Femina*, Jan. 1937.

94. "Le Temps qui court," and René Dubois, "La Presse féminine," *Vendre*, Aug. 1938 and Feb. 1939. According to *Femina*, July 1935, its circulation had reached a high of 40,365.

95. Lisa Tiersten, *Marianne in the Market: Envisioning Consumer Society in Fin-de-Siècle France* (Berkeley: University of California Press, 2001).

96. E.g., "Le Modernisme des meubles" and "Le Cadre moderne de la vie," *Vogue*, 1 Aug. 1925 and Aug. 1929, and "Les Harmonies de la peinture dans un appartement moderne," *Femina*, Feb. 1932.

97. I compared 200 randomly selected ads in 1920s French fashion magazines to Victorian magazine ads as studied by Lori Anne Loeb, *Consuming Angels: Advertising and Victorian Women* (New York: Oxford University Press, 1994), 61.

98. "Les Animateurs de Vogue en Amérique, en Angleterre, en France," *Vogue*, 1 Mar. 1923.

99. Christopher Reed, "A Vogue That Dare Not Speak Its Name: Sexual Subcul-

ture during the Editorship of Dorothy Todd, 1922–26," *Fashion Theory* 10, 1/2 (2006): 39–71.

100. E.g., "Pour être élégante avec économie," in *Vogue*, 1 Mar. 1924.

101. "Pour votre petite couturière" and "Une Robe facile à faire," *Femina*, June 1917 and Dec. 1920.

102. Ad for La Salle automobile, *Vogue*, Sept. 1929.

103. M.H., "L'Evolution de l'automobile et ses rapports avec la mode," *Vogue*, 1 Nov. 1922, and Y.-Georges Prade, "L'Automobile est reine: La Parisienne parmi les roadsters et torpédos," in *L'Officiel de la Couture*, Nov. 1926.

104. *Gazette Dunlop* issue on *La Mode*, Oct. 1937, and Stephen L. Harp, *Marketing Michelin: Advertising and Cultural Identity in Twentieth-Century France* (Baltimore: John Hopkins University Press, 2001), 192–93 and 257. On American practices, see Jenna Weissman Joselit, *A Perfect Fit: Clothes, Character, and the Promise of America* (New York: Henry Holt, 2001), 3.

105. Special contributors are easier to identify than most staffers, who do not have bylines. Among signing contributors, six men wrote at least twice for *Vogue*, whereas two male authors signed articles that appeared two or more times in *Femina*.

106. Pierre Plessis, "Le Plus beau jouet de Madame" and "Le Mardi 24 juin au Théâtre Pigalle . . . le concours d'élégance féminine en automobile," *Femina*, Oct. 1923 and June 1930.

107. "Les Détails charmants de la toilette moderne," *La Mode*, 19 Jan. 1930.

108. E.g., "A Défaut de machine à laver," *La Mode Pratique*, 16 Aug. 1930.

109. Ad for *Françoise* in *Chiffons*, Sept. 1922.

110. *Françoise*, 15 Nov. 1932. *Françoise* folded in mid-1934.

111. Françoise, "Les Jolies choses que j'ai vues," *La Mode Pratique*, 21 Nov. 1936.

112. Marcy Ducray, "La Toilette qui convient à chaque circonstance," *Nos Loisirs*, 1 Nov. 1922, and "Pour un week-end," *La Mode Pratique*, 3 June 1922.

113. Marcy Ducray, "Leçon de la Couturière: Une jupe avec un metre de tissu," *Nos Loisirs*, 1 Sept. 1923, and insert for Académie de la Femme de France in *La Mode du Jour*, 13 Oct. 1932.

114. Christopher Breward, "Patterns of Respectability: Publishing, Home Sewing, and the Dynamics of Class and Gender, 1870–1940," in *The Culture of Sewing: Gender, Consumption, and Home Dressmaking*, ed. Barbara Burman (London: Berg, 1999), 25.

115. See Von Dongon cover "The Fashion Painter" and "Le Programme d'Excelsior-Modes," *Excelsior-Modes*, Oct. 1929.

116. René Dubois, "La Presse féminine," 68, calls *Excelsior-Modes*, *Femina*, and *Vogue* luxury magazines.

117. Coline, "Prévisions" and "La Coquille dactylo," *Les Modes de la Femme de France*, 27 Sept. 1925 and 31 Jan. 1926.

118. See ad for *Les Modes de la Femme de France* in *Annuaire de la Presse*, 1919.

119. E.g., "Les Modestes élégantes que nous représentons," *La Mode du Jour*, 7 Nov 1929, and ad for *La Mode Illustrée*, in *Annuaire de la Presse*, 1936.

120. E.g., Lucy, "Les Robes habillées" and "La Maison," *La Mode du Jour*, 29 Oct. 1929 and 22 Oct. 1933.

121. E.g., "L'Elégance et le luxe," *La Mode Illustrée,* 7 Mar. 1920.

122. On house dresses, see "Revue de la Mode," 12 June 1921. On working-class readers, see "Le Jardin des âmes," 7 Oct. 1923.

123. "Pages féministes," 2 July and 10 Sept. 1922; 28 Oct. 1923, and 10 Feb., 8 June and 14 Sept. 1924.

124. Baron de Clessy, "Revue de la Mode," 1 Jan. 1920.

125. "Revue de la mode" and "Journal des âmes," 25 Mar. 1920 and 7 July 1929.

126. "Pages féministes," 24 Apr. and 9 and 23 Oct. 1921, 21 Apr. 1922, and 12 Feb. and 15 July 1923.

## CHAPTER FOUR. BUSINESS

1. *Annuaire de la Chambre Syndicale de la Confection et de la Couture françaises en gros* (Paris, n.p., 1936).

2. Suzanne Girard, "La Naissance d'une robe," *Nos Loisirs,* 1 Mar. 1921.

3. Bettina Ballard, *In My Fashion* (New York: D. McKay, 1960), 20 and 36.

4. M. Eugène Aine, "La Couture," in Exposition Internationale Urbaine Lyon 1914, *Rapport General du Salon des Industries Parisiennes* (Lyon: n.p., 1914).

5. *Annuaire: Union Syndicale des Tissus, Matières Textiles et Habillement* (Paris: n.p., 1926), and *Annuaire des Industries du Vêtement et des Tissus* (Paris, 1933).

6. Dossier on Succursale de luxe de la Samaritaine at the BNF, Etampes.

7. See ad in *Vogue,* Apr. 1924, and F.A., "Un Centre très parisien: La succursale de luxe de la Samaritaine," and "La Mode à la succursale de luxe de la Samaritiane," *Femina,* Mar. 1933 and Apr. 1934.

8. E.g., *Les Modes élégantes pour le printemps 1922, interpretées par Barbier, Benito, Brissaud, Bruneleschi, Lepape . . .,* and *Nouveautés de printemps et d'été, 1938,* in the catalog collections of the BF. See also Blanche Duverneuil, "La Renaissance du catalogue dans la mode," *La Publicité,* Apr. 1920, 91 and 93.

9. Comparisons based on prices of afternoon gowns from the principal couture houses in 1929 and 1932 in Jean-Marie Boegner, "La Haute Couture à Paris," *Bulletin d'études historiques, géographiques . . . de la region parisienne* 7, 27 (1933): 9, and prices of similar dresses in the Au Printemps, Galeries Lafayette, and Bon Marché catalogs of the same years in the BF and BNF, Etampes.

10. Comparison based on the Au Printemps general catalogs, 1919–32.

11. Robert de Beauplan, "Les Nouvelles silhouettes de l'élégance parisiennne," *L'Illustration,* 25 Nov. 1928.

12. Colin Gale and Jasbir Kaur, *Fashion and Textiles: An Overview* (Oxford: Berg, 2004).

13. ADR, 67J 133, Archives Bianchini-Férier, Grand Livre Clients, 1919–25.

14. Jean Charles Worth, "A Propos de la Mode," extract from *Revue de Paris,* in *Bulletin Officiel de la Chambre Syndicale de la Couture Parisienne,* June 1930; and Vionnet, quoted in Georges Le Fèvre, *Au Secours de la couture (Industrie française)* (Paris: Editions Baudinière, 1929), 22.

15. Stanley Baron, in collaboration with Jacques Damase, *Sonia Delaunay: The Life of an Artist* (London: Thames & Hudson, 1995), 83–84; ad for Jane Regny Prints in

*Vogue* (New York), 15 Jan. 1928; and Amy de la Haye, *Chanel: The Couturière at Work* (London: Victoria & Albert Museum, 1975), 59.

16. Le Fèvre, *Au Secours,* 49 and 64, and Philippe Simon, *Monographie d'une industrie de luxe: La Haute couture* (Paris: PUF, 1931), 58–62.

17. C. Poni, "Fashion as Flexible Production: The Strategies of the Lyon Silk Merchants in the Eighteenth Century," in *World of Possibilities: Flexibility and Mass Production in Western Industrialization,* ed. C. F. Sabel and J. Zeitlin (Cambridge: Cambridge University Press, 1997), 37–74.

18. MTL, Chambre Syndicale des Fabricants de Soieries, Procès-verbaux, Comité syndical, Vice-President Fougère's report to the Assemblée générale of 12 Mar. 1920, and *La Soierie de Lyon,* 1 Nov. 1919.

19. L.deL., "Lyons Silks and Fashion," *La Soierie de Lyon,* 10 June 1919.

20. Fitz Bénard, "Au Chevet de la couture malade," *Vendre,* July 1932, 29–30.

21. Albert Aftalion, *L'Industie textile en France pendant la guerre* (Paris: PUF, 1924), 41ff., and Jean-Claude Daumas, *L'Amour du drap: Blin et Blin, Elbeuf; Histoire d'une entreprise lainière familiale* (Paris: P.U. Franc-Comtoises, 1995), 316.

22. Union des syndicats patronaux des Industries Textiles de France, *Rapport présenté à MM. Les Ministres du Commerce et du Travail sur les Industries textiles en France* (Paris: Imprimerie Nationale, 1915).

23. Daumas, *L'Amour du drap,* 316. For figures on textile exports during and after the war, see *Annuaire statistique de la France* (Paris: Imprimerie Nationale, 1940).

24. ADR, 9M7, Enquêtes sur les industries textiles 1930, dossier on textile industries other than woolens, dossier on Syndicate des Fabricants de Lyon.

25. Giovanni Federico, *An Economic History of the Silk Industry, 1830–1930* (Cambridge: Cambridge University Press, 1994), 12, 77, and 188–89.

26. Pierre Vernus, *Bianchini-Férier, fabricant de soieries à Lyon (1888–1973)* (Thèse, Université de Lyon II, 1997), 149.

27. Rosine, "Propos féminins," *Figaro,* 11 Sept. 1917.

28. L.deL., "Lyons Silks and Fashion," *La Soierie de Lyon,* 19 June 1919, and "A Travers la mode: 'Etoffes nouvelles,'" *La Mode Illustrée,* 12 Jan. 1919.

29. P. Hemp, "La Laine et la soie," *La Renaissance de l'art française,* Sept. 1925, 398–99.

30. F.A., "La Soie artificielle et la lingerie," *Femina,* Feb. 1933.

31. ADR, 67J 363, Archives Bianchini-Férier, Marques déposés, No. 90368 in Miscellaneous binder, and Rosalba in Noms déposé binder; Au Bon Marché, *Eté et printemps 1927,* page on corsets for women; and ad for Vionnet gown, in *Femina,* Dec.1933.

32. MTL, Ducharne collections sample book 4885/1, summer 1920. Of eighty-nine swatches (ten are missing), nine are crepes, two crepes georgette, and four georgettes. By the summer of 1923 (4885/3), almost one-third of the swatches were crepes, followed by georgettes and georgines.

33. Katrin Shultheiss, *Bodies and Souls: Politics and the Professionalization of Nursing in France, 1880–1922* (Cambridge, MA: Harvard University Press, 2001), 148–68.

34. J.F., "La Mode pendant la guerre," *Femina,* Mar. and Sept. 1917; J.R., "L'Esprit de la mode," *La Gazette des Beaux Arts* 59 (1917); L.deL., "Fashion," *La Soierie de*

*Lyon,* 16 Nov. 1920; and A.deL., "Chronique," *La Mode,* 21 Sept. 1919. Also Jeanne Galzy, *La Cavalière* (Paris: Interligne, 2000), 187 and 300.

35. Paul Morand, *L'Allure de Chanel* (Paris: Hermann, 1976), 42–47, and Axel Madsen, *Chanel: A Woman of Her Own* (New York: Henry Holt, 1990), 64, 69, and 80–81.

36. C.D., "Propos féminines," *Figaro,* 24 Apr. 1917, A. deL., "Chronique," *La Mode,* 28 Sept. 1919, and Lucy, "Chronique de la mode," *La Mode du Jour,* 11 May 1933.

37. Michael Lanthier, "Women Alone: Widows in Third Republic France, 1870– 1940" (Ph.D. diss., Simon Fraser University, 2004), app. 2.

38. Ibid., chaps. 2 and 3.

39. The percentage of widows in cases before the Conseil des Prud'hommes, 1919–32, in AP, DIU 10 456, Conseil des Prud'hommes, Tissus, Minutes de jugemens, 1919–32, exceeded the proportion of widows in the female population. The number of widows with war orphans in the apprenticeship contracts are based on AP, D1U 10, 591, Conseil des Prud'hommes, Contrats d'apprentissage, 1928–31.

40. Eleanor Lansing Dulles, *The Dollar, the Franc, and Inflation* (New York: Macmillan, 1933), 10–11 and 23.

41. Benjamin F. Martin, *France and the Après-Guerre, 1918–1924: Illusions and Disllusionment* (Baton Rouge: Louisiana State University Press, 1999).

42. Nada, "Halte-la!" and "Des Robes faciles à faire," *Femina,* June 1917 and Dec. 1920.

43. A.deL., "Chronique," *La Mode,* 12 Jan. 1919, and A. Raymond, "Soyons économes malgré la paix," "Ou nous logerons-nous?," and "Le Travail chez soi," *La Mode Illustrée,* 5 Jan. and 10 Aug. 1919, and 10 Jan. 1920.

44. Claude de Prunières, "La Tenue d'une femme de chambre," and Marthe Pattez, "Le Foyer sans servant: L'organisation du travail ménagère," *Nos Loisirs,* 1 Dec. 1921 and 1 Mar. 1923.

45. Françoise Werner, "Du Ménage à l'art ménager: L'évolution du travail ménager et son écho dans la presse féminine française de 1919 à 1939," *Mouvement Social* 129 (1984): 61–87.

46. "Le Tact dans l'élégance pour diner au restaurant," "Pour votre femme de chambre," and A.G., "Nos domestiques," *La Mode Pratique,* 28 Oct. 1922, 19 Jan. 1929, and 29 Dec. 1934.

47. A.deL., "Chronique," *La Mode,* 21 Aug. 1921, and "Pas de tabliers: Pour menage des robes simples, lavables," *Vogue,* 28 July 1938.

48. Cover drawing by P. Meersen, *Femina,* 1 Nov. 1934.

49. AduN, M541/52A, Renaissance du Nord de France, Exposition internationale Lille, 1920.

50. Edmond Michel, *Les Dommages de Guerre de la France et leur Réparation* (Paris: Berger-Levrault, 1932), 361.

51. United Kingdom, Department of Overseas Trade, *Economic Conditions in France* (London: HMSO, 1934), 309–29.

52. Kenneth Mouré, *The Gold Standard Illusion: France, the Bank of France, and the International Gold Standard, 1914–1939* (Oxford: Oxford University Press, 2002), 43–46.

53. Henry Touraille, *Les Crises économiques et particulièrement la crise de 1920–1921 dans l'industrie textile* (Paris: Crete, 1926), 119, 128, 148, 154–59, 201, 206–12. For the figures on women in textiles and clothing and in the manufacturing sector, in 1921, see T. Deldycke, H. Gelders, and J.-M. Limbor, *The Working Population and Its Structure* (Brussels: Université Libre de Bruxelles, 1968), 172–73, table E4B, 172–73.

54. "Velours et Peluches," *La Soierie de Lyon,* 1 Nov. 1919; M.R., "Le Velours, cette année, sera 'Sans Peur,' " *Femina,* Sept. 1934; and MTL, Ducharne Collections, 48851/2 and 3, winter 1921–22 and summer 1922.

55. International Economic Conference, Geneva, May 1927, *Report on the Natural Silk Industry* (Geneva: League of Nations, 1927), 10.

56. L.deL., "Lyon Silks and Fashion," *La Soierie de Lyon,* 1 July 1922 and 1 Aug. 1923; MTL, Ducharne 48851/16, Unis imprimées sur chaîne, 1922–36.

57. Odile Valenset, "Madeleine Vionnet et la Texture des Tissus," in *Madeleine Vionnet: Les Années d'innovation* (Lyon: Musée des Tissus, 1994), 23ff.

58. Aftalion, *L'Industrie textile,* 246.

59. Paul H. Nystrom, *Economics of Fashion* (New York: Ronald Press, 1928), 169.

60. "Pour les sorties printanières chez Roubaudi," *Les Elégances Parisiennes* 4, 9 (1920); "Tout le monde connait les tissus de Rodier," and "Applications de quelques tissus nouveaux," *L'Illustration des Modes,* 21 Oct. 1920 and 20 Oct. 1921.

61. "Les Lainages de Printemps de Rodier," *Les Elégances Parisiennes* 4, 9 (1920); "Nouveaux Tissus-Nouvelles modes: Vieux artisans—metiers d'autrefois," *Vogue,* 1 Mar. 1924; and "Toute la mode," *Eve,* 16 Mar. 1924 and 15 Mar. 1925.

62. AP, Conseil des Prud'hommes, Classeurs Rodier, nos. 2–11, 1927–33.

63. "La Vie féminine: Les Sports d'hiver," *Le Progres de Lyon,* 29 Jan. 1925.

64. J.F., "La Mode pendant la guerre" and "Des Toilettes pour petits budgets," *Femina,* June 1917 and 1 Nov. 1920, and "Broderies nouvelles," *La Mode Illustrée,* 22 Jan. 1922.

65. Rozsika Parker, *The Subversive Stitch: Embroidery and the Making of the Feminine* (London: Women's Press, 1984), 6.

66. Compare Mamy's "Causerie" columns to Griseline's "Toilettes et parures" columns in *Journal des Ouvrages de Dames,* 1919–20. See also "Deux motifs pour robes" and "Trois dessins pour corsages et robes," in *La Broderie pratique de Lyon,* 15 Nov. and 1 Dec. 1921.

67. See 1 Nov. 1926 issue of *Modes et Travaux féminins* and "Broderons-nous nos robes du soir?," in *La Mode Pratique,* 11 Nov. 1922.

68. Mme. Guibert, "Chiffons à travers la mode," *Chiffon,* 5 Feb. 1919

69. Marie de Russie, *Une Princesse en exil,* trans. H. Archambault-Fauconnier (Paris: Stock, 1933); Alexandre Vassiliev, *Beauty in Exile: The Artists, Models, and Nobility Who Fled the Russian Revolution and Influenced the World of Fashion,* trans. Antonina W. Bouis and Andy Kucharev (New York: Harry N. Abrams, 2000), 135–71 and 189; and Pamela Golbin, "Les Années folles: L'exotisme dans la mode et le textile," in *Touches d'exotisme XIVe–XXe* (Paris: Musée de la Mode et du Textile, 1999), 150.

70. Haye, *Chanel,* 31–32, and "An Interview with Jean Patou" and "Nos informations," *L'Officiel de la Couture,* 20 July 1921.

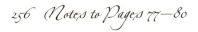

71. Mouré, *The Gold Standard Illusion*, 52–71, and Dulles, *The Dollar, the Franc*, 43, 87, and 92.

72. Kenneth Mouré, *Managing the Franc Poincaré: Economic Understanding and Political Constraint in French Monetary Policy, 1928–1936* (Cambridge: Cambridge University Press, 1991), 13 and 44. On textile production, see Statistique Générale de la France, *Indices généraux du mouvement économique en France de 1901 à 1931* (Paris: Imprimerie Nationale, 1931), 60 and 62.

73. Didier Grumbach, *Histoires de la mode* (Paris: Editions de Seuil, 1993), 32–33, citing *Statistique Générale de France*.

74. "The French Couture," *L'Officiel de la Couture*, May 1924, and *The Buyer's Pocket-Book* (Paris: Les Publications Etrangères, 1927), 553–54.

75. Grumbach, *Histoires*, 32, citing the Exposition des arts décoratifs of 1925.

76. Philippe Simon, *Monographie d'une industrie de luxe: La Haute couture* (Paris PUF, 1931), 8 and 65–85; Jean-Marie Boegner, "La Haute Couture à Paris," *Bulletin d'études historiques, géographiques . . . de la région parisienne* 7, 27 (1933): 9, refers to 200,000 workers and gives the turnover figures.

77. AP, D1U 10, 460, Conseil des Prud'hommes, Textiles, Minutes de jugemens, Patou contre Ballon, 9 July 1920; and 469, Millet contre Brisac, 27 Feb. 1925, and 476, Cyber letterhead, regarding Mme. Zakhwatoff, 1928.

78. AP, D1U 10, 460, Conseil des Prud'hommes, Textiles, Minutes de jugemens, 1920–22, Patou contre Ballon, and Florence Rochefort, "A Propos de la libre-disposition du salaire de la femme mariée: Les ambigüités d'une loi (1907)," *Clio: Histoire, Femmes et Société* 7 (1998): 177–90.

79. M.R., "La Mode des tissus," *Femina*, Mar. 1926.

80. Inventaire and Histoire de la Société anonyme J. Patou, 13 July 1935 in AP, 1049WC 100, 23655, Liquidations Judiciaires, Jean Patou, July 1935.

81. "Mondanités," *L'Officiel de la Couture*, 20 Aug. 1921, and "Le Demeure moderne d'un couturier moderne: Chez M. Jean Patou," *Femina*, Oct. 1925.

82. "Le Home de Renée Devillers," in Madeleine Andral, *Au dela du rideau: Interviews, portraits, bavardages de théâtre* (Paris: Chapelon, 1936), 123, and "La Maison de Colette," *Les Rois de la mode*, Mar. 1926.

83. Rapport regarding judgment of the civil court of the Seine, 20 Oct. 1932, ordering Patou to pay the Monté Carlo Hotel the sum of 162,500 francs, in AP, 1049WC 100, 23655, Liquidations Judiciaires, Jean Patou, July 1935.

84. "Impression sur les modes à venir pour le printemps 1924," *Vogue*, 1 Feb. 1924, and Bonney, *A Shopping Guide to Paris*, 45.

85. Letter from Robert Touboul, director of Cyber, delegating Mme. Maury, head of Cyber's publicity service, in AP, D1U10, 479, Jugemens, 1930–31, and AP, DEM 319, SA Premet, Année 1924, dépôt 243.

86. M.R., "De quoi demain sera-t'il fait?," *Femina*, July 1925.

87. See the fashion photos and illustrations in *Mode 214 bis* 32 (1927–31), in the BAD, Louvre.

88. Vassiliev, *Beauty in Exile*, 171, 175, 181, and 187.

89. Palmer White, *The Master Touch of Lesage: Fashion, Embroidery, Paris* (Paris: Chêne, 1987), 44–75.

90. *Annuaire: Union Syndicale des Tissus. . . .*, 1926.

91. MTL, Chambre syndicale des Fabricants de Soieries, Procès-verbaux, Comité syndical, 19 and 27 June 1927.

92. Ibid., 28 Nov. 1927, 30 Mar. and 31 May 1928, 18 Mar. 1929, 13 June 1932, and 23 June 1933, and Réunion du Bureau syndical, 1 Mar. 1935.

93. MTL, Assemblée générale extraordinaire, 30 Nov. 1932, Réunion du Bureau syndical, 13 Mar. 1935.

94. "M.R., "La Soie artificielle renouvelle l'art du tissu," and F.A., "La Soie naturelle nous donne des tissus de qualité," *Femina,* Jan. 1931 and Oct. 1933. Full-page ads for "Real Silk" began in the Jan. 1929 issue.

95. "La Soie artificielle" and back-page ad for real silk, *Vogue,* Aug. 1928. Variations of this ad appeared through 1935.

96. Daumas, *L'Amour du drap,* 341, 388–95.

97. Situation de l'Industrie lainière pendant l'année 1928, and Letter from Consortium de l'Industrie Textile de Roubaix-Tourcoing, 23 Dec. 1929, in *AduN,* M 571/25, Enquête de décembre 1929.

98. An F[7] 13523, Chômage, 1927, Situation du chômage en France, 24 Sept. 1927, and report to the Ministry of the Interior, 8 Sept. 1927.

99. ADR, 9M7, Enquêtes sur les industries textiles 1930, dossiers on enquête relatif à l'import sur le chiffre d'affaires, offprint from *Journal Officiel,* Chambre de Députés, 19 Dec. 1929, 4849.

100. Mouré, *Managing the Franc Poincaré,* 22.

101. H. Clark Johnson, *Gold, France, and the Great Depression, 1919–1932* (New Haven: Yale University Press, 1997), 145ff., and Patricia Clavin, *The Failure of Economic Diplomacy* (London: Macmillan Press, 1996), 190ff.

102. T. Boyer, "Paradoxes français de la crise des années 1930," *Mouvement social* 154 (Jan.–Mar. 1991): 20–25.

103. "Couturiers Void British Cloth Orders," "Paris Cabinet Meeting on British Tariff," and "British to Continue French Model Imports Despite Duty," *WWD,* 19 and 24 Nov. and 18 Dec. 1931.

104. Mlle. M.-E. Vointot, "Le Paradoxe de la couture française, vue de l'étranger: Allemagne et Amerique, deux centres de la mode parisienne," *Le Conseiller du commerce extérieur,* Dec. 1937.

105. "U.S.-French Luxury Trades to Fight Evils," "U.S. Purchases of Midseason Models Decline," "Paris Commissionnaires Plan Conservative Policy on U.S. Buying," and "Couture Acts to Fight Sharp Seasonal Lull," in *WWD,* 13 and 24 Nov. and 28 and 29 Dec. 1931.

106. "Buy American" file in Box 5 of the Bernis Collection, Sophia Smith Archives, Smith College, and Sarah Berry, *Screen Style: Fashion and Femininity in 1930s Hollywood* (Minneapolis: University of Minnesota Press, 2000), xx, 67–68.

107. Vernus, *Bianchini-Férier,* 265.

108. Rosine columns in *Figaro,* 20 Nov. 1930 and 15 Jan. 1931; Maraine, "Ce qui se porte," *La Mode,* 1 Mar. 1932.

109. Boegner, "La Haute Couture en Paris," 9.

110. Valerie Guillaume, *Haute Couture: Reconquête et "new look," Paris, 1954–1954* (Paris: Autrement, 1995), 97.

111. AP, 1049w, 43119, Faillite Sté A. Premet, Apr. 1932, Extrait du rapport adressé à Messieurs les Créanciers. . . . 13 Feb. 1932, and Bilan M. Boisseraud, . . . sommes dues aux fournisseurs au 12 Sept. 1931.

112. "Histoire de la Société anonyme J. Patou," in P. Planque, Liquidateur-Judiciaire, "Rapport à Messieurs les Créanciers de la Société anonyme Jean Patou" and "Liste des créanciers," in AP, 1049WC 100, 23655, Liquidations Judiciaires, Jean Patou, July 1935.

113. "The Parisian Couture Seen by Lucien Lelong" and "Suite," in *L'Officiel de la Couture,* Aug. and Sept. 1925.

114. "La Mode cinématique," *Les Cahiers du Goût Française.* Offerts aux abonnées parisiennes de *l'Illustration,* no.3, 1925.

115. Colette, "Fards, poudres, parfums," *Femina,* Oct. 1927.

116. "Pour le Lido Lelong fait des 'robes pyjamas' en soie artificielle," *Femina,* June 1933, and Rouff, "Un Peu de psychologie vestimentaire," 130–32.

117. Une Cousette, "L'Evolution de la haute couture," *L'Habillement,* Oct. 1934.

118. Jacques Lanzmann and Pierre Ripert, *Cent ans de prêt-à-porter: Weill* (Paris: PAU, 1992), 65, and Renée Prag, "La Mode d'hiver chez un grand couturier des Champs Elysées: Chez Toutmain, le créateur de la nouvelle formule," *Marie Claire,* 28 Jan. 1938.

119. Janine Hénin, *Paris Haute Couture* (Paris: Editions Philippe Olivier, 1990), 29.

120. "Propos féminins," *Figaro,* 10 Dec. 1933.

121. Marie-France Pochna, *Nina Ricci* (Paris: Editions du Regard, 1992), 9, 15–16, 29–32.

122. Alfred Sauvy, *Histoire économique de la France entre les deux guerres* (Paris: Fayard, 1965), 2: 118, 121, and 507.

123. Vassiliev, *Beauty in Exile,* 177 and 197.

124. AP, 1049W C80, Liquidation judiciaire Prevost Constantin et Cie, Rapport aux Messeurs les Créanciers, Oct. 1930.

125. ADP, 1049W C80 3960, Liquidations judiciaires, Natalie Davydoff, Rapport à Messieurs les Créanciers, 4 Dec. 1930.

126. MTL, 48851/19, Broderies, winter 1935–36.

127. Vernus, *Bianchini-Férier,* 257–60 and 279.

128. According to "Soieries F. Ducharne," *Revue universelle de la soie et des textiles artificiels* 14, 6 (1939), gross profits rose from 7,605,189 francs in 1937 to 9,442,994 francs in 1938. Net profits rose more: from 156,949 to 652,817 francs.

129. Vernus, *Bianchini-Férier,* 266, 272–73, and 278–79.

130. United Kingdom, *Economic Conditions in France,* 330–34; quotation, 330.

131. Fitz Bénard, "Au Chevet de la couture malade," *Vendre,* July 1932, 29–32.

132. MTL, Procès-verbaux, Assemblée générale, 18 Mar. 1929, 18 May and 26 Oct. 1933. See also Reine Bontoux, "The Big Fortnight in Paris," *La Soierie de Lyon,* July 1934.

133. Kevin Passmore, "Business, Corporatism, and the Crisis of the French Third Republic," *Historical Journal* 38 (1995): 968ff.

1. Paul H. Nystrom, *Economics of Fashion* (New York: Ronald Press, 1928), 167–68, and Dudley Kirk, *Europe's Population in the Interwar Years* (Princeton: Princeton University Press, 1946), 34.

2. AP, 1049w, 43119, Faillite Sté Premet, Inventaire 1931, Materiel et Mobilier.

3. Pierre de Trevières, "Une Inauguration," *L'Art et la Mode* 25 (19 June 1926).

4. "La Visite chez les couturiers," *Femina*, Mar. 1924; J.L., "Toute la Mode: La grande quinzaine est commencée!," *Eve*, 1 Feb. 1925, and Marthe Bibesco, *Catherine-Paris* (Paris: Grasset, 1927), 159.

5. Comtesse Riguidi, *L'Epoque: Les moeurs, les modes, le style* (Paris: Berger-Levrault, 1931), 111.

6. Paul Reboux, *La Rue de la Paix* (Paris: Pierre Lafitte, 1927), 15–16, and Colette, *Le Voyage égoiste* (1928), in *Colette: Romans-Récits-Souvenirs (1920–1940)* (Paris: Robert Laffont, 1989), 2: 156.

7. René Richard, "Dans les Coulisses des grandes maisons de couture," *Plaisir de France*, Feb. 1936, and Louis Gillet, "Choses vue," *Marie Claire*, 10 Sept. 1937.

8. C. D., "Vision élégantes," *Chiffons*, 5 Apr. 1926, and Harriet Quick, *Défilés de mode: Une Historie du mannequin* (Courbevoie: Soline, 1997), 32.

9. Gillet, "Choses vues."

10. Lucy Clairin, *Journal d'un mannequin: Feuillets d'une année* (Paris: Fasquelle, 1937), 7–8; "Fashion," *La Soierie de Lyon,* 16 Jan. 1920; "Cabines de Mannequins," *Femina*, Apr. 1934; and Leo Sauvage, "Modes et mannequins," *Peuple*, 1939, in BHVP, Fonds Bouglé, box 2, Articles de presse, couture.

11. Thérèse and Louise Bonney, *A Shopping Guide to Paris* (New York: Robert M. McBride, 1929), 18.

12. "Soyons Minces mais sans aucun excès," *Vogue,* 15 Aug. 1920.

13. "Les Créations 'Schiap' enregistrées de mode par l'illustration," in *Hommage à Elsa Schiaparelli* (Paris: Musée de la Mode et du Costume, 1984), 86.

14. Vionnet ad in *Vogue,* 1 June 1924.

15. Wendy Gambier, *The Female Economy: The Millinery and Dressmaking Trades, 1860–1930* (Urbana: University of Illinois Press, 1997), 99ff.

16. My interpretation draws on conversations with five archivists, curators, and librarians who reminisced about their relations with dressmakers in the late 1930s, and on a description of a visit to a little dressmaker in a letter written by Mary Louise Cahile, 14 Dec. 1936. I am grateful to Whitney Walton for finding this in the Sophia Smith Archives, Box 2110, and sending me a copy.

17. Pierre Bourdieu, *The Logic of Practice* (Cambridge: Polity Press, 1990), chap. 3.

18. René Richard, "Dans les Coulisses des grandes maisons de couture," *Plaisir de France,* Feb. 1936.

19. V. Langlois and Mlle. Gariel, *Le Livret de la couturière: Technologie* (Paris: Librairie de l'Enseignement technique, 1923), 101.

20. Daisy Fellowes, "Des Inquiétudes et des hésitations d'une grande élégante," *Excelsior-Modes,* Dec. 1929.

21. Cecil Beaton, *The Glass of Fashion* (London: Wiedenfeld & Nicolson, 1954), 165.

22. Georges Le Fèvre, *Au Secours de la couture (Industrie française)* (Paris: Editions Baudinière, 1929), 25–26, 42–43, and 59–64, and "La Vie et le secret de Madeleine Vionnet," *Marie Claire,* 28 May 1937.

23. Marthe Pattex, "La Belle industrie parisienne de la grande couture," *Minerva,* 18 June 1926.

24. AP, D1U 10, 603, Contrat de travail du Petit Personnel et des Cadres Supérieurs de la Couture, 7 July 1936. Inexperienced mannequins earned 800 francs.

25. Quick, *Défilés de mode,* 23, 27, and 39. See also Séeberger collection of fashion photographs in the BNF, Etampes, Oa381 to Oa429.

26. Nérine, "Toute la mode," *Eve,* 13 Feb. 1921, and Meredith Etherington-Smith, *Patou* (London: Hutchinson, 1983), 164.

27. Pascal Pia, "Code de mannequin," *Voila: L'Hebdomadaire du reportage* 5, 202 (2 Feb. 1935); Yvette Monier, "La Vie intime des mannequins," *Faits Divers,* 14 Feb. 1932; and Paul Poiret and André Dignimont, *Ce que j'ai vu en chiffonnant la clientèle* (Paris: Libraire des Champs-Elysées, 1938), 65.

28. Colette, "Mannequins," *Vogue,* 1 Apr. 1925; Poiret and Dignimont, *Ce que j'ai vu,* 66; F. de Miomandre, *La Mode* (Paris: Hachette, 1927), 24–26; and Georges-Armand Masson, *Tableau de la mode* (Paris: Editions de la *Nouvelle Revue française,* 1926), 101–2.

29. AP, D1U 10, 601, Procès-verbal de la réunion tenu au Ministère de Travail entre Les Chambres Syndicales Parisiennes Patronales et Ouvrières de l'Industrie du Vêtement, Convention intersyndicale de la Couture, 9 Mar. 1920.

30. AN F[7] 13741, Habillement, Congrès, 1920–29, dossier on 1920–21, Sûreté report on new tariffs, 7 Mar. 1920.

31. With the exception of her argument about apprenticeship, I agree with Helen Chenut, "The Gendering of Skill as a Historical Process," in *Gender and Class in Modern Europe,* ed. Laura L. Frader and Sonya O. Rose (Ithaca, NY: Cornell University Press, 1996). My findings accord with Laura Lee Downs, *Manufacturing Inequality: Gender Division in the French and British Metalworking Industries, 1914–1939* (Ithaca, NY: Cornell University Press, 1995), 89. Apprenticeships played a modest role in higher pay.

32. AP, D1U 10, 603, Contrat de travail du Petit Personnel et des Cadres Supérieurs de la Couture, 7 July 1936.

33. Wage gap figures from Sylvie Schweitzer, *Les Femmes ont toujours travaillé: Une historie de leurs métiers, XIXe et XXe siècles* (Paris: Editions Odile Jacob, 2002), 111–12.

34. See reports on 1923 contract in *L'Ouvrier de l'Habillement,* Aug.–Sept. 1923, 4.

35. AN F[7] 13741, Habillement, Congrès, 1920–29, dossier 1920–21, Sûreté report on general assembly, 11 Jan. 1920. Dues of 2.50 francs for men, l.75 francs for women in January 1920, rose to 5 and 3 francs, respectively, in May 1920.

36. Françoise Blum, *Féminisme et syndicalisme: Les femmes dans la fédération de l'habillement, 1914–1935* (n.p., n.p., n.d.), 70–73. Available at Musée Sociale.

37. Confédération Générale du Travail Unitaire. Fédération nationale des Industries Textile-Vêtement. Congrès de fusion. Compte-rendu sténographique des séances (Paris, 1924), at the Musée Sociale, and AN F[7] 13741, Habillement, Congrès, dossier 1925, 1926, 1927, Sûreté report on clothing union meeting, 6 Oct. 1925.

38. ADR, 10 Mp C61, Strikes, 1919, dossier on Vêtement, May 1919, reports by Commissaire Spécial, 14, 16, and 31 May 1919; ADR 10 Mp C62, Strikes in clothing,

1919–29, reports 7, 17, and May 1919, and "Le Mouvement ouvrier: Dans l'habillement," *Le Progrès,* 22 May 1919, and ADR 10Mp C63, Grèves, 1919–20, reports of 20 and 27 Feb. and 3, 7, 10, 12, 14, and 16 Mar. 1920.

39. AN F⁷ 13741, Habillement, Congrès, 1920–29, dossier 1920–23, reports by the Commissariat spécial, Rhône, 16 Sept. and 30 Dec. 1920; Sûreté, Paris, 24 Mar. 1921; Commissariat spécial, Lille, 3 Apr. and 1 Aug. 1921, and Police d'état, Toulon, 7 Apr. 1921. See also note on Mlle. Bouillot.

40. Dumoulin speech in "Le Congrès de l'Habillement s'est ouvert, hier, à Lille," *Le Peuple,* 2 Aug. 1921.

41. Masson, *Tableau de la mode,* 8.

42. Worth, "A Propos de la Mode," and Pierre Gerber, "Modes et couture," in *La France travaille* (Paris: Horizons de France, 1932), 228.

43. AP, D1U 10, Conseil des Prud'hommes, Textiles, Jugemens, 481, 1931–I, 31 Jan. 1931, two cases involving premières/modellistes. See also BHVP, Fonds Vionnet, Croquis.

44. On costs to a house from a première's mistakes, see AP, D1U 10, 471, Raynaud contre Schaettel, 8 Jan. 1926.

45. AP, D1U 10, 460, Vionnet v. Hermaingue, 16 Nov. 1920 (a seasonal contract); 471, Vout contre Branlard, 2 Apr. 1926 (breaking a two-year contract), 473, Bunel contre Courtisien, 22 Apr. 1927 (firing after giving six months' notice), etc.

46. Masson, *Tableau de la mode,* 90.

47. AP, D1U 10, 603, Contrats de Travail, 1936, Contrat du petit personnel et des cadres supérieurs de la couture, 7 July 1936.

48. Claire B. Shaeffer, *Couture Sewing Techniques* (Newtown, CT: Taunton Press, 2001), 149 and passim.

49. Une Cousette, "L'Evolution de la haute couture," *L'Habillement,* Oct. 1934.

50. AP, D1U 10, 603, Règlement intersyndical signed in June and July 1936.

51. Achille Viallate, *L'Activité économique en France de la fin du XVIIIe siècle à nos jours* (Paris: Marcel Rivière, 1937), 371 and 430. Viallate based his indexes of real wages on the *Statistique générale.*

52. Dossier Chambres Sydicales Patronale Haute Couture et Syndicat des Couturières, Contrat, 20 Aug. 1936, in ADR, 10Mp C122, Conventions Collectives, 1936–39. For differences in average wages in the capital and major provincial cities in 1935, see Philippe Madinier, *Les Disparités géographiques de salaries en France* (Paris: Armand Colin, n.d.), 69.

53. Clairin, *Journal d'un mannequin,* 56.

54. Marthe Louis-Levy, "Ouvrières de la couture et de la confection," *Le Populaire,* 27 Dec. 1932.

55. Marguerite Audoux, *L'Atelier de Marie-Claire* (Paris: Grasset, 1920), reprinted in *Femmes et travail* (Romorantin: Edition Martinsart, 1981), 175–96.

56. Office du Travail, *Enquête sur le travail à domicile dans l'industrie de la lingerie,* vol. 5, *Résultats généraux* (Paris: Imprimerie Nationale, 1911).

57. BHVP, Fonds Bouglé, Manuscrits Jeanne Bouvier, box 19, Travail à domicile, Enquête sur le travail à domicile, 1913.

58. Mary Lynn Stewart, *For Health and Beauty: Physical Culture for Frenchwomen, 1880s–1930s* (Baltimore: Johns Hopkins University Press, 2000), 181–82.

59. AP, D1U 10 456 and 457, Conseil des Prud'hommes, Tissus, Minutes de jugemens, 22 Feb. 1918 and 24 Jan. 1919.

60. BHVP, Fonds Bouglé, Manuscrits Jeanne Bouvier, box 19, Travail à domicile, Jugements Conseils des Prud'hommes, especially letter from Jean Raynal, 30 July 1919, and Fernand Corces, "Le Travail à domicile et le minimum de salaire," *La Loi: Journal du soir judiciaire quotidien,* 25–26 Sept. 1918 and 11–12 Feb. 1918.

61. AP, D1U 10, 461 and 469, Conseil des Prud'hommes, Textiles, Minutes de jugemens, 29 Apr. 1921 and 5 Dec. 1924.

62. BHVP, Fonds Bouglé, Manuscrits Jeanne Bouvier, box 19, Tractes de propagande and Travail à domicile, Modifications de la loi de 1915, proposées en 1925. See also An F[7] 13741, Habillement, Congrès, 1920–29, Commissariat spécial de Lille, 3 Aug. 1921, report on congrès of 1921.

63. "Le Congrès de l'Habillement," *Le Peuple,* 4 Aug. 1921; Louis Gelis, "On Crée un label de l'habillement, " *L'Humanité,* 7 Aug. 1921, in AN F[7] 13741, Habillement, Congrès, 1920–29; *Bulletin d'Information sur l'application du programme . . . élaboré au Congrès de Bordeaux* (1927); and AN F[7] 13584, Confédération Générale du Travail Unitaire, 1922–28, report by Commissaire spéciale in the Rhone on the Congrès de l'Union Régionale des Syndicats Unitaires, 26 Dec. 1928.

64. BHVP, Fonds Bouglé, Travail à domicile, Rapport présenté à l'Office du travail à domicile, 1928.

65. BHVP, Fonds Bouglé, Couture, "L'Application des assurances sociales aux travailleurs à domicile devant le Congrès de l'habillement," *Le Peuple,* 17 Sept. 1930; "Résolution votée par le 18e Congrès de la fédération de l'habillement," *L'Habillement,* 1 Oct. 1934, and "Le Travail à domicile au congrès de l'habillement," *La Française,* 13 Nov. 1937.

66. Eliane Delesalle, *Le Travail de la femme dans l'Industrie textile et du vêtement de l'arrondissement de Lille* (Loos: Danel, 1951), 11.

67. François Faraut, *Histoire de la Belle Jardinière* (Paris: Belin, 1987), 100–109.

68. Une Cousette, "L'Evolution de la haute couture."

69. Contracts for Le Groupement d'Etudes des Grands Magasins and Etablissements Charles Levy in AP, D1U 10, 603.

70. Mlle. Floret, *Travaux manuels: Coupe et couture* (Paris, 1930); AP, D2T1/16, Cours complémentaires, and D2T1/122, Enseignement post-scolaire. Ecole rue Fonday and Ecole Sophie Germain, and AN F[7] 14364, Ecoles professionnelle, Ecole professionnelle de filles de la rue de la Tombe Issoire.

71. Interviews in "Ou va la mode?," *De la mode: Hier-aujourd'hui-demain; Les Cahiers de la République des lettres, des sciences et des arts* (Paris: Les Beaux-Arts, 1927), 85.

72. Nystrom, *Economics of Fashion,* 171, and Elizabeth Hawes, *Fashion Is Spinach* (New York: Random House, 1938), 16–19.

73. AP, D1U 10, 462, 473, Conseil des Prud'hommes, Textiles, Minutes de jugemens, Lapointe contre Gourlay, 16 Dec. 1921; Wormser (Maison Cheruit) contre Perrier, 18 Jan. 1927.

74. Anne Goulet and Olivier Cottarel, "Elément pour une histoire," *Au Temps des ateliers-écoles: La Chambre de Commerce de Paris et l'apprentissage (1921–1939)* (Paris: Chambre de Commerce et d'Industrie de Paris, 1996), 7–10, and Langlois and Gariel, *Le Livret de la couturière.*

75. Yvonne Moustier, "Une Ecole de la haute couture," *La Mode Pratique,* 20 Dec. 1930.

76. AP, DiU 10, 591–95, Contrats d'apprentissage, 1928–35.

77. Comments by Alice Brissat and Juliette Langeois recorded in *Sûreté* notes on a meeting of the Clothing Union, 7 Oct. 1925, in AN F[7] 13741, Habillement, Congrès, 1920–29.

78. AN F[7] 13740, Habillement, Congrès 1912–29, dossier 2, Habillement, 1906–11; "Victoire de femmes: La grève de la maison Esders," *Voix du Peuple,* 7 Aug. 1910; "Une Grève aux Magasins Esders. Six cent ouvrières et ouvriers quittent le travail," *Humanité,* 16 Nov. 1911; "Le Meeting des couturières," *La Petite Republique,* 16 Jan. 1910; "Les Midinettes sont en revolte," *Le Petit Parisien,* 17 Jan. 1910; and "Les Leçons de l'action," *Bataille syndicaliste,* 24 Mar. 1913.

79. AP, DiU 10, 6 Di, Couture. Contrat signé le 8 juin 1917 and Convention in Confection, 26 May 1917.

80. "Femmes et travailleurs étrangers se font concurrence," *L'Humanité,* 2 Dec. 1923.

81. AP, DiUi0, 601, Procès-verbal de la réunion tenu au Ministère de Travail le 10 mai 1919 entre Les Chambres Syndicales Parisiennes Patronales et Ouvrières de l'Industrie du Vêtement, Convention intersyndicale de la Couture, 9 Mar. 1920.

82. Cognacq contre Millerat et al., 1 Aug. 1919, in AP, DiU 10, 458, Conseil des Prud'hommes, Textiles, Minutes de jugemens, 1919.

83. AN F[7] 13741, Habillement, Congrès, 1920–29, 1920–21 dossier, especially reports of 7 and 31 Mar., 2 Apr., and 19 Dec. 1920, and 23 and 25 Jan. and 12 Feb. 1921.

84. Cases involving the houses of Chauvin, Boué Soeurs, Doucet, High Life Taillor, Lanvin, Lelong, Madeleine et Madeleine, Paquin, Patou, Poiret and Vionnet, and the Louvre and Printemps department stores, in AP, DiU 10, 456, 457, 459, 460, and 461, Minutes de jugemens, 1919–21. See also Modification . . . à l'Accord du 25 avril 1923 dated 15 Apr. 1930, in AP, DiU 10, 603 Contrats.

85. Eugène Robert, "Dans la confection administrative et militaire," in *L'Habillement. Bulletin des Syndicats Confédérés des Industries de l'Habillement de la Région Parisienne,* Oct. 1934.

86. Nancy Green, *Ready-to-Wear and Ready-to-Work: A Century of Industry and Immigrants in Paris and New York* (Durham, NC: Duke University Press, 1997), 87.

87. Suzanne Lion, "La Grève des midinettes," *L'Ouvrier de l'habillement* (Organe officiel de la Fédération de l'industrie des Travailleurs de l'Habillement . . . ), Aug.–Sept. 1923; "Les Midinettes en grève," *Le Peuple,* 16 Apr. 1923; and "Les Cousettes parisiennes," *Humanité,* 16 Apr. 1923, and AN F[7] 13882, Grèves, Habillement, 1919–23, notes dated 3, 4, and 5 Apr. 1923.

88. "Les Cousettes revendiquent," "Les Salaires dans la couture," and Suzanne Lion, "Dans la couture parisienne," in *Le Peuple,* 23 Feb., 2 Mar., and 24 May 1924.

89. AN F[7] 13741, Habillement, Congrès, 1920–29, notes of 22 and 31 Mar., 3 and 12 June, 8 Aug., 2 Sept. and 9 Oct. 1926, and "Plus de deux mille travailleurs luttent

depuis une semaine pour une augmentation de salaire," *L'Humanité*, 16 Aug. 1926, in 1925, 1926, 1927 dossier, and "Les Couturiers accordent de ridicules augmentations avec la complicité du Syndicat catholique," *L'Humanité*, 5 Feb. 1929, in 1928–29 dossier.

90. AN F $^7$ 13883, Grèves, Habillement, 1924–34, dossier 1930, notes on Chanel strike, 19 Aug. 1930, and on Société Parisienne strike, Jan. 1930.

91. ADR, 4 M 626, Associations syndicales 1894–1945, see Comité de Chambres syndicales ouvrières, 1907, Syndicat de l'Union de Teinture et parties similaires de Lyon et Banlieu, 1899, and Syndicat réunis du Tissage et Corporations similaire, 1911; and AduN, M 596/52, dossiers on Chambre syndicale ouvrière de l'industrie Textile de Lille et Environs and Syndicat de l'Industrie Textile.

92. MTL, Chambres Syndical, Comité syndicale, minutes of 14 and 19 May, 4, 11, and 15 June 1919.

93. ADR, 10 Mp C62, dossier on grève des ouvriers tullistes, Lyon.

94. ADR, 10Mp C63, dossier Grève dans le textile, general report, letter to the Ministry of the Interior, 31 Oct. 1919, and Conventions dated 31 Oct. 1919 and 2 Mar. 1920. See also dossier on grève des ouvrières mouliniers.

95. E.g., ADR, 10 MP C61 and C64, dossier Grève des ouvriers de tissage mécanique de Thizy, June–Nov. 1919, esp. letter from Prefect to Minister of the Interior, 15 Sept. 1919, and "Questionaires, grève des ouvriers-canuts de Tarare, juin et juillet 1919."

96. ADR, 10Mp/3/71, Grèves 1924, dossier on industrie textile; 10MP/3/75, Grèves 1927–28, dossier on Corporation du Textile, Région de Cours-Thizy-Roanne, and dossier on Fabrique Chaize et Perrin à Cours, 1928, and 10Mp/3/ 76, dossier on usines de textile de la region de Cours, Thizy et Amplepuis, Apr. 1929.

97. Christine Bard, *Les Femmes et la C.F.T.C. à travers le Nord Social, 1920–1935* (Maitrisse, Université de Lille III, 1987), 53–63, 121–23, and 139–40.

98. AduN, M 595 74, Syndicats libres, CFTC, 1924–39, dossier on Textiles, 1924–39, letter from Union de syndicats libres de Roubaix-Tourcoing, 21 Nov. 1924, and AduN, 79J 574, Chambre de Commerce de Roubaix, Commission intersyndicale de l'Industrie Textile de Roubaix-Tourcoing, 1920–25, Note confidentielle, 18 May 1923.

99. AduN, 79J 574, card entitled "*Aux Français*"; correspondence 20 Mar. 1920; Circular no. 138, Aug. 1922, and "L'Oeuvre social du Consortium . . . en 1924."

100. AN F$^7$ 13935, Dossier on general strike in the Nord, 18 July–23 Sept. 1930, esp. Prefect's reports of 31 July and 4 Sept. 1930 and "Ordre du jour." See also ADR, 10MP/3/78, Grèves diverses, 1931.

101. AN F$^7$ 13922, dossier on Armentières strike, esp. Prefect's reports, 23 Dec. 1932; 7, 12, and 24 Jan.; 5, 10, and 21 Feb, and 4, 14, 23, and 24 Mar. 1933. See also AduN, M 619/91, dossier on textile strikes in Amentières-Houplines, Jan.-Apr. 1933.

102. Michael Torigian, *Every Factory a Fortress: The French Labor Movement in the Age of Ford and Hitler* (Athens: Ohio University Press, 1999), chap. 4; and Gary Cross, *A Quest for Time: The Reduction of Work in Britain and France, 1840–1940* (Berkeley: University of California Press, 1989), 220.

103. Paulette Birgi, "Femmes salariées, syndicalisme et grèves des mois de mai-juin 1936 en France" (Université de Paris, Institut des Sciences sociales du Travail, 1969), 16 and 27.

104. ADR, 10MP/3/80, Grèves 1934, dossiers on strikes at Martin Cie. in Tarare,

clothing workers of Lyon, textile factories in Thizy, Bour-de-Thizy, Amplepuis, and Arbresle.

105. AN F[7] 13922, Strike reports on Filatures Vandesmet at St Omer et Watten, 3 Apr.–16 May 1934, especially reports of Commissaire special, 5 Apr., 11 and 15 May 1934, and dossier on épailleuses in Lille.

106. Jacques Delperrié de Bayac, *Histoire du Front populaire* (Paris: Fayard, 1972), 224, and AduN, 603/20 (d), Occupations des usines, 1936, Lille.

107. Delperrie de Bayac, *Histoire du Front Populaire,* 236ff.

## CHAPTER SIX. COPYING AND COPYRIGHTING

1. Edna Woolman Chase and Ilka Chase, *Always in Vogue* (London: Victor Gollancz, 1954), 92.

2. Gilles Lipovetsky, *The Empire of Fashion: Dressing Modern Democracy,* trans. Catherine Porter (Princeton: Princeton University Press, 1994), 56–59.

3. Gini Stephens Frings, *Fashion from Concept to Consumer,* 2nd ed. (Englewood Cliffs, NJ: Prentice Hall, 1987), 6.

4. "Au Travers la mode: Etoffes nouvelles," *C'est la Mode,* 12 Jan. 1919, and B.J. Perkins, "French Fabric Firms Credit Policies Hit," *WWD,* 2 Nov. 1931.

5. E.g., *Les Modes d'Erté par Erté* (Paris: Flammarion, 1972).

6. *Illustrateurs des modes et manières en 1925* (Paris: Galeries du Luxembourg, 1972) and William Packer, *Dessins de mode Vogue, 1923–1983* (London: Condé Nast, 1983), 10–38.

7. Figures are based on the lists of fashion magazines in the *Annuaire de la Presse,* 1919–38. At any one point, the lists included 60 to 165 magazines. Society and women's magazines were listed separately.

8. Françoise Tétart-Vittu, "Couture et nouveautés confectionées," in *Au Paradis des dames: Nouveautés, modes et confection, 1810–1870* (Paris: Editions Paris-Musée, 1992), 37.

9. Ad for Jenny patterns in *Illustration des Modes,* 16 June 1926, and other designers' patterns mentioned in "En Demi-saison printanière," *La Mode Pratique,* 11 Feb. 1928.

10. "Conseils de la couturière," *La Mode Illustrée,* 1920s, and "La Mode de la Femme économe," *Eve,* 1920s.

11. E.g., *Les Modèles pratiques* and *Guide Pratique de la Mode de Paris: Collection complète des modèles nouveaux des patrons-modèles (Patrons bleus)* (Paris, 1932–34).

12. Françoise Tétart-Vittu, "Presse de mode et dessin" and "Notre dessinateur était la," in *Le Dessin sous toutes ses coutures: Croquis, illustrations, modèles, 1760–1994* (Paris: Palais Galliera, 1995).

13. Roland Barthes, "The Photographic Message," in *Image-Music-Text,* trans. Stephen Heath (New York: Hill and Wang, 1977).

14. Séeberger collection of fashion photographs, BNF, Estampes, Oa381 to Oa429.

15. Alice Mackrell, *Paul Poiret* (London: B. T. Batsford, 1990), 78.

16. Anne Ehrenkranz, *A Singular Elegance: The Photographs of Baron Adolph de*

*Meyer* (San Francisco: Chronicle Books, 1992), and Penelope Niven, *Steichen: A Biography* (New York: Clarkson-Potter, 1997), 352, 501, and 506.

17. Nancy Hall-Duncan, *The History of Fashion Photography* (New York: Chanticleer Press, 1977), 26ff.

18. Kennedy Fraser, "Introduction," *On the Edge: Images from 100 Years of Vogue* (Milan: Amilcare Pizzi, 1992), 5.

19. AN, F12 7601, Minutes of Comité technique de la Propriété industrielle, Note sur la photographie des modèles sur les champs de course, 1920–21.

20. Index of Photographers, Worth and Paquin, AAD 4–1990, in NAL/AAD.

21. Paul Jobling, *Fashion Spreads: Word and Image in Fashion Photography since 1980* (Oxford: Berg, 1999), 2.

22. Worth Publicity Albums, 1927–28 and 1928–1929, in Worth Collection, NAL/AAD 1/78–1982 and AAD 1/79–1982.

23. Elizabeth Hawes, *Fashion Is Spinach* (New York: Random House, 1938), 74, suggests that most illustrations were of Parisian couture, but surveys of the New York edition of *Vogue* by my research assistant Alisa Webb and of the London edition of *Vogue* found that about one-third of the illustrations were Parisian.

24. E.g., the Paris Fashion Issue of *Vogue* (London), Sept. 1931.

25. *WWD*, 10, 11, 16, and 17 Nov. 1921 and 9 and 10 Jan. 1922.

26. Lisa Schlansker Kolosek, *The Invention of Chic: Thérèse Bonney and Paris Moderne* (London: Thames & Hudson, 2002), 67–75 and 95–97, and Thérèse and Louise Bonney, *A Shopping Guide to Paris* (New York: Robert M. McBride, 1929).

27. Ad for Chantal, *Vogue* (New York), 15 Jan. 1927.

28. Gaston Derys, "Dans la Royaume de la mode: Les journaux de modes allemands et autrichiens à Paris," *La Renaissance de l'art française*, Jan. 1924, 35ff., and "L'Admission aux présentations de modèles," *Bulletin Officiel de la Chambre Syndicale de la Couture Parisienne*, Dec. 1930.

29. Plans des Classes 67A and 68 B, in Exposition Internationale Urbaine Lyon 1914, *Rapport Général du Salon des Industries Parisiennes*, by M. Frederic Simon (Lyon: n.p., 1914).

30. "Fête de la soie," *La Soierie de Lyon*, 16 Apr. 1923.

31. ADR, 4M507, Expositions, 1920–39, Foire internationale de Lyon, 1925, Compte-rendu des résultats.

32. L.deL., "Zurich," *La Soierie de Lyon*, 16 Oct. 1918.

33. AN, F[12] 9407, Associations professionnels, Couture, letter from Max Brunhes, Director of *L'Officiel de la Couture*, to Sous-direction de l'Expansion commercial, 29 Oct. 1927; "A French Fashion Show in London" and "Une Démonstration française en Egypte," *L'Officiel de la Couture*, Jan. and Feb. 1929.

34. See "Lucien Lelong, ambassadeur du goût français," *Vogue*, Jan 1938.

35. M. Edmond Labbé, "L'Exposition international de 1937 et le commerce extérieur," in *Exportateur français*, 17 Jan. 1937, in AN, F[12] 12143, Exposition internationale 1937, Commerce Extérieure.

36. AN, F[12] 12145, Propagande, Note sur la propagande de l'exposition coloniale de 1931.

37. Exposition coloniale internationale, Paris, 1931, Section Métropolitaine. Groupe XIII B, Classes 84 A, 84 B, et 84 C.

38. Marcy Ducray, "L'Exposition coloniale influence la mode d'été," *Excelsior-Modes,* 6 Sept. 1931, and "A l'exposition coloniale," *La Mode Pratique,* 22 Aug. 1931.

39. E.g., "L'Exposition de 1937 permettra l'accomplissement d'un bienfaisant miracle," *Semaine à Paris,* 8–14 Jan. 1937, in AN, F$^{12}$ 12145, Publicité; "Une Déclaration de l'Union des industries et commerce de luxe," in *L'Echo de Paris,* 1 Oct. 1936, in AN, F$^{12}$ 12131, Commerce de luxe; "Assemblée générale extraordinaire du Commerce Extérieur traditionnel de la France," *L'Industrie du Vêtement,* Oct. 1936, and Achille Ricker, "Le Problème économique," *Jeune gauche,* 1 Nov. 1936, in AN, F$^{12}$ 12131, Commerce Extérieure.

40. Clipping from *Journal Officiel,* 29 Aug. 1937, in AN F$^{12}$ 12145, Publicité.

41. Proposal for first exposition internationale de la publicité, *Journal Officiel,* 9 May 1935, 364, Annexe no. 3291; Le Palais de la Publicité à l'Exposition internationale de Paris 1937," *L'Echo de Paris,* 2 Feb.1937, speech by Paul Mery; and "Un Congrès mondial de la publicité," *Les Temps modernes,* 27 Apr, 1937, in AN, F$^{12}$ 12145, Publicité.

42. Y.-Georges Prade, "Paris convie l'univers à sa prochaine exposition," and "Exposition 1937," *L'Officiel de la Couture,* May 1933 and Mar. 1937.

43. Jean Cocteau, "La Présence," *Vogue,* Sept 1935, and M.R., "La Grande couture à l'Exposition de 1937," and "L'Exposition '37' et ses merveilles," *Femina,* Sept. and Nov. 1936.

44. Sous-groupe A. Parure, Règlement général du groupe, and letter from Lanvin to Mme. Massot, 7 Apr, 1938, in Dossier Sous-groupe A (classes 56, 56bis, 57, et 63), Pavillon de l'Elégance, and Etat de versements effectués par les exposants au 30 juin 1937, in Classe 56 Couture, AN, F$^{12}$ 12345, Exposition Internationale des Arts et Techniques dans la Vie Moderne, Paris, 1937.

45. "Parisiennes de passage," *Vogue,* Dec. 1927, and "Paris-New York," *Femina,* May 1939.

46. Lydie Chantrell, *Les Moires: 1895–1920 (Mesdames Callot soeurs)* (Paris: La Pensée universelle, 1978), 174.

47. Nancy Green, *Ready-to-Wear and Ready-to-Work: A Century of Industry and Immigrants in Paris and New York* (Durham, NC: Duke University Press, 1997), 81.

48. Amy de la Haye, "The Dissemination of Design from Haute Couture to Fashionable Ready-to-Wear during the 1920s," *Textile History* 24, 1 (1993): 39–48.

49. AN, F$^{12}$ 9407, Associations professionels, Couture, letter from Max Brunhes, director of *L'Officiel de la Couture,* 29 Oct. 1927.

50. Germaine Deschamps, *La Crise dans les industries du vêtement et de la mode à Paris pendant la période de 1930 à 1937* (Paris: Librairie technique et économique, 1938), 47.

51. Philippe Simon, *Monographie d'une industrie de luxe: La Haute couture* (Paris: PUF, 1931), 107–9, and "Utilisation des modèles français à l'étranger," *La Soierie de Lyon,* 1 Mar. 1925.

52. Simon, *Monographie,* 77–85.

53. *The Buyers Pocket-Book* (Paris, 1927), 557ff.

54. Paul Poiret and André Dignimont, *Ce que j'ai vu en chiffonnant la clientèle* (Paris: Librairie des Champs-Elysées, 1938), 45.

55. Simon, *Monographie*, 85ff.

56. Hawes, *Fashion Is Spinach*, 11, 52–53, 62, and 88.

57. "U.S. Woman in Paris Court on Piracy Charge," *WWD*, 22 Dec.1931.

58. Deschamps, *La Crise*, 51.

59. Ads for "Nos modèles haute couture," 99 to 250 francs, *Paris-couture: Revue d'informations de la mode féminine* (Rennes, 1933) and *Paris-Couture: Journal d'information de la mode féminine* (Perpignan, 1934–35).

60. Georges Le Fèvre, *Au Secours de la couture (Industrie française)* (Paris: Editions Baudinière, 1929), 117–24.

61. Hawes, *Fashion Is Spinach*, 38.

62. Testimony of Dame Laniel in "Art. 7478," *INPI*, July–Sept. 1937, and M.R., "Dessous et revers de la copie," *Femina*, June 1931.

63. Hawes, *Fashion Is Spinach*, 38ff., and AP, DlU10 456, Conseil des Prud'hommes, Tissus, Minutes de jugemens, 9 July 1920 (Patou contre Ballon) or 27 Feb. 1925 (Millet contre M. Brisac).

64. Valerie Steele, *Women of Fashion: Twentieth-Century Designers* (New York: Rizzoli, 1991), 80.

65. MTL, Chambre syndicale, Réunion du Bureau, 19 Oct. 1924.

66. France, Office national de la propriété industrielle, *Brevets d'inventions* (1923 and 1924), Category XVI, Habillement, no. 576, 334, and Lucien Lelong, "Ma Collection d'hiver," *L'Officiel de la Couture*, Sept. 1925.

67. AN, F$^{12}$ 7497, Office nationale de la propriété industrielle, Congrès de Washington, 1912; AN, F$^{12}$ 7602 and 7603, Propriété industrielle: législation des brevets, 1883 à 1914, Commission technique, 1913–14; and dossier on Brevets d'invention, 1920–21.

68. E. Soleau, Rapport sur le Projet de loi sur les dessins et modèles, in ACCIP, III, 3.91 (17).

69. G. Champtocé, "Les Marques de fabrique," *Publicité*, May 1920, and *Les Marques internationales* (Berne, 1919).

70. R. L. Dupuy, "Si Nous cherchions une marque," *Vendre*, Oct. 1926, 283–86, and Edith Amiot and Jean-Louis Azizollah, *Les Marques françaises [French Trademarks]*, trans. Mary Lefevre (Saint-Cloud: Historicom Editions, n.d.), 367–68.

71. John Mendenhall, *French Trademarks: The Art Deco Era* (San Francisco: Chronicle Books, 1991).

72. ADR, 67J 363, Archives Bianchini-Férier, Marques déposés, dossier of clippings, two drawings of the logo deposited on 20 June 1916.

73. E.g., "A Toutes les lectrices de *Femina*," *Femina*, Aug. 1933.

74. Chase and Chase, *Always in Vogue*, 92–93.

75. Molly Nesbit, "What Was an Author?" *Yale French Studies* 73 (winter 1987): 236.

76. Vionnet and Carel ads, *Vogue*, 1 Feb. and 15 Mar. 1922.

77. B. J. Atkins, "French Manufacturers Seeking Pact with Couture," *WWD*, 6 Nov. 1931.

78. Simon, *Monographie*, 43–45. Simon was director of the Association for the Defense of the Plastic and Applied Arts.

79. Hermine Valabrèque, *La Propriété artistique en matière de modes* (Thèse, Université de Paris, 1935), chap. 2, 75–84.

80. Eugène Pouillet, *Traité théorique et pratique de la propriété littéraire et artistique,* 3rd ed. (Paris, 1908).

81. Soleau, *Rapport,* 6, and Pouillet, *Traité théorique,* 880–81.

82. Soleau, *Rapport,* 1–2.

83. *JO,* 19 July 1909. Loi sur les dessins et modèles, and ACCIP, Minister of Commerce to the Presidents des Conseils de Prud'hommes and Presidents des Tribunaux de Commerce, on application of law of 14 July 1909.

84. G. Champtocé, "Les Modèles de couture," *Publicité,* Apr. 1923, 215, and AP, D5U B2000 Maison Bernard, DEM 9–133, Classeur no. 2, 1924–28.

85. AN, F$^{12}$ 7499, Office national de la propriété industrielle, Soleau, *Rapport,* 1911.

86. In 1924, Madeleine Vionnet deposited 939 photographs of models at the Prud'hommes, according to AP, D5U10 A, Cartons Vionnet, Classeur no. 3, 1924, whereas she publicized three in the *Bulletin Officiel de la Propriété industrielle* (1924).

87. Eric Golaz, *L'Imitation servile des produits et de leur présentation* (Geneva: Droz, 1992), 60–62 and 84.

88. ACCIP, III 3.91 (18) Soleau, *Rapport,* 1905 and 1915; and Taillefer note on protection of designs and models in the United States. See also "Statistique des dessins et modèles pour les années 1921 à 1925," *La Propriété industrielle: Organe officiel du Bureau International de l'Union pour la Protection de la Propriété industrielle* 41 (1925).

89. Ministère de l'Economie, *La Lutte contre la contrefaçon: Colloque du 23 juin 1994,* 16–17, typescript at the Musée de la Contrefaçon, Paris.

90. Rob Walker, "The Acceptable Knockoff," *New York Times Magazine,* 12 Dec. 2004.

91. Touraille, *Les Crises économiques,* 233–36.

92. AN, F$^{12}$ 9494, Associations professionels, Union Syndicale des tissus, matières textiles, habillement, *Bulletin,* July–Aug. 1929, and note, Mar. 1934.

93. "Assemblée générale statutaire," *Bulletin Officiel de la Chambre Syndicale de la Couture Parisienne,* June 1930, and Marjorie Dunton, "La Chambre Syndicale," in *Couture. An Illustrated History of the Great Paris Designers,* ed. Ruth Lyman (Garden City, NJ: Doubleday, 1972), 40.

94. MTL, Procès-verbaux, Chambre syndical, 25 Apr. and 5 and 19 Nov. 1919; 30 Mar. and 30 Apr. 1928.

95. Ibid., 19 Oct. 1924; 14 Nov. 1925; 4 May, 6 July, and 29 Sept. 1926; 11 June 1928.

96. Ibid., 31 Mar. 1930; 31 Mar. and 22 July 1931; 3 Mar. 1933.

97. Ibid., 16 Jan. 1932 and 9 Apr. 1935.

98. Ibid., 29 Mar., 8 Sept., 24 Nov. and 12 Dec. 1933; 12 Apr. and 31 May 1934.

99. Nancy J. Troy, *Couture Culture: A Study in Modern Art and Fashion* (Cambridge, MA: MIT Press, 2003), 4–10, 27, 74–75, 269ff.

100. Palmer White, *Poiret* (London: Studio Vista 1973), 157.

101. Hawes, *Fashion Is Spinach,* 54–61.

102. Amy de la Haye, *Chanel: The Couturière at Work* (London: Victoria & Albert Museum, 1975), 54–57.

103. *Paquin: Une Rétrospective de 60 ans de haute couture* (Lyon: Musée des Tissus, 1989), 9–11, and Steele, *Women of Fashion,* 27–29.

104. *INPI,* 1909, Art. 80, C. de Paris, 1re Chambre, 11 Mar. 1909, Société Paquin contre *Le Chic* and *Le Chic Parisien,* and *La Gazette du Palais,* 1913, 363, Cour de Cassation (Ch. Civ.), 29 July 1913, Bachwitz et autres contre Sté Paquin.

105. Valabrèque, *La Propriété artistique,* 86–88.

106. *Sirey: Réceuil des lois et arrêts* (1914), pt. 1, Cass. Civ., 29 July 1913; *INPI,* 1919, Art. 5169, Cour de Cassation, 31 Dec. 1918, 15–21.

107. "Pas d'élégance à l'instar," *La Mode Illustrée,* 16 Nov. 1919.

108. "A Nos Lecteurs" and "To Those Who Helped Us," *L'Officiel de la Couture,* 20 July and 5 Aug. 1921.

109. "Les Etrennes des Contrefacteurs" and "Points de droit: Madeleine Vionnet contres les copieurs," and Lucien Chassaigne, "Voyez et touchez," *L'Officiel de la Couture,* 4 Dec. 1922 and 15 Jan. 1924.

110. *L'Information féminine: Première revue française du droit et des intérêts féminins,* May 1927, "La Question de la copie," *Femina Bulletin des acheteurs,* 5 and 25 Sept. 1928, and "La Couture contre la copie," *Vogue,* 1 Mar. 1923 and June 1931.

111. "Sur les devoirs d'une modéliste," *Bulletin Officiel de la Couture Parisienne,* Aug. 1930.

112. Betty Kirke, *Madeleine Vionnet* (San Francisco: Chronicle Books, 1998), 30–42.

113. "Une Coupe savante sous une apparente simplicité" and "Une Artiste éprise de la beauté antique et de l'harmonie du corps féminin," *Vogue,* 1 Feb. 1924 and 1 Mar. 1926. See also "Two Recent Imports . . . Vionnet Type," in *WWD,* 11 Nov. 1921.

114. Kirke, *Vionnet,* 129–32.

115. See ads in Le *Jardin des Modes,* 1920, and *Vogue,* 1924.

116. *INPI,* 1922, Art. 5431, Tribunal Correctionnel de la Seine, 31 Dec. 1921 (Vionnet contre Demoiselle Millet et Veuve Boudreau). See also "La Contrefaçon chez le couturier," *Les Elégances* 6 (1921–22), and "La Défense de la Haute Couture," *Vogue,* Feb. 1922.

117. Ad for Henriette Boudreau in *WWD,* 7 Jan. 1926.

118. ACCIP, III–3.91 (17), letter from La Protection Artistique des Industries Saisonnières, 15 Dec. 1930.

119. Louis Dangel, "La Protection des créations d'arts appliqués," *Bulletin Officiel,* Oct.1930.

120. *INPI,* 1923, Art. 6178, 16 June 1923, Vionnet contre Dames Robillard and Gramond et Jeanne Lanvin contre Dames Robillard et Gramond, 1926; Art. 6011, Cour de Paris, 22 June 1926, Patou et Cie contre Touboul (Maison Cyber); *La Gazette du Palais,* 8 May 1930, Tribunal correctionnel de la Seine, 10 Mar. 1930, Vionnet contre dame Muraz.

121. AP, D1U 10, 479, Jugements, 1930–31, 12 Feb. 1930, esp. Rapport du Comité d'enquête and letter from Trouyet to Buhler.

122. "Four More Couture Firms in Anti-Copying Group," *WWD,* 28 Dec. 1931.

123. Ad for Association pour la Défense des Arts plastiques et appliqués en France et à l'étranger, *Bulletin Officiel,* Jan. 1932.

124. *INPI*, 1936, 45–46, Art. 7307. Laniel contre Vionnet et Chanel, 1937, 244–49, and Art. 7478. Vionnet et Chanel contre Laniel.

125. Elizabeth de Gramont, "La Mode en 1930," *Le Correspondant*, 25 Dec.1930.

126. MTL, Chambre syndical, Assemblée générale, 12 Dec. 1933.

127. Deschamps, *La Crise*, 57, and ACCIP, III–3.91, 17, Fabry bill, 22 Oct. 1930, and Bertaut report, 22 Oct. 1930.

128. Axel Madsen, *Sonia Delaunay: Artist of the Lost Generation* (New York: Mc-Graw-Hill, 1989), 191ff., and *Hommage à Elsa Schiaparelli* (Paris: Musée de la Mode, 1984), 36.

129. Jacques Lanzmann et Pierre Ripert, *Cent ans de prêt-à-porter: Weill* (Paris: PAU, 1992), 70.

130. Elsa Schiaparelli, *Shocking Life* (New York: Dutton, 1954), 67 and 86, and "American Buyers Discover Lelong's Robes d'Edition," *WWD*, 2 Mar. 1937.

## CHAPTER SEVEN. SHOPPING AND SEWING

1. Daniel Roche, *The Culture of Clothing: Dress and Fashion in the "Ancien Regime,"* trans. Jean Birrell (Cambridge: Cambridge University Press, 1994), 33, 38, and 41.

2. Daniel Roche, *A History of Everyday Things: The Birth of Consumption in France, 1600–1800,* trans. Brian Pierce (Cambridge: Cambridge University Press, 2000), 218–19.

3. Perrot, Philippe, *Fashioning the Bourgeoisie: A History of Clothing in the Nineteenth Century,* trans. Richard Bienvenu (Princeton: Princeton University Press, 1994).

4. E.g., Le Comte de Bondy, "La Mode et la vie," *De la Mode: Hier-aujourd'hui-demain; Les Cahiers de la République des lettres, des sciences et des arts,* 15 July 1927, 36–41, and Pascale Saisset, "La Démocratisation de la mode," *La Grande Revue,* Jan.–June 1937, 241–43.

5. Michael B. Miller, *The Bon Marché: Bourgeois Culture and the Department Store, 1869–1920* (Princeton: Princeton University Press, 1981), 3 and 4.

6. Rosalind H. Williams, *Dream Worlds: Mass Consumption in Late Nineteenth-Century France* (Berkeley: University of California Press, 1982), 11, 59, 64, and 93, and François Caron, "L'Embellie parisienne à la Belle Epoque: L'invention d'un modèle de consommation," *Vingtième Siècle* 47 (1995): 50.

7. Miller, *The Bon Marché*, 25–28.

8. Thomas Hine, *I Want That! How We All Became Shoppers* (New York: Harper-Collins, 2002), 130–31.

9. Perrot, *Fashioning the Bourgeoisie,* 52–56.

10. *Cent ans après: La vie d'une grande industrie modern dans un vieux quartier de Paris* (Paris: Belle Jardinière, 1930), 11–13.

11. See advertisements in *Femina,* May 1922 and May 1923.

12. Miller, *The Bon Marché,* 40–51; sales figures on 43.

13. V. de Mendez, "Comment les grandes magasins exploitent l'idée de 'service,'" *Vendre,* 16 Feb. 1925, and Christoph Grunenberg, "Wonderland: Spectacles of Display from the Bon Marché to Prada," in *Shopping: A Century of Art and Consumer*

*Culture*, ed. C. Grunenberg and Max Hollein (Ostfildern-Ruit, Germany: Hatje Cantz Publishers, 2002), 21–26.

14. "Une Inauguration bien parisienne: Le premier thé chez Drecoll," *L'Officiel de la Couture*, Jan. 1926.

15. Piedade da Silveira, *Aux Trois Quartiers* (Paris: CCM, 1916), 9–27.

16. *Le Grand Bazar de Lyon de 1886 à nos jours* (Lyon: Charvet, 1990), 7–36, and *Grand Bazar de Lyon: Parfumerie et brosserie* (1913).

17. François Faraut, *Histoire de la Belle Jardinière* (Paris: Belin, 1987), 101.

18. Anne-Sophie Beau, "Les Employées du Grand Bazar de Lyon (1880–1950)," in *Bulletin Centre Pierre Léon d'historie économique et sociale* 4, 4 (1997): 51–64, and Trista Gaston-Breton, *Galeries Lafayette: La Légende d'un siècle* (Paris: Galeries Lafayette Clio Média, 1997), 49.

19. Jean Neuilly, "Une Ecole de Vendeuses: Ce qu'est l'Ecole Technique de Vente pour les jeunes filles," *Vendre*, Feb. 1926, 157–59.

20. *Palais modernes: Les grands magasins du Bon Marché*, in BNF, Etampes.

21. Gaston-Breton, *Galeries Lafayette*, 22–56.

22. Bernard Marrey, *Les Grands magasins* (Paris: Picard, 1979), 8, 89, 97–98, 173–75, and 201.

23. H. Gordon Selfridge, Jean-Louis Vaudoyer, and M. P. Vanginot, respectively, in the Au Printemps brochure on the inauguration of its new store, June 1924, in BNF, Etampes.

24. Mendez, "Comment les grands magasins . . . ," 137; René Herbst, *Nouvelle devantures et agencements de magasins*, 4th ser. (Paris: Editions d'Art Charles Moreau, 1930), and V. de Mendes, "L'Eclairage des vitrines," *Vendre*, Mar. 1926.

25. B.L. (Launois), "A l'Exposition Internationale des Arts Décoratifs: Pour la défense des mannequins modernes d'étalage," and R. Bourgogne, "L'Erreur des étalages modernes," *Publicité*, Nov. 1925, 670–71, and Oct. 1926, 661.

26. Jean Levant, "Pour mieux comprendre le mannequin d'étalage" and "Les Mannequins modernes d'étalage," and M.B. (Boulnois), "Mannequin" and "Le Langage et le mannequin," *Publicité*, Mar. and Apr. 1927 and June and Oct. 1930.

27. See ad for Aux Trois Quartiers in *Le Progrès de Lyon*, 3 Jan. 1925.

28. Henri Lièvre, *Une Forme de la concentration commerciale: Les entreprises à succursales multiples dans l'industrie et le commerce du vêtement* (Paris: n.p., n.d.), 107.

29. Gaston-Breton, *Galeries Lafayette*, 43, and ads in *Le Progrès de Lyon*, 20 July 1920 and 20 Jan. 1925.

30. Gaston-Breton, *Galeries Lafayette*, 44.

31. Xavier Chaumette, *Tissus pour un siècle de Mode: Les Textiles et les modes féminines en France au XXe siècle* (Neuilly-sur-Seine: Michel Lafon, 2002).

32. *Le Grand Bazar de Lyon*, 53–56.

33. André Bovar, *Emile Decré: Un grand commerçant chrétien* (Nantes: Siloë, 1997).

34. Jacques Lanzmann and Pierre Ripert, *Cent ans de prêt-à-porter: Weill* (Paris: PAU, 1992), 17–20 and 54–61.

35. Jean-Jacques Delort, "Préface," in Jacques de Closel, *Les Grands magasins français: Cent ans après* (Paris: Chotard, n.d.), 3.

36. Gaston-Breton, *Galeries Lafayette,* 57–62.

37. Faraut, *Histoire,* 112–13.

38. *Le Grand Bazar,* 57–59.

39. Ad for Grandes Magasins des Cordeliers (Galeries Lafayette) in *Le Progrès de Lyon,* 4 Jan. 1925.

40. *L'Echo du Nord,* 6 Mar. 1927.

41. E.g., ads for Au Bon Marché in *La Mode,* 24 Apr. 1927, and Galeries Lafayette, Louvre, Au Printemps, and Aux Magasins Réunis, in *Eve,* 1922.

42. E.g., insert for Au Printemps men's and ladies' wear in *Femina,* May 1923.

43. See department store ads in *Le Progrès de Lyon,* 18 Apr. 1920 and 4 Jan. and 1 Mar. 1925, and *L'Echo du Nord,* 15 Feb. and 28 Mar. 1920.

44. Ads for "A la Parisienne," in *Le Progrès de Lyon,* 18 Apr. 1920, and for "Aux Modes Parisiennes," in *L'Echo du Nord,* 15 Feb. 1920.

45. Ads for Henri Esders in *Le Progrès de Lyon,* 22 Jan. 1925, and for Aux Dames des France Nouveautés, *L'Echo du Nord,* 30 Sept. 1924.

46. *Au Bon Marché, Mardi 24 avril et jours suivants, 1923. Toilettes d'Eté;* and *Madame: Le Printemps vous prie de bien vouloir honorer de votre visite l'exposition de ses nouveautés pour l'hiver, 25 septembre 1923,* in BNF, Etampes. Also *Présentation des dernières créations été 1927* and *Présentation des toilettes d'été 1928,* in Au Printemps collection at BF.

47. *Le Conseiller de la femme* 2, 13 (1932), and Paul Reboux, "Ah Paris!," in *Agenda des Galeries Lafayette pour 1934* (Paris: Galeries Lafyette, 1933).

48. Elizabeth Sifton, "Montreal's Fashion Mile," in *Fashion: A Canadian Perspective,* ed. Alexandra Palmer (Toronto: University of Toronto Press, 2004), 216–18.

49. Marcel Farges, "La Confection du catalogue d'un grand magasin de nouveautés," *Publicité,* Feb. 1931, 42–47, and Alexandra Keller, "Disseminations of Modernity: Representation and Consumer Desire in Early Mail-Order Catalogs," in *Cinema and the Invention of Modern Life,* ed. L. Charney and V. R. Schwartz (Berkeley: University of California Press, 1995), 157–58.

50. A. Raymond Haas, "Catalogues françaises," *Vendre,* May 1934, 245–50; quotation, 248.

51. L. Manceau, "A Bordeaux: La Publicité des Grands Magasins Aux Dames de France," *La Publicité,* Sept. 1927. Also Colonel Doizan, "Les Enseignes lumineuses," *Figaro Illustrée,* Mar. 1931, 32–34.

52. "Le Catalogue," *La Publicité française: Organe mensuel de propagande commerciale,* Aug. 1920, and Lucien Farnoux-Reynaud, "Du Catalogue," *Publicité,* Feb. 1934, 122–24. For slogan, see Au Bon Marché, *Nouveautés de Printemps et d'Ete 1939,* in BF.

53. Ad for *Les Modes élégantes au Printemps,* in *Femina,* Mar. 1922.

54. Blanche Duverneuil, "La Renaissance du catalogue dans la mode," *La Publicité,* Apr. 1920, 91–93.

55. E.g., *Toilettes d'été lundi 18 avril* (1919) and *Premières nouveautés d'été, 2 mars* (1920), in Printemps collection at BF.

56. E.g., *La Belle saison à la Belle Jardinière: Paris; Eté 1924* and *Pour les beaux jours* (1926), in La Belle Jardinière catalog collection at the BF.

57. E.g., *Nouveautés de Printemps et d'Eté, 1930* and *Nouveautés de Printemps et d'Eté 1934*, in Au Printemps collection at BF.

58. E.g., "Voici la belle saison," in *Bon Marché, Eté 1927*, and captions on the front cover and first page of *Galeries Lafayette, Eté 1936*.

59. "Elégante: Voici les points essentiels," in *Nouveautés de Printemps et d'Eté . . . 1938*, and J.R.F., "Madame," in *Grande Quinzaine des Nouveautés de la Saisons . . . 1939*, in Au Printemps catalog collection at BF.

60. See the short sections labeled "Pour personnes fortes" or "Pour femmes fortes" in *Galeries Lafayette, Hiver 1926–27*, and Au Bon Marché, *Printemps-Eté, 1929*.

61. Rumpf, "Les Catalogues des grands magasins de nouveautés se modernisent," *La Publicité*, May 1928, 71–73.

62. I analyzed cover subjects, settings, and slogans on 100 catalog cover drawings from Galeries Lafayette, Au Printemps, and La Belle Jardinière between 1919 and 1931.

63. "Vêtements de travail" pages in Belle Jardinière, *Catalogue générale*, summer 1919, 1927, and 1931.

64. E.g., Au Bon Marché, *Soldes 1928, Trousseaux, Corsets, Linge de mains*, Jan. 1926; Galeries Lafayette, *Catalogue générale*, winter 1930–31.

65. Au Bon Marche, *Toilettes et modes d'été . . . 1929* and *Printemps-Eté 1929*.

66. Aux Galeries Lafayette, *Toilettes d'été et de campagne, été 1925*, and *Exposition générale le mardi 3 mars et jours suivants 1925*.

67. C.B., "Vertu de l'économie. Efficacité de la dépense" and "A quel minimum peut atteindre le budget de toilette annuel de madame," *La Mode Pratique*, 15 and 27 Sept. 1934.

68. Roger Allard, "Dialogue entre elle et moi sur les grands magasins," *Gazette du Bon Ton* 4, 4 (1921).

69. "Notre Service de Couture" and "Un Trousseau minimum: Sa composition, son prix," *La Mode Officielle*, 12 Aug. 1922 and 16 Jan. 1937.

70. J.L., "Toute la Mode," *Eve*, 3 Dec. 1921 and 29 June 1924.

71. C.D., "Entre Nous," *La Mode Illustrée*, 1 Aug. 1926, and "En mars capricieux," *En la Ville de la soie*, Mar. 1924.

72. Maggy-Rouff, "L'Elégance nait à Paris," *Marie Claire*, 7 May 1937, and Paul Poiret and André Dignimont, *Ce que j'ai vu en chiffonnant la clientèle* (Paris: Librairie des Champs-Elysées, 1938), 44.

73. Comtesse Riguidi, *L'Epoque: Les moeurs, les modes, le style* (Paris: Berger-Levrault, 1931), 12.

74. Marcelle Auclair, *Anne Fauvet ou l'assortiment difficile* (Paris: SEPE, 1931), 58 and 67–73.

75. Colette Yver, *Femmes d'aujourd'hui* (Paris: Calman Levy, 1929), 112 and 117.

76. "Robes toutes faites pour Dames," *La Belle Jardinière, Autumn-Hiver 1926*, 19–20, and *Autumn-Hiver 1930–1931*, 19–20. In the winter 1938 catalogue, prices for "Nos Robes pour Dames" ranged from 95 to 395 francs.

77. Helen Chenut, *The Fabric of Gender: Working-Class Culture in Third Republic France* (University Park: University of Pennsylvania Press, 2005), 316–17.

78. *Traité de pédagogie pour l'enseignement de la coupe et de la couture* (Paris: Librairie Carus, 1920s), 12.

79. Bibliothèque D.M.C., *L'ABC de la Couture* (Mulhouses, Dillmont, n.d.).

80. Ad for *Comment je fais mes robes* in *La Mode du Jour,* 20 Dec. 1934; *Revue très pratique: Pour faire vos robes vous-mémes* (Paris: n.p., 1932).

81. Marie de Grand'Maison, *Le Trésor du Foyer* (Paris: Editions de la *Mode Nationale* 1925), and *Larousse ménager* (Paris: Librairie Larousse, 1926).

82. "Le Nettoyage des étoffes de soie," *La Mode Illustrée,* 14 Feb. 1920; "Le Détachage des robes de soie ou de laine" and "A défaut de machine à laver," *La Mode Pratique,* 22 Mar. and 15 Aug. 1930.

83. "Avec 'Twink' qui nettoie et teint à la fois, vous aurez toujours des robes fraîches" and "N'oubliez pas que 'Lux' savon en paillettes remet à neuf vos lingeries délicates," *La Mode,* 23 Nov. 1926.

84. Margaret Morgenroth Gulette, "The Other End of the Fashion Cycle: Practicing Loss, Learning Decline," in *Figuring Age: Women, Bodies, Generations,* ed. Kathleen Woodward (Bloomington: Indiana University Press, 1999), 36.

85. "Le Portfolio de l'élégance pratique," *Vogue,* 1 Feb. 1925.

86. "Un Mariage à l'automne," *La Mode Pratique,* 27 Sept. 1930.

87. "Savoir coudre est très bien, savoir couper est mieux," *Eve,* 13 Apr. 1920, and *L'Art dans le costume: La Coupe et la mode,* published annually through the interwar decades.

88. E.g., "Robe d'après-midi pour une future maman," *La Mode Pratique,* 12 Mar. 1934.

89. "Les Secrets du métier," *La Mode Pratique,* 8 Sept 1930 and 8 Sept. 1934, and "Toute la Mode: La Vogue des robes imprimées," *Eve,* 11 May 1929.

90. Cover banner on *La Mode,* 7 Nov. 1926; notices about "Notre patron-prime à prix reduit," in *La Mode du Jour,* 1929–32.

91. "Nouveau tarif de *La Mode Illustrée*," "Notre Pochette de patrons," and "Service des patrons," *La Mode Illustrée,* 9 Oct. 1921, 1 Sept. 1929, and 12 Jan. 1930.

92. "*La Mode Pratique* offre à toutes ses lectrices . . . ," and "Tarif de notre service de patrons sur mesures, " *La Mode Pratique,* 16 Apr. 1927 and 16 June 1934.

93. "Une Grande diversité de modèles," *Chiffons,* 5 Apr. 1927.

94. "Pour Vôtre petite couturier" and "Un Tailleur facile à faire," *Femina,* Mar. 1917 and 1 Oct. 1920.

95. "De la Mode," *L'Illustration des Modes,* 21 Oct.1920.

96. *Soyons pratique: Patrons et ouvrages du Jardin de modes* 1, 1 (1933).

97. *Le Miroir des modes* 1, 1 (1922), in *Idées nouvelles* collection at BNF, Etampes.

98. *Patron-journal,* 17 Apr. and 10–19 June 1926, and 10 Mar. 1928.

99. *Guide pratique de la Mode de Paris: Collection complète des modèles nouveaux des patrons-modèles (Patrons bleus)* (Paris: Editions de la Société de *Petit Echo de la Mode,* 1932–34).

100. "Dans Toutes ces villes vous trouverez nos patrons tout faits," *Soyons pratiques,* Mar. 1934 and subsequent issues.

101. See insert and notice in *Hiver 1923–24* catalog in the Au Printemps collection, BF.

102. Prices from Au Printeps *Eté 1923* catalog at the BF and "Journée des tissus" and "Fournitures pour la mode et pour la couture" 14 Mar. and 26 Sept. 1933 Au Printemps flyers in BNF, Etampes, Idées nouvelles collection.

103. Prices for linings are from the Galeries Lafayette summer catalog of 1925 and the Bon Marché, *Grande Quinzaine des Nouveautés de la Saison,* Mar. 1939.

104. Prices from Galeries Lafayette flyer, "Fournitures pour la mode et pour la couture," 26 Sept. 1933, in BNF, Etampes.

105. Judith Coffin, *The Politics of Women's Work* (Princeton: Princeton University Press, 1996), 72ff.

106. E.g., "La Maison jolie," *La Mode du Jour,* 27 Mar. 1930.

107. *Soldes,* Dec. 1923, in Dufayel catalog collection at BF.

108. Pitches from *L'Art et la Mode* 25 (19 June 1926), and *Chiffons,* 20 Nov. 1926.

109. Auclair, *Anne Fauvet,* 14, 27, and 36, and Lucie Delarue-Mardrus, *La Girl: Roman* (Paris: Ferenczi et fils, 1939), 15.

110. See "Pour les sports d'hiver," "Tricoter, Mesdames, ce douillet ensemble pour le sport," *La Mode Illustrée,* 14 Dec. 1924 and 10 Jan. 1932; and "Un Nouvelle marque de premier ordre: Les laines Mode du Jour," in *La Mode du Jour,* 4 Feb. 1932, and insert for courses in 13 Oct. 1932 issue.

111. Francis Petit, Jacqueline Grislain, and Martine le Blan, *Aux Fils du temps: La Redoute* (Paris: Robert Laffont, 1985), esp. 147–66 and 179. See also *Pénélope: Travaux de laine et modes,* at the BF.

## CHAPTER EIGHT. THE POLITICS OF MODERN FASHION

1. Rita Felski, *The Gender of Modernity* (Cambridge, MA: Harvard University Press, 1995), 14.

2. E.g., George Edwin Mowry, *The Twenties: Fords, Flappers, and Fanatics* (Englewood Cliffs, NJ: Prentice Hall, 1963); Sumiko Higashi, *Virgins, Vamps, and Flappers: The American Silent Movie Heroine* (St. Albans, VT: Eden Press, 1978); Martin Pumphrey, "The Flapper, the Housewife, and the Making of Modernity," *Cultural Studies* 1, 2 (1987); Miriam Silverberg, "The Modern Girl as Militant," in *Recreating Japanese Women, 1600–1945,* ed. Gail Lee Bernstein (Berkeley: University of California Press, 1991), 239–66; and Barbara Hamill Sato, "The *Moga* Sensation: Perceptions of MODAN GARU in Japanese Intellectual Circles during the 1920s," *Gender and History* 5, 3 (1993): 363–81.

3. The cultural argument is best articulated by Billie Melman, *Women and the Popular Imagination in the Twenties: Flappers and Nymphs* (Basingstoke, UK: Macmillan Press, 1988), 15ff.

4. Silverberg, "The Modern Girl as Militant," 240.

5. See Anna Gough-Yates, *Understanding Women's Magazines: Publishing, Markets, and Readerships* (London: Routledge, 2003), 56.

6. Pascale Saisset, "La Vie féminine," *La Grande Revue,* Nov. 1922.

7. Irene Guenther, *Nazi Chic? Fashioning Women in the Third Reich* (Oxford: Berg, 2004), chaps. 3 and 4, and Eugenia Paulicelli, *Fashion under Fascism: Beyond the Black Shirt* (Oxford: Berg, 2004), chap. 2.

8. S.A.B., "D'Une chose à l'autre," *Chiffons,* 10 July 1920.

9. Marianna Torgovnick, *Gone Primitive: Savage Intellects, Modern Lives* (Chicago: University of Chicago Press, 1990), 146–47.

10. Edouard Keyser, "L'Eclosion" and "Renaissance du goût français," *L'Officiel de la Couture,* Nov. 1924 and June 1938, and M.R., "La Grande couture à l'Exposition de 1937," *Femina,* Sept. 1936.

11. "La Vie féminine," *Le Progrès de Lyon,* 5 Mar. 1925 and "Chronique de la mode," *L'Echo du Nord,* 16 Dec. 1929.

12. E.g., *La Grande hebdomadaire illustrée de la région Nord,* 1922–24.

13. A.deL., "Chroniques," *La Mode,* 27 Apr. 1919, and L.deL., "Fashion," *La Soierie de Lyon,* 16 Nov. 1920, and 16 Feb. 1921.

14. M.R., "La Mode pour Paris," *Femina,* Jan. 1924; "Entre nous," *La Mode Illustrée,* 12 July 1930; and Countess Riguidi, *L'Epoque: Les moeurs, les modes, le style* (Paris: Berger-Levrault, 1931), 112.

15. "La Vie féminine," *Le Progrès de Lyon,* 15 July 1920.

16. "Très Femina," *Femina,* May 1939, and "La Collection de *Marie Claire,"Marie Claire,* 2 Apr. and 17 Sept. 1937.

17. Mardoche et Desgenais (a.k.a. Gaston Berardi), *Les Parisiennes* (Paris: Dentu, 1882).

18. Ferdinand Bac, *Nos Femmes: Album en couleurs* (Paris: Empis, 1895), Gaston Bonnefont, *Les Parisiennes chez elles* (Paris: Flammarion, 1895), and Henri Boutet, *Autour d'elle* (Paris: Ollendorff, 1897–98).

19. E.g., Remy de Gourmont and Andre Rouveyre, *Parisiennes* (Paris: Cres, 1923).

20. Mireille Dottin-Orsini, *Cette Femme qu'ils disent fatale: Textes et image de la misogynie fin-de-siècle* (Paris: Grasset, 1993), and Edouard Cavailhon, *Les Parisiennes fatales* (Paris: Dentu, 1889).

21. Octave Uzanne, *La Femme à Paris* (Paris: May et Motteroz, 1894), 4–10.

22. Debora L. Silverman, *Art Nouveau in Fin-de-Siècle France* (Berkeley: University of California Press, 1989).

23. Alfred Franklin, *La Vie privée d'autrefois: Les magasins de nouveautés* (Paris: Plon, 1895).

24. Marcel Astruc, "A la Recherche d'un néologisme," *Gazette du Bon Ton* 3, 2 (1920), and "Pour les frileuses épaules féminines," *Vogue,* 15 Sept. 1920.

25. "L'Elégance pour les bourses modestes" and "Pour être élégante avec économie," *Vogue,* 15 July 1920 and 1 Mar. 1924.

26. "Le Duel du Chic et de la Beauté," *Vogue,* 1 Oct. 1920, and Joseph Kessel, "Sous le Signe de Paris," *Femina,* Dec. 1930.

27. "De la Distinction et de la mode," *Vogue,* 1 Nov. 1920.

28. Pierre Bourdieu and Yvette Delsaut, "Le Couturier et sa griffe: Contribution à un théorie de la magie," *Actes de la recherche en sciences sociales* 1 (Jan. 1975): 7, and Bourdieu, *La Distinction: Critique social du jugement* (Paris: Editions du Minuit, 1979).

29. J.L., "Toute la Mode: Il faut avoir du chic," *Eve,* 11 Oct. 1925.

30. "L'Harmonie des attitudes," *Vogue,* Feb. 1938.

31. M.H., "Le Chapeau se transforme suivant le style de la robe," *Vogue,* July 1924, and Astrid, "Harmonie des ensembles," *La Mode Pratique,* 9 June 1934.

32. *La Renaissance de l'art français et des industries de luxe* 9, 1 (1926); for a similar endorsement from Madame Bozier, president of the Chambre syndicale de la Mode in 1929, see *L'Officiel de la Couture,* June 1929.

33. M.H., "Le Chapeau se transforme suivant le style de la robe," *Vogue,* July 1924, and "Un trousseau de chapeaux," *La Mode Pratique,* 31 July 1926.

34. Album des chapeaux, Collection Hélène Meillassoux, Fonds Spony-Blanc, Modèle chapeaux, and Technologie, Musée des Arts et Tradition populaires.

35. "Une Revolution dans la mode," *Excelsior-Modes,* Oct. 1929; "Une Revolution dans la mode," *L'Officiel de la Mode,* Mar. 1930; and "Revolution au pays des chapeaux," *La Mode Pratique,* 19 Sept. 1931.

36. Marraine, "Ce qui se porte," *C'est la mode,* 10 Jan. 1932; "Nos chapeaux penchent sur le cote," *La Mode Pratique,* 2 Apr. 1932; and "Le Chapitre des détails élégants," *Femina,* Aug. 1933.

37. Steven Zdatny, ed., *Hairstyles and Fashion: A Hairdresser's History of Paris, 1910–1920* (Oxford: Berg, 1999), 24–25.

38. "L'Art de Plaire selon votre silhouette," *Femina,* July 1934.

39. M.R., "Le Chapitre des détails élégants," *Femina,* Oct. 1921, and "Du Chic avec peu de chose," *Vogue,* June 1926.

40. Fanny Croisset, "Les Robes à écharpes," *L'Illustration de la Mode,* 7 Apr. 1921; "Avec vos robes imprimées ou vos écharpes de l'an passe," *Le Jardin de la Mode,* 15 Feb. 1926.

41. A.deL., "Chronique," *La Mode,* 29 Aug. 1920; "Les Mille aspects d'une toilette," *La Mode Pratique,* 11 June 1932.

42. "La Mode, comme la nature, créé son renouveau" and "La Mode de jour abonde en détails neufs," *Vogue,* 1 Mar. 1922 and 1 Oct. 1927; M.R., "La Mode est surtout intéressante par la nouveauté de ses détails," *Femina,* Apr. 1933.

43. Lucy, "Les Mélanges de tissues," *La Mode du Jour,* 16 Apr. 1933; "Cache-Mìsères par Anny Blatt," *Femina,* Aug. 1936; and "La Ligne," *La Mode Pratique,* 26 Sept. 1931.

44. "A Paris on voit," *L'Officiel de la Couture,* starting May 1928, and "Feathers" and "New Trimmings" (in English in the original) in the Apr. and Aug. 1924 issues.

45. L.deL., "Fashion," and Henri Algoud, "A Modern Renaissance of the Shawl and Scarf," *La Soierie de Lyon,* 16 Mar. and 16 July 1924.

46. Christine Bard, *Le Mouvement féministe en France, 1914–1939* (D.E.A. d'histoire, Université de Paris VII, 1989), 25 and 29; *Les Féminismes en France: Vers l'intégration des femmes dans la Cité, 1914–1940* (Thèse de doctorat, Université de Paris VII, 1993), 1018ff., and *Les Filles de Marianne: Histoire des féminismes, 1914–1940* (Paris: Fayard, 1995), 235ff.

47. Christine Bard, *La Garçonne: Modes et fantasmes des Années folles* (Paris: Flammarion, 1998).

48. I borrow the term *everyday rebellions* from Gloria Steinem, *Outrageous Acts and Everyday Rebellions* (New York: Henry Holt, 1995).

49. "Conférence: Les Femmes dans le journalisme," in Marguerite Durand, Manuscrit, 3, in BMD, and M. Durand," Quel métier choisir ? Femmes journalistes," *L'Intransigeant,* no date but 1926, BHVP, Fonds Bouglé, Articles de presse, Auteurs, M. Durand.

50. C. de Broutelles (on *Vie heureuse* letterhead) to the director of Les Nouvelles, 20 Apr. 1910, in BMD, 091 BRO.

51. See Maitre Pommay, "La Nationalité de la jeune mariée," *La Mode Pratique,* 14 Jan. 1922.

52. Bard, *Les féminismes en France,* 56, 135, 303, and 487.

53. G. Malaterre-Sellier, "Suffrage des femmes," *La Mode Pratique,* 8, 15, and 29 Dec. 1923.

54. BMD, dossier Hélène Miropolsky, Coupures de presse; Hélène Miropolsky, "Mlle Hélène Miropolsky préconside un referendum," *Journal,* 15 Mar. 1914, and H. Miropolsky, "Les Femmes et les prochaines elections," *Femina,* 1 Apr. 1914.

55. See Miropolsky's article in *Femina,* 1 Feb. 1918. On individualistic and relational feminism, see Karen Offen, "Defining Feminism: A Comparative Historical Perspective," *Signs: Journal of Women in Culture and Society* 14, 1 (1988).

56. Marthe Borely, "Contre le féminisme," *Femina,* May 1918.

57. Marthe Borely, *L'Appel aux françaises: Le Féminisme politique* (Paris: Nouvelle Librairie Nationale, 1919). On prewar antecedents, see Karen Offen, "Depopulation, Nationalism, and Feminism in Fin-de-Siècle France, *American Historical Review* 89, 3 (1984).

58. Jean Elizabeth Pedersen, "Regulating Abortion and Birth Control: Gender, Medicine, and Republican Politics in France, 1870–1920," *French Historical Studies* 19 (spring 1996): 673–98, and *Legislating the French Family: Feminism, Theater, and Republican Politics, 1870–1920* (New Brunswick, NJ: Rutgers University Press, 2003).

59. Hélène Miropolsky, "Le Mouvement social féminin," *Femina,* Mar. 1918.

60. Quote from Steven C. Hause with Anne R. Kenney, *Women's Suffrage and Social Politics in the French Third Republic* (Princeton: Princeton University Press, 1984), 239.

61. "La Femme dans la cité," *Femina,* Mar., May, June, and July 1920.

62. Despite searches in nine libraries, I never found a handful of *Femina* issues. For seven years, the BNF version has been *"incommunicable"* and unfit for microfilming.

63. "Nous allons causer devant vous de la femme et du féminisme avec Mme. Miropolsky," *L'Oeuvre,* 1 Nov. 1926, and "Suzanne Dudit, "Mme Hélène Miopolsky," *Miranda,* 2 Apr. 1933, in BMD, dossiers personnels. On paternity, see K. S. Childers, "Paternity and the Politics of Citizenship in Interwar France," *Journal of Family History* 16, 1 (2001).

64. Hause and Kenney, *Women's Suffrage and Social Politics,* 217–20; and Francine Muel-Dreyfus, *Vichy et l'éternel féminin* (Paris: Editions de Seuil, 1996), 168–69.

65. "La Vie sociale et les femmes," *Le Petit Echo de la Mode,* 12 June and 5 July 1921.

66. Paule Herfort, "Les Etats-généraux du féminisme!," *Minerva,* 3 Mar. 1929.

67. "Jardin des âmes," *Le Petit Echo de la Mode,* 29 Sept. and 6 Oct. 1929.

68. C.D., "Entre Nous," *La Mode Illustrée,* 6 Feb. and 27 Nov. 1927.

69. E.g., Max Dorian, "A Propos de Mlle Chauvin," *Liberté,* Sept. 1926, and "Nous allons causer," *L'Oeuvre,* 1 Nov. 1926.

70. Roberts, *Disruptive Acts,* 60, 70, and 99.

71. *La Femme émancipée: Les Cahiers contemporains* (Paris: Montaigne, 1927), 17; "Comment s'habiller: Comment s'embellir," *Foyer,* Mar. 1927, 90.

72. Duchesse de la Rochefoucauld, "La Mode et la politique," *Excelsior-Modes,* spring 1931, and Bard, *Les Filles de Marianne,* 206 and 268ff.

73. *Eve*, 3 Oct. 1920, and *Annuaire de la Presse*, 1921–35. The BNF put *Eve* the illustrated weekly supplement on the same microfilm as *Eve: Le Premier Quotidien Illustré de la Femme*, possibly because the latter began publishing the year that the former folded. The supplement makes no reference to the earlier, glossier publication.

74. "Modèles féministes," *Eve*, 13 Apr. 1920.

75. René Degy, "Le Costume de la Femme a't'il tendance à se masculiniser?," *Eve*, 28 Aug. 1921.

76. "Tout la Mode," *Eve*, 1 Oct. 1922, 28 Feb. 1925, 11 Sept. 1926, 16 Jan. and 6 Feb. 1927, 28 Nov. 1928, and 16 Feb. 1930.

77. "Toute la Mode," *Eve*, 16 Nov. 1930, 5 Apr., 10 May, and 6 Sept. 1931.

78. Claire Lausnay "Les Caracteristiques de la nouvelle mode," *Femina*, Mar. 1922.

79. Delphine Gardey, "Du Veston au bas de soie: Identité et évolution du groupe des employés de bureau (1890–1930)," *Le Mouvement Socal* 175 (Apr.–June 1996): 55–77, and Linda L. Clark, *The Rise of Professional Women in France: Gender and Public Administration since 1830* (Cambridge: Cambridge University Press, 2000), 125.

80. "La Collaboratrice de l'homme d'affaires reste chic avec sobriété," *Vogue*, 1 Jan. 1925.

81. "Vivre de bonne soupe," *La Mode Illustrée*, 14 Nov. 1920.

82. Brigitte, "Propos sur la mode. Le Centenaire du romantisme, 1830–1930," *La Mode*, 19 Jan. 1930.

83. "Des Métiers pour les femmes qui n'en ont pas," and Henriette, "Le Role de la femme," "Page féministe," and "Le Travail de la femme," *Le Petit Echo de la Mode*, 20 Feb. 1921, 12 Nov. and 3 Dec. 1922, and 11 Mar. 1923.

84. Inquiry cited by Françoise Battagliola, *Histoire du travail des femmes* (Paris: La Découverte, 2000), 61.

85. R.-H. Guerrand and M.-A. Rupp, *Brève histoire du service social en France, 1896–1976* (Paris: Privat, 1978), 64–65ff.

86. "Page féministe," "Les Qualités indispensables à une infirmière"; Pierrette, "Votre premier emploi" and "Revue de la Mode: L'Elégance et le travail," *Le Petit Echo de la Mode*, 2 Aug. 1931, 4 Mar. 1934, 1 Nov. 1936 and 7 Mar. 1937.

87. Christine Bard, *Les Femmes dans la société française au 20e siècle* (Paris: Armand Colin, 2001), 68–69.

88. "Le Trousseau de la femme qui travaille," *La Mode Pratique*, 24 Jan. 1931.

89. Yvonne Ostroga "Professions féminines," *La Mode Pratique*, 1934. See also Ostroga, *Les Indépendantes: Vingt-cinq professions pour les jeunes filles d'aujourd'hui* (Paris: Plon, 1932).

90. "Le Trousseau de la femme qui travaille," *La Mode Pratique*, 2 Apr. 1938.

91. Bard, *Les Femmes*, 68–69, and Clark, *The Rise of Professional Women*, chap. 6.

92. For comparative percentages, see T. Deldycke, H. Gelders, and J.-M. Limbor, *The Working Population and Its Structure* (Belgium: Université Libre de Bruxelles, 1968), table A1, 28ff.; for French female labor force participation, see table A2, 95–96.

93. "La Femme au travail," *C'est la Mode*, 18 July, 5 Sept. and 10 Oct. 1937.

94. Front covers of *La Mode du Jour*, 13 Oct. 1932, 19 Oct. 1934, and 3 Oct. 1935, and notice to readers, with a photo of a workingwoman, in Dec. 1938 issue.

95. Nathan Joseph, *Uniforms and Nonuniforms: Communication through Clothing* (Westport, CT: Greenwood Press, 1986), 17–18 and 55.

96. Valerie Steele, "Appearance and Identity," in *Men and Women: Dressing the Part,* ed. Claudia Brush Kidwell and Valerie Steele (Washington, DC: Smithsonian Institution Press, 1989), and Anne Hollander, *Sex and Suits* (New York: Alfred A. Knopf, 1994), 53.

97. C. de Loris, *La Femme à bicyclette: Ce qu'elles en pensent* (Paris, 1896), and John Grand-Carteret, *La Femme en culotte* (Paris, 1899).

98. Elsa Schiaparelli, *Shocking Life* (New York: Dutton, 1954), 41 and 58.

99. Roger Boutet de Monvel, "Les Masculines," *La Gazette du Bon Ton* 5, 4 (1922).

100. Shari Benstock, *Women of the Left Bank: Paris, 1900–1940* (Austin: University of Texas Press, 1986), chaps. 5–9.

101. *Colette: Romans-Récits-Souvenirs (1920–1940)* (Paris: Robert Laffont, 1989), 2: 907.

102. *Eve* published novels by Lucie Delarue-Mardrus. She contributed to *Nos Loisirs* and published "Comment s'habiller—Comment s'embellir," in *Foyer* (indecipherable month), 1923, 87–93.

103. Lucie Delarue-Mardrus, *The Angel and the Perverts,* trans. Anna Livia (New York: New York University Press, 1995), 75, 82, and 84.

104. Femina-Bibliothèque, *Pour bien faire du sport* (Paris: Lafitte, 1912), 371–73, and "Sportif et élégant!," *Lectures pour tous,* 1 Aug. 1913.

105. Nancy J. Troy, *Couture Culture: A Study in Modern Art and Fashion* (Cambridge, MA: MIT Press, 2003), 120–28.

106. M.R., "A l'instar: Ce que la mode féminine a pris à la mode masculine" and "La Grande Diversité des modes nouvelles," *Femina,* June 1924 and Apr. 1926, and C.D., "Avril en fleurs," *Chiffons,* 7 Apr. 1927.

107. A.deL., "Chronique," *La Mode,* 19 Feb. 1920.

108. J.R.F., "Le Pantalon caracterise le vêtement d'intimité," *Vogue,* Nov. 1929; "Toute la mode: Que préférez-vous? Pyjamas ou déshabillés?," *Eve,* 3 Apr. 1929; "Revue de la Mode," *Le Petit Echo de la Mode,* 2 Aug. 1931.

109. Mme. J. Stirling-Clarke, *Le Cheval et l'amazone: Traité complète de l'équitation des dames* (Paris: Parent et fils, 1894), and Jules Pellier, *La Selle et le costume de l'amazone: Etude historique et pratique de l'équitation des dames* (Paris: Rothschild, 1897).

110. La Belle Jardinière, *Catalogue générale, Eté 1919,* "Vêtements militaries," cover and "Notre couverture," *La Mode,* 5 Oct. 1919; "Le Concours de la plus belle amazone," *Vogue,* 1 June 1926; and "En Amazone ou à califouchon," *Figaro Illustré,* Feb. 1931, 19–20.

111. Lou Taylor, "Wool Cloth and Gender: The Use of Woolen Cloth in Women's Dress in Britain, 1865–85," in *Defining Dress: Dress as Object, Meaning, and Identity,* ed. Amy de la Haye and Elizabeth Wilson (Manchester: Manchester University Press, 1999), 30–47.

112. Rosine, "Paroles féminins," *Figaro,* 23 Sept. 1923.

113. Page on Louiseboulanger, *L'Officiel de la Couture,* Mar. 1928.

114. E.g., "Quel costume de sports préférerez-vous?," *L'Echo du Nord,* 6 Jan. 1929, and "Revue de la Mode," *Le Petit Echo de la Mode,* 5 Sept. 1937.

115. Colette, "Poil et plume," in *Le Voyage égoiste*, in Colette, *Romans-Récits-Souvenirs (1920–1940)*, 169ff., and Coline, "Chasseuse ne sachez pas chasse" and "Invitées de chasse," *Les Modes de la Femme de France*, 12 Sept. 1926 and 1 Sept. 1929.

116. Lenard Berlanstein, "Breeches and Breaches: Cross-Dress Theater and the Culture of Gender Ambiguity in Modern France," *Comparative Studies in Society and History* 38 (Apr. 1996): 343–65.

117. E.g., Marraine, "Ce qui se porte," *C'est la Mode*, 31 Jan. 1932.

118. Mme. Guibert, "A Travers la mode," *Chiffons*, 5 Jan. 1923; J.R.F., "Au Pays des ombres blues: La Culotte, symbole vestimentaire du féminisme," *Vogue*, 1 Mar. 1924; and "Toute la mode," *Eve*, 17 Apr. 1927.

119. "Costumes de chasse," *La Femme, le sport, la mode: Revue féminine des sports mondains*, Jan. 1928; also "La Vie féminine," *Le Progrès de Lyon*, 10 Dec. 1928, and Lucy, "Chronique de la Mode," *La Mode du Jour*, 4 July 1935.

120. The number of sports pants mounted steadily in the 1927–31 collections, according to photographs in the Collection Séeberger, boxes 13–17, 1927–31 in BNF, Etampes.

121. Yvonne Deslandres and Florence Muller, *Histoire de la mode au XXe siècle* (Paris: Samogy, 1986), 165.

### CHAPTER NINE. THE GENDER OF THE MODERN

1. Mary Louise Roberts, *Civilization without Sexes: Reconstructing Gender in Postwar France* (Chicago: University of Chicago Press, 1994), 4, 69, and passim.

2. Ibid., 14.

3. Agatha Brooks Young, *Recurring Cycles of Fashion, 1760–1937* (New York: Cooper Square Publishers, 1966).

4. Claudia Brush Kidwell, "Gender Symbols or Fashionable Details?," in *Men and Women: Dressing the Part*, ed. Claudia Brush Kidwell and Valerie Steele (Washington, DC: Smithsonian Institution Press, 1989).

5. J.F., "La Mode pendant la guerre," *Femina*, Mar. 1917 and 1 Mar. 1920, and A.deL., "Chronique," *La Mode*, 21 Sept.1919. Quote from France Borel, *Le Vêtement incarne: Les Métamorphoses du corps* (Paris: Calmann-Levy, 1992), 97.

6. Coline, "De l'Influence masculine," *Les Modes de la Femme de France*, 15 Feb. 1925, and editorial, *Femina*, July 1928.

7. "La Mode d'hiver telle que la porte la parisienne," *Vogue*, Mar. 1922, and Coline, "De l'Influence masculine," *Les Modes de la Femme de France*, 15 Feb.1925.

8. Dominique Veillon, *Fashion under the Occupation*, trans. Miriam Kochan (Oxford, Berg, 2002).

9. Ad in *Vogue*, 1 Mar. 1923, and notice in *Femina*, Oct. 1923.

10. "War Mourning in Europe and America," *Vogue* (New York), July 15, 1918.

11. Jeanne Galzy, *La Cavalière* (Paris: Double interligne, 2000), 299, and Roger Boutet de Montel, "Deuil," *La Gazette du Bon Ton* 3, 8 (1920).

12. "Robes de deuil," *L'Elégances Parisiennes*, no. 6 (1921); "De la fantaisie dans les deuils" and "Comment porter le deuil," *Vogue*, 1 Nov. 1922 and 1 Dec. 1923; and "Une note blanche dans le deuil," *La Mode Pratique*, 4 Nov. 1922.

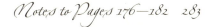

13. "La Vie féminine," *Le Progrès de Lyon,* 8 Nov. 1928.

14. "Le Deuil," *La Mode Pratique,* 31 July 1937.

15. Marcelle Auclair, *Anne Fauvet ou l'assortiment difficile* (Paris: S.E.P.E., 1931), 25.

16. John Harvey, *Men in Black* (Chicago: University of Chicago Press, 1995), 9 and 257.

17. Frances Kennett, *Coco: The Life and Loves of Gabrielle Chanel* (London: Victor Gollancz, 1989), 10 and 42.

18. M.R., "La Femme à la Mode," *Femina,* June 1924; "Pour celles qui aiment le noir et pour celles qui sont en deuil," *La Mode Pratique,* 12 Jan. 1929; and Lucy, "Chronique de la Mode: La Vogue du noir," *La Mode du Jour,* 27 Oct. 1932.

19. "Fashion Report," *Costumes Tailleurs: Précursuer de la Mode,* July and Oct. 1922.

20. Ibid., Jan. 1923, and X. Chaumette and E. Montet, *Le Tailleur: Un vêtement-message* (Paris: Syros-Alternatives, 1992).

21. Eugene Marsan, *Pour habiller Eliante* (Liège: A la Lampe d'Aladdin, 1927), 31.

22. Fany Croisset, "Mademoiselle va au Bois," *L'Illustration des Modes* 1, 5 (1920); Mag Olivier, "Tailleurs et petites robes de Printemps," *Eve,* 24 Feb. 1920; and Marcy Ducray, "La Toilette qui convient a chaque circonstance," *Nos Loisirs,* 1 Nov. 1922.

23. "Une garde-robe complète pour la voyageuse," *Vogue,* 1 June 1924, and "Pour un week-end," *La Mode Pratique,* 3 June 1922.

24. "Les 10 Commandements de la Mode pour 1924," Le *Jardin des Modes* 4, 56 (1924), and C. de S., "La Mode veut" and "Elégances," *Figaro,* 13 Dec. 1934 and 4 June 1935.

25. "Un Trousseau minimum: Sa composition, son prix," *La Mode Pratique,* 16 Jan. 1937, and Kay Boyle, "1923," in Robert McAlmon, *Being Geniuses Together: 1920–1930,* rev. Kay Boyle (Baltimore: Johns Hopkins University Press, 1997), 41–42.

26. "A Paris on voit," *L'Officiel de la Couture,* May 1926.

27. C.D., "Avril en fleurs," *Chiffons,* 5 Apr. 1927, and Eve, "Toute la mode: Raffinements," *La Mode Illustrée,* 2 June 1928.

28. *Paris-Couture-Années Trente* (Paris: Musée de la Mode et du Costume, 1987), 35 and 40.

29. "Haute Couture et tailleurs," *Adam,* 15 Mar, 1931, and "Courrier de la mode," *La Mode Illustrée,* 10 Jan. 1932.

30. "La Mode du jour," *Vogue,* May 1935.

31. "Nos petites robes sont renouvelées par les détails amusants de leurs corsages," *La Mode Pratique,* 26 Mar. 1932.

32. M.R., "La Mode est surtout intéressante par la nouveauté de ses détails," *Femina,* Apr. 1933.

33. "Métamorphoses: La Fille du Régiment est devenue Mélusine," *Vogue,* Oct. 1933.

34. Palmer White, *Elsa Schiaparelli: Empress of Paris Fashion* (New York: Rizzoli, 1986), 100ff., and "Le Mode du jour" and "Les Collections d'hiver," *Vogue,* May 1935 and Sept. 1936.

35. Coline, "La Coquille dactylo," *Les Modes de la Femme de France,* 31 Jan. 1926; "Les petites robes de tout-aller" and covers of *La Mode du Jour,* 22 Oct. 1931 and 19 Oct. 1934.

36. Catherine Horwood, *Keeping Up Appearances: Fashion and Class between the Wars* (Thrupp-Stroud, UK: Sutton, 2005), 48–49.

37. *Lyon-Sténo: Bulletin périodique de la Chambre Syndicale des Secrétaires sténo-Dactylographes de Lyon et de la Région*, 1933–35.

38. Michel Pastouriau, *Blue: The History of a Color* (Princeton: Princeton University Press, 1995), 161, and Elizabeth Kuhns, *The Habit: A History of the Clothing of Catholic Nuns* (New York: Doubleday, 2003), photographs and descriptions in the appendix.

39. "La tenue nette," *Vogue*, Jan. 1933.

40. Colette Yver, *Femmes d'aujourd'hui* (Paris: Calman Levy, 1929), 93.

41. Nathan Joseph, *Uniforms and Nonuniforms: Communication through Clothing* (Westport, CT: Greenwood Press, 1986), 17.

42. Yver, *Femmes d'aujourd'hui*, 9, 132, 136, and 153 (lawyer, editor, civil servant, and notary).

43. Raymonde Machard, *Possession* (London: Boulevard Library, 1932), 117 and 164.

44. White, *Elsa Schiaparelli*, 59, and Joan Rivière, "Womanliness as Masquerade," *International Journal of Psychoanalysis* 10 (1929): 304.

45. Valerie Mendes, *Dressed in Black* (London: Victoria & Albert Publications, 1999), 8.

46. Dani Cavallaro and Alexandra Warwick, *Fashioning the Frame: Boundaries, Dress, and Body* (Oxford: Berg, 1998), 50 and 88ff.

47. Roland Barthes, *The Fashion System*, trans. Matthew Ward and Richard Howard (London: J. Cape, 1985), 172.

48. Mary Lynn Stewart, *For Health and Beauty: Physical Culture for Frenchwomen, 1880s–1930* (Baltimore: Johns Hopkins University Press, 2000), 164–65.

49. "Du Costume simple à la robe du soir," *Vogue*, 1 Jan. 1924, and Lucy, "Le Jersey," *La Mode du Jour*, 5 May 1932.

50. Michel Pastoureau, *L'Etoffe du Diable: Une historie des rayures et des tissus rayés* (Paris: Editions de Seuil, 1991), and "Les industries de la Nouveauté," *L'Officiel de la Couture*, 20 July 1921, and "Nos robes légères d'été," *Chiffons*, 6 May 1922. See also MEIM, Abonnement Coton, no. 41, 1921–23.

51. Pastoureau, *L'Etoffe du Diable*, and Jacqueline, "The Use of Light Fabrics in Haute Couture," *La Soierie de Lyon*, June 1930. See also AP, Conseil des Prud'hommes, Rodier, classeur no. 4, dépôts 1928, for many checked crepes with floral borders.

52. Henri Algoud, "Stripes and Plaids," *La Soierie de Lyon*, 16 Sept. 1924, and Colette, "Printemps de demain," *Vogue*, 1 Feb. 1925. Colette wrote editorial pieces for *Vogue* Paris from Dec. 1924 to Dec. 1925 and from June 1928 to July 1929.

53. Joseph, *Uniforms and Nonuniforms*, 55.

54. MEIM, Abonnement Seide, 1332–36, nos. 52482 to 54200; Mag Olivier, "Elégance de Plein Air" and "Voici les tissus dont seront faites vos toilettes automnales," *Eve*, 28 Mar. 1920, 2 Mar. and 7 Sept. 1924.

55. Quote from Colette's Preface to *28 Composition de Michel Dubost pour des tissus de soie réalisés par les Soieries F. Ducharne* (Lyon: Marius Audin, 1930).

56. Lucy, "Chronique de la mode: La Vogue de l'écossais," *La Mode du Jour*, 2 Dec. 1932.

57. Cecil Beaton, *The Glass of Fashion* (London: Wiedenfeld & Nicolson, 1954), 165; Paul Morand, *L'Allure de Chanel* (Paris: Hermann, 1976), 20 and 46–47; and Kennett, *Coco*, 70.

58. "Tweeds, jerseys et tricot sont largement utilisés," *Vogue,* 1 Nov. 1927, and "Toute la Mode: La Vogue du Tweed," *Eve,* 28 May 1930.

59. Nicole Dantès, "Les Ecossais," *L'Illustration des Modes,* 2 Feb. 1922, and "A Travers la mode: Les écossais" and "Ecossais nouveaux," *La Mode Illustrée,* 20 Apr. 1924 and 22 Mar. 1925.

60. Patrice Hugues, *Le Langage du tissus* (Colombes: Textile/Art/Langage, 1982), 417 and 422–24.

61. MTL, Ducharne collections, 48851/16, Unis imprimées sur chaine 1922–36, and MEIM, Abonnement Siede, 1332, no. 8, Soies imprimés, 1923, and no. 36, Tissus soie, 1921–24, and Abonnement Coton, no. 41, 1921–23. On Egyptian craze, Abonnement coton, 1923, nos. 57553 to 58416.

62. M.R., "A Robes simples, tissus bariolés," *Femina,* Feb. 1924.

63. Nada, "Halte-la!," and J.F., "Les Tissus nouveaux," *Femina,* June 1917 and 1 Mar. 1921, and J.R.F., "Tissus qui enthousiasment la Parisienne," *Vogue,* 15 Apr. 1921. See also M.R., "L'Arc-en-Ciel de la Mode," *Femina,* Dec. 1931.

64. "La Mode d'été exquisément féminine," *Eve,* 7 June 1925.

65. MTL, Ducharne collection, 48851/16 and MEIM, Abonnement Seide, no. 38, 1929–34.

66. L.deL., "Fashion," *La Soierie de Lyon,* 16 Feb. 1921; M.R., "Les Tissus: La Fantaisie des reliefs et le jeu des coloris," *Femina,* Sept. 1934; and "Les Tissus nouveaux," *Vogue,* Sept. 1931.

67. Mme. Doresse, *Les Tissus féminins* (Paris: Librairie de l'Enseignement technique, n.d.), and "Du Choix des formes et des tissus qui leur conviennent," *Revue très pratique: Pour faire vos robes vous-mémes* (Paris: n.p., 1932).

68. J.R.F., "L'Esprit de la mode," *La Gazette des Beaux Arts* 59 (1917): 121–24.

69. "Des Robes pour toutes les heures" and "Toutes sortes de robes de soie," *La Mode Pratique,* 27 Sept. 1919 and 10 June 1922.

70. Lucy, "Chronique de la mode," *La Mode du Jour,* 16 Mar. 1934.

71. F. Klein, *La Publicité textile.* Bibliothèque professionnelle et sociale (Paris: Delachaux et Niestlé, 1933).

72. "Paroles féminins," *Figaro,* 5 Mar, 1917.

73. "Le Plissé roi," *Le Jardin des Modes,* 15 Apr. 1924.

74. M.R., "Les Grandes lignes de la mode nouvelle" and "La Grande Diversité des modes nouvelles," *Femina,* Mar. 1924 and Apr. 1926, and "Paris Favours Tucks, Pleats, and a Circular Cut," *Vogue* (London), June 1926.

75. C.D., "Visions élégantes," *Chiffons,* 5 June 1919; Mag Olivier, "Tailleurs nouveaux, tuniques de ville, et robes de soirée," *Eve,* 10 Apr. 1920; and "A Travers la Mode: Les plissés, leurs employs," *La Mode Illustrée,* 21 May 1925.

76. Elizabeth Hawes, *Fashion Is* Spinach (New York: Random House, 1938), 70–73, and J.R.F., "Les Robes qu'une parisienne élégante choisit cet hiver" and "La Mode de jour abonde en détails neufs," *Vogue,* 1 Oct. 1923, and 1 Oct. 1927.

77. L.N., "Toute la mode," *Eve,* 10 Jan. 1926.

78. M.D., "Quelques Petites choses qui comptant," *Femina,* Oct. 1921; "La Mode de jour abonde en détails neufs" and "La Personnalité s'affirme dans les détails," *Vogue,* 1 Oct. 1927 and 1 Feb. 1929.

79. Pierre Bourdieu, *La Distinction: Critique social du jugement* (Paris: Editions du Minuit, 1979), 204ff., and Beatrix Le Wita, *French Bourgeois Culture,* trans. J. A. Underwood (Cambridge: Cambridge University Press, 1994). J.L., "Toute la Mode," *Eve,* 8 Nov. 1925.

80. Jennifer M. Jones, *Sexing la Mode: Gender, Fashion, and Commercial Culture in Old Regime France* (Oxford: Berg, 2004), 21ff.

81. Rozsika Parker, *The Subversive Stitch: Embroidery and the Making of the Feminine* (London: Women's Press, 1984), 6.

82. Annie Kraatz, *Dentelles* (Paris: Adam Biro, 1988), and *Dentelle de Calais et Haute Couture* (Calais: Musée des Beaux-Arts et de la Dentelle, 1992). Quote from Lucy, "La Dentelle," *La Mode du Jour,* 1 Dec. 1931.

83. L.N., "Toute la mode: Des Fanfreluches" and "Toute la Mode," *Eve,* 29 Jan. and 12 Aug. 1928, and "A Travers la mode," *La Mode Illustrée,* 1 May 1932.

84. L.deL., "Fashion," and Henri Algoud, "A Modern Renaissance of the Shawl and Scarf," *La Soierie de Lyon,* 16 Mar, and 16 July 1924.

85. "Ligne-type d'après-midi de Callot," *Excelsior-Modes,* spring 1930.

86. "Chanel," *L'Officiel de la Couture,* Mar. 1937.

87. "Bonnet et écharpe donnent une note de couleur," *Vogue,* Dec. 1930; "Caractères et Tendances de la Mode pour le Printemps 1932," *Guide Pratique de la Mode de Paris,* summer 1932.

88. "Robes drapées, aux souples enroulement," *Vogue,* 1 Oct. 1922.

89. J.L., "Toute la Mode," *Eve,* 26 Feb. 1922.

90. P. Drecoll, "La Robe et la femme," *La Nouvelle Revue,* 4th ser., 77 (1925): 187–89.

91. "Au Pré Catelan: Le Gala de Mode de Femina," *Femina,* July 1924.

92. Mme. Guibert, "Chiffons à travers la mode," *Chiffons,* 5 Feb. 1919; "Galons et franges," *La Mode Pratique,* 29 Mar. 1919; and "Les Modes nouvelles d'après les grands couturiers," *Femina,* 1 Apr. 1919.

93. Madeleine Delpierre, *Le Costume de 1914 aux années folles* (Paris: Flammarion, 1997), and M.R., "La Retour de la grande élégance," *Femina,* Oct. 1929.

94. Gustave Fréjeville, "Notes et figures: Les petites amazones," *L'Opinion,* Feb. 1917, 153–54.

95. C.D., "Paroles féminins," *Figaro,* 2 Apr. 1917.

96. J.F., "La Mode pendant la guerre," and C. de Monclos, "Conseils de guerre," *Femina,* Mar. and June 1918.

97. See BAD, *Modes 214 bis,* vols. 28–31, 1916–26, especially "Infirmières," by Drian, in vol. 28, 1916–17; "Les métiers féminins de la guerre," *L'Illustration,* "Un tour chez les couturiers and "Les ceintures descendent," in vol. 29, 1918–19. See also "Paroles féminins," *Figaro,* 6 Aug. 1918 and 17 May 1922.

98. Paul Reboux, "Grandeurs, variations et décadence de la mode," 13–17, and "Ou va la mode?," 79–88, *De la mode* (Paris: Les Beaux-Arts, 1927).

99. Abel Hermant, editorial in the first issue of *Monsieur,* 1 Jan. 1920, and captions on covers of *Adam, Revue des Modes masculines* in the mid 1920s.

100. E.g., André de Fouquières, "On ose parler de mode masculine," *Adam,* 15 Jan. 1936.

101. Richard Martin and Harold Koda, *Jocks and Nerds: Men's Style in the Twen-*

*tieth Century* (New York: Rizzoli, 1989), 149 and 181; Sylvie Legrand, "Le XIXe Siècle, 1795–1914," in *L'Album du Musee de la Mode et du Textile* (Paris: Reunion des Musées Nationaux, 1997), 79; and Norah Waugh, *The Cut of Men's Clothes, 1600–1900* (London: Faber & Faber, 1964), 117–19.

102. Farid Chenoune, *A History of Men's Fashion*, trans. Deke Dusinberre (Paris: Flammarion, 1992), 136–38.

103. Philinte, "Le bon choix: De la ligne," *Monsieur*, Oct. 1920.

104. Eric de Coulon, "Chemises de soie pour la mer et les sports," *Monsieur*, June 1920, and "La Laine artificielle" and "Un Aspect nouveau de la soie artificielle," *Adam*, 25 Jan. 1926 and 15 Feb. 1934.

105. "Les ville, le long ruban des cotes," *Adam*, 15 July 1933.

106. Fernand Gregh, "Elégance et civilisation," *Monsieur*, Oct. 1920.

107. "Le Choix d'un tissu chez votre tailleur," *Adam*, 15 Aug. 1931. But see the advertorial "A Propos des costumes de sport," in the 15 Apr. 1931 issue.

108. Paul David, "Pour le bon renom de la mode masculine française," André de Fouquières, "Une Campagne," and Paul Poiret, "Y a-t-il un schisme dans la mode masculine?," *Adam*, 15 Jan. and 15 Apr. 1933 and 15 Apr. 1936.

109. "A la récherche de 'âme française," *Vogue*, 1 Dec. 1922.

110. Compare the grandiose claims of Michel Corday, "L'Influence morale de la tenue," *Monsieur*, Easter 1920, to Claire Lausna, "Le Recueil des modes nouvelles," *Femina*, 1 Apr. 1921.

111. E.g., Frère Philippe de Jésus, *La Modestie et les modes féminines* (Lyon, 1926), and Mlle. de Saint-Seine, *La Mode et la conscience chrétienne* (Paris: Secrétariat National Français, 1926).

112. A.deL., "Chronique," *La Mode*, 4 Dec. 1919.

113. "Les Maisons de la vie sociale" and "Pour Plaire à son mari," *La Mode Illustrée*, 19 Jan. 1919 and 11 Apr. 1920.

114. Compare "De la mode," in *Les Cahiers de la République des lettres, des sciences et des arts* 2, 7 (1927): 7–8, to Guibert, "Chiffons à travers la monde," *Chiffons*, 20 Apr. 1926.

115. Henri Bidou, "Avant-Propos," *Gazette du Bon Ton* 3, 1 (1920).

116. "La Journée d'une Elégante," "La Transformation de la Parisienne suivant l'heure," and "Comment on s'habille selon les heures," *Chiffons*, 5 May 1925, 15 June 1930, and Jan. 1932.

117. Mag Olivier, "L'Elégante sobriété du tailleur," *Eve*, 9 Mar. 1920; Francine, "Les Zephyrs et le soleil ou Soyons toujours dans la note," *Le Jardin des Modes*, 15 Apr. 1923; and Marcy Ducray, "De Paris à la montagne en passant par la Riviera," *Excelsior-Modes*, winter 1931.

118. "Un Tea-gown facile à faire" and "Pour toutes les heures," *La Mode Pratique*, 2 Aug. 1919 and 19 Apr. 1924, and Griseline, "Parlons un peu des robes de dîner," *Journal des Ouvrages de dames*, June 1923.

119. "Les Ensembles," *La Mode Pratique*, 19 Mar. 1928, and "A Travers la Mode: Ensembles élégants," *La Mode Illustrée*, 25 Oct. 1933.

120. J.R.F., "Les robes qu'une parisienne élégante choisit cet hiver," *Vogue*, 1 Oct. 1923.

121. E. Max Brunhes, "Quelques réflexions sur les nouvelles collections d'hiver," *L'Officiel de la Couture*, Sept. 1931.

122. "Vêtement de sport au tricot pour dames et jeunes fille," *Madam*, 21 Oct.1920.

123. Philippe Perrot, *Fashioning the Bourgeoisie: A History of Clothing in the Nineteenth Century*, trans. Richard Bienvenu (Princeton: Princeton University Press, 1994), 91.

124. "Pour le Midi," and M.R., "Les mille détails de la mode d'été," *Femina*, Jan. 1921 and Apr. 1930; "Paroles féminins" columns in *Figaro*, 16 May 1923 and 25 May 1925; and Lucy, "Les Robes imprimées," *La Mode du Jour*, 17 Apr. 1930.

125. "La Mode du jour," *Vogue*, Apr. 1930.

126. A. Muelle, "La Mode masculine redevient virile," *Eve*, 23 Feb. 1920.

127. "La Laine artificielle," "La Silhouette tailleures," "Les Tissus à la Mode," "Parallelisme d'inspiration," "Le Choix d'un tissu chez votre tailleur," "L'Evolution dans les tissus pour les costume légers," and André de Fouquières, "On ose parler de mode masculine," *Adam*, 25 Jan. 1926, 15 Oct. 1928, 15 Mar. and 15 Aug. 1931, 15 May 1935, and 15 Jan. 1936; and Farid Chenoune, *A History of Men's Fashion* (Paris: Flammarion, 1992), 135–80.

128. "Les villes, le long ruban des côtes," and Andre de Fouquières, "On ose parler de mode masculine," *Adam*, 15 July 1933 and 15 Jan. 1936.

### CHAPTER TEN. THE MODERN WOMAN?

1. Brigitte Søland, *Becoming Modern: Young Women and the Reconstruction of Womanhood in the 1920s* (Princeton: Princeton University Press, 2000), 47–48.

2. Yette, "Chronique de la mode: Nos petites enquêtes; Pourquoi fumez-vous, Madame," *L'Echo du Nord*, 2, 9, and 16 Oct. 1925. Yette did not reveal how many women responded.

3. In the Séeberger Frères photographs, fewer than 3 percent of the subjects smoked.

4. "La Question d'Orient" and "Robes de studio," *Femina*, Jan. 1924 and Nov. 1929.

5. J.R.F., "The Parisienne Takes to the Open Road," *Vogue* (New York), 1 May 1921, and "L'Auto qu'une femme peut conduire," *La Mode Pratique*, 17 Jan. 1925.

6. "De l'Uniforme féminine et des fronts nus ou voilés," *Vogue*, 1 Nov. 1924.

7. See notices about Concours d'élégance féminine en automobile, *Femina*, June 1924 and Feb. 1933, and M.H., "L'Evolution de l'automobile et ses rapports avec la mode," *Vogue*, 1 Nov. 1923.

8. "Le Style, c'est la jeune fille," *Femina*, 1 Apr. 1921, and "A Travers la Mode," *La Mode Illustrée*, 17 Apr. and 25 Dec. 1921.

9. George Weiss, *The Emergence of Modern Universities in France, 1963–1914* (Princeton: Princeton University Press, 1983), 221–23, and Roger Boutet de Monvel, "De l'influence des modes sur les mœurs," *Vogue*, 1 Apr. 1922. French society magazines devoted less ink to French debutantes and their social whirl than *Vogue* New York and London did to debutantes and coming-out balls.

10. "La Jeune fille '1930,'" *Femina*, Jan. 1931.

11. "La Coupe Femina de golf" and "Le Coupe de Bridge des Dames organisé par Femina et Paris-Midi," *Femina*, May 1932 and Feb. 1933.

12. "Quand nos filles sont mariées," *La Mode Illustrée,* 22 Feb. 1920, "Paroles féminists," *La Petit Echo de la Mode,* 18 Nov. 1925, and "Au Fil des Heures," *La Mode,* 9 Feb. 1930.

13. "Préliminaries," *La Mode Pratique,* 3 Apr. 1926, and "Revue de la Mode" and "Journal des âmes," *Le Petit Echo de la Mode,* 7 Jan. 1934 and 6 Dec. 1936.

14. A.deL., "Chronique," *La Mode,* 12 Feb. 1922, "La Robe de Mariée," *Femina,* May 1930, and Mme. Clemceau-Jacquemaire, "Mariage d'autrefois et mariage d'aujourd'hui," *Figaro,* 23 Aug. 1930.

15. "Revue de la Mode," *Le Petit Echo de la Mode,* special edition on "Les Modes d'Automne," 1938.

16. "La Nécessité de l'étude," *La Mode Illustrée,* 21 Sept. 1919, and "Jardin des âmes," *Le Petit Echo de la Mode,* 27 Aug. 1922 and 3 July 1927.

17. Franceline, "Des Métiers pour les femmes qui n'en ont pas," and Renée d'Anjou, "L'Histoire de la dot," *Le Petit Echo de la Mode,* 20 Feb. 1921.

18. "Journal de l'âme," *Le Petit Echo de la Mode,* 24 June 1923, and Aline Raymond, "Plus de veilles filles," *La Mode Illustrée,* 21 Nov. 1926.

19. "Quand on ne se marie pas en blanc," *La Mode Pratique,* 14 Apr. 1928.

20. Michael Lanthier, "Women Alone: Widows in Third Republic France, 1870–1940" (Ph.D. diss., Simon Fraser University, 2004), app. 2

21. "Celle qui a vingt ans" section in "La Parisienne à la page" and "La Mode des moins de vingt ans" in special girls' issues of *Femina,* Feb. 1933 and 1935.

22. "Le Trousseau de rentrée," *La Mode Pratique,* Sept. 1922; children's issue of *Femina,* May 1932, and "Un Trousseau bien dans la ligne," *Françoise,* 15 Oct. 1934.

23. *Vogue* (New York), 15 May 1926, and Siàn Reynolds, *France between the Wars: Gender and Politics* (London: Routledge, 1996), 53.

24. "Pour Mademoiselle, Pour Madame," in *Nos Loisirs,* 1 Aug. 1921, and " Nos transformations," *Le Petit Echo de la Mode,* 1 Sept. 1933.

25. Fany Croisset, "Mademoiselle va au cours," *Le Jardin des Modes,* 21 Oct. 1920, and "Le Style c'est la jeune fille: La mode de 10 à 25 ans," *Femina,* 1 Apr. 1921.

26. Mme. Guibert, "A Travers la mode," *Chiffons,* 5 Feb. and 3 June 1922, and Coline, "A une jeune provinciale," *La Mode de la Femme de France,* 17 Nov. 1929.

27. Mary Lynn Stewart, *For Health and Beauty: Physical Culture for Frenchwomen, 1880s–1930s* (Baltimore: Johns Hopkins Press, 2000), chap. 5.

28. Barthes as explicated in Paul Jobling, *Fashion Spreads: Word and Image in Fashion Photography since 1980* (Oxford: Berg, 1999), 76.

29. "La Mode pour les jeunes filles," *La Mode,* 2 Mar. 1930, and Lucy, "Les Coloris en vogue," *La Mode du Jour,* 30 Apr. 1931.

30. "L'Indépendance actuelle de la jeune fille," *Chiffons,* 15 July 1930. This is a rare example of a fashion weekly using the term *independence.*

31. On the Belle Epoque, see *Figaro-Modes,* Feb. 1904, 23.

32. "Pour les jeunes grand-mères" and "Pour les dames qui ne sont plus toute jeune," *L'Illustration des Modes,* 24 Mar. and 21 Apr. 1921, and "A l'heure ou la jeunesse la quitte," *Vogue,* 1 Jan. 1924.

33. Claire Lausnay, "Des Robes pour tous les ages" and "Pour rester jeune," *Femina,* Nov. 1921.

34. A.deL., "Chronique," *La Mode*, 1 Jan. 1922, and "Des Robes du soir pour tous les ages," *La Mode Pratique*, 14 Jan. 1928.

35. Mme. Guibert, "A Travers la mode," *Chiffons*, 20 Sept. 1922 and 5 Oct. 1925.

36. See Tokalon ads in *La Mode*, 1930, *C'est la Mode*, 1932, and *Le Progrès de Lyon*, 3 July 1937.

37. M.R., "Pour les jeunes filles," *Femina*, Feb. 1930, and Nicole, "Premiers élégances," *Figaro*, 29 Nov. 1934.

38. E.g., "L'Art de plaire selon votre silhouette," *Femina*, July 1934, and "Bien choisir robe ou manteau Madame, c'est un art," *La Mode Pratique*, 5 Dec. 1936.

39. E.g., Galeries Lafayette, *Catalogue général, Eté 1925* and Bon Marché, *Nouveautés d'hiver, 1927–1928*.

40. E.g., Galeries Lafayette sale flyer *Soldes, Eté 1933* and Au Printemps flyers in 1935.

41. Gaston Derys, "La Journée de la Parisienne en 1830 et en 1930," *Agenda des Galeries Lafayette pour 1930*.

42. Michael Haber, Henri Bunle, and Fernand Voberat, *La Population de la France: Son évolution et ses perspectives* (Paris: Librairie Hachette, 1965), 51 and table 16. I am grateful to Michael Lanthier, who retrieved this information for me.

43. T. Deldycke, H. Gelders, and J.-M. Limbor, *The Working Population and Its Structure* (Belgium: Université Libre de Bruxelles, 1968), tables E2 and E3, 168–69.

44. Don Slater, *Consumer Culture and Modernity* (Cambridge: Cambridge University Press, 1997).

45. Roland Marchand, *Advertising the American Dream: Making Way for Modernity, 1920–1940* (Berkeley: University of California Press, 1986), and Stanley C. Hollander and Richard Germain, *Was There a Pepsi Generation before Pepsi Discovered It? Youth-Based Segmentation in Marketing* (Chicago: NTC Business Books, 1993).

46. "Toute la Mode: Les Sports et la Ville," *Eve*, 16 Nov. 1930, and "Courrier de la mode, *La Mode Illustrée*, 16 Nov. 1930.

47. M.R., "La Flle fait danser," and Claire Lausna, "Le Recueil des modes nouvelles," *Femina*, 1 Apr. 1921 and Oct. 1922.

48. "Contre l'abus des sports" and "Sport," *La Mode Illustrée*, 18 Apr. 1920 and 13 Mar. 1927, and "Soyons minces mais sans aucun excès" and "La Traditionelle chasse à courre," *Vogue*, 15 Aug. 1920 and 1 Jan. 1924.

49. "Les Devoirs d'une mère" and "Journald'une âme," *Le Petit Echo de la Mode*, 27 Aug. 1922 and 22 and 29 July 1923.

50. "Coupe Femina de la golfe," Au Printemps insert, and Samaritaine ad in *Femina*, May 1932, May 1933, and Mar. 1937.

51. A.deL, "Chronique," *La Mode*, 13 Feb. 1921, and J.L., "Toute la mode," *Eve*, 28 Feb. 1925

52. "La Vie féminine," *Le Progrès de Lyon*, 3 June 1920.

53. Janet and Peter Philips, "History from Below: Women's Underwear and the Rise of Women's Sport," *Journal of Popular Culture* 27, 2 (1993): 129–48, and Sally Sims, "The Bicycle, the Bloomer, and Dress Reform in the 1890s," in *Dress and Popular Culture*, ed. Patricia A. Cunningham and Susan V. Lab (Bowling Green, IN: Bowling Green State University Press, 1991), 126–41.

54. Marie Bourache, *Culture physique de la femme* (Paris: Nilsson, 1920), and Jeanne

Farmant, "Les Modes de janvier" and "Tuniques et ensembles donnent le ton dans toutes les collections de demi-saison," *Vogue,* 1 Jan. 1921 and 1 Sept. 1924.

55. Angela Lumpkin, *Women's Tennis: A Historical Documentary of the Players and Their Game* (Troy, NY: Whitston, 1981), 21, and Gianni Clerici, *Suzanne Lenglen: La Diva du tennis* (Paris: Rochevignes, 1984), 42 and 67–82.

56. Janet Flanner, *Paris Was Yesterday, 1925–1939* (New York: Harcourt, Brace, Javanovich, 1972), 187, and press clippings in the BNF, Collection Rondel, 17.797.

57. Gary H. Schwartz, *The Art of Tennis, 1874–1940* (Tiburon, CA: Wood River Publishing, 1990), 14–16 and 23.

58. Madeleine Delpierre, *Le Costume de 1914 aux années folles* (Paris: Flammarion, 1997), 41, and Valerie Steele, *Women of Fashion: Twentieth-Century Designers* (New York: Rizzoli, 1991), 73.

59. Ad in Le *Jardin des Modes,* 15 Apr. 1924.

60. J.L., "Toute la mode," *Eve,* 20 Aug. 1922 and 11 Jan. 1925; and "La Vie féminine," *Le Progrès de Lyon,* 29 Jan. 1925.

61. J.L., "Toute la mode," *Eve,* 20 Aug. 1922 and 8 Mar. 1925.

62. "Paroles féminines," *Figaro,* 12 Sept. 1923; Claudie, "Pélinerages au pays de la Haute Mode," *Nos Loisirs,* Apr. 1927; Marcy Ducray, "Robes de sport," *Excelsior-Modes,* Dec. 1929; and pages on Germaine Lecomte, Jeanne Lanvin, Schiaparelli, and Jenny in *L'Officiel de la Couture,* Mar. and Sept. 1929, June 1935, and Mar. 1937.

63. "Que l'on voit s'étendre le rôle du costume de sport," "La Femme sportive doit rester élégante," and "Du Costume simple à la robe du soir," *Vogue,* 1 May and 1 July 1923 and 1 Jan. 1924.

64. Rosine, "Paroles féminins," and Comtesse de S., "Autour de la mode," *Figaro,* 19 Oct. 1927, 16 Apr. 1934, and 2 Jan. and 6 June 1935.

65. Lucy, "Chronique de la mode," "Coquetterie sportive," and "Les Tenues sportives," *La Mode du Jour,* 7 Nov. 1929, 18 June 1931, and 9 Mar. 1937.

66. E.g., Aux Trois Quartiers, *Sports, Mer, Campagne,* May 1931 and May 1932, in the library of the Palais Galliera. Ad for Au Louvre Sports Rayon in *Vogue,* May 1933.

67. Claire Lausna, "Les Caractéristiques de la nouvelle mode," *Femina,* Mar, 1922, and Lucy, "Des Robes sans manches," "Les Coloris en vogue," and "La Mode des plissés," *La Mode du Jour,* 25 Apr. 1929, 30 Apr. 1931, and 16 Mar. 1934.

68. Agatha Brooks Young, *Recurring Cycles of Fashion, 1760–1937* (New York: Cooper Square Publishers, 1966).

69. Congrès international de l'Éducation Physique, *Principes de méthodes d'éducation physique* (Paris: n.p., 1922).

70. G. Racine, A. Godier, and L. Leroy, *L'Education physique moderne à l'école: La Méthode française adaptée à la vie moderne* (Paris: n.p., 1937).

71. Dr. Maurice Boigey, *L'Elevage humain,* vol. 1, *Formation du corps, éducation physique* (Paris: Payot, 1917), 90–95, and Nelly Roussel, "La Culture physique de la femme," *La Mère éducatrice,* Jan. 1919.

72. Dr. Yvonne Legrand, *Le Sport et la femme* (Paris: n.p., 1931).

73. Dr. Marie Houdré-Boursin, *Ma doctoresse: Guide pratique d'hygiène et de médecine de la femme moderne* (Strasbourg: Imprimerie des Dernières Nouvelles de Strasbourg, 1930).

74. Stewart, *For Health and Beauty,* chap. 8.

75. Lucy, "Chronique de la mode," *La Mode du Jour,* 20 Dec. 1934.

76. Ellen Furlough, "Making Mass Vacations: Tourism and Consumer Culture in France, 1930s to 1970s," *Comparative Studies in Society and History* 40, 2 (1998): 248.

77. Dr. J. Martinie-Doubousquet, *Les Femmes et les exercices du corps* (Paris: n.p., 1937), 6–15, 20–23, 37–45, and Robert Jeudon, "Le Sport et la femme," in *Congrès international de la médecine appliquée à l'éducation physique et aux sports* (Paris: n.p, 1937), 82–86.

78. J.R.F., "Nos Camarades les sportives," *Figaro Illustré,* Feb. 1933.

79. "Page médicale," *L'Oeuvre,* 8 Nov. 1934.

80. BHVP, Fonds Bouglé, Caroline Kauffmann, dossier 3.

81. E.g., "Atlas de la mode pour le printemps 1926," "Aisance. Mouvement," and "Prévisions sur la mode de printemps," *Vogue,* Apr. 1926, July 1928, and Feb. 1929.

82. "L'Histoire d'une mode qui a enfin changé" and "Le Point de vue de Vogue," *Vogue,* Apr. 1929 and Feb. 1930.

83. Georges Hébert, *L'Education physique féminine: Muscle et beauté plastique,* 2nd ed. (Paris: Vuibert, 1921).

84. Madeleine Rey, *Notre santé et notre charme* (Paris: Gautier-Languereau, 1932).

85. L.N., "La Culture physique féminine," "Pour rester belle," and "Toute la mode," *Eve,* 31 Aug. 1924, 12 Sept. 1926, and 26 Feb. 1928

86. L.N., "Toute la mode: L'influence sportive et la mode," *Eve,* 16 Jan. 1927.

87. E.g., "La Mode d'après-midi gagne en éclat" and "Vogue lit dans les astres l'avenir de la mode," *Vogue,* 1 Oct. 1927 and Feb. 1928, and "Toute la Mode," *Eve,* 24 Apr. 1927 and 28 Feb. 1928.

88. "Toute la Mode," *Eve,* 23 Mar. 1930, 29 June 1930, and 10 May 1931.

89. Marcy Ducray, "Nos Robes ont enfin dégagé leur ligne," *Excelsior-Modes,* Nov. 1930; "Toute la Mode," *Eve,* 16 Nov. 1930, 10 May, and 6 Sept. 1931; and "Courrier de la Mode," *La Mode Illustrée,* 10 Aug. and 30 Nov. 1930.

90. Nicole Parrot, *Mannequins* (Paris: Catherine Donzel, 1981), 70–83, 114, 147–48, and Tag Gronberg, "Beware Beautiful Women: The 1920s Shop Window Mannequin and a Physiogomy of Effacement," *Art History* 20 (1997).

91. Charles Bernheimer, *Figures of Ill Repute: Representing Prostitution in Nineteenth-Century France* (Cambridge: Cambridge University Press, 1989), 173, and Linda Nead, *Female Nude: Art, Obscenity and Sexuality* (London: Routledge, 1992), 6–8 and 17–18.

92. Hébert, *L'Education physique féminine,* 2 and plate 2.

93. Dr. Esther Bensidoun, *La Sport et la femme* (Paris: PUF, 1932), and "La Beauté facile," *L'Illustration,* 2 Apr. 1933.

94. Paul Poiret, *En Habillant l'époque* (Paris: Bernard Grasset, 1930), 52–53, and Georges Le Fèvre, *Au Secours de la couture (Industrie française)* (Paris: Editions Baudinière, 1929), 33, and "La Vie et le secret de Madeleine Vionnet," *Marie Claire,* 28 May 1937.

95. J.M., "Le Trousseau féminin," *La Mode Pratique,* 17 Jan. 1931; "Beau linge, belle lingerie," *La Mode Illustrée,* Jan. 1935, and Comtesse de S., "Elégances," *Figaro,* 13 Jan. 1936. See also "Trousseaux pour dames," in *Aux Trois Quartiers . . . Mardi 24*

*et Mardi 31 janvier 1922,* and "Lingerie trousseaux," in *Dans l'ambiance printanière aux Galeries Lafayette mardi 28 février 1928.*

96. Stewart, *For Health and Beauty,* and Valerie Steele and Dr. Lynn Kutsche, *Fetish: Fashion, Sex, and Power* (New York: Oxford University Press, 1996), 58 and 60.

97. Philippe Perrot, *Fashioning the Bourgeoisie: A History of Clothing in the Nineteenth Century,* trans. Richard Bienvenu (Princeton: Princeton University Press, 1994), 160.

98. Articles by C. Mosse (head midwife at the Maternity Hospital in Paris) reprinted in *Les Dessous élégants,* Aug. 1922–May 1923, and Roger Glénard, *La Silhouette féminine contemporaine* (Paris: Doin, 1933).

99. Mme. Dautet, *Le Costume féminin et ses dangers* (Thèse Méd., Université de Bordeaux, 1919), 94, and Dr. Josephine Gaches-Sarraute, *Le Corset* (Paris: Masson, 1900).

100. Mme. Coullaud-Minier, "Enquête sur le corset," *Le Corset,* June 1935, and ads for sports girdles in Aux Trois Quartiers, *Sports, Mer, Campagne* catalogues of the 1930s.

101. Marcel Astruc, "A la Recherche d'un néologisme," *La Jardin de la Mode,* 21 Apr. 1921, and Une Doctoresse, *Le Guide médical de la femme* (Paris: Editions de *Le Petit Echo de la Mode,* 1923), 186.

102. Georges-Armand Masson, *Tableau de la mode* (Paris: Editions de la *Nouvelle Revue française,* 1926), 22–31; F. De Miomandre, *La Mode* (Paris: Hachette, 1927), 26; and "Jardin des âmes," *Le Petit Echo de la Nord,* 6 Nov. 1927.

103. "Fashions of the Hour," *La Mode Parisienne,* May 1929.

104. Yvette Monier, "La Vie intime des mannequins," *Faits Divers,* 14 Apr. 1932; Pascal Pia, "Code de mannequin," *Voila,* 2 Feb. 1935; and Paul Poiret and André Dignimont, *Ce que j'ai vu en chiffonnant la clientèle* (Paris: Libraire des Champs-Elysées, 1938), 74–75.

105. M. Edmond Labbé, *Maigrir et obesité* (Paris: L'Expansion Scientifique Française, 1932).

106. Note on Féderation National de l'Enseignement Ménager and Comité d'honneur of the Féderation Nationale de l'Enseignement Ménager in AN F12 9408.

107. Dr. E. Monin, *La Santé de la femme* (Paris: Albin Michel, 1928), 82–85, and Rey, *Notre santé et notre charme,* 27–28 and 48–49. Medical advice columns in *C'est la Mode, La Mode du Jour,* and *Le Petit Echo de la Mode. Femina* added a medical column in 1936.

108. Doctoresse, *Guide médical de la femme,* 73ff.

109. Ad for Bains amaigrissants de la Parfumerie Ninon, *Chiffons,* 5 Apr. 1926.

110. Massala, *Rester mince* (Paris: Bernardin-Béchet, 1930), 38–90 and 104–17.

111. Thérèse and Louise Bonney, *A Shopping Guide to Paris* (New York: Robert M. McBride, 1929), 98–101.

112. Mme. Coullaud-Minier, *Le Corset* (Paris: Chambre de Commerce de Paris, 1927), 1–7.

113. "My Corset Maker," in *The Collected Stories of Colette,* ed. Robert Phelps (London: Penguin Books, 1988), 36–38.

114. F. Libron and H. Clouzot, *Le Corset dans l'art et les moeurs du XIIIe au XXe siècles* (Paris: Libron, 1933), 109–18. See reprint of Dr. O'Fallowell, "Medicines et

Couturiers," and interviews with couturiers in *Les Dessous élégants,* Sept.–Oct. 1924 and Nov. 1928–Dec. 1929.

115. "Le Tricot dans les vêtements de dessous élégants," *Les Dessous élégants,* Feb.–June 1924.

116. Ad for Ceinture Maillot du Dr. Clarans and Claverie corsets in *Femina,* 1919–21.

117. *Annuaire: Union Syndicale des Tissus, Matières Textiles et Habillement* (Paris: n.p., 1926).

118. Ministère du Commerce et de l'Industrie, *Exposition française au Caire, Mars-Avril 1929: Rapport de la classe 86 (Industries diverses de la mode, de la parure et des accessoires du vêtement)* (Paris: n.p., 1929), 25, and *Annuaire des Industries du Vêtement et des Tissus* (Paris: Administration, 1933).

119. Au Printemps winter catalogues, 1919–20 and 1925–26. In the latter year, the catalog sold silk stockings with lace inserts for 100 francs. Middle-class fashion magazines dismissed them as "fantasies that women of taste avoid." "Un Coup d'œil au trousseau," *La Mode Pratique,* 17 Oct. 1928.

120. Marny, *Le Bas à travers les ages suivie de Ce qu'il est de bon ton d'acheter* (Paris: Marny, 1925), pt. two.

121. *Dans l'ambiance printanière aux Galeries Lafayette Mardi 28 février 1928* and La Belle Jardinière, summer 1931.

122. "Le Silhouette et le corset," and "Silhouettes nouvelles," *La Mode Pratique,* 19 Mar. and 2 Apr. 1921.

123. "Quelques modèles," *La Mode Illustrée,* 1 Jan. 1922, and Lucy, "Le linge de corps" and "Un patron de corset et un patron de culotte," *La Mode,* 24 Jan. 1929.

124. Claire Lausnay, "Le Recueil des Modes nouvelles"; M.R, "Les Idées nouvelles de la demi-saison," *Femina,* 1 Apr. 1921 and Jan. 1930; and "La ligne nouvelle demande un corset," *Vogue,* 1 Jan. 1926.

125. *L'Officiel de la Couture,* Feb. 1926.

126. "Le Nouvelle ligne apporte de changement appréciable dans la forme de notre lingerie," *Femina,* Apr. 1931, and "Le Caractère de la robe détermine celui du corset," *Vogue,* June 1936.

127. Nancy V. Workman, "From Victorian to Victoria's Secret: The Foundations of Modern Erotic Wear," *Journal of Popular Culture* 30 (fall 1996).

EPILOGUE

1. Dominique Veillon, *Fashion under the Occupation,* trans. Miriam Kochan (Oxford: Berg, 2002), 85–101.

2. Ibid., 13.

3. Roberta S. Kremer, ed., *Broken Threads: The Destruction of the Jewish Fashion Industry in Germany and Austria* (New York: Berg, 2007).

4. Steven Zdatny, *Fashion, Work, and Politics in Modern France* (New York: Palgrave Macmillan, 2006).

5. Donna Evleth, *The Authorized Press in Vichy and German-Occupied France, 1940–1944: A Bibliography* (Westport, CT: Greenwood Press, 1999).

6. Veillon, *Fashion,* 107ff.

7. Ibid., 17, 56, 100, 126, and 133.

8. William L. Hamilton, "Theater of Hope," *Arts and Antiques* 8, 1 (1990): 88–130.

9. Marie-France Pochna, *Christian Dior: The Man Who Made the World Look New,* trans. Joanna Savill (New York: Arcade, 1994).

10. Francine Muel-Dreyfus, *Vichy and the Eternal Feminine: A Contribution to a Political Sociology of Gender,* trans. Kathleen A. Johnson (Durham, NC: Duke University Press, 2001).

11. Ann Heilmann and Margaret Beetham, eds., *New Woman Hybridities: Femininity, Feminism, and International Consumer Culture, 1880–1930* (London: Routledge, 2004).

# Index

*Femina* (magazine) *(continued)*
women, 202; on chemise dresses, 194;
columnists, 58; compared with *Vogue*,
60–61; covers, view of female body on,
112, 214; cross-promotion of automobiles and clothing, 201; department
store advertisements, 136; on fashion
for working women, 170; fashion illustrators, 39; fashion photographs, 115;
and fashion trends, 82; feminism, 167–
68; focus on exclusive products, 60; on
haute couture in theatre, 23; on leisure
as lifestyle, 41, 42–43; on luxury confection, 70; mission statement, 37, 59;
postwar advice to housewives, 75; on
readers' charity work, 229; review of
collections, 160; on servants, 76; on
suits, 184; support for sports, 208;
survey on who women dress for, 51;
on textiles, 56
femininity, xvi, 16, 158. *See also* body,
female; gender, and fashion
feminism: associated with sports clothes,
213; and consumerism, 166; defeat of
female enfranchise-ment bill (1922),
167; economic, 170; and fashion, 50,
169–70; hybrid, xii, 165–73, 179; not
linked with cross-dressing, 173; suffrage, 165, 166, 167, 168–69
*Figaro* (newspaper), 85, 115, 176
film, and fashion, 23
flaneur/flaneuse, xii, 60, 174
furniture, 3, 34–35

Galeries Lafayette (department store), 71,
86, 117, 138, 139, 140, 141, 142, 143–44,
145, 215
"garçonne" look, xiii, 82, 165, 174, 227
*La Gazette du Bon Ton* (magazine), 37–
38, 39, 112, 114, 174
gender and fashion: androgyny, in
Chanel's designs, 9, 16; chemise,
viewed as boyish, 181; cinched waist,
as marker of sexual difference, 181;
clothing workers, feminization of

protests, 104; cross-dressing, 173–77;
fabric, 186–90; in fashion magazines,
xvi; feminization of masculine garments, 175; "garçonne" look, xiii, 82,
165, 174, 227; gendered culture, 3;
gendered work in haute couture workshops, 95, 96–97; identification of
masculinity with creativity, 5; lesbians
and sports, 213; lesbian underground
in Paris, 174; masculine and feminine
clothing lines, xii; masculinized
women's wear, xi, xii, 158, 191–93,
198, 226; pockets in women's clothing, 193–94; vocabulary change
from "masculine" to "boyish," 194;
women fashion illustrators, 39–40
German fashion industry, 225–26
Le Grand Bazar de Lyon (department
store), 137–38, 141
Gres, Mme. *See* Alix, House of
Groult, Nicole, 17–18, 27, 85

*Harper's Bazaar* (magazine), 113, 115
hats, 13, 14, 28, 123, 124, 163, 226
haute couture: advertising techniques,
55–56; and art deco fabric design,
29–33; branding, 4, 21; collections
during World War I, 73–74; copying
models, 81, 118–21; during Depression, 84–89, 91; distinguished from
ready-to-wear, 191; domination of,
1860–1960, xi; economic importance,
90, 92; fashion shows, 93–94; importance of details, 98; industry critique
by Fitz Benard, 89; influenced by art
movements, 27–28; investment dressing in 1930s, 86; limited edition
dresses, 86; multiplier effect of successful models, 90; during Occupation, 224–31; Parisian, as international
style, 158; salon and shop designs,
34–36; separate Parisian and foreign
collections, 160; and textile manufacturers, 71–72; theatre costumes, 23;
workers, 75, 81, 92, 101–2. *See also*

body, female; confection (ready-to-wear); copying; couture workers; couturières /couturiers; democratization of fashion; *les élégantes;* fashion; fashion illustration; fashion magazines; gender, and fashion; models; premières; society monthly magazines; textile manufacturers; textiles

Heim (fur merchant), 71, 118

home sewers, xiv, 60, 62, 135, 136, 148–54, 164, 191, 228

hybrid feminism, 165–73, 231

hybridity, definition, xii

hybrid modern style: characteristics, 230–31; of interwar fashions, 4; and smoking, 201. *See also* art deco

*L'Illustration des Modes* (magazine), xv–xvi, 37, 38–39, 56, 113, 115, 150

individualism, xiii, xiv–xv, 49

investment dressing, 86, 87

Iribe, Paul, 30, 36

jackets, riding, 176

Japanese designs, 6, 8, 31

*Le Jardin des Modes* (magazine), 39, 137–38, 141, 150, 191

Jenny, House of, 16, 17, 25, 113, 116, 192–93, 209, 210

jersey knit fabrics, 10, 74, 78, 186–87

Kitmir, House of, 79–80, 83

knitting patterns, 153

labels, 4, 21, 122

Lagerfeld, Karl, 18

Lanvin, Jeanne: actions against copying, 123, 132; on change in fashion, 47; and collective advertising, 90; as collector of Impressionist art, 27; on customer observation as basis for designs, 49; design characteristics, 18; employees raided by Patou, 81; at exhibitions and fairs, 116, 117, 118; "mother-daughter"

outfits, 18, 204; at Paris World Fair (1937), 118; price cuts during Depression, 85; sportswear, 209

Lelong, Lucien: cutbacks during Depression, 86; diversification, 86; on film, 24; limited-edition dresses, 132–33; during Occupation, 225; organizing against copying, 126; at Paris World Fair (1937), 118; publicity for French haute couture, 117; sportswear, 209

Lepape, Georges, 33, 36, 37, 39

Lesage (embroidery firm), 83, 87

lingerie, 216. *See also* corsets; stockings

Linker, Amy, 17, 25, 176, 209, 210

"little black dress," 16, 182–83

"little" dressmakers. *See* dressmakers, neighborhood

"little hands," 98, 104

Louvre (department store), 136, 140

Lucile, House of, 21–22

Lyonnais silk industry, xiv, 4, 30–31, 32, 56, 72, 73, 77, 83, 87–88, 90, 112. *See also* silk fabrics; textile manufacturers

magazines. *See* fashion magazines; society monthly magazines; women's weekly magazines

maisons de belles copies, 121, 132

mannequins, 82, 93–94, 95–96, 99, 139, 215, 218

*Marie Claire* (magazine), 41, 58, 160

Marioton, Catherine, 39

maternity: concealing pregnancy with clothing, 45; "consuming motherhood," 44; as depicted in mail order catalogs, 144; few depictions in society magazines, 20, 41; physical exercise and pregnancy, 212; promoted during Vichy regime, 231; resistance of Frenchwomen to, 20–21, 44, 231; wedding preparations, 202–203. *See also* body, female

Matignon Accords, 107

men: in dressmaking business, 5; and fashion, 5, 44, 144, 195–96; in mail order catalogs, 144; men's fashions, 195–96, 198–99

Meserole, Harriet, 39, 40

*midinettes* ("little hands"), 98, 104

*Minerva* (feminist magazine), 169

mobility, and changes in fashion, 5, 13, 16, 74, 181. *See also* sports and women

*La Mode* (magazine), 75, 76, 149, 171, 202–3, 214

*La Mode Illustrée* (magazine), 45, 75, 76, 149, 169, 171, 184, 197, 202–4, 221

*La Mode du Jour* (magazine), 45, 149, 173, 205, 210, 212, 226

models: campaign against reproduction of, 7; commercial counterfeiting, 69, 111, 118–21; copies, as publicity, 127; copying by neighborhood dressmakers, 111; as creations, 21; definition, 4; for fuller figures, 94; international protection of, 125; "servile copies," 129; successful, 53, 90

*La Mode Pratique* (magazine), 37, 45, 76, 113, 149–50, 167, 172, 184, 197, 203, 214, 221

modernity: associated with mobility, 181; commodification of youthfulness, 207; definitions, xii; linked to economic and physical emancipation, 157; and smoking, 200. *See also* art deco; modern woman

modern style: characteristics, 6; chemise dress, 180; store mannequins, 215; Vionnet's bias cut and line, 8

modern woman: characteristics, 202; as cultural not political feminist, 158; and cultural preference for young, lean, and limber bodies, 201–2; as depicted in fashion press, 26, 41–45, 157–58, 200, 230; "garçonne" look, xiii, 82, 165, 174, 227; and hybridity, xii; importance of Chanel's designs, 10; and modern decorative arts, 34–35; shift to youthful-looking, 230; and

shopping, 35, 60. *See also* body, female; sports and women

*Monsieur* (magazine), 195, 196

movie stars. *See* film, and fashion

"Munich" style of decoration, 30

Occupation, and haute couture industry, 224–31. *See also* Vichy regime

*L'Officiel de la Couture et de la Mode* (magazine), 28, 56, 61, 115, 129–30, 165, 221, 226

Orientalism. *See* exoticism

pants, 7, 174, 175–76, 177, 178. *See also* sports and women

Paquin, Jeanne: actions against copying, 7, 123, 128–29, 132; beginnings, 7–8; design characteristics, 7, 25; at Exposition des Arts Décoratifs (1925), 34; honors and achievements, 7; theatre costumes, 23

La Parisienne (statue), 7, 34

Patou, Jean: actions against copying, 132; and collective advertising, 90; diversification, 81–82; employee raid on Lanvin, 81; liquidation of couture house, 85–86; military uniforms, 73; and natural waistline in designs, 16, 53–54; at Paris World Fair (1937), 118; perfume, 86; salon decor, 35; sportswear, 16, 209; theatre costumes, 23; use of embroidery, 80

Pavlovna, Maria. *See* Romanova, Maria Pavlovna

perfumes, 81, 86, 224

*Le Petit Echo de la Mode* (magazine), 151, 168–69, 171–72, 202–3, 208, 226, 231

photography, 113–16, 144

Poiret, Paul: compared with Paquin, 7; copying of design in America, 127; design characteristics, 5, 6; designs for film, 24; and Dufy fabric design, 29–30; at Exposition des Arts Décoratifs (1925), 6; and fashion illustrators, 36; harem pants, 175; and L'École

Martines, 29; "liberating women's midriff," 25; orientalism, 6; self-construct as artist, 4; at textile trade fairs, 116; theatre costumes, 23; theatricality of, 21, 30; Western and Eastern influences, 6

popular magazines. *See* fashion magazines; women's weekly magazines

Premet, House of, 82, 85, 92–93, 209

premières, 70, 81, 94, 97–98, 101, 104, 130

*Le Progrès de Lyon* (newspaper), 208

publicity, 54, 57. *See also* advertising

racialized "natives," 32, 33, 40

rayon (artificial silk), 73, 83

ready-to-wear. *See* confection (ready-to-wear)

Regny, Jane, 16, 17, 25, 34, 71, 118, 209, 210

Reilly, Kate, 8, 130

Ricci, Nina, 86–87, 118

Rodier, Jean, 74, 77–78, 86, 123, 226

Rodier, Paul, 31, 32–33, 55

Romanova, Maria Pavlovna, 79–80, 83, 87

Russian-influenced designs, 82–83, 158

La Samaritaine (department store), 70, 136, 147–48

Schiaparelli, Elsa: closure of house during Occupation, 224; color innovations, 13, 28; confection, 132; on copying, 133; on day and evening dressing, 185–86; design characteristics, 8, 11–13, 25; on designing as art, 29; designs for film, 24; embroidery on designs, 87; influenced by surrealist artists, 27–28; at Paris World Fair (1937), 118; sportswear, 210; on suffragettes, 174; suits, 184; theatre costumes, 23; West African images, 11

seamstresses. *See* dressmakers, neighborhood; home sewers; "little hands"; premières; "second hands"

"second hands," 98, 104

Séeberger Frères, 114, 115, 178

servants, presence in postwar years, xiii, 75–76

sewing machine, 136, 152, 153

shopping, 35, 60. *See also* department stores

silk fabrics, 16, 31, 33, 73, 74, 77, 83, 87, 126, 137, 149, 151–52, 175, 189, 216, 221. *See also* Lyonnais silk industry

skirts, 4, 6, 10, 16, 191

smoking, and modernity, 200

social class: bourgeois, importance of dressing appropriately, 49, 52–53; and clothing, xiv; clothing as indicator of, 134, 192; elite, on reasons for clothing purchases, 51–52; and haute couture, xi; and individualism, xiii, xiv–xv, 49; and leisure, 41–42; and sports, 208; and wedding fashions, 203. *See also* bourgeois women; society monthly magazines

society monthly magazines: absence of dominating masculine figures, xiii, 44; attitude toward servants in postwar years, xiii; avoidance of maternal images, 44; couturier-sponsored magazines, 56; on elegance, 161–62; exclusive advertising content, 60; on feminizing masculine features of clothing, 230; focus on leisure, 230; haute couture for young women, 204; on individualization through clothing, xiii, 49; sewing advice for dressmakers, 150; wardrobe advice, 228

*La Soierie de Lyon* (magazine), 117, 160, 165, 187, 189, 192

Sorel, Cecile, 23, 50

sports and women: cross-dressing, 173; dancing, 207–8; debate on appropriateness of, 212–13; depictions in magazines, 42–44; and haute couture, 209–10; as means of staying young, 222; obstacles to physical activity, 211; riding costumes, 176; sportswear, 9, 16,

sports and women *(continued)*
    25, 43, 177, 186–87, 208–10, 222;
    team sports, 211–12
Steichen, Edward, 114
stockings, 83, 221
style bureaus, 84
suits, 14, 16, 176, 183–84, 185, 189
Surrealists, 27–28
sweaters, 12, 16

taste: ascribed to Parisiennes and French-
    women in general, 3, 228–29; disap-
    proval of luxurious dressing during
    Depression, 85; as distinguished from
    style, 3, 4
textile manufacturers: advertising, 55–
    56, 89–90; cooperation with haute
    couture, xiv, 71–72, 89–90; corporate
    structure initiatives, 90; counterfeiting
    of patterns, 122; and democratization
    of fashion, 229; designs as creations,
    33; financing of couturiers, 72, 85, 112;
    group efforts to counteract copying,
    125–26; impact of Depression on,
    87–89; industry critique by Fitz Be-
    nard, 89; popularization of modern
    fabric design, 30; reconstruction after
    World War I, 76–78; trade fairs, 116–
    18; unemployment during postwar
    recession, 77; worker relations, 75,
    105–108; during World War I, 72–73.
    *See also* Lyonnais silk industry
textiles: advertising language in 1930s,
    189; art deco, 29–33, 46; artificial, 195,
    227; brighter colors, 188–89; colonial
    motifs, 33; design by artists, 29–30;
    embroidery, 78–80; fabric: –names,
    22; –new, 89–90; –restrictions dur-
    ing World War I, 73–74; floral motifs,
    29, 31, 77, 78; and gender, 186–90;
    gender coding of patterns, 186–87;
    geometric motifs, 15, 31; plaids, 187,
    188; "shadow brands," 89; stripes,
    187; sturdy, as postwar influence, 185;
    swatches, in mail order catalogs, 151;

texture, as marker of personality and
    distinction, 13; tweeds, 187–88; wool
    jersey, 186–87. *See also* silk fabrics
theatre and fashion, 22–23
Tirtoff, Romain de. *See* Erté
*toiles* (patterns), sale to competitors, 125
Toutmain, 86, 99, 150
trousers. *See* pants

underwear. *See* corsets; lingerie
Union of Russian Artists, 23
unions: clothing workers, 103–105;
    textile workers, 105–108
United States. *See* American fashion
    industry
Universal Exhibition, Paris (1900), 7

Van Dongen, Kees, 27, 28
Vichy regime, 226, 228–29, 231
Vionnet, Madeleine: anti-copying efforts,
    121, 123, 130–31; bias cut, inspired by
    classical sculpture, 8, 9; closure of
    house during Occupation, 224; and
    collective advertising, 90; confection
    designs, 130; during Depression, 85;
    design characteristics, 8, 16–17, 25,
    130; design methods, 16; embroidery
    for, 83; employee benefits, 95; at Expo-
    sition des Arts Décoratifs (1925), 34;
    at Paris World Fair (1937), 118; patents,
    122; sales of successful models, 53;
    sportswear, 210; on textiles, 71; use
    of artificial silk blends, 73, 77
Vogel, Lucien, 37–39, 114
*Vogue* (London) (magazine), 60, 115
*Vogue* (New York) (magazine), 116, 202,
    204
*Vogue* (Paris) (magazine): advertise-
    ment costs, 57; advertisements, 190;
    on the art of dressing, 29; association
    of sports clothes with feminism, 213;
    on Chanel, 48, 191, 209; on chic, 162,
    164; on clothing: –and abstract art, 28;
    –for housework, 76; columnists, 59;
    on copying of models, 111; on couturi-

ers, 50; cover illustrations, 39; covers, view of female body on, 214; on dressing for occasion, 198; on fashion for working women, 170; fashion photographs, 114–15; focus on international set, 61; on models on fuller figures, 94; on modern woman, xv, 41; on Poiret's designs, 5; on suits, 184; wardrobe advice, 59